JET BOMBERS

From the Messerschmitt Me 262
to the Stealth B-2

JET BOMBERS

From the Messerschmitt Me 262
to the Stealth B-2

BILL GUNSTON WITH

PETER GILCHRIST

The editor would like to acknowledge the help of the following individuals who contributed photographs for this volume; Bob Archer, William Green, Neville Beckett, Roy Braybrook, Mike Savage, Phil Jarrett, Lindsay Peacock, Tony Thornborough, Jerry Scutts, Mike Stroud and Randy Jolly.

First published in Great Britain in 1993 by Osprey, an imprint of Reed Consumer Books Limited, Michelin House, 81 Fulham Road, London SW3 6RB, and Auckland, Melbourne, Singapore and Toronto

ISBN 1 85532 258 7

Edited by Tony Holmes
Design by Gwyn Lewis
© Line Drawings by Dennis Punnett

Printed in Great Britain by BAS Printers Ltd, Over Wallop, Hampshire

Contents

Foreword

The very first military aeroplanes to go into action were bombers. The basic aircraft were simply bought from an established maker, such as Monsieur Blériot, and the bombs were grenades or artillery shells fitted with stabilising tails. They were dropped over the side by hand, or even suspended by loops from the pilot's feet and kicked off.

We have come some way since then. The introduction of jet propulsion came at roughly the same time as the first nuclear weapons, and together they multiplied the problems of the defenders perhaps one-millionfold. At a stroke, bombers flew twice as fast and almost twice as high as previously, and it was essential not to let a single bomber get through. One bomber meant one city destroyed.

Another trend at the same time was for an increasing proportion of bombs actually to be dropped by smaller aircraft that not only looked like fighters but might actually be fighters. Sixty years ago fighters of the US Navy almost always could dive on a hostile ship with a couple of 100-lb bombs, and in 1944 the German Panzer armies were being devastated by Typhoons and Stormoviks. Today the tactical attack aircraft is a clearly defined class, and many of this family are featured in this book. So, for example, is the swing-wing F-111, which while ostensibly a fighter, was made to fly so far and carry so many bombs that a version served with Strategic Air Command!

One is inevitably forever looking back at the choice of 'jet bombers'. Many readers will ask 'What, no ....?' An obvious absentee is the F-105, but if we put that in we can hardly leave out the F-100, which did a great bombing job in Vietnam, or the F-84F or the F-84G and F-80C, which flew bombing missions in Korea, as did many US Navy jets ... and so on. We preferred to produce a book readers can afford.

Today the notions of penetrability have long since made bombers – or things like fighters that carry bombs – come down to treetop height and follow the undulations of the terrain even in mountains. Pilots, not given to overstatement, call such missions 'sporty'. Some bombers carry cruise missiles that can be launched up to 2000 miles from the target, while eventually every aeroplane that comes into contact with an enemy will have to be of so-called 'Stealth' design, though when an F-117A arrived at the 1991 Paris Airshow thousands saw a black shape against the blue sky, sunshine glinting from the canopy and making a thunderous noise (and not much can be done about the intense heat emission).

Many students of warfare are surprised to find that, in the B-1B Lancer and Tu-160, the giant 'heavy bomber' is very much alive and well. Bombers as a class are getting on for a century old, and they have been jet-propelled for just half that time. The next century is likely to be even more interesting. It is too much to hope that warfare will then be an extinct activity.

Bill Gunston

HASLEMERE, 1993

In the specification tables the original figures (Imperial or Metric) are given first. Conversions follow in brackets.

Arado Ar 234

First Flight – 15 June 1943

What was the first jet bomber? It was obviously German, but beyond that there are problems. In a nutshell, the first aircraft designed from the start as a jet bomber was the Ju 287. The first jets actually to drop bombs in anger were the Ar 234B-2 and Me 262A-2a, and while the Arado was modified from a reconnaissance aircraft, the Messerschmitt was modified from a fighter. In terms of timing the 262 was unquestionably first, Ekdo Schenck (nominally part of KG 51) having flown its first combat mission on 1 August 1944. But the speedy Messerschmitt *Sturmvogel* was never regarded as anything but an interim machine – as Albert Speer minuted on 25 June 1944, 'Until the 234 can be secured in production'.

The 234 was a strange mixture. It had a nose superficially resembling the Luftwaffe's other bombers, yet it was actually only slightly bigger than many single-seat fighters. It was a sound design, not difficult to fly and used the new means of propulsion to achieve a higher level of performance, yet the overall layout made it difficult to do more than fly the original design mission, which was to carry a couple of cameras. Bombs had to be hung outside, and originally there was not even room for retracted wheels.

The Arado was a company proposal, the E 370 project being submitted by chief designers Walter Blume and Hans Rebeski at the beginning of 1941. It was logical to suggest that the new jet engines should be used to create a reconnaissance aircraft immune to interception, and the idea was quickly taken on board by the RLM (air ministry) in Berlin as the 8-234. Predictably, the airframe outpaced the availability of engines, and it was not until 15 June 1943 that Flugkapitän Selle was able to take the Ar 234 V1 into the air from Rheine, which had been chosen as the 234 flight-test centre even though the aircraft had to complete the 400 miles from Warnemünde by road.

The 234's wing was a simple so-called laminar surface with equal taper, a fixed leading edge, hydraulically-driven plain flaps and manual geared-tab ailerons of curiously narrow chord. It was mounted on top of a simple fuselage with a pressurized cockpit for the pilot in the nose, which from the third prototype was fitted with a primitive

BELOW *Ar 234 V9 taking off. Note the overhead sight above the cockpit, jet-nozzle variable 'bullets' and two drop tanks*

TOP *One of the few high-quality photographs surviving showing an Ar 234B. The overhead sight unit has been removed*

ABOVE RIGHT *Ar 234 V10 taxiing past a Ju 88. This aircraft had no sight fitted*

RIGHT *The V9 pre-production aircraft builds up speed as it accelerates towards rotation*

ejection seat. The pilot had a retractable ladder on the left and entered by hinging the cockpit roof to the right. Behind him was a forward fuel tank which completely filled the next section back to the wing, followed by a centre tank under the flying surface itself, an aft tank filling the section behind the wing, and a simple tail, but again with strangely narrow elevators. The chosen engines, two Jumo 004B turbojets, were hung in nacelles under the wing about one-third of the way out from the centreline.

Arado's main problem had been to meet the required range of 2150 km (1336 miles). No fuel was put in the wing, and to keep down drag the fuselage was slim – the upshot of this design restriction was that there appeared to be no room for retracted landing gear other than a small sprung skid. Accordingly, much time and worry was devoted to perfecting a take-off trolley. This trolley was not only big but also quite complicated. It had a nosewheel and two mainwheels, the latter equipped with automatic brakes which required a safety system to prevent operation until the aircraft's weight had been removed. An electromechanical system enabled the trolley to be jettisoned after the aircraft had reached a height of 60 m (200 ft). Then it was to be recovered by a system of five parachutes.

On the first take-off the trolley was dropped but fell like a stone and was wrecked. On flight two it was again wrecked. On flight three the technique was altered so that the aircraft simply flew off the speeding trolley, but the trolley's presence made it difficult to modify the 234 as a bomber, which is what was increasingly wanted. In any case it was realised that there were operational disadvantages in having airfields littered with immobile twin-jets sitting on skids (one on the centreline and one under each engine). After further agonizing it was decided to fit a conventional landing gear, and this in turn meant replacing the centre tank with bays for the big mainwheels and making the fuselage wider in order to increase the size of the remaining tanks.

The first modified Ar 234B, the ninth prototype, flew on 10 March 1944. Despite the narrow track the aircraft proved satisfactory, and during the summer of 1944 the Ar 234B-1 reconnaissance aircraft came into production at Alt-Lönnewitz, on the Czech border, carrying two big cameras. A standard provision on the B-1 was plumbing for a 300-litre (66-gal) drop tank under each engine nacelle. Some aircraft were fitted with attachments for assisted take-off rockets under the wing out-board of the engines, and another option (rare on the B-1) was a pair of MG 151/20 cannon firing directly to the rear from the bottom of the rear fuselage. To say they transformed Luftwaffe photo-reconnaissance capability is an understatement.

The eagerly awaited bomber version was the B-2. The prototype for this was the V10, flown without pressurization or ejection seat on 2 April 1944.

Production of the B-2, equipped to carry an SC500 bomb of 1102 lb under each nacelle and a third under the fuselage, began in October 1944. The B-2 was to some degree a 'quart in a pint pot', but it demanded much of its pilot. To make a straight diving attack he had to unclip his control column and hinge it to the side to use the Lotfe 7K bombsight and BZA 1 computer, the aircraft being flown by the Patin PDS autopilot. Bearing in mind the fact that with three big bombs the B-2 was slower than Allied fighters, and unable to manoeuvre (except to make required sighting corrections), the courage of the pilots of KG 76 can be appreciated.

The first mission was flown by II/KG 76 from Achmer on Christmas Eve 1944. From then on the 234B-2 proved a valuable weapon, though for obvious operational reasons its effect was never more than a series of pinpricks, even during the later stages of the Ardennes campaign. Their one

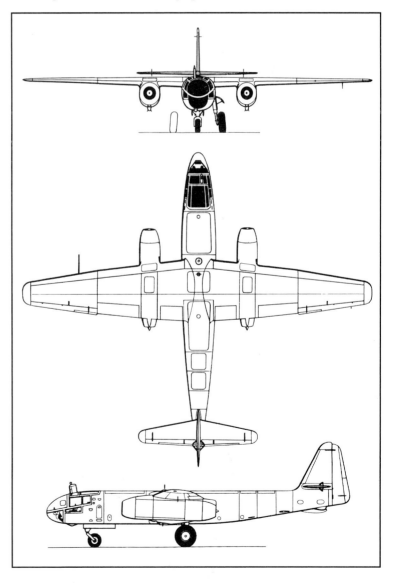

real success, after over 50 bombing runs with bombs up to SC1800 (3086 lb) size, was to collapse the Remagen bridge over the Rhine on 17 March 1945, but by then it was too late.

When Germany capitulated on 8 May many later versions of the 234 were in various stages of development. Notable among these were the 234C series, with four BMW 003A or 003C engines. A wing had been made for the 234 V16 with compound sweep of the type later re-invented by Handley Page as the 'crescent wing'. Numerous 234B Blitz (lightning) aircraft were captured intact, most of these being test flown by Lt Cdr E M 'Winkle' Brown, CO of Aero Flight at Farnborough. More than most aircraft, the slim Arado could have been a real thorn in the side of the Allies, had its development not been so punctuated by rethinks.

SPECIFICATION

Ar 234B-2 Blitz

Two Junkers Jumo 004B-1 turbojets each rated at 900 kg (1984 lb) thrust

Dimensions Span 14.44 m (46 ft 3½ in); length 12.64 m (41 ft 5½ in); wing area 27.3 m² (293.86 sq ft)

Weight Empty 5.2 t (11,464 lb); fuel (kerosene) 3 t (6614 lb); loaded 8.4 t (18,519 lb); maximum with three bombs and tanks 9.8 t (21,605 lb)

Performance Maximum speed (normal weight, 6 km, 19,685 ft) 742 km/h (461 mph); service ceiling 10 km (32,800 ft); range 500 kg bomb 1555 km (966 miles), (1500 kg load) 1100 km (684 miles)

Armament Option of two aft-firing MG 151/20 each with 200 rounds; provision for one PC1400 bomb (3086 lb) or up to three SC500 or one SC1000 and two SC250 or three AB250 or AB500 anti-personnel clusters

Messerschmitt Me 262A-2a Sturmvogel

First Flight – February 1944

The Me 262 is often described as 'the world's first jet fighter'. On almost any count it was not, but it *was* the first jet bomber. What is indisputable is that it was manufactured in greater numbers than any other jet aircraft of World War 2, and also that in many respects it was a superb aircraft. Its engines were unreliable and had a very short life (usually 25 hours), and the 262 killed nearly as many of its own pilots as it did of the enemy. Having said that, it was a dream to fly, simple to build, easy to service, had outstanding performance and, with four 30 mm MK 108 cannon, devastating firepower.

The first prototype flew on 18 April 1941 on the inadequate 700 hp of a Jumo 210G piston engine in the nose, no turbojets being available. The second prototype flew with two 1850 lb-thrust Junkers Jumo 004 turbojets on 18 July 1942, and the production aircraft had 1980 lb Jumo 004B engines, nosewheel landing gear and many other improvements. On 22 April 1943 Generalleutnant Adolf Galland flew the V4 prototype and reported in ecstatic terms, suggesting halting production of all fighters except the Fw 190 in order to put maximum effort into Me 262 production. Soon afterwards Hitler himself became interested; but he was inter-

ested only in attack. He feared an Allied invasion in 1944, and wanted 'terror weapons' that would annihilate the Allied armies.

There are several stories about how the concept of an Me 262 fighter/bomber was born. Certainly, on actually witnessing a demonstration by the V6 prototype on 26 November 1943, Hitler proclaimed 'Here is our Blitzbomber!' (lightning bomber). It is also known that, 24 days earlier, Goering had visited Messerschmitt, asked about bomb-carrying capability and been fobbed off with amazingly casual answers. Knowing Hitler's fixation on the offensive, and that he almost foamed at the mouth at the suggestion that the Me 262 should continue to be regarded as just a fighter, it is extraordinary that the notion of adding bomb racks – which Messerschmitt had said 'might take two weeks' – should not have been pressed ahead with the utmost vigour. Instead, none of the 23 pre-production 262A-0 aircraft had any bombing equipment, and in April 1944 Hitler, learning this, screamed 'Not a single one of my orders has been obeyed!' To soothe his irritation he issued a directive forbidding any production of 262A-1a fighters until the completion of tests of the A-2a bomber.

It has often been claimed that this delayed the

BELOW *Works drawing showing the carriage of side-by-side SC500 bombs*

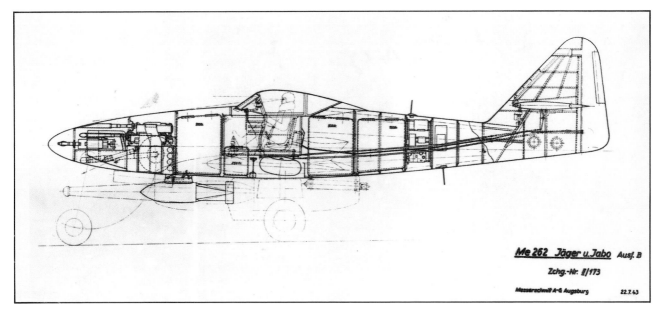

Me 262 Jäger u. Jabo Ausf. B
Zchg.-Nr. II/173
Messerschmitt A-G Augsburg   22.7.43

262's entry to service. This was obviously not the case, and the pacing item was always the production of the 004B engine. It did, however, reduce the numbers available.

Testing of the 262 V10 and A-0 aircraft with bombs began in February 1944. Various schemes were investigated, including a towed bomb in an arrangement similar to those tested with the Ar 234B. SC500 (1102 lb) and SC1000 (2205 lb) bombs were towed, each taking off on a jettisonable trolley and lifted by a 6.1 m (20 ft) wooden wing. Various bombs were also carried conventionally. The arrangement finally adopted was to attach two pylons side-by-side under the forward fuselage, and these carried a SC500 or two SC250 bombs. Of course, bomb fuzing wiring was added, but no sight was provided. Testing showed that in a 30° dive, levelling off at about 1000 m (3300 ft), accuracy was at least as good as in similar attacks with piston-engined fighter-bombers, the chief difficulty being the very short time in which the pilot had to

TOP *One of the best photographs of an A-2a, in this case with both SC500 bombs loaded*

ABOVE *Gun ports taped over, this Me 262A-2a was photographed touching down at Farnborough on 29 October 1945*

identify the target. A single aircraft was modified as the A-2a/U2, with a bomb-aimer lying prone in an extended nose with a Lotfe 7H stabilised sight, the guns being removed. This did not go into production.

Though a special test unit of fighter A-1a aircraft began operating at the end of June 1944, the first regular Luftwaffe unit to be equipped with jet aircraft was the Kommando Schenck, which although a test unit, was nominally made a part of fighter-bomber wing KG 51 in October 1944. The A-2a had actually flown against the enemy with the Kommando Schenck from late August, and indeed

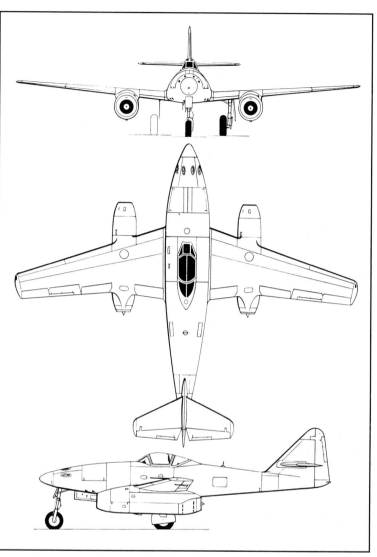

TOP LEFT *Bombing-up an A-2a in frontline service in January 1945*

MIDDLE LEFT *A-2a with both bombs loaded. Many* Sturmvogels *had only two guns*

LEFT *A different bombed-up A-2a, with four guns. The ring behind the canopy is the direction-finding antenna*

had lost one aircraft to P-47s on 28 August. Gradually KG 51 grew in strength and was joined by other KG units (most of which, however, flew the A-1a fighter).

The Sturmvogel accomplished little, despite having a flight performance which made it exceedingly difficult to shoot down with fighters or AA guns. One problem was that most of the pilots were completely inexperienced. The only veteran aircrew had been posted in from bomber units, and a former pilot of an He 111 or even a Ju 88 was hardly the best material for an Me 262 unit, having spent most of his career cruising at medium to high altitudes at around 250 knots.

Dozens of individual attacks were made on the Nijmegen bridge, by day and night. The random bombing never hit the bridge, but it was frustrating to the overwhelming Allied airpower not to shoot down any of the 262s. At last on 5 October one was bagged, having taken hits from *five* Spitfire IXs of No 401 (RCAF) Sqn.

A unique form of bombing trialled by the Luftwaffe saw the A-1a fighter dropping clusters of light bombs on USAAF heavy bomber formations, from December 1944 until March 1945.

TOP *Undamaged, apart from having had the cowls unlatched, an Me 262A-2a sits on a bomb-damaged airfield just taken over by Allied forces*

ABOVE *In the final frantic weeks before surrender hundreds of A-2a Sturmvogels were pressed into service without even being painted. Some GI has scrawled OHIO on the nose*

SPECIFICATION

Me 262A-2a

Two Junkers Jumo 004B (various sub-types) turbojets each rated at 900 kg (1984 lb)

Dimensions Span 12.5 m (40 ft 11.5 in); length 10.58 m (34 ft 9.5 in); wing area 21.73 m² (234 sq ft)

Weight Empty, equipped (four guns), 4.5 t (9921 lb); loaded 7.5 t (16,534 lb)

Performance Maximum speed (with bombs) 750 km/h (466 mph); (clean, medium altitudes) 850 km/h (528 mph); Mach limit 0.83; combat radius (not low altitude) typically 400 km (248 miles)

Armament Usually two SC250 or 500 bombs and four MK 108 30 mm guns, each with 80 rounds. Some aircraft two guns only

Junkers Ju 287

Thanks to Frank Whittle having invented the turbojet in 1929 (and that fact is indisputable), and despite his loss of seven years trying to get someone interested in funding its development, the Allies had the world's best turbojets in the closing stages of World War 2. Yet the expected hordes of jet fighters and bombers were never ordered, and the only Allied jet aircraft to fly during the war were a tiny handful of unimpressive Meteor and Airacomet fighters, and prototypes of the Vampire and Shooting Star. In contrast, dozens of types of jet aircraft were planned in Germany, including three that appear in this book. The Henschel Hs 132 jet dive bomber almost made it too, for the prototype was about to fly when Russian troops captured it.

The subject of this chapter is unique in that it was the first jet bomber to be designed anywhere. The Me 262 was designed as a fighter, and the Ar 234 as a reconnaissance aircraft, but the Ju 287 was specifically planned as a bomber able to outrun Allied fighters.

The design team was led by Dipl-lng Hans Wocke, and he (unlike British designers) realised that the turbojet opened up new possibilities, instead of just being a new kind of engine to be bolted into traditional airframes. Since 1935 – having taken the trouble to do so, which Allied aerodynamicists did not – he had learned all he could about the use of sweepback to delay the onset of excessive drag as the speed of sound was approached. Accordingly he planned the Ju 287 with 25° sweepback, but he was equally aware of the low-speed problems of swept wings, and feared for instability and even loss of control due to stalling at the tips making the ailerons useless. Why not, he reasoned, use forward sweep instead?

There are many valid reasons for doing this (as explained by Grumman when they built the two X-29s), but until quite recently the FSW (forward-swept wing) was structurally unattainable, except at low indicated airspeeds. One has only to hold a sheet of thin card out of a speeding car to see why. Hold it by the leading edge and there is no problem, though it may flutter. Hold it by the trailing edge...!

To explore the FSW full-scale at relatively low speeds Junkers very quickly built the Ju 287 V1. Though this bore the type-number (287) of the proposed bomber, it had no similarity to the bomber except for the basic plan of the wing, with a leading

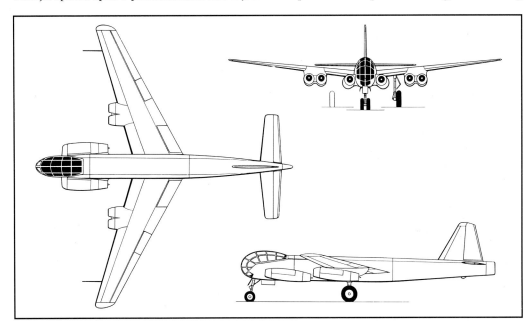

TOP *A remarkable air-to-air picture. The ground shows the true attitude of the aircraft*

ABOVE RIGHT *A surprising number of photographs survive of the Ju 287 V1, built solely to evaluate the low-speed behaviour of the FSW. Note the assisted take-off rockets hung under each jet engine*

RIGHT *The only known photograph of the Ju 287 V2, during its brief flight-test period at Zhukovskii*

edge swept forward at about 18° and a trailing-edge angle of 30°. To save time parts of other aircraft were used, including an He 177, Ju 388, Ju 352 and shot-down B-24! The landing gears were fixed, and power was provided by four Jumo 004B turbojets each of 900 kg (1984 lb) thrust, two on the sides of the nose and two well back under the wings.

Flugkapitän Siegfried Holzbauer made the first flight from Brandis on 16 August 1944. A total of 17 flights confirmed low-speed behaviour, though when the 287 V1 was dived to 650 km/h (404 mph) the potentially dangerous aeroelastic behaviour of the wings became all too evident. Subsequently the V1 was flown to the Rechlin test establishment, where it was bombed.

Despite the fact that in three grandiose plans in July, September and December 1944 the manufacture of bombers had been abandoned, all effort being applied to 'last ditch' fighter production, in March 1945 Junkers was ordered to hasten the Ju 287 into production. By this time the second prototype, the Ju 287 V2, was taking shape at a dispersed factory between Brandis and Leipzig, and work on it continued round the clock.

The V2 was intended to be the true jet bomber, though in the event the planned He 011A turbojets never became available. To help alleviate the dangerous wing twist it was obviously desirable to mount the engines as far out on the wing and as far ahead of the wing as possible, or the opposite of the V1 arrangement. Lacking powerful engines it was decided to fit six BMW 003A tubojets in clover-leaf groups ahead of the wing. This was soon discovered to be aerodynamically unsound, but work rushed ahead while better propulsion was sought. The

wing was little changed, but a definitive fuselage was attempted (though lacking the planned tail turret) with a pressure cabin for a crew of three. The tricycle landing gears retracted into the fuselage.

The incomplete V2 was captured by Soviet troops, and later was taken by rail to the Soviet Union. Here it was assembled by a detachment of Russian-led former Junkers workers and, surprisingly, flown by Flugkapitän Dülgen in 1947. The prototype was rightly regarded by the captors as probably inferior to such bombers as the Il-22 and Type 150, and it was soon abandoned. It appears in the background in photographs of other aircraft under test.

The aircraft assembled in the Soviet Union has been the subject of some confusion. It was the V2, not the fully armed but unbuilt V3. It was flown from Zhukovskii, not Podberzye or Nikolovdskye. It was a completely different aircraft from the projected Junkers EF 131. And, as a final twist, Wocke finally achieved success with an FSW when he led the design of the HFB 320 Hansa business jet, first flown in 1964.

SPECIFICATION

Ju 287 V3 (estimated)
Six BMW 003A-1 turbojets each rated at 800 kg (1760 lb)
Dimensions Span 20.11 m (65 ft 11½ in); length 18.6 m (61 ft 0¼ in); wing area 58.3 m² (627 sq ft)
Weight Empty 11.92t kg (26.278 lb); maximum loaded 21.52t (47,450 lb)
Performance Maximum speed (no bombs) 819 km/h (509 mph) at SL, 856 km/h (537 mph) at 5 km (16,400 ft); service ceiling 12 km (39,370 ft); range at 792 km/h at 7 km (23,000 ft) with max bomb load 1585 km (985 miles); with 2 t, 4409 lb bombload, 2125 km (1320 miles)
Armament Twin MG151 guns in remotely controlled tail turret; up to four tonnes (8818 lb) of bombs

BELOW *The V1 prototype was one of the strangest lash-ups ever to take the air, yet it flew*

Nakajima J9Y1 Kikka

First Flight – 6 August 1945

This Japanese twin-jet is often loosely regarded as a copy of the Me 262. In fact, there was to have been such an aircraft, built under licence as the Nakajima Ki-201 for the Imperial Army, but it was never completed. The Navy's J9Y1 Kikka (Orange Blossom) was similar only in general layout. It had engines of not much more than half the power, so it was considerably smaller. Moreover, it was not a fighter but a Navy 'special attacker', in other words a bomber.

Starting from scratch, aided only by amateur photographs of parts of the BMW 003, a small team formed by Nakajima and the Navy Air Arsenal did wonders in first developing the Ne-12 turbojet, tested at 695 lb thrust in late 1944, and then the more advanced Ne-20, tested at up to 1050 lb thrust in April 1945. These engines were necessarily somewhat crude, with a very low pressure ratio, jetpipe bullets and simple throttle control. Fuel consumption was naturally high, and engine life very short, but nobody was bothered by such shortcomings. What was wanted was something that could drop a few bombs on the enemy. The actual specification called merely for a bomb of 500 or 800 kg (1102 or 1764 lb), and an easily-built structure. Though the aircraft carriers had all been sunk by this late stage in the war, folding wings were needed so that the aircraft could be based in caves and tunnels.

The aircraft was also a joint Nakajima/Navy effort, the company team being headed by Kenichi Matsumura and Kazuo Ohno. The simple stressed-skin structure included a wing of 11 per cent thickness, with most of the pronounced taper on the leading edge, split flaps inboard of the engines, and fixed slots in the outer leading edges. The fuselage had a triangular section similar to that of the Me 262, but was much deeper aft of the cockpit, which had a sliding canopy. The engines were mounted completely ahead of the wings in underslung nacelles, the jetpipes being extended so that the nozzles were aft of the trailing edge. Flight controls

BELOW *Helping Lt-Cdr Susumu Takaoka get aboard*

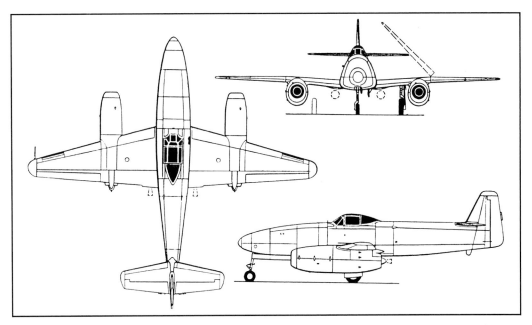

were manual, all surfaces being of generous size and fabric covered, without tabs. Very unusually for a Japanese aircraft, the landing gear was of the nosewheel type, with hydraulic actuation. The main gears retracted inwards, and the long nose leg backwards. Because of the modest engine thrust, provision was made for fitting two ATO (assisted take-off) rockets, each giving 1760 lb for nine seconds. These were attached under the wing roots, and it was essential that they should be jettisoned after use, since they prevented retraction of the main gears or selection of 40° flap for landing.

To avoid destruction by B-29 attack the two Kikka prototypes were built in silkworm huts in a remote area in Gumma prefecture. The first was finished on 25 June 1945. The engines were tested on the following day, after which the aircraft was dismantled and taken to Kisarazu naval airbase on Tokyo Bay. This had only a 6000 ft runway, and in

TOP *Three-view drawing of the J9Y1, emphasising the apparent too far-aft location of the wing*

ABOVE *One of only a handful of photographs of the J9Y1, taken just before the first flight*

view of the limited engine thrust and poor brakes (to save time the wheels and brakes were of A6M Zero type, even though the Kikka was much heavier and expected to land faster) this distance was recognised from the outset as completely inadequate.

There were also many other problems, but Japan's position was desperate. The test pilot, Lt Cdr (later General) Susumu Takaoka started high-speed taxy tests as soon as the aircraft was reassembled, on 29 July. He found the brakes totally inadequate at high speed, but nothing could be done without delaying the programme, and on 6 August – the day

the atomic bomb fell on Hiroshima – Takaoka made the first flight. He did not use the rockets, but everything went well. He said 'It all seemed too calm; it was like flying in a glider!' The second flight was on the 11th. This time the rockets were fired. Immediately Takaoka's view ahead vanished, because the rocket thrust lifted the nose high, the tail scraping along the ground. Suddenly the nose dropped, and it felt as if the aircraft was decelerating. At 90 mph, with less than half the runway left, Takaoka decided the Kikka would not get airborne, and abandoned the take-off. There was no chance of stopping, and the aircraft finally came to rest on the beach with both main gears torn off. Frantic repairs were still going on when, four days later, Japan surrendered. The second aircraft was almost complete, and parts had been made for 20 more.

TOP *Lt-Cdr Takaoka starts the engines on the airstrip alongside the beach on Tokyo Bay*

ABOVE *Manhandling the vital prototype out of its hangar at Kisarazu AB on 7 August 1945 (the day after 'Hiroshima')*

SPECIFICATION

J9Y1 Kikka
Two Ne-20 turbojets each rated at 475 kg (1047 lb)
Dimensions Span 10.0 m (32 ft 9.7 in); length 8.12 m (26 ft 7.7 in); wing area 13.2 m² (142.09 sq ft)
Weight Empty, equipped 2.3t (5071 lb); loaded 3550 kg (7826 lb); maximum 4312 kg (9506 lb)
Performance Maximum speed (with bomb, estimated) 623 km/h (387 mph) at S/L, 697 km/h (433 mph) at 10 km (32,800 ft); range 890 km (553 miles) at 555 km/h (345 mph) at 6 km (19,685 ft)
Armament One bomb of 500 or 800 kg on centreline pylon; no guns

North American B-45 Tornado

This bomber can be regarded from two contrasting viewpoints. From 46 years distance, it can be criticised as merely a traditional bomber on to which jet engines had been fitted, the novel powerplants resulting in a radius of action too short to be of much use to its globally-minded owners, the USAF. The contrary view admires it as the first effective jet bomber in the world, a case of the right aircraft at the right time, and a tough, reliable and valuable aircraft which played a major role not only as a nuclear delivery vehicle but also in various reconnaissance roles.

During World War 2 there were rapid technological changes. The switch from piston engines to jet propulsion was one, and this bomber was designed to a US Army Air Force mission-need statement of October 1944 which led to a formal requirement dated 17 November. This was the first requirement issued outside Germany specifying such engines for a bomber. Another change was the introduction of advanced aerodynamics, such as sweptback wings and tail, and a third was the introduction of nuclear weapons. The B-45 was too early to take advantage of either. A fourth change was merely a matter of terminology. In the early part of the war a bomber weighing 50 tons would have been regarded as exceptionally heavy, especially if it could carry a 22,000-lb bombload. But by the end of the conflict ideas had changed, and from the start the B-45 was actually regarded as a 'light bomber'.

The 1944 requirement resulted in orders being placed for four types of bomber. The XB-45, 46 and 48 were broadly similar in timing, while the XB-47 was deliberately delayed in order to take full advantage of sweepback. The XB-45 was completed ahead of its rivals, and was also cheaper, so it was put into production. From the start, however, the USAAF hoped that the eventual B-47 would succeed, so that the less-advanced B-45 could be an interim aircraft. Three XB-45 prototypes were ordered, North American allotting the company designation NA-130. Serial numbers were 45-59479/59481. The first was trucked in sections from Inglewood to Muroc Field (later named Edwards AFB) and flown by George Krebs and Paul Brewer on 17 March 1947.

It was a handsome machine, with a logical layout. The finely streamlined fuselage had a station for the bombardier/navigator in the nose, which was glazed over its upper half. Opposite his seat, on the left side, was the entrance door, the cutout having a strong frame with a rounded top

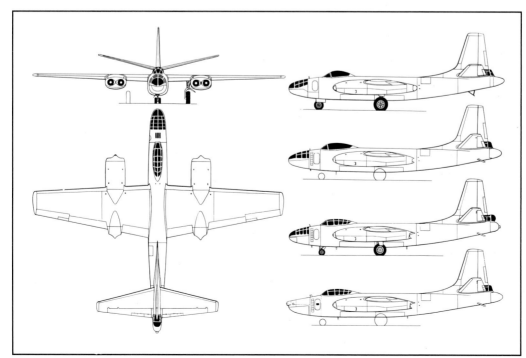

LEFT *From the top: XB-45, B-45A, B-45 and RB-45C*

and bottom because of the high degree of pressurization of the whole crew compartment. Underneath was the very short nose gear, with steerable twin nosewheels, which retracted backwards hydraulically. To the rear, at a much higher level, was the floor of the cockpit with seats for the pilot and copilot in tandem. Over their heads was a large glazed canopy, not normally opened but jettisonable in emergency. Next came the fuselage fuel tank and the wing at the upper level, with the entire lower section being the capacious bomb bay with inner and outer doors on each side sliding over each other when open. In the extreme tail was the fourth crewmember, manning a turret with two 0.5-in guns.

The wing was, of course, unswept, but with a so-called laminar profile. Most of its interior was taken up by flexible fuel cells, the total internal capacity being 2802 Imp gal (12,742 litres). Under each wing, projecting to front and rear, was a nacelle housing two axial turbojets, which in the prototypes were Allison (General Electric TG-180 design) J35-4s rated at 4000 lb. Just inboard of the nacelles were the single-leg main landing gears, retracting hydraulically inwards into the wing. The slotted flaps were also hydraulically driven, and hydraulic boosters provided 95 per cent of the power for the flight-control surfaces. The fixed tailplane had dihedral. All trim tabs were driven electrically.

Plenty of problems were encountered, and in fact the first prototype crashed, but considerable pressure was put on NAA to get a production aircraft qualified. The company subsequently produced 22 B-45A-1 bombers, powered by the 4000 lb Allison J35-11, followed by 74 B-45A-5 bombers powered by the 5200 lb General Electric J47-3. All 96 aircraft were manufactured at the Douglas plant at Long Beach, and all were later retrofitted with the 5200 lb J47-9 or 9A. Compared with the prototypes the B-45A had a larger horizontal tail, revised fuel system, modified tailcone with the turret fitted, a vertical row of powered flaps to create a windbreak ahead of the crew door during an emergency exit by the navigator, and ejection seats for the two pilots. Following inflight structural failures the large Plexiglas canopy was replaced by one with numerous panes in a metal frame, and additional framing

TOP *A truly historic moment captured on film. Before this test over the Mojave Desert with a bombed-up B-45A in 1948, no aircraft had dropped ordnance at speeds over 500 mph. The bombs were wartime 1000-pounders, which were replaced soon after by streamlined 'slick' weapons designed specifically for external carriage by Ed Heinemann*

ABOVE LEFT *Portrait of the B-45C, which was (by modern standards) too heavy for the available thrust*

LEFT *Buzz numbers were in vogue in 1954. BE-047 flew from snow-clad Sculthorpe, England*

was added to the transparent area above the nose.

All 96 aircraft were delivered between February 1948 and June 1949. They were assigned to the 47th Bombardment Group, initially at Biggs Field in Texas but from March 1949 at Barksdale AFB, Louisiana. Late the same year the 47th was deactivated, its aircraft going to reconnaissance units or stored by the maker. After the Korean war broke out things changed, and the 47th was reactivated in March 1951, later being styled the 47th Bomb Wing (Light). The wing moved to Sculthorpe in June 1952, operating throughout Europe until receiving the B-66 in late 1956.

NAA never built the B-45B, with a radar-directed fire-control system, but did receive an order for the B-45C. This improved tactical bomber had a strengthened airframe, 937-gal (4259-litre) tip tanks, J47-13 or -15 turbojets rated at 6000 lb with water injection (supplied from 178-gal, 810-litre jettisonable tanks under the nacelles), and numerous other updates. The USAF ordered 43, but only ten were delivered, the company designation being NA-153. Operationally, the most important variant was the RB-45C reconnaissance aircraft, 33 of which were delivered, but these had no bombing capability.

SPECIFICATION

B-45A-5
Four 5200 lb General Electric J47-9A turbojets
Dimensions Span 89 ft 0.5 in (27.14 m); length 75 ft 3.5 in (22.95 m); wing area 1175.2 sq ft (109.2 m²)
Weight Empty equipped 47,775 lb (21,671 kg); maximum 92,745 lb (42,069 kg), (B-45C, 112,952 lb, 51,235 kg)
Performance Maximum speed 570 mph (917 km/h) at S/L, combat speed 500 mph (805 km/h) at 30,000 ft (ceiling); Mach limit 0.77; range at 25,000 ft (7620 m) with two 416-gal, (1893-litre) auxiliary tanks under the nacelles, 1910 miles (3056 km)
Armament Maximum bomb load 22,000 lb (9979 kg) including 27 500-lb GP bombs; some aircraft modified to carry one Mk 5 or Mk 7 nuclear weapon; two M3 Browning 0.5 in guns, each with 600 rounds

BOTTOM *B-45A 47-047 posed for Lawrence McClaren,* Flight *photographer, in the 1954-55 winter*

BELOW *Late in life the noses of many B-45A Tornados were skinned over. This aircraft (47-082) retains its tail guns*

Convair XB-46

First Flight – 2 April 1947

The same USAAF requirement that produced the B-45 also led to a rival from Convair. This great company had even more experience with bombers than North American, and when their team under Isaac M 'Mac' Laddon began work on the Model 109 – in advance of the requirement – in May 1944, they were sure that this design would win the contract for the first American jet bomber to go into production. They submitted their proposal on 6 November 1944. Following a favourable mock-up review on 29 January 1945, the company received a contract on 27 February for three prototypes designated XB-46, with numbers 45-59582/84. But the war ended, and on 14 August 1945 the San Diego plant received stop-work signals on almost all programmes. The XB-46 was reduced to a single prototype, gutted of military equipment (the other two were to be the XA-44 attack aircraft, and the three-jet XB-53 bomber with forward-swept wings, but in the end these were never built).

After the war the pressure was off. Despite this the sole XB-46 made its maiden flight on 2 April 1947, after a month of taxi testing. The flight took place not at Muroc but at the maker's home base, Lindbergh Field, San Diego. In command was E D 'Sam' Shannon.

Many would consider this single example of a pioneer jet bomber to have been one of the most aesthetically beautiful aircraft ever built. The fuselage was almost perfectly streamlined, with a circular cross-section determined mainly by the pressurised nose section for the crew. Whereas Convair's B-24 had needed a crew of 10 or 11, the larger and heavier XB-46 needed just three. The two pilots sat in tandem high up under a giant fighter-type canopy of blown Plexiglas. The entire nose was a Plexiglas moulding, attached to a very unusual forward fuselage of thick magnesium alloy, with no internal stringers. Inside it was packed with equipment for the man who served as navigator, bombardier and radar operator. Likewise the co-pilot at the back also served as radio operator, systems manager and gunner, it being his responsibility to oversee the tail-warning radar and radar-directed twin M3 0.5-in guns (of course, none of this equipment was actually fitted).

A production B-46 was intended to have General Electric J47 engines with a wet rating of at least 5200 lb, but the only engines available for the XB

BELOW *Almost the only unusual feature of the Convair jet was the startling positive angle of the twin-engine nacelles*

were four Chevrolet-built GE J35 turbojets each rated at 4000 lb. Indeed, Laddon was advised that he might have to settle for prototype TG-180 engines, which did not even have provision for driving a hydraulic pump. Thus, after much agonising, the flaps were made electric and almost everything else pneumatic.

The wing was as beautiful as everything else, with a 13/15 per cent laminar profile and aspect ratio of no less than 11.6. Chief engineer Dick Sebold said that from 40,000 ft the XB-46 could glide over 200 miles. The wing was mounted high to leave room for a bomb bay that could have actually carried more than the limit of 18,000 lb (the AAF requirement was 8000 lb for a 3500-mile range), almost the entire fuselage immediately ahead of and behind the wing being fuel tankage. Slung under each wing were the nacelles, housing two engines apiece. Air entered through flat oval inlets, from where the broad duct curved down and back in a flat S, bifurcating to feed the two engines which were under the trailing edge. The main gears each had a 65-in wheel on a single leg retracting forwards to lie between the ducts inside the nacelle. The steerable nose gear retracted backwards, and an odd feature was that none of the legs had any bracing struts. The pneumatic actuation was set at 2000 lb/sq in.

One of the impressive features of the XB-46 was its superb flaps. These were not only of the super-efficient Fowler type but they extended over 90 per cent of the span. The four sections extended on steel tracks which in cruising flight were inside the wing, carried on the flaps themselves. The electric actuators used current at 24 volts DC. With almost full-span flaps the ailerons were tiny, and this was made possible by using spoilers. Each wing had five, made of curved and perforated magnesium-alloy plate, extended over a distance of 20 ft from 55 to 68 per cent chord. These were powered, but all other flight controls were manually driven via spring tabs. A novel, but surely excellent, idea was that the electric trimmers were all driven via a single cockpit stick on which was mounted a symbolic model XB-46. The pilot had merely to rotate this model in the desired sense to close the appropriate microswitch, springs returning it to neutral when the correct trim had been achieved.

There was never anything very wrong with the XB-46, and some of the Convair pilots considered it 'really smooth'. The chief problems concerned the jetpipe-bleed wing deicing, the cabin-air system, and, above all, vertical oscillations caused by harmonic resonance between the wing and spoilers. There was also disbelief that, in emergency, the three men would be able to get out via the main door on the left, even though it was pneumatically powered against the airstream. They never had to try it: the programme remained a single aircraft, and this ended its days at Eglin AFB in 1950.

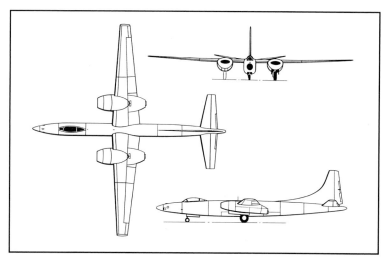

ABOVE *Though aerodynamically unadventurous, the XB-46 was one of the most graceful aircraft ever built. It is seen during high-speed taxy tests at Lindbergh Field, San Diego*

SPECIFICATION

XB-46
Four 4000 lb General Electric J35-C-3 turbojets
Dimensions Span 113 ft 0 in (34.44 m); length 105 ft 9.44 in (32.24 m); wing area 1099 sq ft (102.1 m²)
Weight Empty, equipped as bomber 48,020 lb (21,782 kg); loaded (flight test) 75,200 lb (34,111 kg); loaded (bomber) 91,000 lb (41,278 kg)
Performance Maximum speed (XB) 505 mph (813 km/h, Mach 0.74), (bomber) 565 mph; cruising speed 435 mph (700 km/h); take-off over 50 ft (91,000 lb) 6500 ft (1981 m); range (estimated) 3000 miles (4820 km) with 8000 lb (3629 kg) bombload
Armament Not fitted

Martin XB-48

First Flight – 14 June 1947

We have already seen that on 17 November 1944 the US Army Air Force had issued a formal requirement for a jet bomber. At the time there was some confusion about the terms light, medium and heavy as applied to bombers, but this requirement was originally called a medium border. Prototype contracts were signed with the three principal bomber manufacturers, Convair for the Model 109 (XB-46), Boeing for the Model 450 (XB-47) and Martin for the Model 223 (XB-48). Martin's contract was for two aircraft, numbered consecutively after the planned three XB-46s, 45-59585/6.

Whereas with the Model 179 (B-26 Marauder) in 1939 Martin had been able to design right to the very limits of available technology, with the Model 223 the Baltimore company was specifically instructed to adhere to traditional structures and aerodynamics. While the design was in progress it began to appear that German swept-wing data would make the straight-wing Martin a loser against Boeing, and by mid-1946 the whole project had become slightly half-hearted, with men being pulled off it to work instead on the company's 12 other major aircraft and missile programmes. At least the effort was made very much simpler by forgetting for the moment about advanced avionics and mission equipment, such as the nav/bombing set, radar and gunlaying fire-control. Indeed, when the first XB-48 was at last rolled out on 17 April 1947, the tail turret design had not even been tested.

The original requirement had called for a maximum bomb load of 16,500 lb and range with 8000-lb bomb load of 3500 miles. There was really only one choice of engine, the General Electric TG-180 axial turbojet, which was going into initial production by Chevrolet at a rating of 3750 lb. In September 1946 the entire J35 programme was handed to Allison, while GE got on with the improved TG-190 which became the J47, as used in the production B-47. Convair elected to use just four early J35s, and, despite having a most efficient design, failed to meet the range/load requirement. Like Boeing, Martin decided to use six engines, but installed them in what appeared to be a strange manner (though one that gave good results in tunnel testing).

The engines were installed in groups of three hung directly under the straight, thin wing. Each triple group was placed well out from the fuselage. Each engine was enclosed in a cowling with a square cross-section. Underneath, the three engine pods were joined by a double underskin which was

BELOW *Martin insisted that the narrow channels between the engines did not cause high drag, but the overall layout was too pedestrian*

convex below and flat on top, the flat top forming the bottom of a large duct between each pair of engines. The top of these ducts was made into a venturi by a further double skin, bulged down from the underside of the wing. This was so pronounced that at 400 mph the airspeed between the engines was approximately 600 mph, which seemed extremely undesirable. At the rear the upper bulges ended in open slits at the trailing edge through which discharged various secondary airflows, bleeds and oil vents. It was Martin's intention that the upper bulges should later be used to house large tanks for injection water, as well as the oil tanks. On the front of each engine was a large bullet fairing covering the electric starter, with a small cooling air hole in the centre.

Of course, the wing had a so-called laminar profile, with modest taper. Very small (31-in span) ailerons were provided at the broad tips, the primary roll control being by differential powered spoilers on the upper surface. The upper surface of the wing was extended aft over the triple jetpipes to form a kind of extended-chord flap, while all the rest of the trailing edge was fitted with powerful Fowler flaps of neat design. The wing was mounted high on the bulky fuselage, which had a deep oval section. Crew accommodation was exactly as in the rival bombers: two pilots in tandem under a large fixed canopy, and a navigator/bombardier in the nose. A total of 4163 Imp gal (18,930 litres) of fuel was housed in four fuselage tanks, two ahead of the wing and two behind, plus two tanks in the wing centre section.

Like Boeing, Martin elected to use bicycle landing gears. Large twin-wheel main gears were installed under the front and rear fuselage, the front unit retracting forwards and the rear unit aft. For lateral stability outrigger gears were installed at the outer ends of the engine boxes, retracting forwards. A great deal of development was needed on the landing gear, much of it accomplished with a grossly modified B-26, which was dubbed 'The Middle River stump-jumper'. This aircraft confirmed that steering by differential engine power was useless; nosewheel steering was essential. The XB-48 had insensitive pneumatic brakes worked (most unusually for an American aircraft) by a British-style thumb lever. On the first landing, inability to judge what was happening blew all four main tyres, and during early taxi tests one outrigger was broken.

On the first flight, on 14 June 1947, O E 'Pat' Tibbs and E R 'Dutch' Gelvin took off from Martin's 5000-ft field and landed on the 11,000-ft runway at Naval Air Station Patuxent River, Maryland. Subsequent testing showed nice handling, but it was clear that, contrary to the tunnel indications, the engine installations were causing drag 'like a brick wall'. The first aircraft was 12,000 lb overweight, but No 2 came in 95 lb below estimate, and also had simpler flaps and a revised fuel system. It

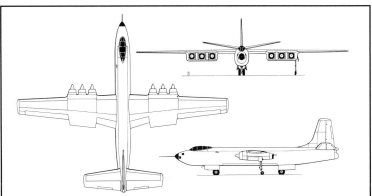

TOP *Martin tried hard with the high-lift system, which (except for the wide nacelles) extended from tip to tip. The landing gear progressed even further into the unknown*

was all rather academic, because it was clear that the Martin was not in the same class as the XB-47. Eventually Martin was reduced to trying to sell the Air Force on a B-48 powered by four Allison XT40 coupled turboprops. When that didn't work, they tried to be allowed to build B-47s. Ironically, Martin never did build the Boeing bomber, whereas two firms who had never even been picked to build the 1944 medium bomber, Douglas and Lockheed, did!

SPECIFICATION

XB-48

Six 3750-lb General Electric J35 turbojets: (No 1) J35-C-7 (Chevrolet), (No 2) J35-A-9 (Allison)

Dimensions Span 108 ft 4 in (33.02 m); length (No 1) 85 ft 9 in (26.14 m), (No 2) 87 ft 2.5 in (26.61 m); wing area 1300 sq ft (120.77 m²)

Weight Empty, equipped (No 1) 58,593 lb (26,578 kg); maximum loaded 102,600 lb (46,539 kg)

Performance Maximum speed 516 mph (830 km/h) at 20,000 ft; tactical radius 'over 800 miles' (1287 km)

Armament (Planned) bomb load of one 22,000 lb (9979 kg) bomb or 36 bombs of 250 lb; twin-0.5 in M7 guns in tail turret

Tupolev Tu-12

First Flight – 27 June 1947

As soon as Rolls-Royce Nene turbojets arrived in the Soviet Union in September 1946 several were assigned to the design bureau of A N Tupolev. To gain immediate experience with these unfamiliar but very impressive engines, two were installed in a series Tu-2S attack bomber, replacing the ASh-82FN piston engines. The tail-wheel landing gear was retained. This aircraft flew in early May 1947.

By this time not only had the design of the Type 77 (service designation Tu-12) been completed, but the first of two flight articles was also ready for flight. This amazing timescale was due in part to the fact that the Tupolev bureau had begun designing a twin-Nene version of the Tu-2 long before the engine arrived in the Soviet Union, the original idea being to design a Soviet copy of it. Thus, the first Type 77 was able to make its first flight, in the hands

of A D Perelyet (who was later killed by the failure of an experimental turboprop being tested in the eight-engined Tu-95/I), as early as 27 June 1947.

Compared with the Tu-2 the jet bomber had thicker wing skins, Nene I engines mounted in long nacelles moved further out than the original piston engines, a deeper fuselage with a longer and redesigned nose, stiffened tail, extra fuel and redesigned pilots' and gunners' stations. The landing gear was completely new, with a long steerable nose gear retracting to the rear and single-leg main gears with large single wheels retracting forwards and rotating to lie flat under the engines, covered by

BELOW *A N Tupolev never regarded the Tu-12 as anything more than an experiment to see how a piston-engined bomber would fly with turbojets*

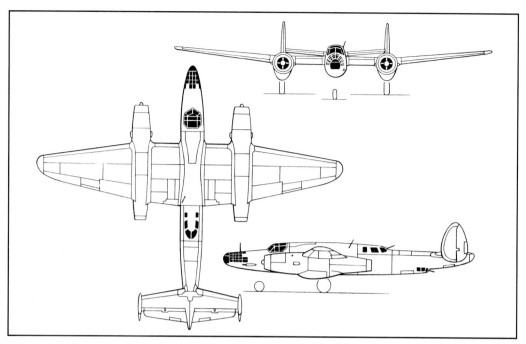

SPECIFICATION

Tu-12 (77)

Two 5000 lb Rolls-Royce Nene I

Dimensions Span 18.86 m (61 ft 10.5 in); length 15.75 m (51 ft 8 in) (second aircraft 16.45 m); wing area 48.8 m² (525.3 sq ft)

Weight Empty 8993 kg (19,826 lb); fuel, normal 4080 kg, max 6727 kg (14,830 lb); loaded (4080 kg fuel) 14,700 kg (32,407 lb), (max fuel, reduced bombload) 15,720 kg (34,656 lb)

Performance Maximum speed 778 km/h (483 mph) at S/L, 783 km/h (487 mph) at 4 km; take-off run 1030 m (3379 ft); range (hi-altitude cruise) 2200 km (1367 miles)

Armament One fixed 23 mm NR-23 gun in the nose, two manually aimed 12.7 mm UBT guns, bombload of 3 tonnes (6614 lb)

bulged doors. Almost all the new design work was done by the Tupolev bureau, no attempt being made to collaborate with the Ilyushin bureau's slightly later work on the Il-28.

So far as is known, the 77 was a satisfactory aircraft, but it was never regarded as a serious bomber for the inventory. To fill in time while better things were designed, the Tupolev OKB did receive an order for at least two further Tu-12 aircraft, generally similar to the first, with RD-45 (Nene-copy) engines. All were flying before October 1947, and one took part in the Aviation Day show at Tushino on 3 August 1947, together with the completely new Il-22.

ABOVE *Heavily retouched, this is one of three known photographs of the Tu-12, or Type 77*

Ilyushin Il-22

First Flight – 24 July 1947

In the summer of 1946 the VVS issued a requirement for a jet bomber. By this time many such aircraft had been captured from the Germans, together with such advanced designs for future production as the Ar 234C, He 343 and Ju 287. In addition, larger and more powerful jet bombers were being built in the USA. In the Soviet Union the problem was the lack of suitable engines, but the requirement stipulated the use of four of Lyulka's TR-1 axial engines. A Mach limit of not less than 0.75 was demanded, together with a speed of 750 km/h and a range at this speed of 1250 km with a two-tonne bombload.

Responses were received from the OKBs (experimental construction bureaux) of S V Ilyushin and P O Sukhoi. The Sukhoi Su-10 was a striking design with the engines in superimposed staggered pairs on the leading edge, the lower engines well ahead of the uppers, but in 1948 it was cancelled. The almost complete aircraft was subsequently used for ground instruction including taxi manoeuvring. In contrast, Ilyushin's design was built and flown, though the high hopes entertained for it were not realised.

The challenge posed by a jet bomber in 1946 needs no emphasizing, and this was especially the case in the Soviet Union. Ilyushin's design staff were aware of sweepback (which had been used at 45° for the vertical tail of the rival Su-10) but, with the agreement of the CAHI (Central Aero- and Hydro-

dynamic Institute) decided not to use it. Instead the wing was given straight taper and a symmetric laminar (CAHI 1A-10) profile, thickness varying from 12 per cent at the root to 10 per cent at the tip. The leading edge was plain, and the trailing edge comprised Fowler flaps and conventional metal-skinned ailerons. After much experiment the decision was taken to mount the engines in four separate pods, widely spaced, hung on pylons well ahead of and below the wing. This arrangement promised low drag, all-round access, easy change to a different engine type, the probability that an exploding engine would not affect its neighbour, and an apparent improvement in flow over the wing, especially at high angles of attack. Much later it was to be made a common arrangement by Boeing.

On the other hand, the slim nacelles could not accommodate the landing gears, and it was concluded that all three units of the gear had to retract into the fuselage. Ilyushin was concerned at the resulting narrow track, and to make this as wide as

BELOW *Admittedly a traditional aircraft with a new kind of engine, the Il-22 was nevertheless the subject of a great deal of design effort. It was the first important aircraft (of many thousands) to be powered by axial turbojets designed by Arkhip Lyul'ka*

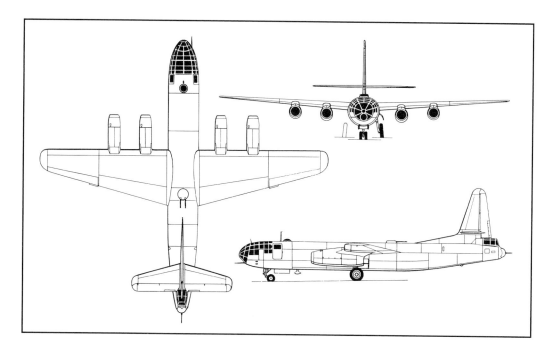

possible the main legs were arranged to extend outwards and downwards diagonally from a fuselage of wide oval cross-section. A few extra inches of track were gained by sloping the large wheels. The unusually wide fuselage was considered to be an advantage, especially in giving plenty of room for the three crew in the pressurised nose. Of fully glazed Germanic appearance, this seated the navigator/bomb aimer in front of the pilot, with the radio operator facing aft under a large transparent dome to aim the dorsal turret. A fourth man, the gunner, was in the extreme tail. The tail was quite conventional, all surfaces being metal-skinned and operated manually. The only unusual feature was that, to avoid the wake behind the wing with flaps extended, the horizontal tail was mounted fairly high up the fin.

The bomb bay was extremely large, the bomb load being limited by weight rather than volume, and easily exceeding the requirement. The twin doors were opened into the slipstream by electric screwjacks. The main gears retracted forwards about skewed axes into compartments ahead of and above the bomb bay, while the castoring twin-wheel nose gear retracted backwards under the cockpit floor. Nearly all the rest of the space in the front and rear fuselage was occupied by the three very large self-sealing fuel tanks, for a total of 9300 kg (11,600 litres). It was hoped later to modify the wing box as an integral tank. The defensive armament comprised one fixed NS-23 cannon with 150 rounds in the right side of the nose, fired by the commander, two B-20E cannon

each with 800 rounds in the VDB-5 dorsal turret, aimed under remote electrical control by the radio operator, and one NS-23 with 225 rounds in the Ilyushin Ku-3 tail turret aimed by the gunner via an electro-hydraulic system over an arc 70° left/right, 35° up and 30° down.

The single Il-22 prototype made its first flight on 24 July 1947, subsequent testing being handled by both the Kokkinaki brothers, V K and K K. This aircraft took part in the Aviation Day display over Tushino on 3 August 1947 (with no picture or report appearing in the West). The brothers were satisfied with the handling, but it was obvious that the Il-22 was an interim species of bomber, with a long take off (despite testing with two added rockets) and short-range, and it was terminated in 1948. The planned Il-24, powered by four RD-45 (Nene) engines in two twin underwing nacelles, was never built.

SPECIFICATION

Il-22

Four Lyulka TR-1 turbojets rated at 1300 kg (2866 lb); intended to fit TR-1A rated at 1500 kg (3307 lb)

Dimensions Span 23.06 m (75 ft 8 in); length 21.05 m (69 ft 0¾ in); wing area 74.5 m² (802 sq ft)

Weight Empty 14,950 kg (32,959 lb); loaded 24 tonnes (52,910 lb); maximum 27.3 tonnes (60,190 lb)

Performance Maximum speed 656 km/h (408 mph) at S/L, 718 km/h (446 mph) at 7 km; range 865 km (537 miles)

Armament One fixed NS-23, one movable NS-23 and twin movable B-20; bombload of 3 tonnes (6614 lb)

Northrop YB-49

First Flight – 21 October 1947

Throughout his life John Knudsen 'Jack' Northrop was convinced that aeroplanes could be made more efficient if everything except the wing was left out. He began trying to prove this with a light single-seater in 1928. In 1940 his first true 'all-wing' aircraft began flight testing, to be followed by the XP-56, a high-speed fighter, and then various other flying wings. By far the greatest was the XB-35 bomber.

This was a true flying wing, with a span of 172 ft. By coincidence, today Northrop is building another flying wing with exactly the same span, the B-2 'stealth bomber'. The XB-35 was hardly stealthy, because it had four enormous six-blade or eight-blade pusher contra-rotating propellers driven by engines of 3000 hp each. The first XB-35 began flight testing on 25 June 1946. It was a truly astonishing sight, and very nearly beat the B-36 to the USAAF production contract.

By 1946 it was looking as if piston-engined bombers would soon be made obsolete by jets, especially as the engines and (especially) the propellers of the giant flying wing were endlessly giving trouble. As early as 1 June 1945 the USAAF had accepted Northrop's proposal that two of the XB-35s should be completed with turbojets instead of the troubled piston engines. Contracts were signed for two of the largest jet aircraft ever built up to that time. Designated YB-49, they were to be Nos 42-102367 and 102368.

Most of the airframe was unchanged. The crew numbered seven. In the XB-35 it had numbered up to 15, included three gunners, manning sighting stations controlling 20 guns in seven remotely-aimed turrets, but this defensive armament was omitted from the two YB-49s in favour of extra fuel. The crew entered through a small hatch in the belly and went to their stations in the pressurised cabin along the centreline. The two pilots sat in tandem cockpits on the left of the centreline under a large 'fighter type' canopy. In the leading edge, to the right of the centreline apex, was a large glazed area in front of the navigator and bombardier. Further back were other specialists, though their stations were not installed in the prototypes, as well as bunks for six reserve crew.

On each side of the crew capsule were the bomb bays, intended to carry an 8000-lb load on each side, or even up to a total of 30,000 lb in an overload condition on take-off. Further out were the long slot inlets in the leading edge feeding the individual ducts to the four axial-compressor turbojets in each wing. In the XB-35 directional stability had been provided by the giant propellers, but in the YB-49 fins had to be added, slightly marring the purity of the flying wing concept. Each close-packed group of four jetpipes had a fin on each side, extended further below the wing than above. The upper fins were extended forwards most of the way across the upper surface of the wing to form a fence.

The landing gear was almost unchanged from the XB-35. The nosewheel, with a 56-in tyre, retracted electrically to the left to lie flat in the leading edge, while the twin-wheel main gears, with 66-in tyres, retracted electrically to the rear inboard of the engines, behind the outer bomb cells. As on the XB-35, enormous split flaps were fitted between the central nacelle and the outer engines for use on landing. Beyond the engines were even larger elevons, each with a span of 34 ft 6 in. Fixed slots in the leading part of the outer wings opened automatically at high angles of attack.

Obviously the flight controls of a flying wing have to be rather special. Northrop had previously

BELOW *First take-off from Northrop's Hawthorne plant of the prototype YB-49. By this time the basic airframe and control system were already mature*

patented surfaces called Decelerons, and these were fitted from the elevons to the tips. They looked like ailerons, but each could split open into upper and lower halves, like the outboard surfaces on the A-6 Intruder. The Decelerons enabled correctly co-ordinated turns to be flown, and the YB-49s also had an autopilot and, after flight testing had shown directional stability even with the four fins to be inadequate, one of the first yaw dampers. Once this was in operation the previous snaking motion vanished, enabling accurate bombing runs to be made even at 30,000 ft.

The prototype YB-49 made its first take-off from the modest airstrip adjacent to Northrop's plant at Hawthorne, Los Angeles, on 21 October 1947. The company test crew comprised pilot Max Stanley, co-pilot Charles F Bretcher and engineer Orva Douglas. This was the same crew that had made the first flight of the XB-35 more than a year earlier, but the difference this time was not only one of sound – the J35 jets poured out eight trails of sooty smoke. Some 32 minutes later they brought the monster jet wing in to Lake Muroc, making a successful flapless landing.

The No 2 YB was delivered to Muroc on 13 January 1948. Flight testing went well until the very last flight in the USAF Phase 2 acceptance programme. The aircraft involved was the No 2 (42-102368), with a test crew headed by Capt Glen Edwards, USAF. The mission included dives to limiting indicated airspeed with CG (centre of gravity) at the fully forward location. On the final dive the design limits were exceeded and the giant wing broke up. None of the crew escaped, and Muroc was renamed Edwards AFB in honour of the YB-49's pilot.

It was known that the amazingly clean wing accelerated very rapidly in a dive, and the accident was put down to too sharp a pull-up at too high a speed. It was not a black mark against the aircraft, and only five days later the USAF announced an order for 30 RB-49A reconnaissance bombers, the only jarring note being that 29 of these were to be built by deadly rival Convair at Fort Worth. In November it was decided that Northrop would rebuild ten YB-35 bombers to a new RB-35B standard with six more powerful turbojets, four in the wing and two in underwing pods.

Soon budget problems led the USAF to cancel all these programmes, leaving just one more of the giant wings to fly. This was the YRB-49A, with the same six-jet arrangement as the RB-35B. It first flew on 4 May 1950, but its mission was pure reconnaissance. Many felt that in rejecting the RB-49 the USAF had made a mistake.

ABOVE *More powerful engines enabled the YRB-49A to have half as many engines inside the wing, plus two in underslung pods*

SPECIFICATION

Northrop YB-49
Eight Allison J35-A-15 turbojets each rated at 4000 lb thrust
Dimensions Span 172 ft 0 in (52.43 m); length 53 ft 1 in (16.15 m); wing area 4000 sq ft (371.6 m²)
Weight Empty 88,100 lb (39,962 kg); loaded 196,193 lb (88,993 kg), max loaded 213,000 lb (96,617 kg)
Performance Maximum speed (max weight) 493 mph (793 km/h); cruising speed 419 mph (675 km/h); service ceiling 40,700 ft (12.4 km); range (with normal bomb load, high altitude) 3155 miles (5077 km)
Armament Normal bomb load 16,000 lb (7.25 t), maximum 30,000 lb (13.6 t)

Boeing B-47 Stratojet

First Flight – 17 December 1947

The widespread transition from piston-engined combat aircraft to jets in the late 1940s produced some truly bizarre airframe changes, but none was more sleekly futuristic than the Boeing B-47 Stratojet. For a brief period in the early 1950s this unique aircraft catapulted bomber performance onto a plateau that was beyond the reach of all but a very select band of experimental fighters, and its crews gained immediate respect from cocky young blades in the 'fast-lane' of Air Force operations. When it went into service in 1951 the B-47 seemed to epitomize the darkening menace of the new atomic age, and even now, some 40 years on, its reputation as one of the all-time classic aircraft designs remains secure.

The development of such an advanced bomber can be traced back to the spring of 1943 when the USAAF Power Plant Laboratory at Wright Field asked General Electric to produce a new turbojet with at least 4000 lb of take-off thrust. This engine, which would more than double the power of anything then available in the United States, was originally wanted for a secret fighter project (later to emerge as the Lockheed P-80 Shooting Star), but its ambitious thrust requirement also made it possible to contemplate much heavier jets, and Air Force strategists soon turned towards a multi-engined

bomber to replace vulnerable B-17s and B-24s.

General Electric responded to the requirement by offering a choice of two engines, each with a different compressor configuration. At the Lynn Works, in Massachusetts, the company had already been working on several preliminary designs using the Whittle-type double-sided centrifugal compressor. One was quickly sized for 4000 lb thrust as the I-40. Meanwhile, 150 miles away at Schenectady, New York, a separate team finished building the prototype TG-100 experimental axial-flow turboprop. Calculations suggested that the axial compressor would be more efficient than the centrifugal. The engineers at Schenectady were anxious to apply the same technology to a turbojet – the result was the 4000 lb TG-180.

The I-40 (later to become the General Electric, and then Allison J33) was selected for the Lockheed fighter. The TG-180 clearly offered tremendous potential, but it could have taken several more years to develop. As soon as the powerplant specifications were known in September 1943, the

BELOW *As 46-065 emerged into the sunshine in December 1947, nobody watching had the slightest idea that another 2000 B-47s would follow*

USAAF circulated details to major airframe manufacturers, and asked for their thoughts on a multi-engined bomber. No official requirement existed for such an aircraft, and to pay for the study a small sum was 'recovered' from an unused allocation for reconnaissance aircraft. This meant that the primary mission had to be 'reconnaissance'. The formal paperwork required the airframe to be 'readily adaptable' as a bomber.

Boeing's first reaction was Model 413, a clumsy marriage between a B-29-style wing and four TG-180 engines in widely-spaced underslung nacelles. This was submitted in January 1944, but the project office at Seattle had doubts, and aerodynamic work continued in the company's new high-speed wind tunnel. In March 1944 the Model 424 was offered. This retained the conventional layout, but the engines were bolted directly to the wing in paired box nacelles.

By the beginning of April 1944 Wright Field had received ideas from Boeing, Convair, Martin and North American. Proper funding was arranged, and, after adding about 10 per cent to the average performance criteria and reducing the suggested weights by a similar margin, the USAAF issued a formal request for proposals. This time the aircraft was designated a medium bomber; the specification called for a speed of 500 mph, service ceiling of 40,000 ft and combat radius of 1000 miles.

Boeing continued work on the 424, but drag problems persisted and in autumn 1944 the 424 was dropped in favour of the 432. This represented a new approach to bomber design. All four engines were grouped together in the bulged upper fuselage, leaving the wing clear of disturbance. The engines were fed by side intakes, and the jetpipes emerged from the rear fuselage to blast each side of the fin. A formal proposal based on the 432 was delivered to Wright Field in December 1944. In March 1945 Boeing was awarded a $150,000 Phase 1 Study contract, as the XB-47.

In spring 1945 Boeing's George Schairer joined a technical mission eager to recover as much enemy research material as possible before it was removed or destroyed. At Völkenrode, near Brunswick, a previously unknown high-speed tunnel complex was discovered, complete with masses of data showing the results of experiments with swept-back wings. Most of this information found its way back to the United States, and the lion's share went to Seattle. Ignorant of swept-wing information published in 1935, Boeing had learned about such wings in April 1945 from Robert T Jones of the

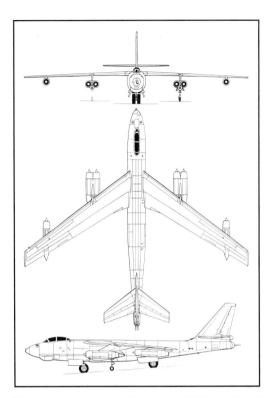

LEFT *The B-47E*

ABOVE RIGHT *Among the last Stratojets in active service were the WB-47s of the Air Weather Service*

RIGHT *A late-model B-47E at readiness – with rocket 'horse-collars' fitted – after conversion to one of five EB-47 configurations*

ABOVE *The 'horse collar' urged the B-47E down the runway through the power of no less than 33 RATO bottles*

NACA. He had predicted that transonic drag-rise would be delayed by sweeping the wing back, but had done no research to prove this. The German papers confirmed everything Jones had said. All work on the Model 432 was stopped, and Boeing embarked on an urgent programme of new tunnel experiments.

The immediate result was the Model 448, which retained the fuselage-mounted engines, but incorporated provision for wing and tail surfaces swept back 30° at the quarter-chordline. In view of the potential performance benefits, Wright Field agreed to a delay on the programme. A revised contract was drawn up in September 1945, confirming the Model 448 as the basis of the XB-47.

By this time the USAAF's flight-safety experts had expressed concern about the buried engine installation. They were worried that a powerplant disintegration or fire (which were uncomfortably

common with early jets) would be impossible to contain in the tightly-packed fuselage, leading to loss of the aircraft. Boeing had recognised this danger, and in any case were considering boosting performance by adding two more engines, so the whole powerplant installation once more came under review. Several configurations were tried, including internal and external mountings, and 'podded' engines – separated from the wing by streamlined pylons – were studied right at the end, almost as an afterthought. These were found to be very efficient, creating much less drag than box-type nacelles, and far enough removed from the primary structure to be safe in almost all circumstances. Boeing incorporated these ideas into the Model 450, and in October 1945 submitted this with a proposal that the contract be amended to include six podded engines. The Air Force agreed, and asked the company to provide a fully costed schedule for two flight prototypes. Following a period of negotiation and design refinement, during which the traditional mock-up was inspected and approved, an $8.4 million Phase II (Hardware) contract was signed in April 1946.

The Model 450 incorporated two twin-engined pods, set well below and forward of the wing at roughly 40 per cent semi-span, and these remained broadly unchanged thereafter. The single nacelles, however, were originally installed directly under the wing, right at the tips. Later, after a more detailed examination of the wing's aeroelastic behaviour, and an assessment of possible flutter and asymmetric problems, they were moved 10 ft inboard, and mounted on vestigial pylons. The prototypes were both initially fitted with General Electric TG-180 (soon to become GE and then Allison J35-GE-2) engines, rated at 3750 lb thrust for take-off.

The wing itself was a supremely elegant piece of

engineering, spanning 116 ft and employing some of the most advanced constructional techniques then available. The primary structure consisted of two massive spars linked by a series of conventional ribs and stringers. Where the wing differed from its predecessors was in the variable thickness of the skin panels covering the top and bottom of the main torsion box. These panels, which had to be manufactured especially for the aircraft, were no less than $\frac{5}{8}$ in (15.9 mm) thick at the wing root, tapering down to $\frac{3}{16}$ in (4.77 mm) at the tip. The wing was unusually heavy as a result, but the Boeing-145 laminar section generated the excellent cruising lift coefficient of 0.35–0.45. With a total area of only 1426 sq ft, the surface supported some of the highest wing-loadings ever attempted. At its optional gross take-off weight of 162,000 lb (73,482 kg) the XB-47 prototype was loaded to over 113 lb/sq ft, and later production aircraft (using exactly the same wing) grossed over 200,000 lb (90,718 kg), which gave peak loadings in excess of 140 lb/sq ft. The wing was unashamedly optimised for high-altitude cruising flight. This was fine at high speeds, and even allowed the bomber to outrun and out-turn most fighters of the day above 20,000 ft, but its field performance was lamentably poor, and it could be a real handful during take-off and landing. There were also obvious piloting problems at high altitudes.

There were no high-lift devices on the leading edge, but large Fowler flaps migrated rearwards for take-off, providing 25 per cent more lift and adding 5 per cent to the total wing area. These were operated by a hydraulic motor in the wing carry-through box, driving long torque-tubes which in turn operated two screw-jacks on each flap section. The flap angle was determined by curved steel tracks mounted on the rear face of the torsion-box. The inboard section was a conventional flap, but the smaller outboard section was a so-called 'fla-peron', linked to the pilot's control yoke to provide additional roll authority at low speeds. All the primary flying control surfaces were fully powered by the duplicated 3000 lb sq in hydraulic system. They were all of the non-reversible servo type, with artificial feel provided by simple torsion springs on the split-section ailerons, and additional 'q-springs' (responding to dynamic pressure) on the elevator and rudder. Two rows of vortex generators were mounted close to the wing leading edge, forward of the tab-controlled inboard aileron. All B-47s began to suffer from control reversal generated by wing twisting at speeds above 425 kt, and by the time the aircraft had reached 460 kt the ailerons were almost totally ineffective. Boeing tried for many years to cure this problem by experimenting on a development B-47 with hydraulically-lifted spoilers. The system worked well enough, but it took a long time to iron out buffet problems, and it was never put to use. Much of this work, however, was later applied to the B-52 and 707.

The wing of the B-47 was so thin and flexible that Boeing decided not to use it for fuel. Instead, all tankage was in the fuselage, clustered around the weapons compartment and main landing-gear bays. Self-sealing bag tanks occupied virtually all the space in the upper fuselage, from a point only 12 in behind the cockpit canopy, right down to the leading-edge of the fin, a distance of over 73 ft. The system capacity varied between 14,600 and 17,000 US gal (12,154–14,153 gal) depending on the model, but the internal tanks could be supplemented by the addition of 1500 US gal (1249 gal) jettisonable tanks under each wing. The aircraft was capable of being refuelled in flight by the new Boeing Flying Boom method, which gave it a theoretical endurance limited only by crew fatigue and the capacity of the engine lubrication system.

The weapons bay was directly beneath the wing carry-through structure, where sudden weight variations would have the least effect on aircraft stability. Early nuclear weapons were huge devices, so the corresponding bomb bay design was more than 20 ft long and occupied all the lower fuselage space between the two main undercarriage trucks. Both of the XB-47 prototypes, and all ten 'pre-production' aircraft (B-47As), were fitted with this big bomb bay. Subsequent work by government scientists managed to miniaturise most of the weapon components, and the 20-megaton B-28IN free fall bomb was eventually reduced in size until it was no bigger than a conventional 2000 lb bomb. As a result, the weapons bay for all production B-47s was reduced in length to only 14 ft. The two bomb doors and the forward airflow deflector were all hydraulically operated.

The undercarriage layout of the B-47 was dictated by the selection of a slender, shoulder-mounted wing, which was unsuitable for the stowage of hefty mainwheel units. Instead, the weight of the aircraft was supported by tandem twin-wheel trucks buried in the fuselage, with roll-over protection supplied by small outrigger wheels under the inboard engine nacelles. All four units retracted forwards, and the whole system was designed for 'pickle-switch' partial extension, so that it could be used as a progressive air-brake below the limiting speed of 305 kt. In general, the configuration worked adequately rather than well. The rear mainwheel was a long way behind the centre of gravity, and the aircraft could not be rotated on the runway by the elevators: this meant that it had to be flown off in a level attitude, and then rotated for the climb. Landing created similar problems: if the forward mainwheel unit touched first, the big braking parachute tended to hold the tail up for a long time, halving the mechanical braking effort and causing the whole aircraft to 'weathercock' around the steerable nosewheel.

The tail surfaces were conventional twin-spar structures, located on big ring-frames set into the tapered rear fuselage. The fixed-incidence horizontal tail mirrored the wing-sweep at 35° on its leading-edge (30° at quarter-chord), but the fin was even more sharply swept at 45°. The short section of fuselage aft of the fuel tanks housed most of the navigation and defence electronics, together with a strike camera and the operating rams for the rudder and elevator. The extreme rear of the fuselage was given over entirely to the seemingly unnecessary tail armament – initially two .50 calibre machine guns but later upgraded to M-24A1 20 mm can-

TOP *General Electric designed the remotely controlled radar-directed tail turret. To build at the rate needed, the Avco Crosley Division was brought in as a second source*

LEFT *With the E-model the trickle became a flood*

nons. These could either be controlled manually from the rear cockpit, or automatically using a small ranging radar set in a 'bullet' fairing just above the turret.

Despite its awesome strike capability, the B-47 was designed to be flown and operated by just three men. The pilot and co-pilot/tail-gunner occupied a tandem, fighter-style canopy, and the navigator/bombardier was buried in the nose: all three entered the aircraft through a forward-hinged, drop-down hatchway on the left-hand side of the fuselage. Both prototypes and all ten B-47As were fitted with US manufactured (Weber or Republic) ejection seats for the three crew members – but the first few batches of production aircraft were not. This illogical change was made because the early examples were all considered to be 'high-risk' development aircraft, whereas the production machines would spend most of their flying hours in high-altitude cruising flight, giving the crew adequate time to escape by conventional means. This decision took no account of the potential horrors of take-off and landing, and completely disregarded the only reason for abandoning an aircraft at high altitude – violent loss of control and imminent break-up. Luckily, someone in the Pentagon saw sense eventually, and the seats were restored on all post-1953 production: early examples of the B-47B were then retrofitted, bringing them up to B-47B-II standard. Both pilots ejected upwards, but the navigator's seat fired down through the floor, which must have limited his chance of survival below about 1500 ft.

All through its career with the USAF the B-47 was grossly underpowered. The aircraft was designed around six General Electric TG-180/J35 turbojets, and both prototypes were powered by the initial production variant of this engine – the 3750 lb thrust J35-GE-2. The J35 concept was quickly developed by General Electric into the much more powerful J47, and this was adopted as the standard powerplant. The ten pre-production aircraft and the first 87 B-47Bs were powered by J47-GE-11s, rated at 5200 lb thrust for take-off, but further development work soon boosted the power of the engine by a further 11 per cent, and the remaining B-47Bs all used the 5800 lb J47-GE-23.

Later B-47Es, which grossed over 200,000 lb for take-off, needed the extra power of the -25A engine, which was fitted with a water/alcohol injection system to boost its available take-off thrust to 7200 lb.

Even with all six engines running at peak efficiency the B-47 was never expected to achieve sparkling acceleration on the runway, so the initial airframe design included provision for auxiliary take-off rockets. All of the early aircraft – right up to the first few batches of B-47Es – were fitted with 18 RATO (rocket-assisted take-off) units manufactured by the Aerojet-General Corporation. These were permanently installed inside the rear fuselage, with their outlet ports in three carefully-angled rows, just above the rear undercarriage bays. Fired some seconds after brake-release, these delivered an extra 1000 lb of thrust each for 12 sec, which would propel a heavily loaded aircraft to 1500 ft and a safe flying speed before exhaustion. As production aircraft began to get heavier, the 18-rocket pack proved inadequate, and the system was re-designed. It was realised fairly quickly that the internal stowage of RATO bottles represented dead weight for 99 per cent of the mission, and the outlet ports encouraged flow breakaway over the rear fuselage, causing unnecessary drag. To overcome these problems the later B-47Es were fitted with an external 'U-frame' collar, which was mounted beneath the rear fuselage, aft of the main undercarriage bay. This could hold either 20 or 30 (depending on aircraft load) 1000 lb-thrust bottles, and could be jettisoned completely after take-off.

The first work-order relating to the XB-47 was issued at Seattle in June 1946, and the first hand-built prototype was rolled out of the factory just 15 months later. For the following few weeks the project engineers were engaged on the final fitting-out process, and then Boeing embarked on one of the most comprehensive ground-test programmes ever undertaken. The aircraft was cleared for flight on 14 December 1947, but the first actual take-off was delayed by bad weather until 17 December.

The XB-47 quickly proved itself to be something quite special in terms of performance and reliability, but the US Air Force seemed curiously reluctant at first to commit itself to full-scale production. The

ABOVE *Ice trials with the XB-47 were completed with little fuss, the brake-chute slowing the bomber up well within the set operational limits. This dramatic photograph was taken on 15 June 1950*

first ten B-47A development machines were not ordered until September 1948 and the first true 'production' contract was limited to a token batch of five B-47Bs, ordered on 9 April 1949. As small as they were, these orders at least allowed Boeing to establish an assembly line at its Wichita plant in Kansas, before starting on a big recruitment and training exercise in preparation for substantial future contracts.

The first major order changed the pace of the whole programme. In June 1950, just a few weeks before the first flight of the B-47A, Seattle negotiated a $303.6 million contract for 82 production-standard B-47Bs. The B-model was remarkably similar in most respects to the earlier development machines, but there were a few visible differences. The Plexiglas bomb-aiming nose was replaced on the production aircraft by a more solid, windowed compartment, with a new periscopic bomb-sight protruding from the apex. The bomb bay was reduced in size, and the fin was noticeably squared-off at the tip: the B-47B was also equipped as standard with the aft-facing gun turret – which had only been fitted to a few of the development airframes. The first two batches of B-47Bs (a total of 87 aircraft) retained the 5200 lb thrust J47-GE-11 engines, but later batches were fitted with the more powerful J47-GE-23. A total of 399 B-47Bs were produced between 1950 and 1953, all but 19 of them being assembled at Wichita.

The first B-47B made its maiden flight on 26 April 1951, by which time Boeing had secured orders for another 590 aircraft. These included the final batches of B-47Bs (312 aircraft, all with -23 engines); the first order for the 'definitive' bomber variant (226 B-47Es); and the first batch of a new reconnaissance variant (52 RB-47Es). At this point it became obvious that even the highly productive Boeing organisation could not keep pace with the delivery demands of SAC, so Lockheed and Douglas were drawn into the programme and contracted to produce B-47Es at government-owned factories in Marietta, Georgia, and Tulsa, Oklahoma. To ease their transition into this new field, Boeing's Wichita plant produced 19 examples of the earlier B-47B in 'kit' form, ten for final-assembly on the Douglas line, and the rest for Lockheed. By the time this second-source programme had finished in 1957, Douglas had produced 264 B-47Es and Lockheed 386.

The E-model itself was a big improvement on the B-47B. The new airframe was strengthened at several key points to improve its fatigue resistance, and the undercarriage was beefed-up to accommodate take-off weights in the region of 200,000 lb. These changes inevitably reduced the usable volume inside the fuselage, which led to a slight reduction in the overall fuel capacity. The defensive guns were upgraded to 20 mm cannon, and a new General Electric A-5 fire-control system was fitted. The B-47E was also the first squadron-level aircraft to incorporate ejection seats for all three crew. The

glazed area around the nose compartment had gradually been getting smaller on succeeding batches of the B-47B, but on the E-model it disappeared almost completely, leaving the navigator/bombardier cocooned in a metal box, with only small 'skylight' windows to relieve the gloom. Higher operating weights obviously demanded more power: the B-47E's basic -25 engine provided just 6000 lb of thrust for take-off, which was quickly seen to be inadequate for hot, high or heavy departures. Later batches were equipped with the water/alcohol injected J47-GE-25A engine and the external RATO, which together boosted the available thrust by 35 per cent. The first B-47E flew from Wichita on 30 January 1953, and by the time production finished in 1957, no fewer than 1341 had been delivered from all three sources. In addition to the new-build aircraft, nearly 200 of the earlier B-47Bs were converted to the E standard during the period 1954–56 – in this guise they were redesignated B-47B-IIs.

The RB-47E was the first of three production-line reconnaissance versions. It used the same engine, armament and equipment-standards as the B-47E, but the fuselage was extended by 34 in forward of the cockpit to accommodate a fixed radar camera. The weapons compartment was virtually the same as that on the bomber (indeed, the RB-47E retained a residual bombing capability), but its operational load normally consisted of pre-prepared reconnaissance pallets, each equipped with up to 11 cameras: the bomb doors were not fitted with windows, so they had to be opened during the actual photographic run. Two pilots were retained, but the navigator/bombardier was replaced by a specialist navigator/photographer. The first of 240 RB-47Es flew from Wichita on 3 July 1953, and the type eventually equipped five medium Strategic Reconnaissance Wings during the mid-1950s. Unfortunately, the value of conventional photo-recon missions was beginning to diminish by the time the aircraft came into service, and the RB-47E wings began to deactivate as early as October 1957.

By far the most successful and longest-serving of the reconnaissance variants was the RB-47H, which was wholly dedicated to electronic-intelligence gathering. These aircraft carried a crew of six, including three EWOs (Electronic Warfare Officers – or 'Ravens' as they were known colloquially) in a cramped, pressurised compartment built into the former bomb bay. Instantly recognisable by their black dielectric nose-cones and continually changing selection of bulges, pods and antennas, the RB-47Hs were largely engaged on clandestine missions around the fringes – and sometimes deep inside – the airspace of the Soviet Union and China. Several of them were shot down during more than a decade of these highly provocative overflights. Only 35 RB-47Hs were built, all of them operated by units of the 55th SRW(M), where they remained active right up until the end of 1967.

Among the last B-47s built by Boeing's Wichita plant were 15 RB-47Ks, which were primarily dedicated to weather reconnaissance missions, but had a secondary photo-reconnaissance role. Originally ordered as RB-47Es, these aircraft were re-designated before final assembly began, and therefore qualify for the 'new-build' name-tag. They were all operated by just one squadron of the 55th SRW(M), and spent most of their time gathering continuous weather data on the proposed wartime attack routes of SAC. All 15 were delivered in 1955–56, and they remained in service until the summer of 1963.

More than 90 of the original B-47Bs were temporarily switched to a photo-reconnaissance role under the designations YRB-47B or RB-47B. These aircraft were equipped with eight cameras in the bomb bay, and were used to train crews for the new RB-47Es: when the true reconnaissance models arrived, the bombers reverted to their primary role and designation. At least 70 B-47Bs were also slated for conversion to DB-47B standard – these were unarmed drone director aircraft destined to take part in the cancelled GAM-63 Rascal missile programme. Some were certainly completed, though exactly how many is unknown. The only other major conversion of the B-47Bs resulted in the TB-47B trainer. On these aircraft the rear guns were removed, and an extra seat was installed in the cockpit to allow either a navigator or pilot instructor to be carried. Sixty-six of these were converted, all serving with the 3520th TFW at McConnell AFB in Kansas. Several one-off conversions were also applied to the B-47B airframe, most of them relating to individual trials programmes.

Although the B-47E was far more plentiful, only about 100 were converted into other designations. Several were rebuilt as YDB-47E/DB-47Es as part of the aborted GAM-63 programme, and an unknown number were reassigned to electronic deception/disruption tasking as EB-47Es: these particular aircraft carried two EWOs in the bomb bay. A separate EB-47E(TT) designation was used to describe aircraft tasked with the monitoring of Soviet space stations. ETB-47Es were modified to train specialist electronics crews, but because of the classified nature of such programmes, the numbers involved are not known. The two relatively big conversion programmes based on the B-47E resulted in the WB-47E (34 completed) and EB-47L (35). The first of these was specially prepared as a survey aircraft for the MATS Weather Service, and the second was a dedicated communications relay aircraft – the first recognition by SAC that nuclear warfare would devastate normal ground-based systems. Again, several minor conversion programmes were conducted, including the single YB-47J, which was used to test the radar bombing and navigation systems for the B-52.

Relatively few of the RB-47Es were converted – perhaps because they were more expensive air-

ABOVE *First take-off (from Boeing Field) of the XB-47D, with the four inboard jets replaced by two Wright T49 turboprops. Date, 26 August 1955*

frames in the first place. Fourteen were used as target drones under the twin designations JQB-47E and QB-47E. As is common with unmanned aircraft, these were equipped and maintained to immaculate standards, and their modifications included an arrestor hook in the aft fuselage and modified wing pods to hold cine-cameras. Three RB-47Es were also converted into ERB-47H electronic intelligence gatherers for the 55th SRW: these aircraft are known to have carried two EWOs in the bomb bay, but the exact nature of their tasking remains classified.

SPECIFICATION

Boeing B-47E
Six General Electric J47-25E single-shaft turbojets each rated at 5970 lb (7200 lb with water injection for take-off)
Dimensions Span 116 ft (35.36 m); length 109 ft 10 in (33.5 m); height 27 ft 11 in (8.52 m); wing area 1426 sq ft (132.5 m²)
Weight Empty 78,200 lb (36,281 kg); loaded 206,700 lb (93,760 kg); maximum permissible 220,000 lb (99,790 kg)
Performance Maximum speed (max weight) 606 mph (980 km/h); cruise Mach number 0.75 (early) to 0.82 (later); service ceiling 32,000 ft (9754 m) (early in mission) to 38,000 ft (11,582 m) (later) – increase in speed due to burnoff of fuel; range with maximum bomb load 3600 miles (5794 km)
Armament Remotely controlled tail turret with twin 20 mm cannon. Internal bomb load of up to 22,000 lb (9979 kg), all free-fall

Tupolev Tu-73

First Flight – 29 December 1947

In September 1946 the VVS (Soviet air force) issued a requirement for a medium attack jet bomber. It was clear from the start that the favoured powerplant would be two of the Soviet-built Nene engines, designated RD-45. Ilyushin and Tupolev responded at once, and it was taken for granted that neither the Il-22 nor the Tu-12 could be used as a starting point. Tupolev assigned the project to A A Arkhangelskii, who began work on what the bureau called Aircraft 72. He adopted many features from existing Tu bombers, including an aft-facing sight station controlling remotely directed turrets. Curiously, two of the established historians of Soviet aircraft, V B Shavrov and Václav Němček, have published totally different accounts of the resulting programmes. Indeed the Czech writer even gives the engines of the earlier Type 77 (which he calls Tu-77) as Derwents. There seems no reason to doubt that the Soviet histories, by Shavrov and K Yuriev, are correct.

According to them, Aircraft 72 remained a paper design, the first version built was the three-engined 73 and the next was the Type 78, with the mission changed to reconnaissance. There was no 78R, and both the 73 and 78 had the same engines. These comprised two imported Nene I turbojets in underwing nacelles and a Derwent V in the rear fuselage, fed by an S-duct from a simple inlet in the front of the dorsal fin. At the time this tail engine installation was unique, and it was seen next on the Martin XB-51. The third engine was adopted because Arkhangelskii calculated that two Nenes were insufficient power for a bomber weighing over 20 tonnes. It was added reluctantly; complication was to be avoided, and the third engine made it impossible to fit a tail turret.

The Tupolev OKB was aware of swept-wing data, but deliberately ignored the possibilities of such wings with this programme. Accordingly, the wing was designed with the common SR-5s profile, the thickness being 12 per cent. The engines were mounted in nacelles very similar to those designed for Type 77, hung under the ends of a straight centre section. Outboard were tapered outer wings with 5° dihedral. Inboard and outboard of the engines were hydraulically driven flaps virtually indentical to the Fowler type. All flight controls were conventional and manual, the only unusual feature being that, to avoid feared compressibility problems with the horizontal tail, that surface was swept at no less than 40°, besides being mounted half-way up the fin.

As in the Type 77 the nacelles were slung under the wing, with the Nene engines right at the front. Four inlet struts were joined to a central fairing over the accessories upstream of the compressor front bearing. A long jetpipe then extended under the wing to the propelling nozzle well aft of the trailing edge. The main landing gears resembled those of the Type 77 but were designed for much greater weights. Even though the wheels and tyres were larger they could retract into the nacelle, rotating to lie flat, without the two large doors having to be bulged. The steerable nose gear retracted to the rear, and there was also a retractable sprung tailskid.

The fuselage was completely new (if one discounts the stillborn No 72), though the crew compartment had some features in common with the Tu-2. This was Tupolev's first original design for a pressurised aircraft, and many parts were based on the technology of the B-29. The glazed nose was equipped for the navigator/bombardier, using for the first time a Soviet sight based on that of the B-29. The pilot was on the centreline, with a good view all round (as in the Tu-2, but unlike the Type 77) and behind him, facing aft, was the radio operator/gunner. The pilot fired the forward-facing guns, while the gunner had charge of twin cannon in an extremely attractive low-drag dorsal turret. Immediately aft of the wing was a separate, isolated pressure cabin for a second gunner who sighted through two lateral blisters to aim the twin ventral guns. Though the guns were newer, the whole aft armament scheme was virtually identical to that of the piston-engined Tu-8, 80 and 85. There was ample room for fuel in the fuselage and wings, and for the required fuselage bomb bay.

Aircraft 73 was first flown by F F Opadchii at the end of 1947 (most Soviet accounts say 29 December, the new edition of Shavrov says 20 December and the most recent account, by Yuriev, says merely 'at the end of December'). It proved a fine aircraft, flying 38 hours in the first month. Nevertheless, rapid development of the Nene, via the RD-45 to the VK-1, made it possible to return to

ABOVE *The Tu-73 began flight testing with the tail engine blanked off*

a much better twin-engined layout in the Type 81 and 89, which went into production. The only other three-engined prototype was Aircraft 78, a derivative of No 73 for the reconnaissance mission. It differed from No 73 in having a longer fuselage, greater fuel capacity and unspecified changes to the fin and rudder. The bombing equipment was removed. The Type 78 was first flown by Opadchii on 7 May 1948. The story has it that at the end of 1948 Marshal Vershinin ordered direct competitive evaluation of the Type 78 and the Il-28 by three regular VVS crews. All three picked the Ilyushin.

SPECIFICATION

Types 73 and 78
Two 5000 lb Rolls-Royce Nene I turbojets and one 3500 lb Derwent V turbojet
Dimensions Span 21.71 m (71 ft 2.7 in); length (73) 20.32 m (66 ft 6.7 in), (78) 20.63 m (67 ft 7.8 in); wing area 67.36 m² (725.1 sq ft)
Weight Empty (73) 14,340 kg (31,614 lb); normal loaded (73) 21,100 kg (46,517 lb), (78) 18,500 kg (40,785 lb); maximum (73) 24,200 kg (53,351 lb), (78) 23,790 kg (52,447 lb)
Performance Maximum speed at S/L (73) 840 km/h (522 mph), at 5 km (73) 872 km/h (542 mph), (78) 840 km/h; take-off run (73) 740 m (2428 ft); time to climb to 5 km (16,400 ft) (73) 9.5 min, (78) 7.7 min; range (both) 2810 km (1746 miles)
Armament (Both) Two fixed and four turret-mounted NR-23; (73 only) 3 tonnes (6614 lb) of various bombs

Ilyushin Il-28

First Flight – 8 July 1948

Thanks in part to experience gained with the Il-22, the development of this neat 'front-line' (ie, tactical) bomber could hardly have been more successful. The project was begun as a private venture by the Ilyushin OKB in December 1947, and this early start played a part in enabling the bureau to stay ahead of rival Tupolev. Another factor was that, whilst using exactly the same layout and engines, Ilyushin produced a smaller, faster and significantly more agile machine which, when it came to the crunch fly-off, resulted in a walk-over.

Despite its small size and high performance, Ilyushin was required to burden the aircraft with a heavy pressurised manned tail turret with two heavy cannon. Apart from this the crew numbered just two, a navigator/bomb aimer to the right of centre in the glazed nose and the pilot on the centreline in a fighter-type cockpit. Magnesium alloy was used for the window frames. In emergency both front crew could eject upwards, while the radio-operator/gunner could escape through his entrance hatch, as illustrated in this chapter. All crew stations were armoured, either by steel sheet nominally 10 mm thick or by D16-T dural (the material used throughout the airframe) no less than 32 mm (1.26 in) thick. Steel armour covered the two 225-round magazines for the tail guns, and the turret windows were 68 mm thick at the sides and 102 mm (over 4 in) at the rear. The total weight of armour was just over 1000 lb (455 kg).

The wing was smaller than that of the Il-22, and whereas the tail was given sweepback, to ensure good control even in a high-Mach dive, the wing had all its taper on the trailing edge. Aerofoil profile was SR-5s, with a thickness of 12 per cent. Dihedral was almost zero (0°38'). The leading edge was fixed, while the trailing edge comprised slotted flaps inboard and outboard of the engine nacelles, driven hydraulically to a maximum setting of 50°, and balanced ailerons worked by rods and bellcranks. An unusual structural feature was that almost every part of the aircraft, including the left and right wings, was divided into upper/lower or left/right halves. Each portion was completed with its internal equipment, wiring, control runs and other parts and then joined to its partner. The system needed a lot of precision tooling but worked very well.

Sweepback of all tail surfaces was 35°. The tailplane was fixed to the fin at a height that kept it clear of the jets, and it was given 7° dihedral. All tail controls were driven manually by cables and pulleys, and like the left aileron they were driven via small electrically-powered screwjacks.

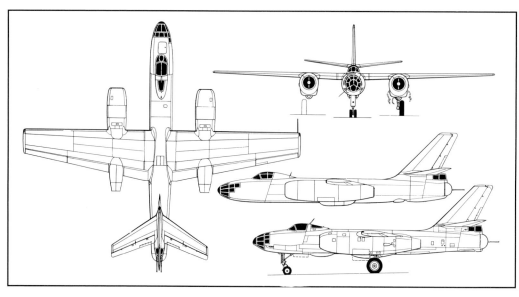

A key to the Il-28 was the export to Moscow of the best and most powerful turbojet in the world at that time, the Rolls-Royce Nene. Somehow the British government of the day thought this would curry favour with their otherwise 'difficult' former Allies. All that happened was that, while almost nothing was done with the Nene in England, it was rushed into mass production at two factories in the USSR as the RD-45, and then urgently further developed as the VK-1 (named for design leader Vladimir Klimov).

The prototype Il-28 naturally had imported Nene engines. These were mounted on steel-tube frames completely ahead of the main firewall bulkhead integral with the front spar. By simply unclipping the complete front part of the nacelle the entire engine was exposed for maintenance. The jetpipe went straight back to the nozzle well behind the trailing edge. A total of 7908 litres (1740 gallons) of fuel could be housed in three protected fuselage bag tanks ahead of the wing and two more behind. During production two 333-litre tanks were added to the wingtips of the 28R version, though these were not filled if maximum bomb load was carried.

The main landing gears were simple short legs hinged to the bottom of the third nacelle bulkhead, hydraulically retracting forwards while the wheel rotated 90° to lie flat under the jetpipe, the bay being closed by left and right doors. Tyre size was 1150 mm × 355 mm, the pressure of 7 atm even in overload condition (102 lb/sq in) being low enough for operation from rough front-line strips. The nose gear had twin wheels with 600 × 180 (later 600 × 155V) tyres and retracted backwards into a bay under the cockpit with three doors.

The fuselage had a circular section and was of the simplest possible construction. The wing was mounted almost at the top, above the bomb bay. The latter was amply large enough for the specified bombload of one tonne (2205 lb), with the overload capability of carrying one FAB-3000 bomb weighing 6614 lb. The left/right bomb doors merely hinged outwards, driven pneumatically, with an emergency standby system. Just ahead was the navigation and bombing radar. The pilot needed a ladder to reach his canopy, which hinged open to the right. He had a reflector sight for a single fixed cannon on the right side of the nose. The navigator also had to climb up to his jettisonable roof hatch. He had the radar display and M-9 visual sight copied from the American Norden.

Vladimir K Kokkinaki made the first flight on 8 July 1948. By this time the Tu-73 had been flying more than six months and already been improved into the Tu-78. A lot was riding on the decision, and in October 1948 Marshal Vershinin, Chief of Staff, boldly ordered three test crews to wring out the competing prototypes and recommend which should be selected. All had no hesitation in picking the Ilyushin. Stalin immediately announced that 25 should participate in the 1950 May Day flypast

over Red Square. Fortunately time-wasting hand-building was not necessary, because the simplicity of the aircraft and extent of the tooling, mainly at GAZ-53, enabled quantity deliveries to commence before the end of 1949. Most early aircraft had the RD-45 engine, rated at 2268 kg (5000 lb), but early in 1950 the standard engine became the VK-1A. By September 1950 a complete Frontal Aviation regiment was operational.

Over 2000 Il-28s were delivered in four years. The Il-28T was a torpedo-bomber version for the AV-MF with different radar and sight, and provision for carrying two short 533 mm torpedoes. The Il-28R with wingtip tanks first flew on 19 April 1950 and quickly became standard. The 28U was a trainer version, first flown on 18 March 1950. Without radar or armament, it replaced the navigator station by a cockpit for a pupil pilot; many served for over 25 years. A large number of Il-28s were built or converted as dedicated reconnaissance, electronic-warfare or target-towing aircraft, and from 1956 Aeroflot used a few Il-20 transport versions for carrying urgent cargo.

An estimated 1100 were eventually exported

ABOVE *Ilyushin was the leading supplier of tail turrets for Soviet bombers. The powerful door ram was needed for emergency escape*

from the Soviet Union, 500 of them to China. Czechoslovakia and Poland maintained several regiments into the late 1960s, and a small number were built under licence in the former country as the B-228. Il-28s were used by 21 air forces, and performed active war missions with Egypt, Iraq, North Korea, Nigeria, Syria, North Vietnam and both Yemens (YAR and PDRY).

In China the basic aircraft was put into mass production at Harbin as the H-5, and several hundred exported aircraft came from this source. Even today dozens of these easily-operated aircraft are still flying, though none as front line bombers. NATO called the Il-28 'Type 27', later changed to *Butcher* and then to *Beagle*. The 28U was called *Mascot*.

SPECIFICATION

Il-28
Two VK-1A turbojets each rated at 2700 kg (5952 lb)
Dimensions Span (excluding tip tanks) 21.45 m (70 ft 4½ in); length (excluding guns) 17.65 m (57 ft 11 in); wing area 60.8 m² (654.5 sq ft)
Weight Empty 12.89 t (28,417 lb); fuel 6.4 t (14,109 lb); loaded 18.4 t (40,565 lb), maximum 21.2 t (46,737 lb)
Performance Maximum speed 786 km/h (488 mph) at S/L, 902 km/h (560 mph) at 4.5 km (14,760 ft); S/L climb (normal TO weight) 900 m (2952 ft)/min; service ceiling 12.3 km (40,350 ft); range (low level) 1135 km (705 miles), (high) 2180 km (1335 miles); take-off/landing run at max allowable weights both 1.15 km (3773 ft)
Armament Two NR-23 in K-6 tail turret, each with 225 rounds; one fixed NR-23 with 100 rounds; internal bay for various bomb loads up to 3 t (6614 lb) or two torpedoes

Tupolev 82 (Tu-22)

First Flight – 24 March 1949

The first swept-wing bomber in the Soviet Union, this aircraft has always been something of a mystery. Even today several accepted authorities, including Němeček's book and the East German *Flug Revue*, have got several basic facts and figures wrong, whilst getting others correct. For example the first flight, in the hands of A D Perelyet, was not in February 1949 but on 24 March, and the engines were not VK-1s.

While Tupolev's OKB was busy with what became the Tu-14 series, Arkhangelskii suggested that they should use as many existing parts as possible in building a prototype bomber with a swept wing. In fact, though major parts of the fuselage, tail, engine nacelles and landing gear were almost identical with those of existing machines, the overall dimensions were appreciably smaller, and weights were reduced by some 30 per cent. While the Type 82 was being designed the decision was taken to change it from an experimental type to a 'frontal' (tactical) bomber, and it received the service designation Tu-22 (a number to be used again a decade later).

If the most recent Soviet drawings are to be believed, the change of mission resulted in the fuselage cross-section being changed from circular to a slim oval. This reduced the fuel capacity and weights, whilst retaining the same crew as before: navigator/bombardier in the nose, pilot behind on the centreline and gunner/radio operator in a separate pressure cabin in the tail. Compared with the earlier designs, the nose had extra glazing on top, and the pilot's canopy was of fighter type, with only two transverse and no longitudinal frames. The sole Type 82 had no tail turret fitted, but it was the intention to fit a turret of a new type with two superimposed guns. According to a recent account by K Yuriev, the guns were to be of 'calibre 20 *and* 23 mm'.

The wing was completely new, and the CAHI (Central Aero- and Hydrodynamic Institute) assisted the OKB in its design. Sweep at the quarter-chord line was 34°05′, and whereas other contemporary swept wings had an aspect ratio of 5 or less, suitable for fighters, this one had an aspect ratio of 6.9. The leading edge was fixed, and the trailing edge had

BELOW *Few photographs were ever taken of the first swept-back Tupolev, the Tu-82*

conventional flaps and ailerons. An indication of the wish to avoid too much spanwise flow is provided by the inclusion of no fewer than four fences on the upper surface of each wing, one of them inboard of the nacelles. The latter, and the landing gears, were almost identical with those of the Types 73 and 78. The horizontal tail, with its sweep of 40°, was changed only in reducing the chord and modifying the root, whereas the swept vertical tail was completely new. In most respects the No 82 tail resembled that of the later Tu-88 and Tu-95, though of course on a much smaller scale.

Clearly No 82 was intended as an attack aircraft rather than as a traditional bomber, because the modest weapon bay carried only a single weapon of 1 t (2205 lb) or combinations of smaller stores. Yet, strangely, no forward-firing guns were fitted, nor provided for, unlike the bigger Tupolev bombers and torpedo aircraft. Work began on a second prototype, with OKB number 83, with the fuselage lengthened to 19,925 m, the extra length accommodating radar, a remotely sighted dorsal turret

ahead of the fin and a larger bomb bay. This aircraft was never completed. In early 1951 the OKB was working on Type 86, a larger aircraft with two AM-2 or TR-3 (AL-5) engines. Like No 82, all these projects were dropped so that the maximum effort could be put behind the No 88, which became the Tu-16, still in service today.

SPECIFICATION

Type 82
Two 2270 kg (5000 b) RD-45F turbojets (Soviet Nene copy)
Dimensions Span 17.81 m (58 ft 5.2 in); length 17.57 m (57 ft 7.7 in); wing area 46.24 m² (497.7 sq ft)
Weight Empty 11,226 kg (24,749 lb); fuel/oil (normal) 2250 kg (4960 lb), (max) 5670 kg (12,500 lb); loaded (normal) 14,919 kg (32,890 lb), (max) 18,339 kg (40,430 lb)
Performance Maximum speed (S/L) 870 km/h (541 mph), (4 km) 931 km/h (579 mph); service ceiling 11.4 km (37,400 ft); take-off run 1100 m (3600 ft); combat range 2395 km (1488 miles)
Armament Two cannon (20 and/or 23 mm) in tail turret, 1000 kg (2205 lb) bombload

RIGHT *The bottom side view shows the unbuilt Type 83*

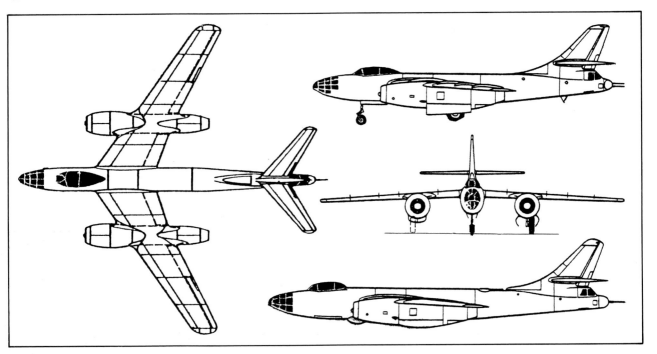

English Electric Canberra

First Flight – 13 May 1949

Bearing in mind the appearance of the XB-47, flown by Boeing in December 1947, and of the many other futuristic American jet bombers of the immediate post-war period, the English Electric A.1, which did not emerge until May 1949, seemed to suggest that Britain could no longer compete. At first glance it was not only small, but also appeared to be a pedestrian piston-engined design which just happened, precociously, to have jet engines. Not many people – outside English Electric, at least – would have dreamed that it would have one of the longest and most successful careers of any military aircraft.

English Electric (EECo) was formed in 1918 by the merger of five of Britain's biggest electrical firms, several of which had mass-produced aircraft in the recent war. The company built a few aircraft of its own design, but really got back into planemaking from 1938 with 770 Hampdens, 2145 Halifaxes and 1369 Vampires. So good was its performance – and political clout – that in 1944 it was invited to join the close-knit and jealous club of British companies which not only built other people's aircraft, but also designed their own. EECo was included in the companies invited in November 1943 to discuss the possibility of designing a jet bomber.

Managing Director Sir George Nelson decided to stay in this uncertain business, and to lead the design team picked W E W 'Teddy' Petter, previously Technical Director of Westland Aircraft. Here Petter was busy with a tactical jet bomber, personally assigned to him by Air Marshal Sir Ralph Sorley. In some ways he appeared to make a bad move. Instead of being a director, with a fine office in pleasant Yeovil, he had become a Chief Engineer with a barren office in Barton Motors' bus garage in Corporation Street in the grey rainswept Lancashire mill-town of Preston. But he knew exactly what he was doing, and proceeded to gather a design team of outstanding merit. Over the years this team has grown in political power also; despite the written belief of the 1965 Labour government that the whole Preston operation should be closed down, it is today the undisputed king of British Aerospace, while BAe factories elsewhere are closed down one after another.

It all began with this vague idea for a tactical jet bomber, which eventually supported specification E.3/45 and then B.3/45. Nobody in the Air Staff or

BELOW *Previously the sole B.5, this black machine became the prototype B(1).8*

MAP (Ministry of Aircraft Production) knew quite what to ask for, apart from 'a two-seat high-altitude bomber with jet engines and a radar bomb sight'. Petter's thinking was, from the start, polarised around a conventional aerodynamic design for easy handling and good performance to very high altitudes. He thought in terms of a wing loading of 40 lb/sq ft, compared with 54 for the Lancaster and 81 for the B-29. He soon calculated he could meet the requirement with a sea-level thrust of 13,000 lb, and that there was no point in sweeping back the wing or tail. He was, however, interested in minimum drag, and in discussions with Rolls-Royce schemed B.3/45 with a single huge centrifugal engine (a scaled-up Nene) in the rear fuselage, the latter being of exactly the same circular diameter as the engine.

When Sorley had first discussed the concept with Petter he had in mind a kind of jet version of the Mosquito. After this informal talk the project had grown to the class of the B-25 or B-26 or even larger, in the 40,000-lb class and thus roughly twice as heavy as typical Mosquitoes. Like the Mosquito but unlike the big medium bombers, the jet was considered not to need defensive armament. A crucial factor was that Sorley, as Controller of Research and Development at the MAP, was well aware of the prospects for radar bombsights which would eliminate the need for a bomb-aimer with an optical sight in a glazed nose, and this enabled the crew to be reduced to two.

Unfortunately, there was no way even Petter could reconcile the single giant engine, with its plenum chamber and inlet ducts, with the need to put a substantial bomb bay evenly disposed around the CG (centre of gravity). Yet, even these 'first thoughts', showed several of the features that were to endure, including a broad wing in the mid-position on a circular fuselage, with a conventional tail and fuselage-mounted tailplane with mild dihedral, pilot and navigator in tandem in a nose

pressure cabin with the pilot under a large full-width semi-spherical canopy moulded from a single sandwich of Perspex, and tricycle landing gear with big single main wheels retracting inwards into the inner wing.

Reluctantly Petter decided in June 1945 to split the required thrust among two 6500-lb engines, and this was (as its designation implied) the design thrust of the first Rolls-Royce axial jet, the AJ.65. At first these slimmer engines were put in the wing roots, fed by leading-edge slot inlets, and this not only left the fuselage free for fuel on top and a bomb bay underneath, but the gross weight came out 13 per cent lighter. This might have worked well, but after much thought and discussion with his team – notably Dai Ellis, Don Crowe, Freddy Page, 'Harry' Harrison and, especially, aerodynamicist Ray Creasey – Petter decided that with such ample wing thickness to play with he could move the engines out and put them completely ahead of the main spar. This improved CG position and gave all-round access to the engines and accessories. Unlike the Meteor, the resulting nacelles did not project far above and below the wing, and the only adverse features were greater engine-out yaw and slightly higher losses in the long jetpipes.

On 7 January 1946 EECo received a contract for four prototypes, which received the SBAC designation A.1. As design progressed, so did manufacture at the company's Strand Road factory, with many details assembled at Barton Motors (the Vampire production was east of the city at Samlesbury). The only major problem appeared to be very slow progress by Rolls-Royce with the engine, which they named the Avon, to the extent that in October 1947 it was decided to modify the second aircraft to have Nene engines. In 1948 the design team moved six miles west of Preston to the former USAAF airfield called Warton. Here a flight-test organisation was set up, and No 25 hangar prepared for A.1 assembly.

The first prototype, VN799, was in fact fitted with two Avons of the RA.2 type. These had the inner diameter of the axial compressor increased to reduce airflow by 10 per cent, and this at last moved the surge line clear of normal operating regions. The RA.2 still had a massive single-stage turbine with an extremely poor efficiency (76 per cent) and it was pegged at a take-off thrust of 6000 lb. Two RA.2s at last got airborne in a Rolls-Royce Lancastrian on 15 August 1948, but until quite near VN799's first flight it was uncertain whether the second A.1, with Nenes, might not have to be the first to fly. Gradually the Avon improved, and VN799 was rolled out for engine runs on 2 May 1949. Chief test pilot R P 'Bee' Beamont, who had worked closely with Petter since 1947, made the first hop on 9 May, showing that the new bomber could easily accelerate, fly for over 1500 ft and then without violent braking came to a stop on a 5700 ft runway.

Beamont made the first flight on Friday the 13th (of May 1949). Apart from severe rudder overbalance the aircraft handled beautifully. From this day onwards the British media were less inclined to point out how foolish it had been to entrust Britain's first jet bomber to 'an electrical firm with no idea how to design aeroplanes'.

Painted the grey-blue colour (officially, Cerulean blue) used by RAF photo-reconnaissance aircraft, VN799 differed mainly in its engines from its wartime predecessors. It was made from the same thicknesses of the same aluminium alloys, fabricated by the same methods. The broad wing had a thickness/chord ratio of 12 per cent at the root and 9 per cent at the tip, and the simplest possible structure with just one main spar. The leading edge was fixed, and the hydraulically driven flaps were of the conventional split type. All flight controls were boldly manual, with cables replaced by push-rods. The ailerons had shrouded beak (pressure-balanced) noses and spring tabs, the rudder a spring tab and large horn balance, and the horn-balanced elevators a spring tab on the left and a geared tab on the right. The elevators were hinged to a tailplane driven by an electric screwjack for trimming. The only thing not seen on wartime aircraft was the unusual airbrake, comprising a row of ten vertical fingers (four inboard and six slightly further out) raised hydraulically above and below the wings just behind the spar (40 fingers in all).

Mounting of the engines could hardly have been simpler, with loads taken by tubular trusses and short links direct from the main mounts to the adjacent leading edge. The capacious wing was empty, all fuel being housed in three tanks in the upper part of the fuselage, with traditional gravity fillers. Ahead of the massive wing-spar bulkhead were tanks 1 and 2, of the internally supported self-sealing type with capacities of 512 and 317 gal, and behind the bulkhead was tank 3, a lace-supported bag housing 545 gal. Later testing cleared the

TOP *VX185 was built as the sole B.5, with the navigator's position intended to be occupied by the radar that was supposed to be fitted in the first aircraft (note the flat panel in case a bombsight had to be added)*

ABOVE *The first prototype Canberra B.2 flew on 23 April 1950*

addition of a 250-gal drop tank on each wingtip. The other systems were little different from those of wartime aircraft, each engine driving a 6-kW generator for the 28-V electrics, a Lockheed pump for the single 2700 lb/sq in hydraulics and a Marshall blower plus engine bleed to serve the cabin pressurisation.

The cabin, or rather cockpit, was more like that of a fighter than a bomber. At the front was a pressure bulkhead leaving room in the nose for the nav/bombing radar. Pilot and navigator sat in tandem in Martin-Baker Mk 1C seats, the very first production pattern, the pilot left of centre. The rear pressure bulkhead provided the mounting for the navigator's

ABOVE *Canberras from Nos 13, 17 and 100 Sqns at Luqa, Malta, in 1974. In the foreground is a T.4 with Day-Glo bar markings*

seat and sloped at the angle of the seat-back. Once demisting had been perfected, the giant blown canopy was popular, giving unimpeded vision with little distortion. A circular direct-vision aperture was included to the left of centre, and a small internal windscreen was added to protect the pilot in case the canopy jettison circuit should be fired accidentally. After Beamont had demonstrated 450 kt with the canopy removed, this was replaced by a shallow deflector plate. The pilot had a spectacles wheel carried on a control column from the floor, with traditional hand-operated wheel-brakes. Entry was via a low upward-hinged door on the right.

Like many other equipment items, the main landing gears were of English Electric design and manufacture. Each comprised a single leg outboard of a single wheel with a tyre pressure which was originally only 80 lb/sq in. There was no pneumatic system, the brakes being of the disc type applied hydraulically. Each main unit retracted hydraulically inwards to lie in the wing in a bay covered by doors on the leg and hinged under the wing root. The twin-wheel nose unit was a Dowty product, with Liquid Spring levered suspension. The Canberra sat lower on the ground than any other aircraft of its size, and the tops of the nosewheels were almost level with the underside of the fuselage. Freely castoring, but without steering, the nosewheel unit retracted hydraulically to the rear into a bay closed by two rectangular doors. Above it were the radio and most of the few systems components.

The whole lower section of the centre fuselage was the impressive bomb bay, normally closed by twin hinged doors driven by a hydraulic jack. At that time nuclear weapons were expected to be too bulky and heavy for such an aircraft, and the baseline load was six 1000-lb GP bombs in two triple clutches. Alternative loads comprised one 5000-lb or two 4000-lb light-case 'blockbusters', and with maximum accelerative loading reduced

from 5 g to 3.5 g a maximum load of 10,000 lb was permitted. Provision was made for an F24 camera to be mounted vertically immediately aft of the bomb bay, and in theory various other cameras or a chaff dispenser could be installed.

In the nose was to be the vital radar bombing system. Other equipment was generally of wartime origin, comprising Gee-H navigation, Rebecca beacon-interrogation DME (distance-measuring equipment), a VHF radio, radio compass, radar altimeter for low-level operations and, in production aircraft, IFF (identification friend or foe) Mk 10 and an Orange Putter radar warning receiver and cockpit indicator.

From the start it was clear the B.3/45 was a winner. Once the rudder and elevator horns and balances had been rectified, to eliminate buffet problems, it handled like a fighter in a way not seen since the early Boulton Paul bombers. Lifting off at 80 knots, it could do virtually any manoeuvre at speeds double what Bomber Command was used to. The Service limit was to be set at 450 kt (518 mph), but every production aircraft was cleared to an indicated airspeed of 500 kt. As for altitude performance, there was nothing else in the same class in the world, one early prototype still climbing at 54,500 ft. From the viewpoint of demonstration flying, the impact of VN799 at the Farnborough airshow on 6 September 1949 was probably greater than that of any other aircraft before or since, because it was so unexpected.

The one crippling problem was complete failure – of the Telecommunications Research (later Royal Radar) Establishment at Malvern and of two firms in the industry – to produce the radar bombing system. Petter had always had a feeling this would happen, and did not demur when on 12 November 1947 a revised specification, B.5/47, was issued. This called for a completely new crew compartment, with the nose redesigned with a glazed tip and flat panel for visual bombing. This in turn meant the addition of a bomb-aimer to the crew. The navigator (officially now called the observer) was moved to the extreme left, so that the ejection seat for the bomb-aimer (who was called the nav-plotter) could go alongside. For bombing, the aimer had to go forward and lie in traditional fashion and use his T.2 optical sight. The jettisonable roof over the backseaters was given a window on each side. The pilot's seat, six inches left of centre, left room for the prone bomb-aimer on the right.

The need for a third man was obviously a retrograde step, but far more serious was the fact that the primary mission was no longer viable. There is no way a traditional bombsight could aim bombs from around 50,000 ft, unless a CEP (circular error probable) of something in excess of a quarter-mile was acceptable. This alone could well have resulted in cancellation of the whole programme, but by 1949 the desperate need of the RAF for some kind of jet other than crude day fighters resulted not only in EECo being told to continue but – remarkably, in view of the fact that this was a time of an anti-defence Labour government, and that the first prototype had not even flown – in March 1949 the company received an ITP (instruction to proceed) for production. While the various Preston factories tooled up, a welcome order arrived in July 1949 for no fewer than 132 aircraft: 90 B.5/47 bombers, 34 photo-reconnaissance aircraft to PR.31/46 and eight trainers to T.2/49. Production aircraft were all assembled at Samlesbury, the company's Vampire work tailing off to make room for the new bombers.

As noted, VN799 flew on 13 May 1949. Prototype No 2, VN813, flew on 9 November 1949, distinguished by its bulged nacelles for Nene engines which reduced normal Mach limit from 0.85 to 0.80. The third, VN828, was assembled at Samlesbury, flying to Warton on 22 November 1949. The fourth, VN850, made its first flight on 20 December 1949.

By this time the aircraft had received the unexpected name of Canberra. This choice followed interest by the Australian government, at first in an unbuilt version with Tay engines. Accordingly, the B.5/47 bomber became the Canberra B.2 (the two-seat prototypes becoming B.1s), the reconnaissance version the PR.3 and the trainer the T.4. EECo built two prototypes of the B.2, VX165 and 169, the former flying on 23 April 1950. These were the first to be powered by the greatly improved RA.3, Mk 101, engine, with a two-stage turbine, variable inlet vanes and cartridge starter. The first production B.2, WD929, flew on 8 October 1950. The first to clear production testing was WD936, and Beamont delivered it to No 101 Sqn at Binbrook on 25 May 1951. Subsequent B.2s were ferried by RAF pilots to No 27 MU at Shawbury for distribution to squadrons. All service testing was handled at Binbrook by a crew comprising Wg Cdr Hamish Mahaddie, DSO, DFC, AFC, CZMC, and navigators

Flt Lt Barlow and Plt Off (later AVM) Brownlow.

On 25 June 1950 the Korean War had broken out. This threw the British government into a near-panic, trying to organise war production to make up for five years of almost complete neglect. Orders were quickly placed for Canberra B.2s with Avro, Handley Page, and Short Brothers, and for the Avon 101 with Bristol Napier and Standard Motors. Altogether, despite its obvious operational limitations, EECo built 196 B.2s (plus others for the USA, Australia and Venezuela), Avro and Handley Page 75 each, and Short 60. The total of 418 exceeded that of any other version. From the start the Canberra was very popular, with superb handling and the ability to fly missions up to 10,000 ft higher than any intercepting fighters. The only real problems were a succession of hard-over tailplane runaways (caused by simple sticking of the trim switch), progressive jamming of the ailerons (caused by unequal contraction of metals in colder air) and the basic inability to drop bombs accurately. For a time the accident rate was serious because, as with the Meteor T.7, inexperienced pilots were being misled by sustained acceleration on overshoots, making the horizon indicate a completely false steep climb. There were other sources of controversy, notably that a number of aircraft (and sometimes crews) were lost because, to save an obscenely trivial sum, the customer consistently failed to fit the powered rudder which EECo demonstrated could reduce single-engine safety speed by at least 25 kt.

As described in the Martin B-57, WD932 was

BELOW *Another long-serving B.2 was WD953, used by Ferranti at Edinburgh on avionic testing*

flown to the USA in February 1951 to take part in an evaluation that led to the remarkable adoption of the Canberra by the USAF. In August 1951 two B.2s bought by Australia, WD939 and 983, were flown to the RAAF where they became A84-307 and A84-125. While Commonwealth Aircraft produced the Avon Mk 109 (7500-lb RA.7 rating), Government Aircraft Factories built under licence 48 Canberra B.20s, essentially a B.2 with an integral tank in each wing leading edge which together added a valuable 900 gallons. The B.20 also had some Australian or US equipment.

In late 1954 the RAF had 32 Canberra B.2 squadrons, though their only battle honour was the doubtful one of bombing Egyptian airfields in November 1956. No 45 Sqn operated against Malayan guerrillas, and other units saw active service in Cyprus and Kuwait. In contrast RAAF No 2 Sqn, with just eight B.20s, flew almost 12,000 exceedingly successful missions over Vietnam, mainly at very low level directed by USAF FACs (Forward Air Controllers). They lost two aircraft (one to a SAM hit) and one crew.

The RAAF also used T.21 trainers which, like the RAF's T.4, seated two pilots side-by-side with a navigator at the rear. The PR.3, the fifth example of which won a tough race from London to Christchurch, New Zealand, in under 24 hours in 1953, was basically a B.2 with two seats, a 14-in bay spliced into the fuselage to increase fuselage fuel from 1374 to 1917 gal, Green Satin doppler and various arrangements of cameras and flares.

In 1948 the Air Staff decided the RAF could use special target markers with airframes stressed for high indicated airspeeds, so that they could make full-power runs at low level and mark targets using radar guidance. Like the Valiant B.2, the resulting Canberra B.5 remained a single prototype, in this case the second prototype PR.3, VX185. It was completed in July 1951 with two seats and, the vital radar again failing to appear, a flat glass pane under the otherwise opaque nose for visual marking. Later it was the first British Canberra with the leading-edge integral tanks, RA.7 (Mk 109) engines and Maxaret anti-skid brake control. As well as giving 1000 lb more thrust the RA.7 had a bigger intake 'bullet' housing a triple-breech starter. Previously, every time an engine failed to start someone had to fetch another cartridge from the small magazine behind the bomb bay and spend at least five minutes loading it. VX185 few the North Atlantic in both directions in 10 hr 5 min on 26 August 1952, despite failure of all navaids except a trial-installation radio compass, the magnetic compass and a plotting chart and pencil.

The obvious next move was to replace the B.2 in production with a version that boasted the wing fuel, RA.7 and Maxaret – the resulting B.6 first flew on 26 January 1954. EECo built 45 for the RAF, and

BELOW *In 1976 they hadn't built a 'Can' for years, but in No 4 Shed Jim Hayle and Bob Ainsworth were rushed off their feet with rebuilds*

ABOVE *'Bee' Beamont extends the unusual airbrakes in order to come close to the photographic C-119 in the first B.2. They were surprisingly effective*

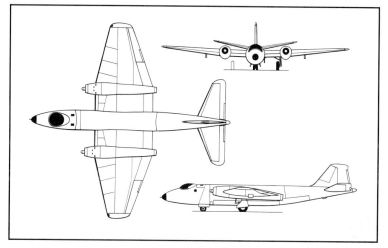

49 were licence-built by Short. EECo followed from March 1955 with 22 B(I).6, an interim 'Bomber (Intruder)' which not only added two wing pylons for 1000-lb bombs or rocket launchers but could also carry a gun pack in the rear half of the bomb bay. Produced by Boulton Paul, this pack contained four 20 mm Hispano Mk 5 cannon, each with 525 rounds, which allowed for 50 sec of continuous firing. From 1960 many Canberras became surplus, and the B(PR).6, also designated B.6R, was a reconnaissance conversion with cameras in the bomb bay and the Blue Shadow side-looking radar along the ventral centreline, which was used for navigation as well as reconnaissance. The PR.7, of which EECo built 71 for the RAF, was a PR.3 with the wing fuel, RA.7 and Maxaret, plus several new avionic and sensor items.

Next came the the definitive intruder, B(I).8. This not only looked much better, but it at last accepted that stooging about with a T.2 sight at 50,000 ft was pointless, and that a tough manoeuvrable vehicle like the Canberra was really an ideal attack aircraft. Naturally incorporating the wing fuel, Mk 109 engine and Maxaret, the Mk 8 had a totally rethought crew compartment. The pilot was moved to the rear and seated higher up in a Mk 2CB or 3CS seat (many Martin-Baker sub-types were fitted to different Canberras) under a fixed but jettisonable fighter-type canopy on the left. This gave the pilot a far better all-round view, plus a birdproof windscreen and other advantages. In the glazed nose was a non-ejection seat for the navigator/bombaimer facing to the left beside the entrance (or his emergency exit) door on the right. Armament options were the same as for the B(I).6. Arguably, this is how the Canberra should have been from the start. As it was, EECo converted the B.5 to serve as the prototype and then built just 44 for the RAF,

plus 12 assembled by Short from EECo parts. This outstandingly useful aircraft served with squadrons in 2nd ATAF in Germany, where its ability to make LABS nuclear toss-deliveries formed a major part of NATO's front line.

The final new-build RAF version was the PR.9. Fitted with much more powerful Avon RA.24s and with a new inner wing and many other changes, including a crew compartment based on that of the Mk 8 but with a hinged nose and upward-hinged canopy, it was produced with EECo assistance by Short at Belfast. It closed out manufacture of 925 Canberras in Britain (631 by EECo and BAC), and a further 451 were produced in the USA and Australia making a total of 1376. Of the British production, 146 were exported new to Argentina, Australia, Ecuador, Ethiopia, France, West Germany, India, New Zealand, Peru, Rhodesia, South Africa, Sweden, the USA and Venezuela, plus a further 91 export rebuilds.

Rebuilds in Britain led to Mark numbers reaching 22. These included pilotless targets, radar trainers, target tugs, radar calibration aircraft and special electronic countermeasures trainers. Also included were two bombers, or more precisely low-level tactical strike versions. Marshall of Cambridge and Bristol converted 39 B.6 to B.15 standard, adding the wing racks, new UHF and HF radio, doppler radar feeding a Decca roller-map display, a forward-facing F95 camera in the nose and a G45 ciné camera in the starboard leading edge.

The first B.15 was flown in this form on 4 October 1960. In parallel, the same two companies also converted 19 B.6 to B.16 standard. These were very similar, but instead of being intended for Near and Far East service they went to RAF Germany. Equipment was similar to the B.15 but included Blue Shadow side-looking radar, and they were similarly tasked with low-level attack with bombs, rockets and (like the B(I).8) tactical nuclear weapons. From 1963 both marks were cleared to launch the French-built Nord AS.30 command-guidance missile from each wing pylon.

Canberras retired from RAF Bomber Command in October 1961. The Akrotiri, Cyprus, Strike Wing of B.15s was disbanded in February 1969, and No 45 Sqn in the Far East (with the PR.7s of 81 Sqn) served until January 1970. On 12/13 May 1989 RAF Wyton hosted a celebration of 40 years of Canberras, and even today more than 100 are in use in various roles in eight countries. One, WD955, has been in RAF service over 40 years. That may answer the media expert who in 1948 wrote 'How irresponsible to award such an important project to a company with no experience in designing aircraft'.

BELOW *The prototype PR.3 introduced a stretched fuselage with extra fuel and a camera bay. It was PRU Blue overall*

SPECIFICATION

Canberra B.2
Two 6500-lb Rolls-Royce Avon Mk 101 turbojets
Dimensions Span 64 ft 0 in (19.51 m); length 65 ft 6 in (19.96 m); wing area 960 sq ft (89.19 m²)
Weight Empty 22,205 lb (10.072 kg); max take-off 46,000 lb (20,866 kg)
Performance Maximum speed 570 mph (917 km/hr) at optimum height (Service Mach limit 0.84), 518 mph (834 km/hr) at sea level; service ceiling (nominal) 48,000 ft (14,630 m); mission radius, hi-lo-hi, tip-tanks retained (2000 lb bombload) 1060 nm (1220 miles, 1965 km), (8000 lb bombload) 730 nm (841 miles, 1353 km)
Armament Six ballistic or four retarded 1000-lb GP bombs, or one nuclear weapon or various smaller or practice bombs, or 300-gal auxiliary tank

Canberra B.6
Two 7500-lb Rolls-Royce Avon Mk 109 turbojets. *As above except:*
Weight Empty 22,265 lb (10,099 kg); max take-off 53,000 lb (24,041 kg)
Performance Maximum speed (clean) 605 mph (973 km/hr) over medium altitudes; combat radius, hi-lo-hi, tip tanks retained (2000-lb bombload) 1415 nm (1630 miles, 2623 km), (8000-lb bombload) 1095 nm (1261 miles, 2030 km)
Armament As above, or option of three 1000-lb bombs plus 4 × 20-mm gun pack; B(I).6, B.15, B.16, in addition two wing pylons for 1000-lb bomb, rocket launcher (37 × 2 in or 18 × 68 mm), AS.30 missile or various 7.62 mm gun pods

Canberra B(I).8. *As B.6 except:*
Weight Empty 24,140 lb (10,950 kg); max take-off 54,950 lb (24,925 kg)

Ilyushin Il-30

First Flight – August 1949

In mid-1948, with the Il-28 assured of success, the Ilyushin OKB was assigned the harder task of designing a frontal bomber to carry a 2 t (4409 lb) bombload at the magic speed of 1000 km/h (621 mph), over ranges up to 3500 km (2175 miles). The task appeared possible by combining swept wings and tail surfaces with the new TR-3 turbojet under development at the engine KB of A M Lyulka, who had provided the engines for the Il-22. Intensive research in partnership with CAHI led to the decision to use a conventional wing of SR-12S (12 per cent) profile, swept at what had become the usual angle of 35°. Despite the absence of radical features this wing was to give considerable aerodynamic difficulty and to be partly responsible for the Il-30 remaining a prototype.

Though not very much larger than the Il-28, the Il-30 proved to need much heavier structure, and various vicious circles resulted in empty and gross weights double those of the earlier bomber. The weight problem was not helped by the decision to fit a defensive armament of six NR-23 cannon, two in the Il-K6 tail turret and two each in the upper and lower remotely controlled Il-V12 turrets. Thus, the crew numbered four: navigator/bombardier in the glazed nose, pilot under the fighter-type transparent canopy, radio operator/gunner with his back to the pilot to look through a complex optical sight system, and tail gunner. The bomb bay was eventually developed to carry double the specified maximum load.

The axial engines were installed in conventional nacelles hung under the wing, projecting far to the front and rear. The leading edge was fixed, while the trailing edge had slotted flaps, divided on each side by the nacelles, and conventional ailerons. The entire tail section was very much like that of the Il-28, though the horizontal tail had slightly greater span, no dihedral and was mounted slightly higher up the fin. One major change in this aircraft was that, for the first time on a Soviet bomber, the *velociped* (bicycle) type of landing gear was adopted. Careful study was made of the landing gears of the B-47 and XB-48, and the twin-wheel main units were placed as close to the bomb bay as possible to minimise fuselage bending stresses whilst still keeping the centre of gravity roughly half way between them. The front unit was made long

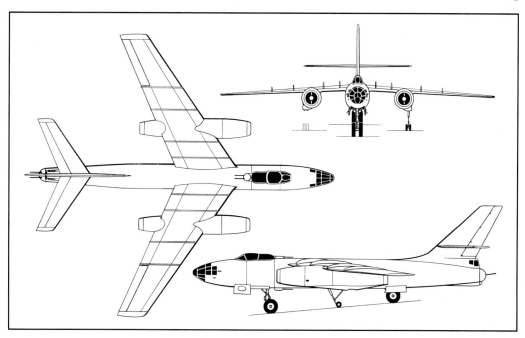

enough to give a wing angle of attack of about 9°30′; this angle hardly varied with changes in weight. Small stabilising outrigger gears were fitted under the outer sides of the nacelles, each with two small wheels retracting to the rear. A satisfactory escape system for the crew was never worked out. The pilot had an upward ejection seat, his cockpit being very similar to that of the Il-28. The other three crew had to make do, as in British V-bombers, with an emergency hatch each. These were said to open to form windbreaks to assist egress.

The single prototype made its first flight in the hands of V K Kokkinaki around the end of August 1949. By this time two airbrakes had been added to the rear fuselage, but it was here that the scanner for the panoramic radar would have had to be installed. There were problems with cabin pressurisation, and there were other shortcomings. Strangely, the official history of the S V Ilyushin OKB includes no illustration whatever of this prototype, neither are any figures given for take-off or landing distance, landing speed or various other parameters which appear for every other type.

A wordy explanation is given that the technical

features of the Il-30, and the data derived from it, were eventually put to use in the design of a new bomber to carry a bombload of 3 t over a distance of 3000 km, with the intention that at overload weight it should be possible to carry 5 t for 5000 km. The latter figures were completely beyond the capability of the Il-30, though it is not clear why this early swept wing bomber was such a disappointment. A root cause may have been the endemic aerodynamic problem with the wing, which eventually sprouted no fewer than four full-chord fences on each side, two inboard and two outboard of the engines.

SPECIFICATION

Il-30

Two Lyulka TR-3 turbojets each rated at 4600 kg (10,141 lb)

Dimensions Span 16.5 m (54 ft 2 in); length 18.7 m (61 ft 4 in); wing area 100 m² (1076 sq ft)

Weight Empty 22,967 kg (50,633 lb); loaded 32,552 kg (71,764 lb); maximum 37,552 kg (82,787 lb)

Performance Maximum speed 900 km/h at S/L, 1000 km/h (621 mph) at 5 km (16,400 ft); range 3500 km (2175 miles) at 850 km/h with 2 t bombload

Armament Three pairs of NR-23 guns in three turrets; maximum bombload 4 t (8818 lb)

BELOW *The only known photograph of the Il-30*

Tupolev Tu-14

Though the somewhat unprofessional choice of the Il-28 over the trijet Tupolev was probably correct, the latter aircraft was basically larger and could offer either heavier bombload or greater range. Arkhangelskii's brigade at the Tupolev bureau had from the start of the Type 72 been in contact with the MA (naval aviation), which throughout had favoured the Tupolev designs because of their longer range. The problem had been the third engine. Nobody had liked it, it compromised the whole design and it appeared difficult to establish the best cruise technique (Type 73 was flown with a centre-engine inlet door, cruising on the wing engines only). In early 1948, before rejection of Aircraft 73 by the VVS, V Ya Klimov informed Tupolev of the greater thrust possible at an early date from the VK-1 engine, which his team had developed from the Nene and RD-45. The decision was quickly taken to start again with an aircraft combining the best features of Types 72 and 73, using just two of the new engines. The result was Type 81, first flown by F F Opadchii on 13 October 1949.

Though major parts, notably the wing, were little changed, most of Type 81 was refined and improved in detail and design compared with Aircraft 73. By far the most important change was to fit VK-1 engines, the nacelles being changed only slightly (in such matters as access doors and auxiliary ram air inlets). This made possible elimination of the tail engine, and its replacement by a gun turret, with a pressurised compartment for the gunner. This in turn allowed the previous armament of dorsal and ventral remotely-controlled turrets, with sighting stations at the rear of the crew compartment and aft of the wing, to be deleted. This major change also permitted an increase in internal fuel capacity and a reduction in the crew from four to three.

The tail turret, ammunition and gunner weighed approximately the same as the previously installed tail engine, but other changes, notably removal of the dorsal and ventral turrets, required the forward fuselage to be lengthened to preserve CG position. The Ilyushin OKB assisted with the design of the tail turret. As originally fitted this had a lateral arc of fire of $\pm 50°$. This was one of the features criticised during the first MA (later AVMF) evaluation in May 1950, and after some redesign a modified turret was produced with the angle increased to $\pm 70°$. Further redesign took place to make better use of the extra fuselage length, and comprehensive mission avionics were installed including PSB-N navigation and bombing radar, ILS and twin radar altimeters. According to K Kosminkov many aspects of the Type 81 were 'almost ignored', including speed, take-off/landing characteristics and rate of climb. The only advantage of the big Tupolev over the little Ilyushin was longer range and endurance.

At the end of 1950 the Type 81 was accepted for production for the Aviatsiya VMF, a run of 500

BELOW *Tu-81, almost a production Tu-14T*

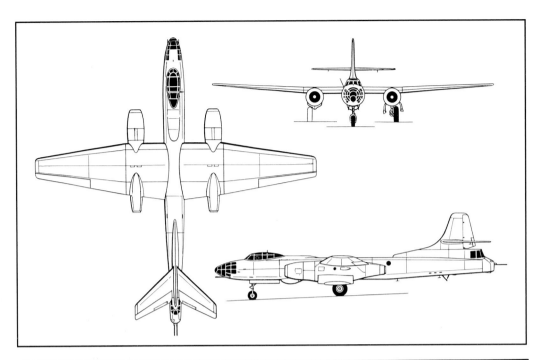

RIGHT *When the VVS picked the Il-28 the Tu-14 was shunted off to the AV-MF as a torpedo-dropper*

being funded. Service designation was to be Tu-14, but before any were completed the decision was taken to equip the aircraft as torpedo carriers. The Type 81T was the prototype, and it differed from the 81 in many details. Two NS-23 cannon; were mounted to fire ahead, controlled by the pilot; the tail turret was modified to have two NR-23 guns controlled by electric PV-23 servo circuits; the bomb bay was modified to carry two Type 45-36A torpedoes and a considerable amount of additional armour was added. Despite a weight-reduction programme the maximum weight grew from 24.6 tonnes to the figure given in the data. According to Shavrov two further NR-23 guns were added aft of the cockpit for upper defence, making six in all.

The series Tu-14T entered service with the AVMF in February 1951, and remained in front-line service for ten years. It was quite popular, though a somewhat pedestrian aircraft. In the course of operational service various modifications were made, including the addition of an ejection seat for the navigator in the nose (the pilot had one from the start) and a large ribbon-type braking parachute. A few Tu-14Ts were still flying in the 1980s.

In February 1951 Tupolev flew the sole Type 89, intended to lead to the Tu-14R recce variant. This had increased fuel capacity, and instead of bombs or torpedoes carried AFA-33-20, 30-50/75 and 33-100 cameras, a drift sight, flares and other recce equipment. It was not built in series.

SPECIFICATION

Tu-14T

Two 2700 kg (5952 lb) Klimov VK-1 turbojets

Dimensions Span 21.686 m (71 ft 1.8 in) (**89** same, **81** 21.71 m); length 21.945 m (72 ft 0 in) (**89** same, **81** 21.4 m); wing area 67.36 m² (725.1 sq ft) (**89** same, **81** 67.38 m²)

Weight Empty 14,930 kg (32,914 lb) (**81** 14,430, **89** 14,490); normal loaded (4300 kg fuel/oil) 21 t (46,296 lb); maximum (8445 kg fuel/oil) 25,350 kg (55,886 lb) (**81** 24,600 kg, **89** 25,604 kg)

Performance Maximum speed (S/L) 800 km/h (497 mph), (5 km) 845 km/h (525 mph), (**81**) 861 km/h, (**89**) 859 km/h; take-off run 1200 m (3937 ft); landing run 1020 m (with parachute 700 m, 2297 ft); service ceiling 11.2 km (36.745 ft); range 2870 km (1783 miles), (**81**) 3150 km, (**89**) 3240 km

Armament Six 23 mm cannon in three pairs; two 45-36A torpedoes or 3 t (6614 lb) of bombs

Martin XB-51

First Flight – 28 October 1949

It is curious that in both the Korean and Vietnam wars the US Air Force lacked a really effective attack aircraft, combining jet speed with long endurance, heavy weapon load and the ability to hit point targets at night. It is curious because attempts were made to procure just such an aircraft in November 1944. Admittedly at that time the speed demanded was 525 mph, and it was thought the winner might be a turboprop. In 1945, however, it was considered that swept wings probably made older ideas obsolete, so in late January 1947 the requirement for an advanced attack aircraft was reissued. Whereas the bomb load was halved, to only 4000 lb, the speed was raised to 640 mph. Moreover, the combat radius with this load was set at 600 miles, and to make matters even more challenging the aircraft was required to operate from 'front-line bases', which presumably meant relatively short unpaved strips.

Three designs submitted to the 1944 requirement had been the Curtiss XA-43, Convair XA-44 and Martin XA-45. All were two-seaters powered by turbojets. To meet the revised specification the Martin proposal was considerably modified by a special task force headed by William Van Zelm, and their proposal, the Model 234, was picked on 13 September 1947. Following a good mock-up review, the contract for Phase II design plus two prototypes was awarded in April 1948. The two aircraft were redesignated XB-51, with serials 46-685/6. The No. 1 aircraft was rolled out from the Baltimore plant on 29 July 1949, and O E 'Pat' Tibbs, flying solo, made a highly successful first flight on 28 October 1949.

In almost every way the XB-51 was breathtaking. Parked among piston-engined aircraft it looked amazing, with a colossal fuselage, tiny fighter-type canopy, two engines hung under the front and one inside the tail, a tiny swept wing, T-tail, bicycle

BELOW *Nobody could decide if the 51 was a box-car with wings or a glimpse of the future*

BOTTOM *Hardly anything about the XB-51 was normal, yet in fact its pilots were impressed*

ABOVE *One of a handful of photographs showing both prototypes together. They could almost pass for aircraft of the 1990s, in appearance at least*

landing gear, a large bomb bay and (at least in theory) eight cannon in the nose.

Martin's Marauder had frightened everyone with its wing loading of 50 lb/sq ft; the figure for the XB-51 was over 100 lb/sq ft! Martin pulled out all the stops to make this super-loaded wing give high lift for short fields by pivoting it to the fuselage, the settings normally being 2° for cruising flight and 7°30' for landing. The outer 69 per cent of the leading edge was fitted with powerful hydraulically-driven slats, while almost the entire trailing edge was occupied with slotted flaps each extended hydraulically on three external hinges to give a lift coefficient of 2.95 at 50° depression. The variable incidence was needed because, as in the XB-48, bicycle landing gear had been adopted, and this made it essential to land with the fuselage horizontal. Each twin-wheel truck retracted rearwards hydraulically, the nose unit being steerable (this also was essential). Advanced multi-plate brakes were fitted, controlled by the newly-patented Westinghouse Decelostat anti-skid system. Outrigger wheels were fitted under the wingtips, retracting

forwards into shallow compartments with rear and outer-side doors. Four assisted-take-off rockets could be attached on the sides of the huge rear fuselage, each giving 1000 lb of thrust for 14 seconds. A large ribbon-type braking parachute was housed in the fairing at the base of the rudder.

The three J47 engines were mounted in a unique way. Two were in very efficient pods carried on short pylons on the lower sides of the forward fuselage. The third was inside the extreme tail of the rear fuselage, fed by an S-duct with the inlet at the front of the fairing ahead of the fin. Common today, this had never been done before (except, unknown to Martin, by Tupolev). To facilitate cruising with the forward engines at maximum continuous rpm and the tail engine shut down, the dorsal inlet could be shut off by a 180° rotating fairing. JP-3 fuel was carried in three protected flexible cells, No 1 of 533 Imp gal above the foward landing truck, No 2 of 621 gal above the wing centre section, and No 3 of 1207 gal filling the space above the rear weapon bay and rear truck. For ferrying, two 291-gal tanks could be mounted in the weapon bay. Between tanks 1 and 2 was a tank of 117 gal capacity to provide water/alcohol for injection during take-off.

Hot-air deicing was pumped along the wing leading edges for ice protection, escaping through a slit around the wingtip. Thermal deicing was also a

ABOVE *The F-80 chase aircraft would have had no chance of staying with the XB-51 at full throttle*

feature of the tail, the shape of which caused gasps of astonishment. The rudder and elevators were hydraulically boosted, and the tailplane, on top of the fin, was hydraulically driven via an irreversible screwjack for trim and dive recovery. The entire lower half of the tail-end of the fuselage could be detached for access to the middle engine, or its removal. Immediately ahead of this removable portion was a hydraulically-powered ventral air-brake for adjustment of the glidepath. Lateral control was by very small all-speed ailerons at the wingtips plus large one-piece spoilers which could be used symmetrically after landing as lift dumpers.

The pilot and systems operator entered via a small ventral door just ahead of the front truck bay. They climbed up to ejection seats in the pressurised crew compartment, the backseater having windows above and on the right side. From the outset the XB-51 was judged a winner, and it was extremely popular with pilots and line crews alike. It was everything the XB-48 was not: fast, agile and more than able to meet every specified demand placed on it. At 55,923 lb, close to the maximum, it got off the ground in zero wind in 4340 ft, and at

645 mph could outrun everything in the USAF except the F-86. Initial climb was 7130 ft/min, and this was combined with superb handling and comprehensive avionics and weapons capability. As for serviceability, 'Chuck' Yeager flew five missions, each time being reloaded with live bombs, in 2 hr 30 min.

Researching the XB-51 in the 1970s, historian Walt Boyne found that almost all the documents had disappeared. In his view, rejection of this remarkable aircraft stemmed from the long-established antipathy of the USAF towards Martin.

SPECIFICATION

XB-51
Three General Electric J47-7 turbojets rated with water injection at 5820 lb

Dimensions Span 53 ft 1.3 in (16.18 m); length 85 ft 1.3 in (25.94 m); wing area 548 sq ft (50.91 m²)

Weight Empty 29,584 lb (13,419 kg); basic attack mission 55,923 lb (25,367 kg); maximum 62,452 lb (28,328 kg)

Performance Maximum speed at 55,923 lb (S/L) 645 mph (1038 km/h), (35,600 ft) 578 mph (930 km/h); combat radius (lo-lo) 435 miles (700 km)

Armament Eight 20 mm guns firing ahead, each with 160 rounds; up to 10,400 lb (4717 kg) of bombs up to 4000 lb size or eight 5 in rockets all carried on rotary weapon-bay door

Sud-Ouest 4000

First Flight – 16 March 1951

In the years immediately following World War 2 the French aircraft industry made tremendous efforts to rebuild its shattered factories, re-form its design teams, learn the new technologies of jet engines and transonic aerodynamics and, at the same time, become progressively less reliant on imported hardware. One of the greatest challenges was to build a jet bomber. Discounting the S.E. Grognard series, which were ground-attack fighters, the first French jet bomber prototype was the S.O.4000, produced by the SNCA du Sud-Ouest (south-west). It was a strange design, almost the only conventional thing about it being the use of two Hispano-Suiza Nene engines, the licence-built British turbojet which at the time (1947–51) powered almost every French jet aircraft.

These engines were installed close side-by-side at the tail of the extremely large, but beautifully streamlined fuselage. The only marring feature was the rather primitive shape of the inlets, on each side of the forward fuselage. Boundary-layer air was diverted by a splitter and dumped overboard through slits above and below the inlet duct. The ducts then continued for over 30 ft under the shoulder-mounted wing to reach the engines. Engine access was via large doors under the rear fuselage. The tailplanes, with elevators, were attached beside each jetpipe, and a bizarre feature was that the fin was continued down to the bottom

of the fuselage, separating the jet nozzles. Another odd feature was that the fuel capacity was a mere 1430 gal, in long shallow tanks in the top of the centre fuselage.

The nose was an empty fairing leading to the pressurised drum containing the crew of two, which in the only example built comprised a pilot and test engineer, or observer. The pilot had a fighter-type canopy and the observer a roof hatch, both hinged to open to the right. In the centre fuselage there was provision for a large bomb bay under the centre section of the wing. The wing had constant thickness of 10 per cent and a sweep at the quarter-chord line of 31°. Very large slotted flaps covered most of the trailing edge. Outboard of the flaps were small ailerons, used for roll control in conjunction with powered spoilers, which were then a novel idea. All flight controls were manual, with nearly full-span spring tabs, but it was intended to fit powered surfaces eventually.

One of the many odd features of the S.O.4000 was the landing gear. The nose unit was noteworthy mainly for its great height. It was intended to make

BELOW *The sole SO.4000 was hardly one of France's better efforts at aircraft design. Even the design team felt that they ought to start afresh – which they did with the 4050*

it steerable, and it retracted backwards into a long compartment under the pressure cabin. The main gear comprised two individual units in tandem on each side, hinged only just outboard of the wing root. All four units retracted outwards into the wings, the tandem wheels being covered by very large rectangular doors extending over 65 per cent of the wing chord. These enormous cut-outs were in the most highly stressed part of the whole aircraft! All units of the landing gear had very long levered-suspension arms allowing vertical leg travel of 1 m (39.4 in). Like the flaps, landing-gear operation was hydraulic. It was largely because of these main gears that no fuel was carried in the wings.

Because of the bomber's odd features it was preceded by two research aircraft. The S.O.M1 was a glider, while the M2 was a powered aircraft, both being models of the S.O.4000 on a 0.5 linear scale. The glider made several captive flights riding on the AAS.01 (Heinkel He 274) in 1948, but for some reason was never released. So, unexpectedly, the M2 flew first, on 13 April 1949. Powered by a single Rolls-Royce Derwent of 3500 lb thrust, it was the first French aircraft to exceed 1000 km/h (621 mph) in level flight. It had a nosewheel and three tandem mainwheels, all on the centreline, and outrigger wheels at the wingtips. The intention was that, like the original scheme for the bomber, the pilot should sit under a flush transparent roof, raising his seat to look ahead through a small hinged windscreen for landing. In the event, the M2 was given a conventional blister canopy. The M1 glider began flying on 26 September 1949, launched from the back of a Languedoc transport at 16,400 ft. Like the M2 it was used to research such features as swept wings, pilot escape through a ventral chute, spoiler control and leading-edge slats (which were locked shut on the bomber).

By the time the S.O.4000 was built – fitted like the M2 with a conventional pilot canopy – it could be seen to be not only obsolete but to have useless capabilities. It lacked power, was far too heavy, had

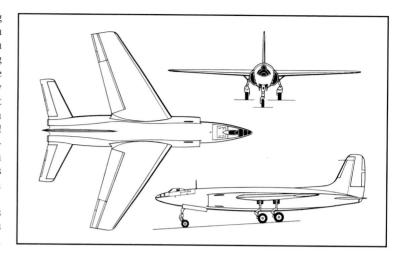

extremely poor ratio of empty to gross weight, and could not fly any useful mission. Chief test pilot Jacques Guignard flew it on 16 March 1951, just to show that it could fly. It never flew again. The planned defensive armament of twin-20 mm guns on the wingtips were never installed.

SPECIFICATION

S.O.4000
Two 2268 kg (5000 lb) Hispano-Suiza Nene 102 turbojets
Dimensions Span 17.86 m (58 ft 7 in); length 19.75 m (64 ft 10 in); wing area 75.0 m² (807 sq ft)
Weight Empty 16,583 kg (36,558 lb); maximum loaded 22 tonnes (48,510 lb)
Performance Maximum speed (estimated) 850 km/h (528 mph) at 9 km (29,530 ft); combat radius about 610 km (380 miles)
Armament Was designed to include twin-20 mm gun barbette on each wingtip and internal bombload of at least 3 tonnes (6614 lb)

BELOW *Uncertain, and wishing to proceed in small steps, SNCASO first built the S.O.M2. This at least solved problems with the landing gear – in time for the bomber to use a different arrangement!*

Alekseyev Type 150

First Flight – 14 May 1951

This bomber was for many years something of a mystery, except within a very small group in the Soviet Union. Nothing was known about it at all until 1983, when preliminary details began to emerge of a bomber called Type 150 designed in the Soviet Union by Prof Brunolf Baade, a former chief aircraft designer of Junkers. Baade had masterminded the Junkers EF 131 and EF 150, probably the most advanced bomber designs in the world in 1944. When the news of the Type 150 leaked out in the 1980s it was taken for granted that Baade had merely carried on in the Soviet Union where his team had been forced to leave off in Germany, and that the two designs were the same.

What had been known previously was that on 4 December 1958 a four-jet passenger airliner, the Baade BB 152, had made its first flight at Dresden, in what was then the German Democratic Republic. It was a product of the VEB, the East German aircraft factory, and Prof Baade was named as chief designer. Its overall configuration was an impossible one for a commercial jet, but an excellent one for a bomber. Nobody in 1958 commented on the similarity of the BB 152 to Baade's EF 150 bomber project of 14 years earlier, despite the similarity of the type numbers.

Now at last the story can be told, and the only problem is that, as told by official Soviet historian I Sultanov, history may have been slightly re-written. The official Soviet account makes only the most cursory mention of Baade, or indeed of any German input whatsoever. Perhaps Sultanov intended the type number 150 and the close similarity to the wartime EF 150 to speak for itself. According to his account, the project was launched in 1948 by the well-known OKB of S M Alekseyev, basing the design on work done at the CAHI (Central Aero- and Hydrodynamic Institute) by V N Belyaev, A N Makarevskii, G P Saishchyev and S A Christianovich.

The striking configuration was that of a bomber with swept wings and tail, the wings being mounted in the shoulder position and having two jet engines in underslung pods, and the tail being of T-type. Because of the basic layout a bicycle landing gear had to be used, with outriggers at the wingtips. Just as Martin had explored the behaviour of bicycle landing gear with a B-26, so did Alekseyev,

rebuilding one of his I-215 fighter prototypes into the I-215D. The geometry had to be slightly different because the outer stabilising wheels were mounted under the engines, well inboard, but at least the 215D showed that there were no serious problems, and also that wing angle of attack during take-off should be about 3°30'.

The single prototype, called simply Samolyet (Aircraft) 150, made its first flight on 14 May 1951 in the hands of Ya I Vernikov. It was certainly an impressive aircraft, even though, after heated arguments, it had been decided to use A M Lyulka's AL-5 engine instead of the bigger and more powerful AM-3. These turbojets were hung in pods 6639 mm (21 ft 9.4 in) long, giving all-round access to the engines, well below and ahead of the wings. The wings were almost untapered, and this certainly reduced aerodynamic efficiency. Sweep angle was 35°, and though CAHI had recommended the use of aerofoil profile S-10s-9 it was decided to use the less challenging SR-3-12, of 12 per cent thickness. The leading edge was fixed, and the trailing edge comprised large slotted flaps in two sections and conventional outboard ailerons. Two large fences were added above each wing, starting at the leading edge and terminating at the flap.

The fuselage was typically Russian, with the pressurised forward section dictating an almost circular cross-section. In the glazed nose was the navigator/bombardier, and at the upper level were the pilot, co-pilot/commander and aft-facing radar operator, the latter also manning the dorsal guns. In the tail was a small capsule for a tail gunner. Under the nose was the Argon mapping/bombing radar, and under the wing the bomb compartment 7 m (23 ft) long and 2.7 m (106 in) in diameter, with two hydraulically-driven doors. Ahead of and behind this bay were the compartments for the nose and main landing gears, both with two levered-suspension wheels and the forward unit being steerable. At full load the aft-gear oleo compressed to give a ground angle of 3°. The oleo's upper end was pinned to a forged trunnion at the extreme top of the fuselage, so that on retraction the levered leg could rotate through 92° to house the unit in its bay. The wingtip outriggers were long, even though the wings had 4° anhedral outboard of the engines. Each unit retracted rearwards into a pod fairing.

ABOVE *One of the few surviving photographs of the Type 150, in the melting slush shortly before the first flight. Both outrigger wheels are touching the ground*

RIGHT *Type 150 was essentially an attempt to build a German wartime project for service in the 1950s*

Today it is hard to imagine the visual impact of the T-tail. The sweep angle of the fin was no less than 45°, whereas that of the horizontal surface was only 33°. The latter had 8° dihedral, and the tailplane could be driven through 3°30′ for trimming, a large fairing acorn being added at the junction with the fin. Along the underside of the rear fuselage were long ventral strakes spaced at 90°. An unusual feature was that all the control surfaces were driven by electric screwjacks. An emergency wind-driven generator was installed in the fuselage.

In many ways the Type 150 exceeded the requirement. For example, speed at sea level was 850 km/h instead of the requested 790. Waiting for engines brought it into the same timescale as the Tu-88, against which it never had a chance. On the 16th flight, on 9 May 1952, the braking parachute streamed inadvertently during the landing approach, resulting in a heavy arrival which severely damaged the landing gear, fuselage and an engine pod. It was never repaired.

At the end of Sultanov's history terse mention is made of the group under Baade who 'played a part' in creating the Type 150. It is noted that Baade then returned to the German Democratic Republic, where he led the team which built two forms of BB 152, basing this design on the Type 150.

SPECIFICATION

Type 150
Two 4600 kg (10,140 lb) Lyulka AL-5 turbojets
Dimensions Span 24.1 m (79 ft 1 in); length 26.74 m (87 ft 8.8 in); wing area 125 m² (1346 sq ft)
Weight Not reported (like the dimensions, those given in many Western accounts are pure invention)
Performance Maximum speed (S/L) 850 km/h (528 mph), (at 10 km, 32,800 ft) 930 km/h (578 mph)
Armament Two pairs of NR-23 guns in two turrets; various bombs up to a maximum of 6000 kg (13,228 lb)

Vickers-Armstrongs Valiant

First Flight – 18 May 1951

At the end of World War 2 the Weybridge complex of Vickers-Armstrongs (Aircraft) Ltd was one of the world's pre-eminent centres of aeronautical expertise. The chief designer, R K (Rex) Pierson had in B N (later Sir Barnes) Wallis a colleague with exceptional talents in the stressing of basketwork structures, and incidentally, the creator of a variety of very large and unconventional bombs. No fewer than 11,461 Wellingtons had been built, using his flexible and easily-repaired Geodetic type of airframe, but experience with the four-engined Windsor suggested that even special forms of fabric covering would tear off at jet speeds. Fortunately, another designer, G R (later Sir George) Edwards, was showing promise as a master not only of modern stressed-skin structures but also of programme management and sound judgement. Other talented engineers included Maj P L Teed on basic materials research, Henry Gardner on stressing, Basil Stephenson on structure design, Elfyn Richards on aerodynamics, and (not least in the context of this chapter) Harry Zeffert on electrical systems.

As explained in the stories of the Vulcan and Victor, all the advanced thinking of the Air Staff where strategic bombers were concerned was encapsulated in specification B.35/46, issued on 9 January 1947. It is difficult for us today to comprehend how daring the notion of a large jet bomber *with swept wings* seemed at the time. Just how the resulting aircraft were considered likely to fail was never explained, because an aerodynamicist would suggest there are few problems of drag, stability or control that cannot be cured. Be that as it may, it was almost immediately decided to issue a second but earlier and less-challenging specification, B.14/46, which called for little more than a traditional aircraft fitted with jet engines; this resulted in the SA.4 Sperrin.

Britain's post-war Labour government not unnaturally put defence near the bottom of its priorities. The idea of a costly jet bomber was anathema, and by applying the traditional 'ten-year rule', a cloud-cuckoo idea which arbitrarily assumed that no war would take place in the next ten years, so nobody need show any urgency in the provision of newer weapons, the Treasury could save a lot of money each year. B.35/46 was thus seen as a very long-term effort – and, in fact, it was not to make the slightest difference to RAF Bomber Command until over 11 years after the war had ended. But many people in the corridors of power suffered inward twinges of unease, and when in June 1948 the Russians began a total blockade of Berlin, it was very suddenly obvious that the cosy ten-year rule was nonsense. Almost overnight, the need for the RAF to have jet bombers was seen as urgent.

In retrospect the whole business could hardly have been more completely mismanaged. What was needed was the best and most advanced jet bomber at the earliest possible date. This clearly meant a quick decision in choosing the best design, followed by the application of maximum effort (by a collaborative group of companies) to getting a prototype into the air in, say, 18 months, a production aircraft in a further year, followed by production of 15 aircraft per month not long thereafter. Britain certainly had the design expertise and industrial strength to do this, and the MoS (Ministry of Supply, which succeeded the Ministry of Aircraft Production on 1 April 1946) should have found no difficulty in knocking together the heads of such entrenched rivals as Sir Roy Dobson of Avro and Sir Frederick Handley Page, just by saying 'Collaborate, or you don't get a contract'. Instead the MoS ordered prototypes of three different large bombers from Avro, Handley Page and Short, and then ordered a fourth from Vickers! Even more incredibly, three of the four went into full-scale service. Just to help things along, the loser, the Short, was the only one whose prototypes were built in full production jigging.

The rationale behind the order for a fourth type was the perfectly correct belief that Vickers could, by actually pulling out all the stops, produce a bomber almost as advanced as B.35/46 but in about half the time. The company had submitted what Edwards called 'an unfunny design' to that specification, and seen it rejected for not being sufficiently 'funny'. They needed the work. The piston-engined Viking/Valetta was a short-term programme, and despite its obvious superiority the turboprop Viscount had (apparently) been rejected by BEA in favour of a fleet of Ambassadors. Thus, the Type 660 jet bomber appeared to make all the difference between, as Edwards put it, 'whether we

could pay the chaps on the shop floor to come to work' or close down. But to get the job, Edwards really had to take a gigantic risk. He had been pushing the Type 660 from late 1947, and when he at last got an Instruction To Proceed with two prototypes, on 16 April 1948, he had to agree to fly the first by mid-1951, the first production aircraft before the end of 1953 and to begin serial deliveries in early 1955. Specification B.9/48 was written around the Vickers aircraft. It had been submitted to B.35/46 with six engines of 6500 lb thrust, but with much more powerful engines in prospect, the number was cut by 1948 to four.

Today aviation enthusiasts around the world are very familiar with Lockheed's 'Skunk Works', famed for its ability to produce advanced designs quickly and in secret. Hardly any of them know that Vickers had an exactly similar organisation as part of the Weybridge complex (so, for that matter, did de Havilland, at Salisbury Hall). Deep in woods not much more than a mile from the main factory at Brooklands was Foxwarren Park. Here, under A W E (Charlie) Houghton, many secret wartime programmes had yielded results in days rather than months, and here in 1949 actual manufacture began of WB210 and WB215, the prototypes of the Type 660. It was the start of what Sir George Edwards was later to regard as 'the best aeroplane that I ever did'.

TOP *Official Ministry of Supply photo of the first prototype 'Vickers-Armstrongs B.9/48'. Note the slot intake and flaps at maximum depression*

ABOVE *Unpainted, a B.1 retained by the maker as a trials aircraft is seen at Wisley during tanker conversion*

Today the British are perhaps less locked-in to the whims of fashion. Almost entirely because we thought it meant minimum drag, we designed all three of our advanced bombers – Avro, Handley Page and now Vickers – with four tubojets buried inside the roots of the wings. The fashion had been set by de Havilland with the Comet. Today we can see that hanging the engines in separate widely spaced 'pods' below and ahead of the wings had a lot to commend it. It does not interfere with the most heavily stressed part of the structure, greatly reduces the dangers of structural failure through engine fire and the possibility of a damaged engine affecting its neighbour, can ensure that an exploded turbine wheel will not send fragments through either the crew cabin or a fuel tank, can improve airflow over the wing (by proper design of the pylon strut), provides valuable distributed mass along the span to damp out flutter, facilitates all-round access to the engines and makes it much easier to change to a completely different type of engine in the future.

Instead, burying the engines in the wing roots was accepted as a law of nature.

Vickers adopted a design Mach number of 0.84, which was compatible with a wing of 9 per cent laminar profile with the modest sweep angle of 20°. Of course, the effective thickness at the root was affected by the flow through the 'letter-box' slot inlet along the leading edge into the four Rolls-Royce Avon engines and out through their jetpipes projecting just behind the trailing edge. Early in the work aerodynamicist Richards discovered that it was a good idea if this inboard section of wing was altered so that the maximum thickness was swept sharply forward. Not only was the inboard leading edge swept at an angle of no less than 45°, but the line of peak thickness (or peak lifting suction) swept at an even sharper angle. The nominal thickness at the root was 12 per cent, and the chord no less than 35 ft 6 in, which naturally caused losses from the long inlet ducts and even longer jetpipes. Richards patented the discovery, which was later followed on

TOP *WJ954, the black B.2, is the Valiant the RAF obviously ought to have bought instead of the relatively flimsy high-altitude bomber*

ABOVE *Ready for thermonuclear radiation, aircraft and crews take a photocall before demonstrating a scramble departure in 1960 at Farnborough*

such aircraft as the Tu-16 and B-52.

A key feature of the new bombers was that, following the Mosquito's success, they would rely on speed rather than gun turrets for defence. Thus, the crew could be reduced to five, all in one pressurised compartment in the nose. At the upper level were two pilots, side-by-side on an airline-type flight deck. Below and behind were three more crew, a wireless operator (later called the Air Electronics Officer) and two navigators. The entire pressure cabin formed the fuselage between the nose and wing, naturally having a circular cross-section. In the nose was the H₂S Mk 9 radar, much bigger and more powerful than the wartime patterns and with the scanner rotating inside a giant glassfibre radome forming the entire lower half of the nose. Then came the pressure cabin, whose front bulkhead was a dish braced by radial struts and (surprisingly, on first sight) made concave to give more room for the radar, oxygen and nitrogen bottles and other items. To speed production the manufacture of the entire pressurised section was subcontracted to Saro on the Isle of Wight. In it were the two Martin-Baker Mk 3A seats for the pilots, who escaped by firing 26 explosive bolts which severed the large metal canopy in which were incorporated the seven windscreen panels and various radio antennas. It was judged that the lower-deck crew could get out in emergency through the oval main entrance door, which for this purpose was provided with a windbreak immediately upstream. Repeatedly it was shown that this idea would kill V-bomber aircrew, but despite prolonged campaigning nothing was ever done, because it would cost a little money – in sharp contrast to the supposed unfeeling Russians who took meticulous care to ensure 100 per cent safe escape for every bomber crew-member. Under the lower floor was a visual bomb-sight at the front of a blister fairing. The rear pressure bulkhead was of the conventional convex form, the periphery being joined to the rest of the fuselage. The section ahead of the wing contained avionics, air conditioning, the short steerable twin-wheel nose gear which retracted backwards into a bay with two doors (the right door carrying the HF 'towel rail' antenna), and in the extreme top of this section the dinghy and the ADF antenna.

Then came the main centre fuselage, with immensely strong cross-beams linking the two spars of the wing and supporting the weight of the five protected fuels cells along the top and the enormous bomb bay with two doors opening upward and inwards. An obvious requirement had been to accommodate a 'special weapon', and by 1952 this had come to mean not only a fission 'atom bomb' but also the bigger thermonuclear H-bomb, packaged into a shape called Blue Danube. The aft fuselage was a capacious semi-monocoque structure which, unlike the central section, did not need massively strong components machined from solid slabs of light alloy. To it was attached the simple tail, with taper rather than sweep. Mounted high enough up the fin to be well clear of the jets, the tailplane was pivoted to a fixed triangular forward root section and could be driven through a small angular range for longitudinal trim.

The wings had two main spars, far apart. Between them, at the root, were the closely-spaced engines in fireproof bays. Then came a large bay occupied by the main landing gears, which were designed at Weybridge but subcontracted to Dowty-Rotol for production. After carefully looking at

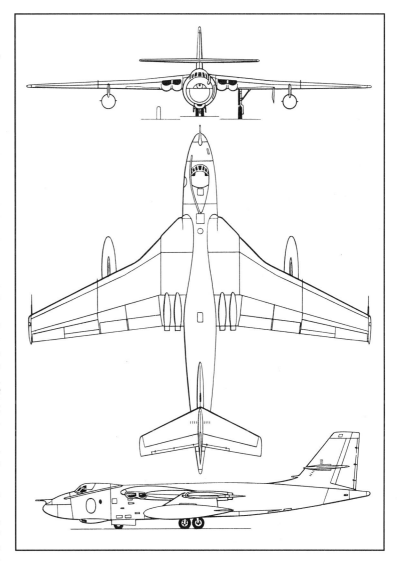

alternatives the arrangement judged best was to use two main gears on each side, in tandem. Each of the vertical legs, of S.99 high-tensile steel, carried a curved arm on which, on the inner side, was mounted a wheel with multipad anti-skid disc brakes. The two legs were joined by a telescopic link so that a single drive would pull both units out and up into the giant aperture in the wing, closed by a large door open on the ground. One of the penalties was obviously loss of fuel capacity, though fuel cells occupied almost the entire inter-spar space further outboard. To bring capacity up to the 9972 gal needed, each wing was stressed to carry a 1645-gal external tank on a deep pylon outboard of the landing, gear. Aiming mainly at the Comet 4, Boeing quipped, 'The Brits put their engines inside and fuel outside'.

The wing was horizontal, and mounted high enough for the thickest parts almost to meet at the top of the fuselage. The leading edge was fixed, but the trailing edge incorporated large outboard ailerons made in two segments moving together, the inner having geared and trim tabs, and even larger double-slotted flaps, again in inboard and outboard sections, plus similar split flaps curved to fit round the underside of the jetpipes. There were no spoilers, but four sections of perforated airbrake, again moving as one unit, were hinged to the underside of each wing ahead of the inboard flaps.

Bearing in mind the need to move fast and reduce risk, the most unexpected feature of the 660 was that, like the Fw 190 fighter, it was all-electric. In collaboration with Rotax Ltd a scheme was worked out under Zeffert's leadership whereby the only items driven by the four Avon engines (apart from such things as fuel pumps and tachometers) were big DC generators each rated at 22.5 kW. These generated all the secondary power needed throughout the aircraft. Zeffert had calculated that by generating at the exceptional potential of 112 volts the weight of cables needed would be much less than the weight of equivalent hydraulics. Using conventional hydraulics would in any case have needed electrical power at the point of application, to provide control functions and limit switches, and of course considerable electrical power would always be needed for the radar and other avionics. All-round, the all-electric high-voltage aircraft could be shown to be much simpler.

Accordingly, virtually every item requiring a mechanical powered input was driven electrically. The ailerons, elevators and rudder were all driven by Boulton Paul electro-hydraulic power units in the rear fuselage, connected via mechanical linkages. The electric power drove a variable-displacement hydraulic pump in a tiny self-contained circuit which in turn powered the hydraulic actuator. The direct electric drives to the flaps turned torque shafts which, via gearboxes and bevel gears, turned irreversible Acme-threaded drives to the carriages mounted on the flaps. Each main landing gear was driven by a ball-bearing screwjack rotated via a reduction gear by a large motor with a second half-power motor alongside as stand-by. Other motors drove the nose gear and bomb doors, as well as a row of triangular flow spoilers immediately ahead of the bay to ensure clean store separation, and the large, hinged bottom section of the rear fuselage which, on opening the bomb doors, hinged upwards to let the air flow cleanly downstream.

Hot air to drive the pressurisation and air-conditioning was tapped (bled) from the engines. Raw DC electric power was fed to Napier Spraymat heaters to deice the engine inlets. Other hot air was passed through heat exchangers ahead of the main landing gears to provide hot air to deice the wings, while further ducts supplied hot air to the tail, augmented by an unobtrusive ram inlet in the leading edge of the small dorsal fin. Immediately above this was a more prominent inlet providing dynamic 'q' pressure for the artificial-feel units in the three axes of the flight-control system. Access to the flight-control power and feel units, and to many

RIGHT *Landing at Farnborough, the B.2 shows its bogie undercarriage gears*

BELOW *Anti-flash white if anything enhanced the Valiant's appearance*

avionic items, was gained by entering the bottom of the rear fuselage and walking along a catwalk. This climbed steps up the top of the aft bomb bay, but the steepness was alleviated by the fact the aircraft sat nose-down when parked.

Smiths provided the autopilot, and navigation was to be by Marconi doppler (called Green Satin), Gee, ADF (with a flush antenna in the top of the fuselage), radar and traditional wartime methods, later supplemented by VOR/DME with sense antennas in the centre of each wingtip. Twin radar altimeters were fitted, together with ILS for bad-weather landing. There was no braking parachute, because the entire aircraft had been designed to operate easily from even quite short (6000 ft) runways.

The parts for WB210 were trucked the half-mile or so to the grass airfield at Wisley, because it offered a much longer run than tiny (3600 ft) Brooklands, and there the company's veteran test pilot Capt 'Mutt' Summers, assisted by G R 'Jock' Bryce, made a very successful maiden flight well within the agreed schedule on 18 May 1951. Brightly polished all over, it was one of the aerodynamically cleanest aircraft ever built. Apart from the thin slit inlets, the only items marring a perfect outline were the visual bombing blister, the big bulge over the cockpit (the same structural arrangement was seen on the Viscount), modest fences in line with the flap/aileron junction, the pitot tubes on the wingtips and the tiny q-feel inlet. Later the wings were given a short row of vortex generators ahead of the ailerons and fuel vents projecting behind the tips, and small vortex generators were added to the fin.

In June 1951 the 660 was named Valiant. From Flight 4 the test programme moved to another company base, Hurn, near Bournemouth (where Viscount production shops were soon in action) while Wisley was given a paved runway. Here, during a routine test on 12 January 1952 which involved repeated shut-downs and air starts, fuel built up in one engine bay where no fire-detection equipment had seemed necessary. The fuel caught fire, and by the time it was discovered the starboard wing appeared about to come off. Tragically, Sqn Ldr B H D Foster's ejection seat struck the tail, and he was killed.

WB215, the second aircraft, flew from Wisley on 11 April 1952. It had been intended to fit it with 8000-lb Armstrong Siddeley Sapphires, and accordingly the inlets and ducts were enlarged to form two distinctive shapes resembling a pair of goggles. In fact Avons were again fitted, but the larger inlets were needed to handle the much greater power of the 200-series Avons being developed for the production aircraft.

An initial order for 25 Vickers-Armstrongs Type 674 Valiant B.1 bombers had been placed in April 1951, and this was crucial in getting production going quickly. Despite shortages of everything – notably of steel, so that the jigging and tooling was

ABOVE *Loading clutches (3s and 5s) of thousand-pounders at Luqa for delivery to Egyptian targets in November 1956*

mainly concrete – the completely new Valiant shop built on the West side of Brooklands soon contained a visible assembly line. The first five Valiants to come off it were completed as Type 674 pre-production aircraft, the first of which, WP199, flew on schedule direct from the Brooklands runway on 21 December 1953. Not only did this meet the challenging 'first production' timescale but by this time Edwards' men had surpassed themselves, because on 4 September 1953 they had also flown a shiny black Valiant meeting an even tougher specification. This was WJ954, dubbed 'the Pathfinder'.

It was built to meet a far-seeing requirement for a bomber able to fly at full throttle at low level. Whereas the regular Valiant, built for the thin air of the stratosphere, was redlined at 414 mph at sea level on the grounds of inadequate structural strength and stiffness, the Type 673 was made strong enough to fly at full power at sea level, reaching 552 mph. The most obvious change in the 673 was the main landing gear. The huge cutout in the most highly stressed part of the wing was skinned over, and a completely new four-wheel

was installed in a large nacelle complete with a complex system of jettisoning, stabilisation and parachute recovery, finally landing on cushioning air bags. De Havilland Engines and the GQ Parachute company worked for over four years before the system flew on a Valiant in 1956. Then, after numerous costly packs had been delivered against a production order, the whole scheme was junked, just as were the more powerful Spectre packs for the Vulcan and Victor.

Production Type 706 Valiant B.1 bombers were distinguished by having the radar fitted, together with a longer tailcone housing warning radar. Vickers had previously schemed a neat installation of two 20 mm cannon in the tailcone, but this never got off the drawing board. Deliveries began to No 232 OCU at Gaydon spot on schedule in January 1955. From then onwards the Brooklands works regularly despatched 104 production aircraft on time and below budget, the last being XD875 flown out on 27 August 1957. They came in four main variants. Inserted into the line among 29 Valiant B.1 bombers came 11 aircraft designated B(PR).1, Type 710. This fulfilled the original B.9/48 requirement that photo-reconnaissance had to be a secondary role, the cameras (and provision for later sensors such as side-looking radar and infra-red linescan, not available in 1955) being mounted on removable pallets in the bomb bay, with windows in the doors. Next came 14 'all can do' aircraft rejoicing in the designation B.PR(K).1. The definitive aircraft was simply called B(K).1, these being the last 45 on the line.

The letter K denoted the ability to serve as an air-refuelling tanker. Amazingly, though the RAF had eagerly participated in flight-refuelling trials from 1949, using the probe and drogue system perfected by Flight Refuelling Ltd, nothing was done to fit either hose-drum units or even receiving probes to the V-bombers. When the last Valiant was on the

bogie main gear was designed which did not cut into the wing at all. Instead it retracted backwards, folding into a streamlined box (of the kind later to become familiar on Tupolev designs) with the four-wheel truck lying inverted. This gear also catered for a significant increase in weight, partly because of the much stronger airframe and partly because of extra role equipment which resulted in an increase in length of the fuselage ahead of the wing. The engines were meant to be specially designed Rolls-Royce RB.80 bypass jets, the first of that company's important series of engines later named Conway. In fact, WJ954 was to be completed with Avon RA.14s of the uprated 200-series earmarked for production Valiants. It was the last aircraft built at Foxwarren. It was also called the Valiant B.2, but foolishly it was never ordered into production, and the impressive aircraft was scrapped in 1958.

Instead of ordering the low-level bomber, millions were wasted on developing a jettisonable rocket pack to boost take-off acceleration on hot and high tropical airfields, which in the early 1950s were expected to be routine bases for RAF bombers. The original idea had been merely to clip 14 small Scarab solid motors, in two packages of seven, to strong points on the rear fuselage, but this was soon judged nothing like grand enough. Instead a special rocket engine was developed by de Havilland as the Super Sprite, which with HTP peroxide and kerosene fuel gave a mean thrust of 4200 lb for 40 sec. It

ABOVE *The camouflaged multi-role low-level aircraft resembled the early versions externally, except for the fuel pipe past the pressure cabin*

assembly line the Air Staff woke up to the fact that flight refuelling could be an important force-enhancer, and trials were urgently started using the 41st Valiant as the tanker, with an FR hose-drum unit in the rear of the bomb bay, and the 51st aircraft as the receiver with a fixed probe on the nose feeding via a pipe scabbed on the outside around the left side of the canopy to avoid penetrating the pressure cabin.

Valiant crews were the first of the RAF's élite 'V-Force', which emulated USAF Strategic Air Command. All were initially veterans, most being decorated for war service. In addition to the OCU already mentioned, the Valiant equipped, in chronological order: No 138 Sqn at Gaydon, later at Wittering; No 543, a PR unit, at Wyton; No 214 at Marham; No 49 at Wittering, later at Marham; Nos 207 and 148, completing the Wing at Marham; No 7 at Honington, later at Wittering; No 90 and then No 199, completing the Honington Wing; and finally No 18 at Finningley.

Valiants had a much more active Service career than the later V-bombers. One was entered by the RAF in the Christchurch race to New Zealand in October 1953, and would probably have won had it not been scratched at the last moment. On 11 October 1956, while a crew of No 138 Sqn were embarrassed by being given helpful homings from the tower of an Egyptian airfield they were about to bomb during the Suez campaign, Sqn Ldr E J Flavell and crew, flying WZ366, accurately dropped a live nuclear bomb over the Maralinga range in South Australia. In contrast to World War 2, when dedicated crews were often 'lost as soon as we left the airfield', Valiant crews were able to put down practice bombs from 45,000 ft with an accuracy of a few metres.

The most serious task was dropping a live thermonuclear bomb. The assignment fell to Wg Cdr Ken Hubbard, OC No 49 Sqn, and crew flying XD818 on 15 May 1957. By this time all Valiants in front-line service were painted in anti-flash white overall, with pale markings and protective blinds over the windows. The megaton-yield weapon was aimed to detonate at a point 10,000 ft above Malden Island, an atoll 400 miles south of the Christmas Island base in the Pacific. When the weapon was triggered XD818 was over ten miles away. Four more bombs, with even larger yields, were dropped before the tests, called Operation *Grapple*, were completed in November 1958.

Valiants performed extremely well in SAC Bombing Competitions and took part in numerous research and test programmes, including those for the Blue Steel cruise missile and BS.53 Pegasus vectored-thrust engine (mounted in the bomb bay). But by 1960 it was obvious (as it had been from 1951) that to penetrate hostile airspace it was necessary to fly as low as possible, to try to escape radar detection. By 1963 the remaining four units, Nos 49, 148, 207 and 214 Sqns, were assigned to SACEUR (NATO Supreme Allied Commander Europe) in the conventional low-level role, painted in grey/green camouflage with normal markings. As anyone could have predicted – and the Weybridge structures experts of what had become British Aircraft Corporation thus advised the RAF – flying Valiants at low level for any long period was courting disaster. Despite a reduction in flying rates, by August 1964 the front and rear spars of many aircraft were starting to crack. In January 1965 the decision was taken to ground the whole force, except for aircraft on special trials, and to scrap the lot. Among other things, this took away overnight the RAF's entire force of tankers, causing a near-

ABOVE *WB215, the second prototype, later carried out trials with the DH Super Sprite rocket engines*

TOP *WZ365 was one of the original silver Valiant B.1s, seen here with open airbrakes*

crisis. There was little point in commenting that, had they been Mk 2 aircraft, their attack speed would have been 140 mph faster and the trouble would have been avoided.

In a lecture to The Fellowship of Engineering, Sir George Edwards recalled a visit made to Wisley by the five most senior generals of the USAF. He said 'Impressed by the Valiant's take-off performance, they were even toying with the idea of putting it on an aircraft carrier. There was plenty of top-level American interest, but all that came of it was that Gen LeMay bullied Boeing into putting side-by-side seating in the B-52'.

One Valiant exists today. It is '818, the H-bomb dropper, and it is in the Bomber Command Museum at Hendon.

SPECIFICATION

Valiant BK.1

Four Rolls-Royce Avon Mk 204 turbojets of 10,050 lb each

Dimensions Span 34.85 m (114 ft 4 in); length 33.0 m (108 ft 3 in); wing area 219.43 m² (2362 ft²)

Weight Empty 23,419 kg (75,880 lb); normal loaded 63,504 kg (140,000 lb), max 79,380 kg (175,000 lb)

Performance Maximum speed S/L, 666 km/h (414 mph), (high altitude) 912 km/h (567 mph); service ceiling 16.46 km (54,000 ft); range (TO 140,000 lb, hi-alt, dropping 10,000-lb bomb half-way) 5550 km (3450 miles); max range with underwing tanks 7240 km (4500 miles); TO run at 140,000 lb, 1.1 km (3600 ft); landing distance from 50 ft at 110,000 lb, 1676 m (5500 ft)

Armament One thermonuclear store or 21 bombs of 454 kg (1000 lb) grouped 5/5/5/3/3

Short SA.4 Sperrin

In the Valiant chapter it was explained how the British Air Staff laboriously wrote Specification B.35/46 telling the aircraft industry – at that time comprising over a dozen companies all powerful enough to tender – what it thought it would require for a future jet bomber. A little earlier a much less-demanding specification, B.14/46, had been written, but not immediately issued. It called for a four-jet bomber to replace the piston-engined Avro Lincoln. The key elements were the ability to carry a 'special weapon' (at that time a closely guarded secret, but translated as a shape 10 feet × 10 feet × 30 feet) at 'the highest possible speed' over a round-trip distance of 3350 nautical miles (3858 miles) with an over-target height of 45,000 ft. It also included such routine items as the ability to operate from a base 'anywhere in the world', carrying 'an advanced H_2S radar', with provision for 'rapid bale-out' for the crew prior to the departure of the pilot who alone was required to have an ejection seat.

Nothing was said about giving the wing sweepback or a delta shape, in order to fly faster. This is odd, because such shapes had been openly discussed at a conference as far back as 1935, and were known to hundreds of aerodynamicists around the world. Yet, for the past 50 years, the party line has been (according to an official document) 'the practical importance of sweepback had not been appreciated until German documents had been analysed after the War'. By the time B.14/46 was written, this 'practical importance' had begun to seep through into the minds of the people of importance, but it was specifically ignored in the specification. Instead, B.14/46 was to lead to an interim bomber quickly; later the B.35/46 bomber, with 'some unorthodox shape of wing', was expected to replace it.

Four leading bomber firms tendered to B.14/46, and to the astonishment of many the submission judged best came from Short Brothers & Harland Ltd. Virtually nationalised in 1943, this 'the first aircraft company in the world' was in a sorry state. Among other headwinds, the design team under C P T Lipscomb were still at the original factory at Rochester, in Kent, whereas new manufacturing was centred at Queen's Island, Belfast, next door to chief shareholder, the Harland & Wolff shipyard.

ABOVE *Looking into the open bomb bay of the first SA.4, after the aircraft had been painted grey, red and black*

Despite this, the Short company not only came up with a perfectly sound B.14/46 design, but got it 100 per cent right first time. When it is realised that the firm had no high-speed wind tunnel, and worked out their shapes on the basis of models towed through the water of the firm's seaplane tank, one is driven to conclude that they enjoyed a fair element of luck. Moreover, they built the two prototypes in production jigs, and had anyone given them an order might have had the first Bomber Command squadron equipped before the end of 1953.

Short's order was for two prototypes, VX158 and VX161, plus a structural-test airframe. The company designation was S.42, the SBAC designation was SA.4, and later the name Sperrin was bestowed, after Ulster's chief range of mountains. Under almost every kind of difficulty, the process of design and manufacture slowly proceeded, until at last the pieces of VX158 could be taken by road, mostly in January and February 1951, from Queen's Island to the RAF airfield at Aldergrove (today Belfast Airport). The tiny city airport of Sydenham, conveniently adjacent to the Queen's Island factory, was far too small for testing a big jet bomber. Putting '158 together and completing the complex ground testing took five months, and it was not until 10 August 1951 that chief test pilot Tom Brooke-Smith was able to make the first flight. He was later joined by Wally Runciman and 'Jock' Eassie.

Except for the flight controls and the striking engine installation the SA.4 was a very straightforward aircraft. The wing had a symmetric laminar profile (A.D.7, also called RAE.103) with a thickness of 12 per cent. Most of the taper was on the leading edge. The wing was set mid-high, the obvious location between the bomb bay and fuselage tanks, at an incidence of 4°30', and with 1° dihedral. There were no root fillets. In effect there were three spars, and the skins were ordinary sheet. The only unusual structural features were that much of the airframe was of 75ST light alloy and the external rivets were inserted into hot-dimpled countersinks and then milled flush to leave a very smooth surface. The leading edge was fixed, and in contrast to the junction with the fuselage there were huge curved fillets at the junction with the engine nacelles. On the trailing edge were simple plain flaps inboard and outboard of the nacelles, and large ailerons described later. Originally the outer flaps were designed to incorporate an airbrake hinged at mid-chord, to rotate open broadside-on (similar brakes were seen on the Vampire). Before first flight this idea was replaced by split brakes opening above and below, provided the flaps were up or at the 7° setting. Maximum flap was 40°.

The enormous whale-like fuselage was made so deep in order to obtain the required 10-foot depth under the four massive beams joining the wing root ribs. The upper part of the 24 ft 4 in forward fuselage was occupied by the pressure drum for the

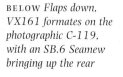

BELOW *Flaps down, VX161 formates on the photographic C-119, with an SB.6 Seamew bringing up the rear*

crew of five. At the top was the pilot, in a Martin-Baker Mk 1D seat under a jettisonable roof panel, whilst on his right was the co-pilot, in a normal fixed seat. Above the instrument panel were ten windows, one on the left being openable. At the lower level were the radio operator and two navigators, facing aft. Apart from the pilot, everyone in an emergency had to make their way to the central lower seat, fold this back, scramble through a pressure-tight door under the navigators' console and table and worm their way along a tunnel to the main entrance door, which could be power-opened to serve as a wind-break. The co-pilot's chances of escape can be left to the imagination.

As originally built, the lower part of the forward fuselage contained a block of concrete and the nose was a hemispherical cap. Later the H_2S Mk 9 radar was installed, with the scanner in a giant glassfibre radome, and the nose cap was replaced by a longer and more pointed nose incorporating a flat visual bombing window underneath. To get to this sight the bomb-aimer (one of the downstairs navigators) had to climb to the cockpit, get under the instrument panel and go down a sloping tunnel riding luge-style on a tiny powered trolley.

The tail could hardly have been simpler, though to check its ability to handle the engine-out case the vertical tail was tested on a Sunderland V with the fin mounted on a plinth simulating the bomber's fuselage. Again, there was no attempt at sweepback, though the fixed tailplane had 13° dihedral. The actual flight-control system, however, was of absorbing interest. Like the contemporary Bristol Britannia airliner, there was no connection at all between the pilot's controls and the control surfaces! Movement of any of the cockpit controls drove a gearbox which, via various pulleys and cables,

TOP *VX158 began flight-testing the de Havilland Gyron with a single example in the lower left position*

ABOVE *VX161 was the second prototype*

rapidly rotated ball-screw jacks acting on servotabs occupying the full trailing edge of each surface. The aerodynamic load on the tab then moved the main surface. The system was simple, light, reliable, free from stiction and lost motion, and the friction in the long control runs was almost non-existent. Thanks to an artificial-feel system the control loads appeared to vary in an almost perfect manner; one wondered why anyone should go to the weight and cost of devising complex powered systems. A g-restrictor limited vertical acceleration to 1.8g. Remarkably, nobody got around to fitting an autopilot.

The other startling feature was the engine installation. VX158 was powered by four of the first Avons ever sent to a customer, while '161 had the RA.3 version with the dramatically superior two-stage turbine. Each pair of engines was carried on steel-tube spaceframes in a double-deck nacelle set at the same positive angle of incidence as the wing (though the lower jetpipes ended horizontal). Once one had got over the initial shock the installation could be seen to be – like the rest of the aircraft –

basically conventional, efficient, easily accessible and a very good solution. Measured drag was remarkably low.

A total of 6170 gal (28,049 litres) of fuel could be carried in 14 bag tanks in the wings and eight in the fuselage. The fuel was fed via a proportioner, and to relieve wing bending as quickly as possible the wing fuel could not be used until no fuselage cell held more than 100 gal. To prevent the tanks from collapsing in a fast dive they were pressurised from various ram inlets.

Again like the Britannia, the SA.4 had landing gears by British Messier, with a twin-wheel nose unit and four-wheel bogies (then a novel feature) on the single long main struts. The latter retracted straight in to stow the neat bogies in the root of the wing in a bay closed by a large door which was open

on the ground. An equally large door was attached to the leg. The nose gear retracted backwards into a bay covered by twin doors below the crew drum. It had one of the first British attempts at steering, the pedal link soon being replaced by one connected to the aileron handwheel. Tyre pressures were from 98 to 105 lb/sq in, which seemed high compared to a Lancaster but still low enough for operation from an unpaved surface. There was provision for twin braking parachutes in the tailcone.

Operation of the landing gear, like the flaps, airbrakes, the two enormous outward-opening bomb doors and the wheel brakes, was effected by the British Messier hydraulic system. Again like the Britannia, this worked at the unprecedented pressure of 4000 lb/sq in to save weight. The electrical system was a traditional 24/28-volt DC network fed by four 6-kW generators, with inverters to supply AC to the radar. The cabin air system, pressurised to 8.5 lb/sq in (reduced to 3.5 in imminent combat), was fed by a supercharger by Sir George Godfrey & Partners driven off each accessory gearbox, one in each leading edge. The radar was unpressurised.

No armament was specified, and no attempt was made to install any kind of countermeasures. The required bombload of 20,000 lb could easily have been increased. Loading of large (for example, 10,000-lb) bombs was accomplished by opening the bomb doors to a special high position.

Before the first flight it was known that the rapid progress with the Valiant had eliminated the need for the Short bomber, which would almost certainly have proved popular in service and cheap to buy and operate. Not a lot needed to be done to it, though (because the pressure was off) aileron flutter at the ceiling held Mach number to 0.78 instead of the planned 0.85. Other modifications included adjustments to the wing/nacelle fillets, adding small 'boat tails' between the jetpipes and adding an anti-

buffet rake immediately ahead of the bomb bay.

VX161 came into the flight programme on 12 August 1952. Subsequently, this aircraft was gainfully employed at Farnborough, Boscombe Down and Woodbridge helping the specially-built Avro Ashtons develop radar bombing for the V-bombers, bomb loading (eventually using a crane lifting through hatches in the fuselage above the bomb bay) and dropping concrete models of the proposed Blue Danube and guided Blue Boar. Its partner, '158, was picked as the flying testbed for the big de Havilland Gyron turbojet, and Eassie flew it with a Gyron in the lower left position on 7 July 1955. On 26 June 1956 testing began with Gyrons in both lower positions, but over the Irish Sea the right-hand main-leg door came adrift. A spare was obtained from VX161, which never flew again, and within a year the Gyron had been abandoned, consigning both Sperrins to the scrap heap.

SPECIFICATION

SA.4 Sperrin
Two Rolls-Royce Avon turbojets, (VX158) 6000-lb RA.2, (VX161) 6500-lb RA.3
Dimensions Span 109 ft 1⅛ in (33.25 m); length (visual bombing) 103 ft 6 in (33.96 m); wing area 1896.77 ft² (176.2 m²)
Weight Empty 72,000 lb (32,659 kg); normal loaded 115,000 lb (52,164 kg); max landing 81,310 lb (36,882 kg)
Performance Maximum speed (10,000 ft) 496 kt (571 mph, 919 km/h); initial climb 3500 ft/min; service ceiling 42,000 ft (12.8 km); range 3860 miles (6212 km); take-off run (max wt, RA.2) 3120 ft (950 m)

Ilyushin Il-46

First Flight – 3 March 1952

Having by the start of 1950 abandoned the Il-30, the OKB of S V Ilyushin found it difficult to come up with a better design. The only positive factor was that, again, the engine KB of Arkhip Lyulka had come up with a new powerplant, in this case the TR-3A (a refined version of the Il-30 engine) rated at 5 t thrust. While the new bomber was being schemed to use it, Lyulka was permitted to use his own initials, and this engine accordingly became the AL-5. As noted earlier, the broad design objective facing Ilyushin was to carry a 3 t bombload 3000 km, with the potential for development to overload weights which would permit a 5 t bombload to be carried 5000 km. From the outset there appeared to be a choice between adopting a 35° swept wing and meeting the 1000 km/h speed objective (this was merely desirable, not mandatory) or of using a straight wing and meeting the range/load requirement, with satisfactory field performance, but with maximum speed limited to 900–925 km/h.

Design of the straight-wing Il-46 went ahead in October 1951, but two months later a detailed parallel study was undertaken of the Il-46s (the suffix 's' meaning *strelovidnost*, swept wing).

Problems were encountered with structural strength at the root, fuel capacity in relation to centre of gravity and other factors. The engine nacelles would also have been extremely long, with the inlets beside the pilot. Accordingly, the straight-wing design was continued, though retaining the concept of a swept tail unit which had proved so successful on the Il-28. Another important advantage of the unswept wing was that it brought the engine nacelles much further back and made it possible to use the same conventional landing gear configuration as in the Il-28, but with differences. The twin-wheel nose unit was made hydraulically steerable, and retracted to the rear. The main gears comprised four separate single-leg units, pivoted to strong frames surrounding the very long (4.9 m) jetpipes. With the gear extended, the result looked from a distance like a conventional twin-wheel unit, but one part of it retracted to the rear and the other went forwards, both wheels rotating 90° to lie flat under the jetpipe. The Il-46 was cleared to land with any one main gear retracted.

The crew numbered three, in two pressure cabins as before. In the glazed nose, with an optically flat bomb-aiming window, was the navigator, who was

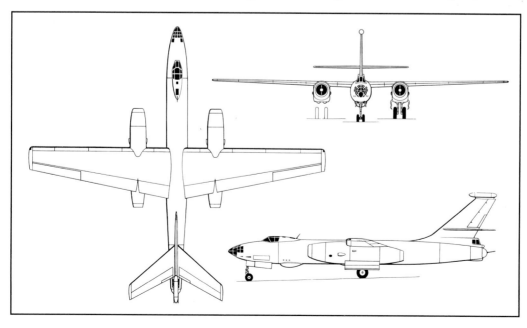

ABOVE *One of the few known photographs of the Il-46*

also the bombardier and radar operator. He had a ventral emergency escape hatch, and had easy access to the pilot, who was seated in an upward ejection seat under a large metal canopy with numerous panes of Plexiglas (quite unlike the fighter-style canopy of the Il-30). Access to the forward pressure cabin was via a door on the right side. In the tail was the pressurised compartment for the gunner, who was also the radio operator. His Il-K8 turret was the next generation on from the K6, and though it had the same twin NR-23 guns, these had 320 rounds each. The electrohydraulic control system could rapidly train the guns through 105° in azimuth and from 58° up to 39° down. All crew positions were armoured, the total weight of armour being 880 kg (1940 lb). In many ways the 46 remained simple, with a fixed leading edge, conventional slotted flaps and manual flight controls. Of course, no fences were needed. In the overload condition tankage in the wings and fuselage could accommodate 25,000 litres (5500 Imp gal) of fuel, more than enough to meet the range requirement.

The prototype of this experimental bomber made its first flight in the hands of V K Kokkinaki on 3 March 1952. He found it a pleasant aircraft to fly, stable and posing no problems, though at maximum weight engine-out performance was marginal. Unfortunately, the Tu-88 (Tu-16) could do about four times as big a job, and by 1952 it was becoming clear that a scaled-up Il-28 was obsolescent from the outset. At some time the Il-46 may have been fitted with a streamlined container at the top of the fin, shown in some drawings. This is believed to have been to test experimental front/rear passive radar warning receivers.

SPECIFICATION

Il-46
Two Lyulka AL-5 turbojets each rated at 5 t (11,023 lb)
Dimensions Span 29.0 m (95 ft 2 in); length 24.5 m (80 ft 5 in); wing area 105 m² (1130 sq ft)
Weight Empty 26,300 kg (57,981 lb); loaded 41,840 kg (92,240 lb); maximum 52,425 kg (115,575 lb)
Performance Maximum speed 800 km/h at S/L, 928 km/h (577 mph) at 5 km (16,400 ft); range with 3 t of bombs at 700 km/h 4970 km (3090 miles)
Armament Two fixed NR-23 guns in nose firing ahead, two NR-23 in tail turret, and bomb bay with normal capacity of 3 t (6614 lb) and overload capacity of 6 t (13,228 lb)

Boeing B-52 Stratofortress

First Flight – 15 April 1952

It would be pointless to suggest that the B-52 is the 'greatest' of all jet bombers, but its story is certainly unique – not only among jet bombers but among aircraft of all time. At the start, the US Air Force's requirement could not be met by any jet aircraft at all. Under intense pressure, and thanks to a complex and massive new turbojet which promised to reduce specific fuel consumption by some 30 per cent, Boeing found a way to come some way to meeting the long mission radius with a jet bomber; and with air refuelling, the global missions of SAC looked like being flown at over 500 mph instead of the 200/225 mph of the B-36.

But, like other combat aircraft of over 40 years ago, the giant Boeing was designed to have quite a short active life. By 1954 Weapon Systems 110A and 125A were being developed to replace it, as explained in the chapter of the XB-70. After 1957 it was confidently predicted that the B-52 would soon be phased out from SAC's Bomb Wings in favour of a bomber that either would cruise at supersonic speed (WS-110A) or have a flight endurance measured in days or weeks (WS-125A). Nobody would have believed that 36 years later the B-52 would be one of the dwindling number of USAF aircraft assured of a continuing front-line status!

In the late 1940s SAC was equipped with the Boeing B-29 and B-50, and was wondering whether the gigantic Convair B-36 was really the best choice for 'global deterrence' in view of the excellent performance of the rather smaller Northrop B-35 flying wing. Northrop was already flying prototypes of a jet version of the B-35, the YB-49, and rejecting this was seen by some as short-sighted. Admittedly, the B-49 appeared unlikely ever to have the 605-mph speed of Boeing's B-47, but the sleek B-47 fell far short of meeting the SAC mission radius. Even Boeing could see no way of scaling up the B-47 to fly much further – the range had to be more than doubled – so the design team at Seattle concentrated on a succession of Model 464 bombers powered by four turboprops, such as the 5500 hp Wright T35. Other engines of greater power were in prospect, opening the way to better mission radius, but there appeared to be no way of making a propeller-driven aircraft go faster than 400 mph (the Russians were cleverer, but their Tu-95/Tu-142 family cannot be included in this book).

Thus, when on 21 October 1948 a team from Seattle arrived at Wright Field to present their definitive proposals for the XB-52, their truckload of paper described an improved turboprop aircraft, the 464-35, with slightly swept wings and T35 engines uprated to 8900 hp. Thousands of man-hours had gone into this presentation, and the team were taken aback when Col Pete Warden hardly looked at it. Instead he asked how quickly the team could come up with a Model 464 powered by turbojets, in particular the Pratt & Whitney JT3, which was under Air Force contract as the XJ57. This was a pioneer two-spool engine, with separate low-pressure (LP) and high-pressure (HP) compressors driven at different speeds by their own LP and HP tubines. Rated at about 8800 lb thrust, it was to prove not only the key element in switching the XB-52 from propellers to jets, but also in salvaging several important Navy programmes from the wreck of the Westinghouse J40, and also in enabling the USA to enter the commercial jet age with the 707 and DC-8.

BELOW *An unusual view of the first B-52 to fly: 49-231, the YB. Like the XB it had a tandem cockpit for the pilots*

It is part of Boeing's legendary history that their team went back to their hotel room in Dayton on that Thursday night and worked non-stop for four nights and three days, finally reporting back in Col Warden's office at 8 am on the Monday with a complete package of typed and bound documents, working drawings and even a nicely finished desktop model of the B-52 powered by eight J57 engines arranged in four twin pods. Called Model 464-49, it had the same span as the 464-35 but considerably greater wing area, partly because the wings were swept at 35°. Fuel capacity was increased by over 40 per cent, giving an estimated range close to 6000 miles.

A week later the Dash-35 was formally terminated, and it was 'all systems go' on the Dash-49, which very soon became the Dash-67 with a slightly longer nose, smaller dorsal fin, broader tailplane, provision for spoilers along the top of the wings, provision for outboard underwing fuel tanks and various other refinements. Boeing received an order for test airframes and two flight articles, an XB-52 (construction number 16248, AF serial 49-0230) and a YB-52 (No 16249, 49-0231). The XB was rolled out hidden under about an acre of white cloth on the night of 29 November 1951, carried out systems and taxi testing and then went back inside for modifications. Meanwhile the YB was rolled out on 15 March 1952 and made a very successful first flight on 15 April, in the hands of A M 'Tex' Johnston and Lt Col Guy M Townsend, finally landing at the B-52's test centre at Larson AFB, Moses Lake. Though originally almost outwardly identical to the YB, the XB incorporated various changes and did not fly until 2 October 1952.

The two giant prototypes embodied a blend of conventional and radical solutions to the many problems encountered. The wing had straight taper from root to tip, and a thickness/chord ratio of 8 per cent at the tip, quite normal for a late-1940s jet. As the wing came inboard the t/c gradually increased, to 9 per cent at the half-way point. Further in, the wing got rapidly thicker, reaching the surprising value of 15 per cent at the junction with the massive bridge frame on each side of the slab-sided fuselage. Moreover, the wing was twisted (technically called washout), so that the root was at a much greater incidence (8°) than the tip, the highest part of the root being well forward and almost meeting at the top of the body, as on the British V-bombers. The leading edge was fixed, but on the trailing edge were giant sections of Fowler flap, driven electrically with a gap between them in the wake of the inner pair of engines.

One of the main imponderables was the flight-control system. At the start lateral control was by combined flaps and ailerons, or flaperons. These were soon abandoned, and replaced on the XB by three sections of slotted spoiler ahead of each outer flap. The YB then received six sections of spoiler,

backed up by outboard flaperons, while the XB was given small 'flipper' ailerons between the inner and outer flaps, driven manually by two servo tabs extending across the trailing edge. When the lateral control system was finally judged to be adequate there were not three or six but seven sections of spoiler on each wing, each with its own hydraulic jack and with a deeply serrated trailing edge. All 14 sections could be opened symmetrically as airbrakes (when the small inboard ailerons suddenly became much more effective). The enormous delta-shaped horizontal tail was boldly made the primary surface for longitudinal control, as well as trimming, and pivoted at 65 per cent chord. It was driven by an irreversible screwjack. On its trailing edge were relatively tiny elevators, driven manually by trailing-edge tabs. The gigantic fin was mounted on hinges, with a hydraulic drive to fold it to the right prior to entering a hangar. On its trailing edge was the relatively insignificant rudder, again driven manually by a trailing-edge tab. Throughout its life the B-52 has always had limitations in asymmetric flight, even with full asymmetric use of the spoilers. Indeed, with any twin-engine pod inoperative it is virtually impossible to overshoot from a landing, without suffering uncontrollable roll and structural damage (in other words, with two engines out on one side you have just one chance at a landing).

As in the B-47, the main landing gears had to be on the fuselage, the wheelbase being 49 ft 9 in. In turn this made it impossible to rotate the aircraft nose-up as take-off speed was reached because no horizontal tail would have the necessary power to rotate the aircraft about the rear main wheels. Therefore, the B-52 had to take off in a level attitude, hence the pronounced positive incidence of the wing. In fact, the drill is to pull back on the yoke as unstick speed is reached to prevent 'wheelbarrowing' (running along on the front wheels with the tail in the air), but even with a strong pull the take-off is in a nose-down attitude, which is unnerving to pilots making their first familiarisation flight. It is rather like a VTO, or going up in a powerful lift.

The weight of the new bomber made it necessary to use four main gears, each with a twin-wheel truck. This gave a track (distance between the vertical oleo struts of the left and right gears at either front or rear) of 11 ft 4 in, which in completely calm conditions might have been sufficient to keep the aircraft from ever rolling over sideways or hitting a wingtip or fuel pod on the ground. In practice, of course, outrigger gears were needed, as on the B-47. These took the form of small single-wheel units, retracting inwards to lie flush with the underside of the wing, the wheel itself being faired by an inboard-hinged door. Such is the flexibility of the wing that, as the fuel tanks are filled, the outrigger gears slowly move down about 6 ft until they are both pressing firmly on the ground. As they are 148 ft apart, the pilot has then to take care that

ABOVE *Features of the B-52G – the most numerous model – included small tanks and a short fin. This is how a G looked when it was young*

RIGHT *Big tanks and a tall fin were features of the B-52D, which late in life was rebuilt to carry 40 tons of conventional bombs and went to war from Guam with the underside painted black*

neither gear runs off a paved taxyway on to soft ground.

In many respects each main gear was almost identical to those of the B-47, with similar tyres and multi-disc anti-skid brakes. There would have been room for the front and rear pairs to retract in the same direction to lie in a single transverse bay side-by-side. In the event, the solution was to mount each gear on a skewed axis so that it swung in and up, the left gears retracting forwards and the right gears aft, so that all four lie along the centreline in separate bays closed by large triangular doors. Crosswinds were clearly going to be even more of a problem with this aircraft than they were with the B-47, and as at least one set of trucks had to be steerable the obvious (but unique) answer was to arrange for all four trucks to be hydraulically steered up to 20° left or right. For manoeuvring on the ground or taxiing, the front and rear pairs can be steered in opposite directions, while for landing all four can be slewed in unison so that the aircraft approaches the runway crabwise, the wheels being the only part aligned with the runway. The pilot has a wind/weight crab chart, the wind being measured relative to the runway direction and the weight determining the BFS (best flare speed), which may be 15 kt higher than the 1g stalling speed. Throughout the B-52's life the BFS climbed from 118 to about 140 kt (161 mph) as its landing weight went up with natural development. Like the take-off, the final touchdown tends to be nose-down, though in theory all eight main tyres should hit together. Then the braking parachute is streamed (in early B-52s dropping out of the rear fuselage) as speed

falls below 135 kt, the crabbing of the landing gears simultaneously being cancelled. The standard drag chute has always been a circular ribbon-type, with a diameter of 44 ft. Reverse thrust has never been fitted.

To return briefly to the wing, this was designed around a two-spar torsion box which, in most strength aspects, exceeded anything seen previously. The static-test wing was bent 10 ft downwards and 22 ft upwards at each tip without breaking! In the air flexure is thus considerable, though damped by the five-ton masses of the pods hung 34 ft 2 in and 60 ft 0 in from the centreline. Another record was set by the fuel capacity, which even in the prototypes was 38,865 US gal, compared with 21,000 for the previous greatest, the B-36. Most of the fuel was in the seven wing tanks, there being six more in the fuselage, all of them being self-sealing flexible cells. This enormous fuel capacity meant that even the prototypes could take off at 405,000 lb (390,000 was the usual limit set during test flying).

Though the YJ57-P-3 engines fitted to the prototypes were rated at only 8700 lb thrust, the engine had potential for well over 10,000 lb, and for even greater thrust with water injection. The latter was not fitted to the prototypes, which in any case usually flew at relatively light weights. Each engine was hung on the left or right side of a stainless-steel

ABOVE *Late on in its life, this G was photographed being refuelled at RAF Fairford*

firewall dividing each nacelle into two. In turn the complete pod was hung on a large pylon angled sharply forward below the leading edge, with the upper edge of the strut extended back over the wing as a short fence. Later in development the airflow over the inboard, sharply cambered upper surface of the wing was re-energised by adding a row of vortex generators at 40 per cent chord from the root to the inboard pylon strut.

Together with the landing gear the most unconventional of the new bomber's features was the accessory power system. Since World War 2, a new company, AiResearch, had been building a business based on small gas tubines of one kind or another. One of their families was based on driving small turbines with the hot high-pressure air bled from the main engines of a jet aircraft. The twin-spool J57 appeared peculiarly suitable for supplying such air, because delivery from the HP spool could be at a pressure of 250 lb/sq in and a temperature of 750°F (400°C). AiResearch managed by early 1950 to convince Boeing that using bleed-air turbines was the lightest and most versatile answer to the problem of the giant bomber's accessory power. A quite complex system was devised in which the bleed air, controlled by numerous valves and other devices, was taken through stainless-steel ducts with a diameter of 2.5 in to 5 in along the pylon struts and leading edges to groups of air turbines in the front landing-gear compartments. As the ducts glowed red-hot they had to be lagged in glass wool and asbestos sheet. The turbine packages screamed and hissed at either 40,000 or 60,000 rpm, mostly driving alternators. Four 40-kVA alternators provided raw AC to power not only the electrical systems, but also hydraulic pumps, the cabin environmental system, deicing and, later, the water-injection pumps. Of course, Boeing and AiResearch built giant test rigs simulating the entire system to try to eliminate faults.

From the outset the accommodation for the crew was pressurised. The only defensive armament, envisaged as radar-directed guns of 0.5 in or 20 mm calibre, was in the tail. Here a pressurised compartment was provided for the gunner, who in emergency could jettison the entire turret to escape. The other crew members originally numbered four, in the pressurised forward fuselage, entered by a door with a long integral ladder, hinged down from the rear to touch the ground when open. As in the B-47 the pilot and co-pilot sat in tandem ejection seats, though their canopy comprised 15 Plexiglas panes set in a strong metal frame. The navigator and bombardier sat at a lower level in downward-ejecting seats, and remarkably (because Boeing knew about fatigue) had square windows with sharp 90° corners. No armament provision was made in the prototypes. The tailcone was merely a streamlined fairing, and the bomb bays contained instrumentation.

While the test-flight programe was generally encouraging, the overall programme was a mess. At the start, though Boeing had received a letter of intent for no fewer than 500 B-52s, nothing had actually been ordered apart from the two flight articles and the static-test airframe. Then on 25 June 1950 war broke out in Korea, and panic ensued. Convair's rival YB-60 had always been almost a non-starter, and it was no great surprise when the Air Force picked the more costly B-52 instead. But with the pressure suddenly full-on there was no time for proper planning. It was normal to proceed with 13 development aircraft, but, with so much to do, this would have delayed matters. Instead, just three B-52As were funded, serial 52-0001/0003, known to Boeing as Model 464-201-0, C/n 16491/3, to continue the test programme. The other ten aircraft became B-52Bs, regarded as production articles.

The first B-52A was rolled out on 18 March 1954 and flown on 5 August of that year. Its most obvious difference was that the cockpit had been completely redesigned, with the pilots on an airline-style flight deck in side-by-side ejection seats, each looking ahead through the big windscreen panels. Boeing had not made a side-by-side mock-up, and what tipped the scales was a visit by Generals Vanden-berg, LeMay and Griswold to Vickers-Armstrongs to study the Valiant. All that came of this visit was a new cockpit for the B-52, which despite higher drag, offered much better crew co-ordination and made better use of the available space. This space was in any case significantly increased by lengthening the forward fuselage by 4 ft to make room for a sixth crew-member, an ECM (electronic counter-measures) operator. Ship 2001 also introduced the row of three bomb bays, each with its own pair of hydraulically driven doors, and each able to accommodate either a nuclear weapon (single examples of several early Marks or a quad pack of B28s) or nine GP bombs of 500 or 750 lb size, a total of 20,000 lb. This was academic, however, as the radar and nav/bombing system had yet to be cleared for flight and was absent. The defensive fire control was fitted, however, the A-3A having a giant cheese-shape radar scanner in a flat round radome which totally blocked the gunner's rear view. The performance of this radar matched the effective range of the two 20 mm guns, though in fact '2001 had a different tail, with a prototype of the MD-5 system with four 0.5 in guns.

Over 600 other engineering changes in the A-model hardly showed. Among the more important were the 9700-lb thrust J57-P-1W engines, with water injected on take-off by bleed-air turbopumps from a 360-US gal tank in the rear fuselage under the fin. With water injection the J57s pumped out excruciating noise and clouds of black smoke, and with later B-52s that boasted even greater take-off power, the noise was so intense that the flaps began to crack and had to be reskinned or replaced every few flights.

A more obvious change was provision to carry a 1000-US gal external cylindrical tank under each outer wing, though this was not initially fitted to '2001. Mission radius was further improved by adding a receptacle for a Flying Boom air-refuelling connection in the top of the fuselage immediately behind the cockpit, normally closed by two skew-hinged doors. The normal pressure-fuelling socket remained in the left front truck bay. Other changes included the swivelling main landing gears (those of the prototypes having only front-wheel steering), a mechanical 200:1 geared drive through which, in an emergency, the rear gunner could alter the incidence of the tailplane, and an increase in gross weight to 420,000 lb, a record for any aircraft at that time.

As before, testing was generally successful, though at first there were hairy problems with the main gears. On one occasion one truck refused to extend, and the landing had to be made (without trouble) on the other three. On another, one truck jammed at the maximum 20° crosswind setting, and the tyres covered the fuselage downstream with rubber. Later a few SAC crews even suffered the frustration of split gears, the two front trucks having turned in opposite directions simultaneously! These difficulties took a little while to sort out.

Though the B-52 was never going to be ordered in numbers even approaching the 12,731 total of the B-17, or even the 2032 of the B-47, its size and complexity made its production far too much even for mighty Boeing to handle alone, especially coming on top of huge orders for the B-47 and KC-97. Accordingly, by late 1950 Boeing had put together the greatest nationwide manufacturing programme ever seen in the United States, even surpassing the numbers of major contributors needed in programmes of World War 2. For a start, the giant Wichita Division (originally the little

LEFT *The B-52H*

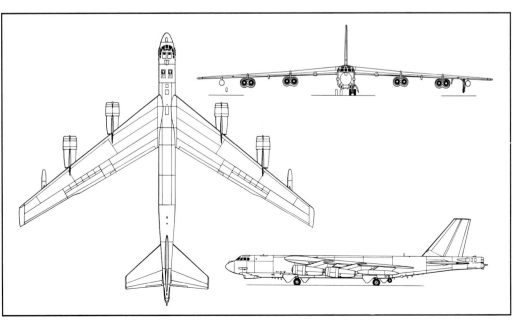

TOP *Nearing retirement, 57-6492 proudly displays 54 Gulf War mission symbols with the 379th BW*

ABOVE *'Buffs' have dropped vast tonnages of conventional bombs in anger. Among the last were these M117 750-pounders about to leave RAF Fairford en route to Iraq*

Stearman plant, but vastly expanded over ten years from 1935) was tooled up to build the B-52 complete, but like the parent plant at Seattle, it mainly assembled airframe sections built elsewhere.

Among the principal subcontractors were Goodyear (centre fuselage, wing centre section, fuel cells and decks), Fairchild (outer wings, rear fuselage from wing to near tail, assisted by Temco, top panels, fin and tip-protection gears), Aeronca (bomb doors, landing-gear doors, access panels, rudder, elevators, spoilers and ailerons), Cessna

(tailplane), Rohr (aft fuselage, nacelles, pylon struts and external tanks) and Cleveland Pneumatic Tool (main gears). The J57 engine went into second-source production at the Ford Motor Co plant at East Wacker Drive, Chicago, and Ford-built J57s became standard on later production B-52s as noted later. As for the subsystems and equipment, they involved a large fraction of the whole US aerospace industry.

As noted, the last ten B-52As were completed as B-52Bs. This was another result of the delay in getting started caused by failure to order production earlier (another result was that the side-by-side cockpit, which was not expected to be introduced until the 14th production aircraft, was actually on the first!). Orders were placed for 40 B-52Bs, which were intended to be the first bombers for the SAC inventory, but the numbers were further altered. Addition of ten A-models brought the total up to 50, but only 23 were completed as Bs, the other 27 being RB-52Bs.

The 23 Bs were Boeing Model 464-201-3, C/n 16852/16855, USAF 53-0373/0376, and C/n 16859/16877, USAF 53-0380/0398. The obvious new feature of the B-52B was its operational capability. Overcoming countless, often serious problems, the MA-6A nav/bombing system was cleared for service in 1955. It was a descendant of the wartime Sperry-Rand K-System, packed with thermionic valves which pumped out heat and frequently malfunctioned. The system included the ASB-4 radar which filled the lower half of the nose and weighed nearly 6000 lb. In the tail was the gunner with the A-3A fire-control system and a periscopic optical sight to aim the two 20 mm cannon.

Empty weight of the B climbed to about 169,300 lb, roughly 10,000 lb more than for the prototypes, and maximum takeoff weight remained 420,000 lb. This was made possible by the installation of the J57-F-19W, -29W or -29WA, all uprated to 12,000 lb with water injection. Of course, whereas the prototypes and A-models had been essentially unpainted, the B carried full USAF titles and, a few months after entry to service, a complete underside, engine nacelles and, in a few cases, vertical tail, all painted in anti-flash white to offer some protection against the radiation from nuclear bombs.

The B was actually cleared for duty on 29 June 1955. As this was the very last day allowed by the contract one suspects that a few items were still missing or not fully proven, but the important thing is that, if the President had picked up the red telephone, the B-52Bs would have gone to war. The unit was the 93rd Bomb Wing at Castle AFB, outside Merced, California. Crews were converted at the 4017th Combat Crew Training Squadron at the same base. Parts of the aircraft were by this time mature, and on a 500-h overhaul cycle.

Other parts, however, were anything but mature, and from 1955 until well into 1957 the main accessory-power system was the cause of frantic further development effort. One aircraft was destroyed at Travis AFB in late 1955. Six weeks later another blew up in flight, and it was found that the cause was failure of one of the air turbines, which had exploded the fuel cell above it. In February 1956 the 78 aircraft (B and C models) then in service were grounded, and inspection of the accessory power system resulted in 31 aircraft being rejected. A panic ensued, Fairchild Stratos, GE, Thompson Products and Solar being brought in to help Boeing and AiResearch incorporate fixes in days rather than months. Turbine wheels had to be made capable of holding together even during severe overspeeding. Flak curtains and armour were added to contain the pieces of any that failed. Not least, the duct systems were redesigned to avoid fatigue failures (which inevitably caused fires) due to turbulence and resonance in the near-sonic airflow. These were just the first of several ongoing dangerous problems.

The RB-52B, which had originally been ordered as the XR-16, was, as its designation implied, a dual-mission aircraft, able to undertake bombing or strategic reconnaissance. Aeronca produced a unique pressurised capsule which could be winched up into the bomb bay on four cables, and then locked in place, the bomb doors being removed. The capsule was equipped with seats and controls for two crew who could manage either a suite of up to six cameras or various ECM installations. Usually four large cameras and two jammers were fitted, but the capsule was not particularly popular, and the idea was abandoned before 1956 was out. The RBs had C/n 16494/16503, 16838/16844, 16845/ 16851 and 16856/16858, the corresponding USAF serials being 52-0004/0013, 52-8710/ 8716, 53-0366/0372 and 53-0377/0379.

Next came the B-52C. The rising tempo of production, combined with the natural learning curve of human operatives, resulted in the price of each aircraft falling with each production block. The $29,000,000 price tag of each B-52A reflected the bill for original development. With the B-52B the figure came down to $14.4m, and in the C to $8.3m. It was to continue to fall until in 1957–58 the B-52E, despite an ever-increasing list of equipment items, was being produced for less than $6.1m, which today seems fantastic. (Later, much more than this was to be spent upgrading each surviving aircraft.)

The B-52C was Boeing Model 464-201-6, and 35 were built. This pushed the available propulsive power back to the limit by raising maximum take-off weight to 450,000 lb. This was done by increasing the size of the external underwing tanks to 3000 US gal, the largest on any regular service aircraft, bringing total fuel to 41,700 US gal (34,724 Imp gal, about 275,000 lb). The engine water system was made more sensible and less vulnerable by replacing the tank in the tail with a 150-US-gal tank in each wing root. The C was also the first variant painted with anti-flash white from the start. Incidentally, with so large an aircraft, care had to be taken to apply the paint with some precision, because an extra 0.005 in thickness (about the thickness of fine tissue or metal foil) meant an extra 450 lb in weight.

These were the visible changes, but the ones that meant the biggest engineering effort were inside. The greatest change was the introduction of a completely new nav/bombing system, owing nothing to wartime hardware. Designated ASQ-48(V), it incorporated the ASB-15 bombing radar under the nose and the APN-108 navigation radar looking ahead, as well as many new interfaces and displays. At the back was a completely new tail turret, outwardly resembling that flown on the first

BELOW *Boomer's view of a G of the 379th BW returning to Morón AB, Spain, after a mission over Iraq during the Gulf War*

B-52A, with four 0.5 in M3 guns. These were arranged in square formation in a large package pivoted on a horizontal axis to elevate or depress. This package in turn was mounted in the main barbette carried on a vertical axis on the fuselage. Above the four 600-round ammunition feedways was the gunner's pressurised compartment, extended aft to house units of the MD-5 fire-control system, developed by Bosch Arma, which used as sensors a small radar with a circular dish antenna in a radome which was either conical or hemi-spherical, above which was the bore-sighted optical sight with a hemispherical cap. This new armament was fitted to the final 34 aircraft, which also differed from the first in having no provision for the RB capsule.

The B-52C first flew on 9 March 1956. There were two production blocks, C/n 16878/16887, 53-0399/0408, and 17159/17183, 54-2664/2688. They were built under great political pres-sure. The 'Bison' (M-4), and other Soviet bombers, had thrown the Pentagon into a near-panic, and predictably a so-called 'bomber gap' was invented based on the totally unwarranted supposition that SAC was being outnumbered by enemy strategic aircraft coming off the assembly line in enormous numbers. Accordingly, the US Administration launched a crash programme to convert eight complete B-36 wings to B-52s by 30 June 1958. As even the B-52 needed tanker support, and the piston-engined KC-97 was the only tanker actually available, this meant accelerating production to 20 B-52s and 20 KC-135s per month. Coming on top of the rapidly expanding 707 programme, and conti-nued development of all these aircraft, this strained

the Seattle, Renton and Boeing Wichita plants.

The next model, the B-52D, was the first to be assembled at Wichita. The Kansas facility was also progressively made the centre for all B-52 flight testing, so it was fortunate that the D-model differed from the C only in details. Designated Model 464-201-7, it retained the standard Ford-built Dash-29W or WA engines, but incorporated internal structural strengthening which added 921 lb to the airframe weight. By far the most significant change was that the tail fire-control system was replaced by the Bosch Arma MD-9, with a General Electric monopulse radar and improved ammunition supply system. The first B-52D was actually the first built at Wichita, which retained the old Stearman series of construction numbers based on Model number. Thus, their 69 aircraft were as follows:

```
B-52D-1-BW, 464001/464003, 55-0049/0051
B-52D-5-BW, 464004/464006, 55-0052/0054
B-52D-10-BW, 464007/464012, 55-0055/0060
B-52D-15-BW, 464013/464016, 55-0061/0064
B-52D-20-BW, 464017/464019, 55-0065/0067
              464020/464022, 55-0673/0675
B-52D-25-BW, 464023/464027, 55-0676/0680
B-52D-30-BW, 464028/464039, 56-0657/0668
B-52D-35-BW, 464040/464051, 56-0669/0680
B-52D-40-BW, 464052/464069, 56-0681/0698
```

BELOW *Possibly the last major weapon deployed by the 'Buff', the AGM-142 Popeye is also known as Have Nap (though the operator of the TV guidance stays very much awake). This B-52G of Barksdale's 2nd BW did not use Have Nap in the Gulf War because of its Israeli manufacture*

LEFT *A major hiccup in the planning of the RAF, as well as SAC, came when GAM-87A Skybolt was cancelled. The B-52H carried four*

BELOW *One of the first wet hook-ups, with landing gear extended to match performance of the KC-97*

These were the smallest sustained production blocks in USAF history to that time, reflecting the careful control over the start of second-source production. Seattle's blocks were of normal (ie, quite modest) size for B-52 production, the total being 101 for a B-52D total of 170:

B-52D-55-BO, 17184/17204, 55-0068/0088
B-52D-60-BO, 17205/17220, 55-0089/0104
B-52D-65-BO, 17221/17233, 55-0105/0117
B-52D-70-BO, 17263/17273, 56-0580/0590
B-52D-75-BO, 17274/17293, 56-0591/0610
B-52D-80-BO, 17294/17313, 56-0611/0630

The first delivery of the D to SAC took place only one month after first flight, despite the new gunfire control system. But, while the aircraft naturally matured, serious troubles persisted, and four aircraft were lost between September and December 1956. The USAF grounded the B-52 for a second time, and described the safety record as 'grave, but not evidence of a defective system' (the final word meaning the entire aircraft, not just the air-turbine drives, which continued to improve). Before the end of 1956 a second unit, the 42nd BW at Loring AFB, Maine, was operational with the C- and D-models. Meanwhile, on 16 Janury 1957 the 93rd BW sent three B-52Bs on a non-stop flight round the world, using air refuelling. They returned to Castle AFB on the 18th in an elapsed time of 45 h 19 min for the 24,325 miles, compared with the previous record of over 94 h set by a SAC B-50A in 1949. One B-52 gunner got into the *Guinness Book of Records*

by circling the globe backwards during a sortie!

Years of work behind the scenes by a large contractor team led by IBM resulted in another completely new, and much more capable, nav/bombing system designated ASQ-38(V). This incorporated nine of IBM's own computers and displays, and these in turn led to a redesign of the crew compartment which also improved convenience and access. Consideration was given to further rearrangement to enable all crew to eject upwards in an emergency, because the downward ejection of the two navigator/bombardiers (the man on the left usually navigating and his partner sighting bombs) was not cleared for use except above 1000 ft altitude. In the mid-1950s this did not seem serious, and the change would have been a major modification. Other parts of ASQ-38(V) included the ASB-4 or -4A radar, APN-89 doppler, Kollsman astro compass, Kearfott true-heading indicator and GE radar strike camera.

When all this was put together and fitted into a B-52 the resulting production model was the B-52E, Boeing Model 464-259. The first flew on 3 October 1957, and despite the new electronics the E was the lowest-priced of all B-52s, as noted earlier. Total production was 100, as follow:

Seattle:
B-52E-85-BO, 17314/17332, 56-0631/0649
B-52E-90-BO, 17333/17339, 56-0650/0656
　　　　　　 17408/17416, 57-0014/0022
B-52E-95-BO, 17417/17423, 57-0023/0029

Wichita:
B-52E-45-BW, 464070/464083, 56-0699/0712
B-52E-50-BW, 464084/464098, 57-0095/0109
B-52E-55-BW, 464099/464119, 57-0110/0130
B-52E-60-BW, 464120/464127, 57-0131/0138

BELOW *How the crew finally got together in the G-model*

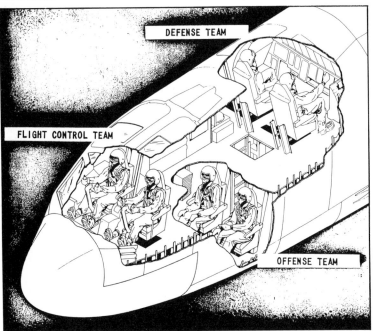

DEFENSE TEAM

FLIGHT CONTROL TEAM

OFFENSE TEAM

Despite all the attractions of the air-turbine drive accessory power, and the years of effort to perfect it, the USAF and Boeing finally decided it had to go. The alternative was to move the big alternators alongside the engines and drive them through a gearbox from the HP shaft. The drive had to be taken via a Sundstrand hydraulic CSD (constant-speed drive), so that all the four alternators in the aircraft could run at precisely the same speed, with their alternating current supplies in parallel, no matter what variation in engine shaft speed might be needed. Of course, the package of the CSD and 40-kVA alternator was both big and heavy, but it hardly affected the engine's frontal area, because, like the engine's oil tank, it fitted snugly into the J57's wasp-waisted mid-portion. On the other hand, it was decided to use aircooled alternators, instead of using oil or other liquid cooling, and this did result in a large blister around the lower left side of each twin-engine pod, the new package being driven by the left engine of each pair. The ram air cooling inlet was near the front of the pod.

Arguments raged for some time over what this change did for the B-52. The catastrophic air-turbine explosions were, by 1958, receding into history, and the fact that B-52Ds equipped with this system were retained in service after the B-52E and F had gone to the 'boneyard' shows that safety was no longer an issue. Several authorities claimed that the shaft-driven alternators increased the distance flown per gallon of fuel, but there was no change in the published ranges or mission radius. Removal of the armoured accessory-drive packages from the front truck bays did open up extra space which eventually was put to good use in housing extra equipment. Perhaps the crucial advantage was removal of the red-hot ducting from the wing, which, especially in view of the increasing likelihood of combat damage from guided missiles, did pose a real threat of fire. Their removal made it possible to do what Boeing had really wanted to do at the very start: use integral-tank wings.

This fundamental change took a little longer, and while it was being designed Boeing went into production with the B-52F, the Model 464-260. This incorporated the new engine pods, which not only housed the alternators but also new engines. The Dash-43W, 43WA or 43WB were all broadly similar, the most significant change being uprating to 13,750 lb for take-off with increased water injection. The LP spool was largely redesigned, with titanium replacing steel in discs and blades to cut over 300 lb off the weight. The HP spool had a higher-capacity tower shaft to drive the CSD/alternator, and the oil cooler was removed from the nose of each engine and replaced by a bullet fairing. Instead a large oil cooler was airframe-mounted under the centre of each pod, with a ram air inlet at front centre. A further change in the B-52F was to move the water tanks to where they would have been in the first place, had it not been for the big bleed-air ducts: in the wing leading edge. Capacity was again increased, with four tanks adjacent to the four pylon struts.

The first B-52F flew on 6 May 1958. Between then and November of that year Seattle delivered 44 jets, completing their manufacture of bombers:

B-52F-100-BO, 17424/17431, 57-0030/0037
B-52F-105-BO, 17432/17446, 57-0038/0052
B-52F-110-BO, 17447/17467, 57-0053/0073

A further block, B-52F-115-BO, 17468/17488, 57-0074/0094, was cancelled. But production continued at Wichita, which delivered 45 of this model for an F total of 89:

B-52F-65-BW, 464128/464143, 57-0139/0154
B-52F-70-BW, 464144/464172, 57-0155/0183.

A further Wichita block, No 75, to have been 57-0184/0228, was cancelled and funds transferred to the B-52G. Of all the eight major original versions of B-52, the G, arriving almost ten years after the start, represented the greatest single advance. In fact, though the only obvious difference was its shorter vertical tail, the G was almost a new aircraft entirely. Hardly a single portion of airframe escaped either being refined and strengthened, or being completely redesigned.

The B-52G, Model 464-253, introduced what was the largest integral-tank wing put into production at that time. The spars were not greatly modified but the upper and lower skins were redesigned as giant machined panels without joints. The main torsion box was bolted together using eight layers of primers and sealants. Each half-

wing, 115 ft long, was then sloshed with thousands of gallons of pungent sealer, after which a 15-man skin-diving team in wet suits inspected every nook and cranny to ensure that the sealing was perfect, and to cut away any surplus. This change not only saved weight but increased internal fuel capacity from 35,550 US gal to 46,575. As a result it was possible to replace the huge 3000-gal jettisonable underwing tanks with simple 700 US gal fixed tanks. Another change in the liquid systems was to redesign the water supply yet again, this time feeding from a giant 1200-gal (10,000 lb) tank filling the upper fuselage between the crew compartment and the No 1 fuselage fuel tank. This enabled water to be supplied for 110 sec, fed by four pumps in a front truck bay delivering to the four pods. The system was armed before reaching the runway, and started to feed as power passed through the 86 per cent level. Should supply to any engine have been lost, the adjacent engine also received no water, which may have required an abort. Nothing was ever done about the dense black smoke on take-off, though the flap skins and internal structure were repeatedly strengthened against noise fatigue.

It is remarkable that it took ten years for Boeing to come to a firm conclusion about the flight controls. This conclusion was that the spoilers alone could provide adequate lateral control at all indicated airspeeds, as well as handling all survivable engine-out asymmetric problems. Accordingly, in the B-52G the ailerons were omitted, the trailing edge between the flaps being a fixed section housing the Lundy ALE-27 chaff dispenser with five large channels feeding many miles of chaff cut automatically to length to match the hostile threats. The reassessment of the asymmetric case, and especially of crosswind landings, showed that the vertical tail

BELOW *On take-off the engines of the B-52G's Hound Dog missiles made their contribution*

could be reduced in height by almost 8 ft, but that the rudder and elevators should be hydraulically powered. The G horizontal tail thus linked the quick-response elevator and slower-moving tail-plane (stabiliser), the pilot always having to remember that the authority of the latter was many times greater than that of the small elevators. Driving too much nose-down stab on landing, for example, could not be countered by hauling back on the wheel.

These vital flight controls were driven by two separate electrically powered hydraulic systems, but the other hydraulic services were powered by pumps on engines 1, 3, 4, 5, 6 and 7. Amazingly, each pump served a particular group of services, so that no amount of manual juggling with valves or cross-feeds could provide power to a lost service. Thus, loss of pumps 4 (serving left body) or 5 (right body) created a real problem, resulting, for example, in one truck extending with braking available, the possibility of emergency extension of the other truck on that side but with no hope of brakes, and no knowledge of which way the wheels were pointing, so crosswind landings had to be made with wheels centred.

Another visible change in the G was to move the gunner into the main crew compartment. This enabled the tail pressure cabin and all its services to be eliminated, and also gave the gunner a much more comfortable ride in turbulence. The armament and ammunition feed was unchanged, but the fire-control was replaced by the ASG-15, still by Arma and with the tracking radome centred between the four guns. At the top of the fuselage tail-end is the tracking radar, with a hemispherical radome (replacing the previous optical sight) and between the two radomes is an ECM sensor which by 1970 comprised the APR-25 threat warning receiver and ALQ-117 active X-band jammer, both covering the supposedly more dangerous aft hemisphere. The installation of the ALQ-117, which also used an auxiliary antenna (when required, it is hinged out from the top of the rear fuselage) resulted in the tail being extended by 40 in. A 12 in increase in nose length raised the overall length from 156 ft 6.9 in to 160 ft 10.9 in.

A less-obvious change in the G-model is that the crew compartment was again considerably modified. The cockpit floor was lowered by 2 in to improve the view of the pilots during air refuelling. Despite this, crew of normal size cannot stand upright. Both the upper and lower-deck seating and consoles were again changed, and the entry door moved and hinged at the front instead of the rear. From the start the G had improved Weber seats, retrofitted to most earlier aircraft, which in theory enabled the downward-fired nav/bomb and other lower-deck occupants to survive at an altitude of 250 ft. In practice 500 ft is considered marginal. The limit for the upper-deck seats is zero height but 90 kt airspeed.

As with so many B-52 modifications, arguments continued over some of the G changes. Shortening the vertical tail made the aircraft noticeably more prone to Dutch roll. Bringing the gunner forward denied the crew a pair of eyes who could watch for hostile aircraft or SAMs, or for fuel leaks, engine fires, combat damage or other happenings invisible from the forward compartment. With the tail compartment eliminated it was decided to relocate the braking parachute in the space thus vacated, immediately ahead of the ALQ-117 retractable antenna.

The B-52G bomb bay was little changed, nominal bomb load remaining 20,000 rather than 27,000 lb. A completely new development was to add provision for two large air-breathing cruise missiles carried on deep pylons under the inner wings. The weapon chosen was the North American Hound Dog, originally called GAM-77 (Guided Air Missile) and from 1962 redesignated AGM-28 (Air/Ground Missile). Carrying a single warhead of 1 MT or 4 MT yield, Hound Dog could fly up to 710 miles at speeds up to Mach 2.1. It weighed about 10,140 lb and was 42 ft 6 in long, so the pair were quite a burden. On the other hand its Pratt & Whitney J52 turbojet of 7500 lb thrust could assist the bomber on take-off. During the long cruise to the target area the B-52 crew could if necessary then top up the missile's tanks before restarting its engine and dropping it, to fly on independently with astro-inertial guidance. This missile was operational with B-52G units in 1961–76.

Another new vehicle carried by the B-52G was the McDonnell Quail, initially the GAM-72 and from 1962 the ADM-20 (Air Defense Missile). This was a diminutive aeroplane, powered by a GE J85 turbojet that could fly about 250 miles in 30 min mimicking the radar signature of the B-52. Weighing about 1100 lb, it had an airframe mainly of glass-fibre which folded up to fit in a B-52 bomb bay. Either the fore or aft bomb bay could carry two Quails. In 1963, when SAC had 593 Hound Dogs, it also had 492 Quails. Training launches and attrition wiped Quail out by the late 1970s, planned successors failing to reach production.

In 1957, before the first wet-wing G-model had flown, it was taken for granted that this would be the final model. The 'bomber gap' was beginning to be questioned, production of the B-52 had been reduced from 20 to 15 a month (all at Wichita), and the planned SAC force had been fixed at 11 wings of 45 aircraft, requiring total production of 603 aircraft. It was equally taken for granted that from about 1961 the B-52 would be progressively replaced by the supersonic B-70. It did not work out like that, the first change being that, because of the slowed production, and the transfer of funds from the last blocks of the B-52F, B-52G production could be increased, to equip not two wings but three.

Wichita actually built 193, making this numerically the most important of all versions:

B-52G-75-BW, 464173/464180, 57-6468/6475
B-52G-80-BW, 464181/464190, 57-6476/6485
B-52G-85-BW, 464191/464204, 57-6486/6499
B-52G-90-BW, 464205/464225, 57-6500/6520
B-52G-95-BW, 464226/464255, 58-0158/0187
B-52G-100-BW, 464256/464279, 58-0188/0211
B-52G-105-BW, 464280/464300, 58-0213/0232
B-52G-110-BW, 464301/464314, 58-0233/0246
B-52G-115-BW, 464315/464326, 58-0247/0258
B-52G-120-BW, 464327/464365, 59-2564/2602

The first B-52G flew on 27 October 1958, the first delivery to SAC was in February 1959, and the last was delivered in January 1961. What happened next was the result of such diverse factors as the continuing Cold War (which almost became a Hot War in October 1962 during the Cuban missile crisis), the increasing doubt over production of the B-70, the development by Douglas of an ALBM (air-launched ballistic missile) and the development by Pratt & Whitney of a startlingly improved engine derived from the obsolescent J57.

The J57 had been essential in 1950, but ten years later could be seen to be heavy, short on power (even with high-rate water injection), and no longer regarded as fuel-efficient. Though such issues seemed unimportant in the 1950s, its noise and smoke on take-off were appalling. Pratt & Whitney simply removed the first three stages of the LP compressor and replaced them by two stages of far longer fan blades, held on pivoted roots so that, as the engine spooled down after a flight, they clicked and clacked against the discs. To supply the greater shaft-power to drive the fan a new LP turbine was fitted, and there were various other changes. It was decided not to duct the fan airflow to a common mixer nozzle but to eject it through a

separate peripheral nozzle immediately downstream of the fan. For the 707 this was no problem, but the twin-engine nacelles of the B-52 required the air to be discharged through 'banana nozzles' (so-called because of their cross-section shape) on the outer side of the engine only. From here the cool jet scrubbed at about the speed of sound across the big access door covering that side of the engine.

The new engine was designated TF33-P-1 or P-3, and rated at 17,000 lb. At a stroke it added about 30 per cent to the take-off thrust while reducing specific fuel consumption by 15 per cent, take-off smoke by over 90 per cent and noise by over 99 per cent. It also, at last, got rid of the need for water. Whereas the 'wet wing' of the B-52G had increased still-air range at high altitude from 7370 miles to 8406, the fan engine extended it to a nominal 10,130. In fact in January 1962 a B-52H flew from Kadena AB, Okinawa, to Torrejon AB, Madrid, a distance of 12,532 miles. Six months later another flew non-stop from Seymour Johnson AFB to Bermuda, Greenland, Alaska, California and Florida and back to its base, a closed-circuit record of 11,337 miles which stood for 25 years.

Rapidly growing demand for electrical power resulted in bigger alternators being fitted, each with a continuous rating of 90 kVA. These were retrofitted to the B-52G. The TF33 nacelle had visibly bigger inlets, handling not only the 2.5-times greater airflow for the engine but also that needed to cool the oil radiator and the alternator on the left engine of each pair. Still no attempt was made to fit reversers, as on the civil 707. To help the totally new propulsion system gain experience, a B-52G, 57-6471, was completely re-engined in 1959.

Fitting the TF33 resulted in the B-52H, Model 464-261. Another visible change in this aircraft was to fit a new tail-end housing the ASG-21 fire control, with improved sensors, for a single M61A1 'Gatling gun' of 20 mm calibre, with 1200 rounds. A further defence upgrade was to be the addition of small forward-firing rocket pods hung under the leading edge. Developed by Northrop Nortronics, these were to fire chaff several miles ahead to confuse the defences, but in the event they were not fitted to production aircraft.

During the late 1950s fundamental changes were being imposed on bombers everywhere. Advanced SAMs made high altitudes no longer a safe haven, and SAC was forced to accept that the only way to penetrate hostile airspace would henceforth be at the lowest safe height, to try to get 'under the radar'. This meant flying with reduced throttle settings, at modest airspeeds not much over 300 kt. In turbulence, weight is limited to 420,000 lb and indicated speed to 310 kt. In any case, the B-52 was never built to be thrown about at low level, the manoeuvre limit being 2g at 450,000 lb, falling to only 1.8g at 488,000. Thus, in low-level turbulence the airframe accrues fatigue damage rapidly. From 1962 onwards the B-52s had endless structural problems, but repeated strengthening and incessant inspection kept them flying.

Another new problem was the possibility of the B-52's own base being wiped off the map by an ICBM or, with even less warning, an SLBM fired from just off the US coast. Accordingly it became essential to scramble quickly, and all front-line B-52s were subjected to various 'Quick Start' modifications, one of which was to add ammonium-nitrate cartridge starters to two of the H's TF33 engines (Nos 4 and 5). Pushing the buttons for these, running them cautiously up to 90 per cent followed by 'gang-starting' the other six with ground and bleed air takes only two minutes, and for a real emergency the B-52G and H were later fitted with cartridge starters on all eight engines. A simultaneous eight-engine start is quite a spectacle.

Further fundamental changes concerned what weapons the B-52 carried. The G had introduced the Hound Dog, and this was an option on the H, but the latter was really designed to carry the new ALBM mentioned earlier. Developed by Douglas as the GAM-87A Skybolt, this weapon was a perfect streamlined shape, apart from having four large fins

and four small guidance controls, and it was to carry a thermonuclear warhead 1150 miles. With its tail fairing Skybolt was 38 ft 3 in long, and the launch weight was 11,300 lb. As it was wingless two Skybolts could be hung close side-by-side, so the B-52 was designed to carry four, the twin pylons being bolted to the same attachments as those for Hound Dog.

In fact, the Skybolt was developed not so much to help the B-52 penetrate as to free ballistic missiles from the vulnerability of fixed silos. For most targets Skybolt could have been launched from a C-130! Nevertheless Boeing were glad to have an order in September 1959 for 102 of the new bombers, bringing total procurement up to 744 aircraft. Wichita rolled out the first H on 30 September 1960, but it did not fly until 6 March 1961. The final aircraft was rolled out on 22 June 1962 and delivered to SAC on 26 October 1962. Wichita's final group was:

B-52H-125-BW, 464366/464372, 60-0001/0007
B-52H-130-BW, 464373/464379, 60-0008/0014
B-52H-135-BW, 464380/464386, 60-0015/0021
B-52H-140-BW, 464387/464393, 60-0022/0028
B-52H-145-BW, 464394/464400, 60-0029/0035
B-52H-150-BW, 464401/464407, 60-0036/0042
B-52H-155-BW, 464408/464414, 60-0043/0049
B-52H-160-BW, 464415/464421, 60-0050/0056
B-52H-165-BW, 464422/464427, 60-0057/0062
B-52H-170-BW, 464428/464467, 61-0001/0040

Completion of the manufacturing programme was merely the end of the beginning. In a way never dreamed of previously, the B-52 fleet was repeatedly denied a replacement and instead was continually upgraded to continue in service. Moreover the missions expanded and altered, at first by being flown at low level and then by using new weapons, navaids and sensors, the latter diversifying into defensive avionics and offensive avionics. In the more than 30 years since the last B-52 was delivered these aircraft have been subjected to over 600 ECPs (Engineering Change Proposals), some of them amounting almost to major rebuilds, to a total cost varying from 7 to 10 times the price of the new aircraft. Significant modifications are depicted in an accompanying graphical plot. Each entry here is really a major story in itself, and the outward expression of a ceaseless process which has also included numerous less-important changes and upgrades.

In 1959 all models except the B were still in service, but by 1965 the B, C and E had been withdrawn. The 'low-level mod' was in fact an ongoing series of structural changes, almost all involving the addition of metal and modified parts to give the required much greater stiffness and strength for turbulence in dense air. The changes varied according to sub-type, and from one aircraft to the next, but most involved extensive rebuilding of the wing, widespread introduction of T-2024 alloy, reskinning of parts of the fuselage and, especially, numerous secondary modifications. Included here are the addition of terrain-avoidance radar, an improved radio altimeter, much greater avionic-cooling capacity and shock-absorbing mounts for over 150 LRUs (line-replaceable units, mainly avionic). The biggest airframe rebuilds are listed for the G/H only in 1963–71. Low-level missions are tough, and in the early 1960s 'airborne alerts' piled up the hours as well, and on many occasions cracks or even failures showed that planned modifications were not enough. Ship 58-0187 suffered a catastrophic wing fatigue failure; in January 1963 two aircraft suffered catastrophic failure of the bulkhead 1.655 in from the nose datum *after modification*; and on 10 January 1964 a low-time B-52 lost its entire vertical tail.

The ADM-20 and AGM-28 have been mentioned, as have the G/H structural mods. High-density bombing was something extra, never dreamed of when the B-52 was designed. War in South-east Asia called not for nuclear weapons but for 'iron bombs', and it had always been obvious that the B-52 could fly long round trips with conventional bomb loads far heavier than the limit of 20,000 lb. In December 1965 work began at Wichita on B-52D and F models. These received ECP 1208, which added the Hound Dog pylon. This in turn received a locally-produced adapter rail for four triple tandem clutches of bombs, adding 24 bombs of 500-lb (actually 580-lb) or 750-lb size (actual nominal mass 825-lb). In addition the B-52D, which proved surprisingly efficient and effective, received the 'Big Belly' rework which, without altering the size of the bomb bay, enabled it to carry 42 bombs of 750-lb size or 84 of 500-lb. Thus the conventional bomb load was increased from 20,000 lb to 68,520 lb.

The fuselage-life mod (ECP 1185-5) was major, especially on the G/H. The stability-augmentation system was needed to fight Dutch roll by the small-fin G and H and reduce structural loads in turbulence. It replaced the original yaw-damper system by much faster electronics with greater authority to multiply the speed of response of the rudder and elevators. Next came SRAM. The Lockheed AGM-69A Short-range Attack Missile was developed to take out hostile radars, airfields and other defence centres up to 105 miles ahead of the bomber. A perfectly streamlined shape, it was given a tail fairing (increasing length to 190 in) for triple tandem external carriage on a modified Hound Dog pylon, or without the fairing (168 in) for loading on an eight-shot rotary launcher in the aft bomb bay. Thus, a B-52G/H could launch up to 20 of these 2230-lb rocket missiles, each with independent inertial guidance and a 200 kT W-69 warhead.

EVS (Electro-optical Viewing System) was the most visible of all updates. Introduced from 1973, it transformed the ability of the G/H to fly safely at low level; it also assists post-strike assessment. Desig-

ABOVE *Adding the twin EVS sensors was just the beginning of the 'aerodynamic dirtying' process. This is an H-model*

nated ASQ-151, its sensors comprise a Westinghouse AVQ-22 low-light TV scanning over much of the forward hemisphere with 3:1 zoom capability, and a Hughes AAQ-6 FLIR (forward-looking infra-red). These are respectively housed in left and right turrets under the nose, normally rotated 180° to minimise abrasion and foreign-object damage. These sensors were tied in with the main radar, terrain-avoidance radar and flight-director imagery to feed new 10 in displays.

Phase VI ECM was an even more costly upgrade which added 17 avionics LRUs, some in large subsystems, to guard against hostile transmissions, radars and heat-homing missiles. It included SNOE (Smart Noise Operation Equipment), which listens for enemy signals and jams them automatically on the correct wavelength. Quick Start was mentioned earlier. ALR-46, by Itek, was a digital threat-warning system welcomed by D-model crews. AFSATCOM, Air Force SATellite COMmunications, gave the G/H global voice or encryption contact via satellite from 1979. PMS, Performance Management System, saves a lot of fuel and refines mission accuracy. ASQ-48 was the last and most costly of all D upgrades, replacing the entire nav/bomb system with modern digital microelectronics.

After a false start with ALQ-27 the Tail Warning programme was finally implemented to tell G/H crews not only about interceptors and big SAMs but also tiny AAMs and even cannon fire. Its sensor, Westinghouse's ALQ-153 pulse-doppler radar, automatically manages chaff/flare ejection, using a single scanner which at first was on the left tailplane tip but later moved over half-way up the fin; 321 sets were installed by 1985.

Biggest of all the upgrades, the OAS (Offensive Avionics System) cleaned out the entire ASQ-38 and gave the G/H a comprehensive nav/bombing system, using nuclear-hardened digital microelectronics. It has to work right down to 300 ft altitude, with nuclear or 'iron' bombs, SRAMs and cruise missiles. The CMI (shown on the chart as external and internal carriage) was the Cruise Missile Interface. In a typically pragmatic and purely political decision in June 1977, President Carter cancelled the B-1, saying that SAC could manage with the B-52 converted to carry 'a completely new weapon', the cruise missile (apparently ignorant of the cruise missiles developed in both world wars). The missile chosen was Boeing's own AGM-86B, a miniature turbofan-engined aircraft with a length of 20 ft 9 in, launch weight of 3200 lb and ability to deliver its 150-kT W-80 warhead anywhere within 1550 miles at 500 mph. Wings, tail and engine inlet folded so that tandem triplets could be hung on the long adapter on each underwing pylon. The original programme of 1980 involved ACMI Ext (12 missiles) on 173 B-52Gs, but this was later changed to convert 99 Gs and 96 Hs. The rebuild of the aft bomb bay to carry eight ALCMs (Air-Launched Cruise Missiles), which were too long for the bay or rotary launcher as originally built, was never carried out. Under the SALT (Strategic Arms Limitation Treaty) the CMI G-model aircraft were given a wing leading-edge/body fairing called a strakelet so that they could be thus identified. Such a cosmetic change was not needed on the H, which was visibly identifiable from its engines.

Adding cruise missiles seemed of paramount importance to the credibility of this ancient bomber in 1982. Nobody then thought that over ten years later ten wings of B-52s would be soldiering on with the main emphasis on dropping 'iron bombs', a role carried out with telling effect in the 1991 Gulf War. Having eliminated its proudest element, SAC, the USAF has designed a *Bomber Road Map* to guide its use of bombers over the next decade in what it sees as conventional wars in any part of the globe.

All the trusty B-52Ds have gone, and the Gs are following to the boneyard in 1991–95. In late 1992 the force had dwindled to 15 Gs and 80 Hs, deployed in the following units: 2nd BW, Barksdale AFB, LA; 5th BW, Minot, ND; 7th BW, Carswell, TX; 42nd BW, Loring, ME; 92nd BW, Fairchild, WA; 92rd BW, Castle, CA; 97th BW, Eaker (ex-Blytheville), ARK; 279th BW, Wurtsmith, MICH; 410th BW, K I Sawyer, MICH; and 416th BW, Griffiss, NY. They are tasked in conventional bombing, having to relearn high-altitude free-fall delivery after 20 years at under 500 ft. Alternative roles include anti-ship attack, with 12 AGM-84A Harpoon cruise missiles carried on the external pylons. Nuclear war is seen as unlikely, but four B28s can still be carried in the front bay, plus the eight SRAMs on the rotary launcher and 12 ALCMs outside.

In what must be the last major upgrades 47 of the Hs are being equipped to carry TSSAM (Tri-Service Stand-off Attack Missile) from 1997, while the other 33 will get Heavy Stores Adapter Beams, STD-1760 interfaces and GPS precision nav receivers for the heavy conventional role. All will be Harpoon-capable, and new weapons will include the first-generation JDAM (Joint Direct Attack Munition), a precision-guided Mk 84 (2000-lb) bomb. From 1991 the 42nd BW (B-52G) also carried the AGM-142A Have Nap conventional cruise weapon, which is being added to ten Hs in 1995. Upgrades to B-52 equipment were approved in the October 1992 Defense Budget, together with $15 million added by Congress for testing the Have Lite version of Have Nap. As this book goes to press in mid-1993, Boeing Defense and Space Group is delivering kits (in part with hardware removed from retired B-52Gs) to convert up to all 95 active H-models to carry 12 Harpoons or four Have Naps or eight JDAMs on a stub pylon, or 16 Harpoons or six Have Naps or 12 JDAMs on a lengthened ALCM pylon. TSSAM numbers remain classified.

The story of the B-52 is unique, not only among bombers but among man's vehicles for air, land or sea. Created in a frantic hurry to last a few years, these huge and distinctive machines have been forced by circumstance to stay in the frontline almost 50 years. To do as much, Sopwith Camels would have had to remain operational to 1968. Now the bombers are fading away at last.

SPECIFICATION

B-52G/H

Eight Pratt & Whitney jet engines: (G) J57-43WB turbojets rated at 13,750 lb with water injection, (H) TF33-3 turbofans each rated at 16,500 lb (originally 17,000)

Dimensions Span 185 ft 0 in (56.39 m); length (G) 160 ft 10.9 in (50.26 m), (H) 164 ft 0 in (49.99 m); wing area 4000 sq ft (371.6 m²)

Weight Empty 184,250–186,720 lb (c84 t); max fuel 312,195 lb (141,612 kg); max take-off (G, max g limit 1.8) 488,000 lb (221,357 kg), starting TO roll at 495,000; (H) 505,000 lb (229,068 kg) with war limit after air refuelling of 566,000 lb (256,738 kg)

Performance Maximum speed cited as '650 mph' (1046 km/h) at high altitude; normal penetration speed at low level 310 kt (357 mph, 575 km/h) reducing in turbulence (max weight 420,000 lb) to 270 kt indicated; combat ceiling (both) c46,000 ft (14 km); unrefuelled range at high altitude (G) 8406 miles (13,528 km), (H) 10,130 miles (16,300 km); TO run about 4000 ft (1219 m); landing run (max 325,000 lb) typically from 3300 ft with chute on dry runway to 9900 ft without chute on wet

Armament Defensive guns (G) four 0.5 in M3 each with 600 rounds, (H) one M61A1 with 1200 rounds; max bombloads, see text

Convair YB-60

Having established the B-36 as the only truly strategic bomber in the USAF's Strategic Air Command, Convair was naturally anxious to keep it competitive and also fend off outsiders. The B-36's chief weakness was its lack of speed, and in February 1950 the division's engineering staff under Dick Sebold began designing a version with swept wings and tail. The chief imponderable was what engines to use, and at first the favoured solution was six turboprops (an answer also favoured at that time by Boeing). It was soon obvious that a far superior propulsion system would be eight J57 turbojets, which combined high power with good fuel economy. The level of performance possible put Convair in a quandary. Starting with the B-36, they could never hope to equal the performance of an all-new aircraft, such as the Boeing B-52. The only hope appeared to do the best they could, and rely on commonality with the B-36 to carry the day.

On 15 March (also reported as 5 March) 1951 the Air Force authorised Convair to complete two B-36F bombers, Nos 151 and 165, as B-36Gs, with swept surfaces and eight J57 engines. Later in that year it was decided, on Convair's insistence, that these aircraft should receive a new designation entirely, and YB-60 was allotted. Convair claimed that the YB-60 used '72 per cent of the parts of the B-36', but this is clearly nonsense. Again, it was claimed that 'the wing centre section and the fuselage apart from the nose' were unchanged, but this is similar nonsense. Where there was a lot of commonality was in the on-board systems, bomb bay and landing gear.

The wing of the YB-60 was almost completely new. Incidentally, though the span was considerably less than that of the B-36, it was greater than that of any other jet bomber. Sweepback was 35° at the leading edge and about 31° at the quarter-chord line. Chord of the centre section was greatly increased in order to preserve virtually the full original depth and still achieve the reduced thickness ratio of 13 per cent. Maximum use was made of both wing and fuselage volume in increasing the fuel capacity from 29,995 US gal (B-36D) to 38,500. The YJ57–3 engines, each rated at 8700 lb, were carried in twin pods hung on sharply swept pylons which extended back across the top of

BELOW *Small humans before pre-flighting the only YB-60 to fly*

LEFT *It's 30 September 1951 and the world's biggest jet-bomber wing has yet to fly*

ABOVE *It's still 30 September 1951, and the first YB-60 is on the ramp alongside its giant predecessors*

the wing to serve as fences. Each trailing edge carried four sections of Fowler flap.

The fuselage resembled the B-36 only superficially, the main points of similarity being the bomb bay and cockpit (though it was intended to fit a new cabin air system with increased pressure). The interior was greatly simplified, first by eliminating the three front gun turrets (nose and twin dorsal) and then the four retractable rear turrets (two dorsal, two ventral). This left only the single tail turret with twin 20 mm M24 guns with 575 rounds each, controlled by APG-32 or -41A radar. This reduced the crew from 22 to five, all housed in the forward pressure cabin. In any case, Convair made no attempt to fit any armament or operational equipment to ship 49-2676, the YB-60-1, but rushed it through carrying nothing more potent than instrumentation in order to confirm the predicted performance quickly.

Although the tail had to be totally redesigned, Convair went to great lengths to adhere to manual

ABOVE *Now it is 25 April 1952 and the monster jet takes off on its second test flight. The aircraft's brief flying programme with Convair was not continued by the USAF after June 1954, and it was scrapped soon after*

flight controls, though it meant having spring-tab drives covering virtually the entire trailing edge of each surface. Another dimension in which the YB-60 set a record for jet bombers was in height on the ground. Often reported as 50 ft, the actual figure was 60 ft 5 in. Overall length was increased over that of the B-36F by more than 13 ft, but this was partly accounted for by the instrumentation boom on the nose and partly by the swept tail. As the swept wing made the YB-60 land at a much greater angle of attack than the B-36, a retractable tailwheel was added.

The YB-60-1 made its first flight from Carswell AFB, adjacent to the Fort Worth plant, on 18 April 1952. Convair thought they had done well to get the first 'jet B-36' into the air so quickly, and were disheartened to find that they were three days behind the all-new B-52. They knew they could never equal the Boeing's performance, and in fact their aircraft was almost 100 mph slower. With fully-developed engines they calculated a maximum speed of nearly 550 mph, but the USAF remained unimpressed by both this and the supposed savings in commonality with the B-36. The YB-60-1 flew only 40 hours before it was handed over to the USAF on 25 June 1954. The YB-60-5, No 49-2684, was to have been fully equipped with bomb-carrying systems, tail guns, K-3A radar-bombing system and ECM, but it never even received its engines. It was handed over as an engineless hulk on 8 July 1954, and both YB-60s were scrapped soon afterwards.

SPECIFICATION

YB-60
Eight 8700 lb Pratt & Whitney YJ57-P-3 turbojets
Dimensions Span 206 ft 5 in (62.92 m); length 175 ft 2 in (53.39 m); wing area 5239 sq ft (486.7 m²)
Weight Empty 153,016 lb (69.408 kg); combat 260,250 lb (118,050 kg); maximum 410,000 lb (185,976 kg)
Performance Maximum speed 508 mph (818 km/h) at 39,250 ft; combat ceiling 44,650 ft (13.6 km); combat radius with 10,000 lb (4536 kg) bombload 2920 miles (4700 km)
Armament Two 20 mm M24A1 guns each with 575 rounds; bombload not specified but intended to be the same as the B-36, maximum 84,000 lb (38,100 kg)

Tupolev Tu-16

First Flight – 27 April 1952

Development by the engine KB (design bureau) of Gen A A Mikulin of a large axial-compressor turbojet known initially as the M-209, and later put into production as the AM-3, was the key to the development of the first really capable jet bombers in the Soviet Union. One was the four-engined Myasishchyev M-4. The other was the twin-jet which is the subject of this chapter.

Along with the VVS-ADD, the long-range force of the Soviet air force, the Tupolev design bureau had long sought to create a bomber combining jet speed with the range and bombload of the Tu-4 (Soviet copy of the B-29). In the summer of 1950 the bureau dropped the smaller Tu-86 and 90 and received an order for two Tu-88 prototypes plus a static-test specimen. Internally the project was called N, the design team being led by Dmitri S Markov (today a Tu chief designer). Professor A N Tupolev himself decided on the location of the engines, A A Judin then designing novel main landing gears which became an OKB 'trademark'. The basic requirement was to carry 5 t (11,020 lb) of bombs for 5000 km (3125 miles), and also to carry the largest bomb, the FAB-9000. This dic-

tated the width of the bomb bay, and to reduce drag and bring the engines closer together Tupolev discarded the circular section in the centre fuselage and drew the engines in close beside the FAB-9000, 1.9 m (75 in) apart, curving in the inlets and curving out the jetpipes. This unwittingly gave an Area Rule shape, and the splayed-out jetpipe angle avoided scrubbing of the rear fuselage.

The aerofoil profile of the wing was PR-1-10S-9, with a theoretical thickness/chord ratio of 15.7 per cent on the centreline and 12 per cent on the outer panels. Leading-edge sweepback was 41° from the root to the structural joint at 6.5 m, and then 37° to the tip. Mean aerodynamic chord was 5021 mm (198 in) and wing anhedral −3°. The main structural box had thick machined skins, forming integral tanks throughout, and the leading edge incorporated hot-air anti-icing with the exhaust from tip slits. On the trailing edge were arranged track-mounted slotted flaps inboard and outboard of the main landing gears with a total area of 25.17 m². driven by electric ball-screws to 35° for landing. Outboard were fitted balanced Frise ailerons of 14.77 m². A fence 200 mm deep (extended to

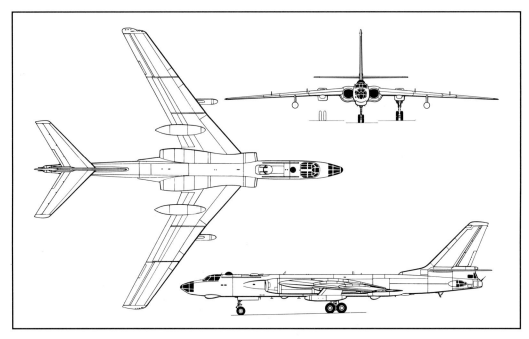

TOP *Trials aircraft used to develop the strange 'looped hose' air refuelling system*

ABOVE *The first time Western analysts had a close look at Tu-16s was on 4 December 1967 when nine flew to Cairo on a 'goodwill' visit. They were of the K2R version*

the leading edge during production) was added at the structural break and another at the flap/aileron junction. The tail was almost scaled-up from the Tu-82, with a fin of 23.3 m² area, swept on the leading edge at 40°, carrying a rudder of 5.21 m². The fixed tailplane had an area of 34.45 m², the leading edge being swept sharply at 42°, carrying elevators of 8.65 m². All the control surfaces were tabbed and balanced for manual control. Production aircraft switched to full hydraulic boost, but retained the tabs.

The fuselage was of circular section, with a diameter of 2.5 m (98.4 in) except over the centre section, and it was constructed in five sections. First, the glazed nose, with the main radar under the cockpit, and the ventral crew door with a telescopic ladder under the main avionics/systems compartment, bounded by the convex rear pressure bulkhead. Next was the section housing the nose landing gear, forward tanks, dorsal turret, cameras and landing lights. This was followed by the long centre section with protected fuel tanks and the 6.5 m (256 in) bomb bay with two hydraulic doors, plus a bay for target indicators (or other loads in other versions). Next, a section housing the Nos 5 and 6 tanks and ventral turret, followed by the rear pressurised compartment (linked by a tunnel in the first prototype) with a ventral door, side blister windows, retractable bumper, PTK-16 braking parachute and tail turret. There were a total of 36 main frames, those in the centre section being of KhGSA chrome steel with extra side rings for the engine duct or engine and picking up the wing spars at the top, leaving large engine access doors under the wing. The navigator/bomb-aimer normally sat in the nose on an armoured seat, next came the side-by-side pilots, and then the *radist* to operate the RPB-4 *Rubin 1* navigation and bombing radar, and the dorsal gunner who also managed the electrical system and signals. In the tail was a ventral gunner with an optical sight at lateral blisters and the tail gunner with his radar-turret, the defensive system being described later. The pilots were arranged to blow off roof hatches and eject upwards, all other crew-members ejecting downwards. Fuel was housed in no fewer than 27 tanks with inert-gas protection, self-sealing in the fuselage and integral in the wings. The total capacity added up to 43,800 litres (9635 gal), fed to the engines via a flow proportioner.

TOP *Today almost all surviving Tu-16s have been repeatedly upgraded and converted for different missions. This was one of several species of Tu-16Ye*

ABOVE *A Tu-16K-10 photographed near Japan on 28 February 1963 by an RF-8A from USS Kitty Hawk (CV-63)*

For the first time in the Soviet Union, bogie main landing gears were fitted. The track came out to 9775 mm (32 ft), the tyres being of size 1100×330 to enable pressure to be compatible with unpaved runways. Each wheel had a multi-disc anti-skid brake, the complete bogie having hydraulic retraction backwards with the truck somersaulting to lie inverted in a box fairing with twin doors entirely behind the wing. At first strikingly unusual, this was an efficient arrangement which avoided cutting into the highly stressed wing skins. The twin-wheel nose gear was fitted with tyres 900×275, with hydraulic steering and retracting to the rear into a bay with twin doors, the wheelbase being 10.91 m (35 ft 10 in).

Hydraulic system pressure was set at 3000 lb/in², and was completely duplex to ensure the availability of stand-by power. Electric power was generated as mainly DC at 28 volts to drive the flaps and gun turrets, and for starting the AM-3 main engines and (in later versions) the S-300M gas-turbine starter of the RD-3M engine. In addition, raw AC could be supplied for deicing the tail and windscreens. The air-cycle cabin environmental system operated at a maximum pressure differential of 0.05 kg/cm² (7.1 lb/sq in). A KP-23 gaseous-oxygen system was installed, together with two IAS-5M dinghies.

Tupolev was distressed by serious weight growth to over 80 t, which threatened to make flight performance sluggish. He bitterly contested a design requirement for Mach 0.9 to be demonstrated at low level, and got this downgraded to 700 km/h, enabling airframe weight to be reduced by no less than 5.5 tonnes (12,125 lb). The first prototype, burdened by the heavy structure, was first flown by a test crew headed by N S Rybko on 27 April 1952. Despite indifferent performance, and the arguably better handling of the rival Il-46, the potential of the big Tu-88 was clearly much greater, and production was ordered in December 1952. Tupolev asked for, and eventually got, permission to delay the programme while the lighter No 2 aircraft was built, and flown in early 1953. This reduced take-off weight to 71,560 kg and had other improvements. Full production at two GAZ (state aircraft factories) was begun in October 1953, and nine series aircraft flew over Red Square, Moscow, on the 1954 May Day. Service designation was Tu-16.

The initial production version was powered by the AM-3A engine. A small number were supplied to the DA and also to the AV-MF (naval air force), most being retained for test and training. Not knowing what it was, NATO called these aircraft 'Type 39', and later *Badger*. The Tu-16 was quickly followed by the Tu-16A, the major production version *Atomnyi*. This version was powered by the more powerful RD-3M engine, and the weapon bay was configured for the FAB-9000, as an alternative to five types of nuclear bomb or various other loads to a maximum of 9 tonnes (19,840 lb).

At last the PV-23 fire control was installed, governing all the defensive guns, linked to the PRS-1 *Argon* tail radar under the rudder. At the rear of the main crew compartment was the DT-V7 dorsal turret twin short-barrel AM-23 cannon, each with 500 rounds, with 360° traverse and elevation $+90°/-3°$ with an electrical safety cutout to prevent the turret firing on the aircraft's own tail. The ventral turret was a DT-N7S, with the same 23 mm guns but with 700 rounds, slewing through $\pm 95°$, elevation $+2°/-90°$. The tail turret was a DK-7 with twin AM-23 with 1000 rounds, slewing $\pm 70°$, and elevating $+60°/-40°$. A single PU-88 installation was fitted on the right side of the nose, with a long-barrel AM-23 (100 rounds), aimed with a PKI pilot reflector sight. The PV-23 system added as S-13 (forward) and PAU-457-1 and -2 (turret) ciné cameras.

Basic avionics included an SPU-10 intercom, R-807 and (pilot) -808 HF, RSIU-3 UHF, RSIU-4 VHF, RPB-4 *Rubin* main radar, TV-17 (high-altitude) and RV-2 (low-altitude) radar altimeters. The AP-28 autopilot was linked to the NAS-1 integrated navigation system including DISS- *Trassa* doppler, MRP-48P ADF, KRP-F VOR and SD-1M DME. ILS linked the DME with a GRP-2 glide-slope receiver into the SP-50 ILS. SRO-2 IFF was naturally fitted, with three rod-like antennas, as well as a Sirena-2 RWR (radar warning receiver). Standard cameras were the AFA-33M (day) and NAFA-8S (night).

During production, upgrades included the AP-6E autopilot, RV-5 and -18 radar altimeters, SOD series ATC/SIF, ARK-15 ADF, ARK-5 tanker homing and *Khrom-Nikel* IFF. In 1965 the ILS was upgraded to SP-50M standard for Cat III landing, in almost blind conditions. In some versions the RSDN *Chaika* Loran and even the *Glonass* navigation-satellite receiver have been added.

Total production of the Tu-16A was over 800, out of a total for all versions which exceeds 1800. Most Tu-16A were rebuilt for other purposes after 1960. NATO called them *Badger-A*.

Chronologically, the next version was the Tu-16R for reconnaissance, followed in 1959 by the Tu-16T, a torpedo-bomber version for the AV-MF. This had the bomb bay equipped to carry four torpedoes, and a special sight was installed in the glazed nose. Alternative loads could include mines or other stores. Because it did not look very different NATO still called this *Badger-A*. Another AV-MF version is the Tu-16S. This is a SAR (search and rescue) version carrying a large lifeboat, para-dropped and guided by radio from the aircraft to the rescuees. Though it is still in use with the CIA Navy, the NATO name is unknown.

From the mid-1950s the AV-MF played a prominent role in the Tu-16 programme. In 1948 it had funded development of the KS-1 *Komet*, a high-subsonic cruise missile for long-range stand-off attacks on surface ships and other clearly definable radar targets. The missile was developed by the fighter OKB of A I Mikoyan (MiG), and Tupolev was instructed to produce a version of the Tu-16A modified to carry one KS-1 under each wing. The resulting Tu-16KS was fitted with a special pylon under each wing 7.75 m (25 ft 5 in) from the centreline. A considerable amount of test gear was needed in the development aircraft, but the production required few other changes. Over 100 conversions served with the AV-MF, as well as with the AURI No 41/42 Sqns (Indonesia) and with Egypt. Those in the former USSR have now been converted to later versions. The NATO name was *Badger-B*

One of the most important versions was the Tu-16K-10. This was a substantially modified AV-MF missile carrier – the Russian category being 'rocket launcher' – with a K-10 cruise missile (NATO name

AS-2 *Kipper*) recessed into the weapon bay with a multi-pin guidance cable link and fuel connection. This required the A-329Z guidance system, with the nose navigator station replaced by a powerful radar with a 2 m (80 in) antenna scanning through a limited forward arc to provide a guidance offset to the missile autopilot out to a distance of 250 km. About 100 of this version were built new from 1959. All were rebuilt from the late 1960s as EW platforms. NATO called this variant *Badger-C*.

Because they acted as a bomber force-multiplier, mention should be made of the Tu-16Z. This was, and remains, a dedicated air-refuelling tanker.

BELOW *This prototype tail turret still operates after 40 Russian winters*

BOTTOM *Designed to knock out almost any warship, except the biggest carriers, the KSR-5P homes in on its target at supersonic speed*

Initially the Z retained standard tankage and bombing capability. Refuelling was carried out through a hose trailed from the right wingtip, picked up by the left tip of the receiver, many in-service Tu-16s being equipped as receivers. From 1960 the dedicated Tu-16N tanker became available, with weapon-bay tanks and a 1000 litre (220 gal)/min hose-drum unit in the rear fuselage for refuelling the Tu-20/22/22M and MS2. The maximum transfer fuel capacity was usually 54,000 litres (11,800 gal). All N-versions were conversions of 16A or M aircraft, the total (1993) being estimated at 20 with Air Armies and 70 with the CIS Navy. The NATO name is unknown.

The first reconnaissance version was the Tu-16R, built from 1955. Based on the Tu-16A, the weapon bay was reconfigured for pallets carrying various arrangements of optical cameras. Some aircraft were fitted with an Elint (electronic-intelligence) installation, usually with two steerable parabolic receivers in dielectric blisters ahead of and behind the camera bay, but this was merely the first of almost 20 recon/EW versions with a profusion of sensor fits. Today's total with Air Armies is estimated at 15. The NATO name is *Badger-D*.

A number of K-10 aircraft were rebuilt to Tu-16KR standard with various suites of cameras and Elint receivers. The latter typically included three steerable antennas in blisters and six with flush antennas. Normally, the flight crew number three or four and the mission specialists five. The NATO name is *Badger-D*. Two related AV-MF R versions added forward-looking receivers in pods carried on underwing pylons, as well as small fixed pods and steerable fuselage receivers to cover virtually all hostile radar wavebands. These entered service in 1962, and the total of recce versions with the CIS Navy in 1993 was estimated at 30; NATO name is *Badger-F*.

Most DA and AV-MF aircraft still serving as free-fall bombers were converted in 1962–66 with the RD-3M-500 engine and previously listed avionic updates. Some were prepared with wiring for future EW conversion. NATO kept the name *Badger-A*.

Yet another variant was the Tu-16Ye, an active and passive jammer platform to escort AV-MF strike aircraft. These were mostly rebuilt Tu-16K-10s with both steerable (including a small 360° scanner in a hemispherical radome) and fixed (flush and blade) receiver antennas to establish hostile wavelengths and control cut lengths of chaff dispensed from a bulk (c9t, 19,800 lb) three-channel installation in the weapon bay feeding through chutes in the left weapon-bay door. Some Yes have blade antennas above the cockpit and on underwing pylons. The NATO name is *Badger-H*.

Most remaining KS-1 aircraft were modified into the Tu-16K-11-16, retaining the same pylons but with the on-board command radio system modified to control KSR-II or -2 (NATO AS-5 *Kelt*) cruise missiles. A few were used by Egypt in the 1967 war, firing 25 missiles at Israel with patchy results. All CIS Navy examples have been rebuilt into later versions. NATO called this *Badger-G*.

The Tu-16K-11-16 is a rebuilt AV-MF Tu-16A with wing pylons (often on the right wing only) to carry a single KSR-5P cruise missile (NATO AS-6 *Kingfish*), with guidance radar added ahead of the bomb bay using a steerable antenna in a radome, and air-data sensors on the nose. Variants are the Tu-16K-10-26 of 1962, carrying a K-10 and two KSR-5s, and the Tu-16K-26 of 1965, able to launch KSR-5Ps or K-26s from either or both wings. The clumsy NATO name is *Badger-G Mod*.

The first AV-MF version to carry an ECM (electronic countermeasures) station in a large ventral installation entered service in 1970. The weapon bay is occupied by jamming pallets carrying power units, eight exciters, transmitters, RF couplers and antennas for Bands (usually) A or B to J plus a control computer. External intakes and exhausts serve the power units and cooling radiators. Some of these PP or PPM aircraft have large horizontal plate antennas extending beyond modified wingtips, plus a *Chaika*-M 'towel rail' Loran antenna. These Tu-16RMs are on their second rebuild, NATO calling them *Badger-J*.

Yet a further group of EW platforms rebuilt from

the Tu-16M have as their primary role active and passive jamming with two steerable antennas under the centre fuselage, together with four fixed forward receiver antennas in separate pylon-mounted pods. The associated power units, exciters, tuners and other ancillaries are in the weapon bay, their output governing the chop length of large chaff dispensers behind the weapon bay. This version remains in CIS Air Army service, the total of EW platforms (excluding the AV-MF) being estimated at 90. The NATO name is *Badger-K*.

These 1959-vintage EW platforms were all converted from Tu-16K versions and retain the original broad chin radome but with an added 'thimble' radome on the nose, the tail turret replaced with a long tailcone (as seen on the Tu-126 and Tu-95K-22 versions) and variable pylon-mounted pods under fuselage and/or wings. All these Tu-16Ps are associated with active jammers. In service with the CIS Navy, whose total of EW versions is estimated at 60, the NATO name is *Badger-L*.

Early production Tu-16s were demilitarised and equipped with civil navaids to serve as GVF crew trainers and to undertake route-proving prior to the entry into service of the Tu-104 airliner, being redesignated Tu-16G or even Tu-104G. Another variant was the Tu-104Sh; in the early 1960s about ten Tu-16A bombers were fitted with radar, missile guidance and navigation systems of the Tu-22 to serve as crew trainers. Survivors were rebuilt for other roles. The NATO name is unknown.

The story of the Tu-16 has lasted 45 years, and many are still active; in mid-1993 the DA alone was operating over 300 aircraft. French historian Jacques Marmain has identified over 20 major versions so far.

In September 1957 the People's Republic of China was granted a licence to manufacture the basic Tu-16 bomber. Almost two years later two pattern aircraft were delivered, one dismantled and the other completely 'knocked down' into small sections. The former was assembled at Harbin and flown on 27 September 1959. Subsequently, relations between the two countries were severed, but in 1961 it was decided that a Chinese version would be produced as the H-6 (Hongzhaji 6, bomber 6) at what became XAC, the Xian Aircraft Manufacturing Co. The engine was also put into production at the Xian aero-engine factory as the WP-8.

Progress was understandably slow, but the first H-6A flew on 24 December 1968. Since then both production and improvement have continued, and in 1993 it was estimated that well over 120 aircraft had been delivered to the PLA air force and navy, plus four to Iraq and numerous major spare parts to Egypt. The current version is described as the H-6D (B-6D in Westernised notation). There are several variations, some having no main radar, but the standard 6D version has a large Chinese radar with an antenna revolving in a circular radome. This provides targeting information for two C-601 anti-ship cruise missiles carried on wing pylons. Unlike the 6A, the 6D has no fixed nose gun. Many other variants have been studied, and in 1986 Flight Refuelling Ltd completed a design study for a tanker version to refuel the Q-5 and H-7 attack aircraft, but this remains in abeyance. Manufacture of the H-6 has been tapered off, but there are plans for major conversions to other roles. NATO simply calls all H-6 versions *Badger*.

SPECIFICATION

Tu-16 and H-6

Two Mikulin AM-3 (**Tu-88**) or AM-3M turbojets, each rated at 19,285 lb, or (main production, here abbreviated to M) RD-3M-500 turbojets rated at 20,950 lb
Dimensions Span (**88**) 35.5 m (109 ft 11 in), (production, excl tip antennas on some) 33.4 or 34,189 m (112 ft 2 in); length (basic) 34.8 m (114 ft 2 in), (M) up to 37.9 m (124 ft 4 in); wing area 164.65 m² (1772 ft²), (**B-6D**) 167.55 m²
Weight Empty (**88 No 1**) 37.2 t, (**16A, M**) 36.6 t (80,688 lb), (max EW versions) 38 t, (**H-6D**) 38.53 t (84,944 lb); fuel (**16M**) 34.36 t (equivalent to 41,400 lit T-1 or 43,750 lit TS-1), (**H-6D**) 33 t; normal loaded (**88 No 1**) 80 t, (production, all) 72 t (158,730 lb), (maximum, all) 75.8 t (167,108 lb); maximum landing weight (paved) 50 t, (unpaved) 48 t, (**H-6D**) 55 t
Performance Max IAS (excl **88 No 1**) 700 km/h; max speed at 6 km (**88 No 1**) 945 km/h, (production) 1050 km/h (642 mph), (10 km) 1010 km/h (628 mph, Mach 0.95); maximum cruising speed of **H-6D** with C-601 missiles 786 km/h (488 mph); service ceiling (**88 No 1**) 11 km, (production) 15 km (49,200 ft), (**H-6D**) 12 km (39,370 ft); range with 3 t bombload 7200 km (4475 miles), with 9 t bombload 4800 km; combat radius of **H-6D** with missiles 1800 km (1118 miles); TO run 1250 m (H-601D at full load) 2100 m; landing speed/run 223 km/h, 1100 m (**H-6D**) 1540 m

BELOW *The first air-refuelling method adopted by Long-range Aviation was this odd looped-hose technique, here demonstrated by a Tu-16Z tanker and (nearer) a prototype Tu-16K-10-26*

Avro Vulcan

First Flight – 30 August 1952

When the Chadderton, Manchester, projects office of A V Roe Ltd (Avro) received Ministry of Supply specification B.35/46, it was assumed that in some way the drafting team had gone too far in their performance demands, and asked for something that existing technology could not provide. The specification was the technical follow-up to Air Staff Operational Requirement OR.229, and was issued on 7 January 1947.

Major elements of the requirement were demanding, but not unreasonable. The RAF wanted a strategic jet bomber capable of transporting a 10,000 lb 'special store' (nuclear weapon) over a combat radius of 1500 nm (1727 miles): alternatively, a conventional bomb load of at least 20,000 lb should be carried over unspecified shorter ranges. Altitude performance included a cruise-climb at 450–500 kt to 35,000 ft, eventually rising to not less than 50,000 ft over hostile territory. The speed component stipulated a high-

altitude cruise of 500 kt (576 mph), a short-duration dash over the target of at least Mach 0.85, and an approach speed of not more than 120 mph. The five-man crew – pilot, co-pilot, nav-plotter, nav-radar and signaller (later upgraded to air electronics officer, AEO) – were to be provided with a jettisonable pressure cabin, which would incorporate ejection seats only for the two pilots. Cabin pressure differential was to be 9 lb/sq in during the cruise (equivalent to about 8000 ft at 45,000 ft), reducing to 3.5 lb/sq in over the target area to lessen the risk of explosive decompression. The weapons bay would have to accept a single bomb at least 25 ft long and 5 ft diameter, and the aircraft would need equipment for radar and visual bombing.

With the possible exception of the capsule (which was later abandoned), all these requirements were technically achievable. What worried Avro, and the other contenders, was the arbitrary imposition of a 100,000 lb gross-weight limit. This seemed to ignore the fact that the 6000 Imp gal of kerosene needed would weigh 48,600 lb on its own. Add to this the 10,000 lb bomb, at least 12,000 lb for the four installed engines and probably another 10,000 lb for the landing gear, a mere 19,400 lb was left for the rest of the aircraft.

Avro's first thoughts on B.35/46 were similar to those of Vickers: a conventional streamlined fuselage with a high shoulder wing swept at 45°, four engines buried in the wing roots and a traditional tailplane. The performance criteria suggested that this was the logical way to go, but the aircraft would have been bigger than the Air Staff wanted, and its gross weight was estimated at 193,000 lb. So, in early February 1947, technical director Roy Chadwick and chief designer Stuart Davies began to look at tailless designs as a means of saving weight. These needed a shorter fuselage, and the 45° wing could be reconfigured to make use of elevons for lateral and longitudinal control. Directional control was maintained by mounting the fin and rudder close to each wingtip. At this time a bicycle-type undercarriage was being considered, with small outrigger wheels. The truncated fuselage obviously reduced structural weight, and it also created less drag, which in turn made the aircraft more efficient and reduced the fuel needed. Taken together, these

BELOW *XA891 in silver finish in 1955*

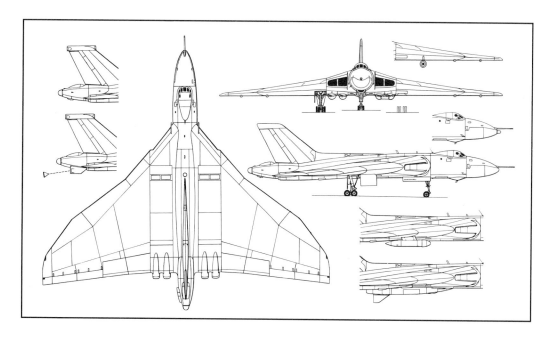

changes resulted in an estimated weight of 140,000 lb, but the new layout was prone to centre-of-gravity problems, particularly during fuel burn-off and bomb release.

The wing was now the heaviest part, and the design team knew that its weight could be reduced if it were made deeper. This would allow lighter fabrication techniques to be used, but it would also drastically increase the thickness/chord ratio, which would have an adverse effect on the critical Mach number. This conflict was resolved by the simple expedient of filling-in the gap behind the trailing-edge, effectively creating the biggest delta (triangular) planform in the world. This was a bold move at a time when delta control-technology was still in its infancy, but it transformed the aircraft's potential. Although the root chord was stretched to over 70 ft, the wing retained its high-speed cross-section, yet was now deep enough to house the engines, undercarriage, bombs and fuel. There were no centre-of-gravity problems, and the enormous wing area provided good low-speed control and excellent high-altitude performance.

Everyone at Chadderton was delighted with the new configuration, and the following weeks were spent refining the basic concept into something that could be formally submitted. By May 1947 the aircraft had become the Avro 698, but at this stage it had no fuselage. Instead, all five crew were housed in a projecting 'centre-body' that blended into the thickness of the wing, leaving the top surface completely smooth. On each side of the crew compartment were two large (6–7 ft diameter) circular intakes for superimposed pairs of Bristol BE.10 engines mounted near the centreline, the upper pair being forward of the lower ones. The top nozzles emerged through the upper surface at about 70 per cent chord, the lower nozzles being in the trailing edge. Immediately outboard of the engines were two separate bomb compartments, one for the 'special-store' and the other for HE bombs or additional tanks (for a non-nuclear strike, both compartments could carry conventional weapons). The twin-wheeled main landing gears were outboard of the bomb bays, giving an unusually wide track.

The 698 was clearly seen by the Ministry as a high-risk project. On the other hand it had tremendous potential, and was backed by some of the world's best aeronautical engineers. During the summer of 1947 Chadwick was often seen in Whitehall, encouraging Ministry officials to accept something unusual. His reputation alone often carried a meeting that would otherwise have been lost. It came as a terrible blow therefore, when he was killed on 23 August 1947. This could have been a real disaster for Avro, and at one point it seemed certain that the contract would be lost. But Chadwick had laid a firm foundation for the project, and the appointment of W S (later Sir William) Farren as technical director did much to calm official concern. Farren had been director of the Royal Aircraft Establishment at Farnborough during 1941–45. On 27 November 1947 it was announced that the Avro design would go forward into more detailed discussions; a similar decision in favour of Handley Page had been announced a week earlier.

The discussion period for both manufacturers was initially taken up by consultations at Farnborough, where it was quickly discovered that the 500 kt cruising speed would not be economically possible unless the thickness of the wing was reduced. Avro took some persuading of this, because their whole philosophy had been based on the deep wing section. But the results of Farnbor-

ough's tunnel testing were convincing. Accepting the findings resulted in profound changes. The vertical pairing of engines would not be possible inside a thinner wing, nor would the provision of separate outboard bomb compartments. Instead, it was decided to use a conventional fuselage, with a forward pressurised cabin, a weapons bay amidships, and an aft compartment for avionics and tail warning radar. The circular inlets were retained, but the engines were installed side-by-side, the jetpipes projecting slightly beyond the trailing edge. The tip rudders were retained, but the elevons were divided into two, with dual actuator systems.

By spring 1948 there was talk of using pivoting wing-tips. These would be flutter-free, and could serve as elevators or as ailerons. The scheme for the 698 involved moving the fins inboard by about 10 ft to provide clearance for the pivoting tips, but these were found to be less positive than expected and the idea was dropped.

In 1948 there was still a degree of uncertainty about the longitudinal stability of the triangular shape, particularly at low speeds or high altitudes. These doubts suggested the 698 might need a horizontal tail. The existing arrangement would have been difficult to modify, so in the summer of 1948 it was dropped in favour of a large single fin. Also, the split elevons were replaced by elevators

TOP *A pair of B.1 Vulcans in original configuration. XA912 and XH505 were later to get both more weight and more thrust from Mk 104 engines*

ABOVE *The Mk 1 converted to act as the prototype B.2 in 1958*

(inboard) and ailerons, and the circular inlets were replaced by slots set into a forward extension of the wing root. Nobody had used anything quite like it, so there was a high risk of airflow problems. To prevent ingestion of the turbulent boundary layer, a large semicircular splitter-plate was wrapped around the leading edge to separate the intakes from the fuselage.

On 1 January 1948 Avro had been given an Instruction to Proceed with two prototypes. Theoretical work suggested the delta would be a great success, but tunnel testing had its limitations, and there was no 'hands on' experience, and Avro decided to build two delta research aircraft. The Avro 707 was to be a simple, Derwent-powered single-seater, designed to investigate handling at 90–350 kt, and the Avro 710 a twin-Avon machine for Mach 0.95 and 60,000 ft.

The 707, VX784, turned out to be the first of five Avro 707s. Their first-flight dates were spread over a four-year period, and only two had any direct input into the 698. The 710 was never built.

The 707 was a roughly one-third scale of the wing, tail and control configurations of the 698, but the first two were unrepresentative in that they had a dorsal intake. The later 707A and 707C had wing-root intakes, but flew too late to help influence the design of the Avro bomber.

The first 707 flew on 4 September 1949, but it crashed 26 days later. Wreckage analysis showed that the aircraft had stalled and spun vertically near Blackbushe, killing test pilot Sammy Esler. The accident caused great concern until the investigation cleared the wing aerodynamics and identified a fault in the airbrake circuit as the most likely cause of the initial stall. The much-modified 707B, VX790, flew on 6 September 1950, piloted by Avro's chief test pilot, Roly Falk. Several lessons were learned from the 707, but the 698 detail design was virtually complete so there was little scope for change. As it turned out, the 707s were all pleasant to fly, which gave the Chadderton team confidence.

On 28 July 1948 the ITP was converted into a contract for two prototypes, VX770 and 777, plus a static test airframe. There was also discussion about building a 'stripped down' 698 to gain early flight experience, but it could never have been effective as a research vehicle unless the main programme had been shut down to await the results.

Just as the final aerodynamic design was nearing completion, the RAE decided that the wing profile needed 'minor' changes. What they were asking for was a totally new wing section, which occupied the time of nearly 200 engineers and draughtsmen. The point of maximum thickness had to be moved forward at the root until it was very close to the leading edge: this avoided uneven pressure distribution on the original Avro-designed section, which was caused by airflow interference from the fuselage.

Manufacture of the first prototype began in spring 1951. The outer wings were built at Woodford, but the remainder of the aircraft, including the massive fuselage/wing centre-section, was built at Chadderton and then transferred to Woodford by road. By this stage it had become obvious that the chosen Bristol BE.10 (later Olympus) engines would not be ready on time. Avro studied the Sapphire and Avon as temporary replacements, and chose the Avon RA.3 rated at 6500 lb.

Although the 698 was radically new in shape, its underlying structure was simple. At its heart was a 30 ft long by 27 ft wide box-section, which contained the four engine bays and the arched girder over the big weapons compartment. This assembly was immensely strong, and over the years it gave the Vulcan more fatigue resistance than the RAF could ever reasonably have hoped for, especially considering the low-level battering that was later imposed on what was basically a high-level design.

The nose, tail and outer wing sections were bolted-on to its four faces.

Its front and rear faces were the massive carry-through wing spars, each of which was 'perforated' to accommodate the engine inlet ducts or jetpipes. The swept outer spars were joined to the four corners of the central box, each supported by multiple ribs coupled to spanwise stringers and overlain with parallel skin panels. The fixed leading edge had a similar rib construction, but instead of stringers the skin was reinforced by internal corrugations. The entire leading edge incorporated a hot-air de-icing duct. The rear spar carried the power units for the two sections of aileron and two of elevator on each wing.

On early aircraft, the rear fuselage tapered to a small cone designed to house a Red Garter tail-warning radar (never fitted). The tailpipes were angled down slightly, thanks to the 707; they emerged from the underside of the wing at roughly 30 per cent chord, and by the time they reached the trailing edge more than 90 per cent of their diameter was below the wing. On early aircraft these pipes extended only a few inches behind the wing, but later, as more powerful engines were fitted, they were made about 3 ft longer. The fin had a light-alloy leading edge incorporating a duct for hot-air de-icing. The rudder was pivoted to the fin torsion-box, and operated via a long torque-tube driven by a power unit buried in the fuselage.

Forward of the arched girders over the bomb compartment, the construction changed to more

BELOW *Three B.1s in anti-flash white. The span was actually less than that of a Lancaster, but weight was roughly multiplied by four*

ABOVE *The Blue Steel cruise missile was a formidable weapon, but it was withdrawn when politicians decided they preferred low-level ops with HE. This photo was taken in February 1963 with No 617 Sqn at Scampton*

conventional circular frames, with stringers to support the skin. Superimposed on each side was a contoured box forming the non-load-bearing intakes and inner leading edge. This box included the engine ducts and inlet de-icing pipes. The upper fuselage between the bomb bay and pressure cabin housed fuel, while the lower compartments were occupied by the nosewheel bay, electrical and hydraulic services, and other equipment. A reinforced frame just forward of the wing root carried the nose gear and rear pressure bulkhead.

The crew compartment was small in relation to the size of the aircraft, but it had operational positions on three levels. For long-range deployments a servicing crew of two could also be carried, but with seven on board the cabin could seem crowded. The two pilots were provided with Martin-Baker ejection seats under a teardrop canopy. If escape became necessary the metal rear part of the canopy was released by explosive bolts as part of the automatic ejection sequence, but the windscreen remained in place. Below and behind the pilots, three other crew were provided with conventional aft-facing seats, and any escape had to be made through the door. This was on the underside, immediately aft of the visual bomb-aiming position. It was pneumatically lowered to about 45°, an extending ladder covering the last few feet. In an emergency, the ladder system could be removed to create an angled slide giving airflow protection. This was far better for a 'normal' escape than the side doors of the Valiant and Victor. However, the nose gear was just 6 ft behind the slide, which made escape with the undercarriage down hazardous. The difficulty of escape from the rear seats of all three V-bombers caused much bitterness. Even the

Vulcan suffered at least four accidents where the pilots escaped but the rear crew did not.

The domed forward pressure bulkhead was immediately below the windscreen. Cantilevered ahead was the main H_2S radar. Its parabolic scanner was close to 80 in (2 m) across, which meant that the drive had to be some way forward of the primary structure. This was achieved by hanging the scanner from triangular beams in the top half of the nose only. The scanner was then enclosed by a dielectric cover that extended from the tip of the nose to the pressure bulkhead.

The cockpit layout was considered good for its time. Heavily influenced by Roly Falk, it featured airline-style blind-flying and engine monitoring panels, with throttles and trim switches between the two pilots. All vital controls and indicators were within reach of both seats. The captain was responsible for engine start, radio selection, bomb-door sequencing and trim. The co-pilot looked after pressurisation, air-conditioning and de-icing, and dealt with fuel management if the automatic system failed. The pilots had fighter-type control columns. This was logical in view of the performance and manoeuvrability of the aircraft, and it also made ejection much quicker, and therefore safer.

The flying-control surfaces were electro-hydraulically operated, but mechanically signalled via rods and levers. Each control axis (pitch, roll and yaw) was operated by multiple Boulton Paul actuators to prevent loss of control in the event of individual system failure. The ailerons and elevators were independently-powered split-section surfaces, and the rudder was operated by two jacks in tandem. Being a delta, the aircraft had no flaps. Artificial feel was provided by springs. Their feedback was electrically adjusted according to the manually-selected trim, and automatically modified by the 'q-feel' system. Any runaway failure in the high-IAS mode – which would have made landing very difficult – could be disabled from the cockpit. The air brakes were very small, but, because they were deployed well clear of the boundary-layer, they could multiply the drag of the aircraft by a factor of 2.5. They were driven vertically away from the wing by electric actuators, and then rotated through 45° or 90° to the airflow. Both prototypes had twin brake units above and below each wing, but the underside outer panels were deleted from production aircraft.

The Vulcan had so much internal fuel that external tanks were never considered. Three offset ribs supporting the elevator pivots were carried forward to the front spar. These bays were used to house ten self-sealing bag tanks, two in each outer bay and three in the inner bays. More fuel was carried in the upper part of the fuselage, and ferry tanks could be fitted in the bomb compartment. An automatic system maintained CG (centre of gravity) position while fuel was burned. This was done by two sequence timers, which drew fuel from each tank in proportion to its original capacity. In the event of any failure, fuel could be pumped around by manual selection. The refuel/defuel panels were in the main undercarriage bays.

Four engine-driven generators supplied the 112V DC electrical system, which powered fuel pumps, radar inverters, power-control pumps, airbrakes and many other items. It also supplied three rotary transformers for the 28V DC system, and six inverters for the AC supply. Between them, these low-power circuits looked after secondary equipment such as small pumps, motors and fans, windscreen wipers, radios, radar, lighting and instrumentation. On all early Vulcans most 112V services were supplied by a single busbar. This was later split into two separate systems, after a simple short-circuit resulted in one aircraft losing all its power-controls at the same time, and crashing into a residential area of Detroit.

The main hydraulic system was unusual because it operated at 4000 lb/sq in. Using engine-driven pumps and electrical selector valves, it served undercarriage retraction, wheel-brake operation, nosewheel steering and bomb-door opening. Air from all four engines was used for pressurisation and de-icing, and hot air was pumped into the bomb compartment to prevent the release mechanisms from freezing during a long high-altitude cruise.

By August 1952 the first prototype was almost complete. There was a tremendous team spirit, with everyone trying to get the new bomber airborne before the HP.80, and in time for the Farnborough air display. VX770 was rolled out in mid-August, and engine runs began a day later. Just before the first flight, Avro received a Ministry of Supply order for 25 production aircraft. It had been assumed that one of the B.35/46 contenders would be killed-off by some kind of competitive evaluation, so it came as a surprise when Handley Page were given an order for 25 HP.80s.

On Saturday 30 August Roly Falk took-off in VX770 for what should have been a brief handling assessment. As it turned out, the flight had to be extended almost to the limit of the fuel, because observers had seen debris falling as Falk lowered the undercarriage for landing. A Vampire and one of the company's 707s were dispatched to carry out a visual inspection, and it soon became clear that both trailing closure-doors had been torn away from the undercarriage legs. There appeared to be no other damage, so Falk landed normally. From a handling point of view the flight had gone extremely well.

Several more flights were made over that weekend, and on Monday 1 September the aircraft was flown to Boscombe Down, which was its base for five appearances at Farnborough. The new bomber was staggeringly impressive during these demonstrations – especially on the limited power of its Avon engines – and immediately became the star of the show. It was painted a brilliant white, and was

ABOVE *Trial installation of Skybolt ALBMs on XH537*

accompanied every day by the red Avro 707A and blue 707B. This patriotic trio split up after a sedate initial flypast, and Falk opened the throttles of the 698 to thunder round Farnborough like a demented fighter – far removed from the kind of bomb-truck people were used to.

After Farnborough, VX770 returned to Woodford and grounded for completion of the pressurisation, strengthening of the undercarriage doors, and fitting of a second pilot's seat. It was flying again from the end of October until in May 1953 it was fitted with 7500 lb-thrust Armstrong Siddeley Sapphire ASSa.6s. Installation of the wing tanks gave it the range for 'cold soak' flights at representative weights. Flying was resumed in July 1953.

In late 1952 the 698 had been named Vulcan. The Chief of the Air Staff, Sir John Slessor, suggested a family of 'V-bombers' following choice of the name Valiant, inspired by Churchill's wartime 'V for Victory' campaign.

The second prototype, VX777, was flown on 3 September 1953. It was more representative of the service aircraft, and was powered from the start by 9750 lb Olympus Mk 100 engines. It also had a 16 in-longer nose, which enabled the forward wheel bay to be slightly extended. Trials with the 707B had shown that the take-off could be shortened if the angle of the fuselage was set at $3\frac{1}{2}°$. A longer nose gear on the first prototype proved the point, but the new leg had to be telescoped to allow it to retract: the longer bay avoided that complication. The second prototype was equipped for high-altitude navigation and bombing trials. Its pressurisation was complete, and equipment included observer seats, an operations panel, the visual bomb-aiming position, and a full H_2S Mk 9A radar and its NBC Mk 2 computer.

VX777 appeared at the 1953 Farnborough display with all four Avro 707s. It then became a bit of a 'hangar queen' at Boscombe, with problems with the engines, fuel system and pressurisation. It had just embarked on its high-altitude trials pro-

an almost perfect triangular planform. The Phase 2 wing was less elegant, with 52°/42°/52° sweep, and a thinner, sharply cambered leading edge which increased the chord on the outer panels by up to 20 per cent. Vortex generators were also added upstream of the ailerons, but later discarded. The new shape delayed shockwave formation and pushed the buffet boundary beyond the anticipated performance of even future Vulcans. During 1954 it was tried in crude form on the 707A, but the full-scale Phase 2 was not flown until October 1955.

Development of Phase 2 was completed too late to be incorporated in the first production aircraft, XA889, which flew on 4 February 1955. It was initially powered by the Olympus 100, but later that year it was re-engined with production-standard Mk 101s. Service-acceptance trials culminated in CA (Controller, Aircraft) release on 29 May 1956 as the Vulcan B.1.

The second prototype rejoined the programme in February 1955, becoming the lead airframe involved in the Phase 2 wing tests. It was then fitted with an Avro (but Louis Newmark-manufactured) autostabilisation system. This provided damping in pitch and yaw, and a Mach trimmer which slightly deflected the elevators to balance-out centre-of-pressure movements with changing Mach number.

An additional order for 37 Vulcan B.1s was placed on 30 September 1954, and another eight in March 1955, bringing the total to 70. The first six, XA889–894, were absorbed into the trials pro-grame by 1956, and allocated to various trials. The first to reach the RAF was '897, delivered to No 230 Operational Conversion Unit (OCU) at Waddington on 20 July 1956. After minor changes it took off from Boscombe on 9 September on a three-week tour of Australia and New Zealand. The tour itself was a great success. The final leg ended at London's Heathrow Airport, where a reception committee was waiting. The approach to Runway 10L, in bad visibility but under GCA control, went horribly

gramme when it was badly damaged by a heavy landing at Farnborough. This was a bitter blow, because Olympus engines were needed for the high-altitude work.

By being pushed to its limits in a shallow dive, the Sapphire-powered 770 could just explore the high-speed end of the envelope, but representative altitudes were beyond it. Speed was becoming an important issue, because trials with the 707A had identified severe buffet on the outer wings when pulling 'g' at Mach 0.80 or above. This would eat into fatigue life if allowed to continue. VX770 ran into similar problems even with low-power engines, but the 11,000-lb Olympus Mk101 had flown in a Canberra, and the 12,000-lb Mk 102 was being bench tested. With such power a Vulcan pilot would push his aircraft to the buffet boundary just by opening the throttles.

The problem was caused by airflow breaking away from the upper surface, in the onset of a classic compressibility stall. Fences and vortex generators were tried on the 707, but did not provide the answer. The leading edge had to be substantially redesigned, which could have been avoided if the high-speed 707 had flown a year or two earlier.

The original edge was swept at 52°, which gave

wrong. The Vulcan touched down over 2000 ft (610 m) short of the threshold, tearing off both main landing gears and critically damaging the elevators. A full-power climb was initiated immediately, but the aircraft began to roll to starboard and was clearly out of control. Both pilots ejected from about 300 ft, but the four men in the rear perished as the Vulcan crashed and exploded inside the airport boundary. This was the first Vulcan crash of any kind. Occurring as it did in a very public arena, the accident attracted massive publicity, especially as one of the escapees was C-in-C Bomber Command, Air Marshal Sir Harry Broadhurst.

The crash left No 230 OCU with one aircraft until '898 arrived on 3 January 1957. Three more were delivered by mid-May and the first Aircrew Course qualified on 20 May. This group formed A Flight of No 83 Sqn at Waddington. At Finningley No 101 Sqn formed on 15 October 1957, followed by No 617 at Scampton on 1 May 1958. Each unit was nominally allocated eight aircraft.

While the aircraft had been working-up towards its service entry, Bristol Aero-Engines had been making remarkable progress with the Olympus. The 13,500-lb-thrust Mk 104 was run in 1956, and by January 1957 the early 200-series engines were achieving over 16,000 lb, and the 20,000-lb 300-series was planned. Accordingly Avro's new chief designer, Roy Ewans, started work on an improved Vulcan with a higher gross weight and better high-altitude performance. Span was increased from 99 ft to 111 ft. This increased wing area by over 500 sq ft, allowing take-off weights in excess of 200,000 lb. Thickness/chord ratio was reduced on the outer panels, and instead of elevators and ailerons the trailing edge was fitted with eight elevons.

The new wing was approved in October 1955, for the Vulcan B.2. In March 1956 Avro received a contract to convert the second prototype (VX777) into a B.2 trials aircraft, and this flew from Woodford on 31 August 1957, powered by the 12,000-lb Olympus Mk 102s. The 200-series engines were tested on XA891, and a new constant-frequency 200V AC electrical system was installed in XA893.

In June 1956 an order was received for 24 Vulcan B.2s. It was decided to cease manufacturing the B.1 at XH532 (the 45th airframe) and convert the 25 remaining to B.2 standard. The first production B.2 was therefore XH533, which flew on 19 August 1958. It incorporated the changes mentioned, plus enlarged intakes, 'splayed-out' jet nozzles, stronger main gears and a gas-turbine APU in the starboard wing.

In late 1958 the Air Staff realised that Vulcan B.2s should carry electronic countermeasures, to enable the crew to analyse and jam Soviet radars and VHF communications. The only space that could be found for the bulky ECM boxes was in a bulged 34 in extension of the rear fuselage. The 35 ft GQ ribbon parachute was moved up into a bulge on top. Red Steer ECM was first carried by XH534, which also introduced a flat antenna box bridging the starboard jetpipes. Final clearances were endorsed in May 1960, and the first operational example (XH558) reached No 230 OCU on 1 July 1960.

The Vulcan force was then rearranged. The OCU moved to Finningley. No 44 (Rhodesia) Sqn formed at Waddington on 10 August 1960, to take over the B.1s from No 83. No 44 was then joined by the B.1s of No 101. No 50 re-formed at Waddington on 1 August 1961 with the B.1s previously operated by No 617. Armstrong Whitworth fitted Red Steer to 29 B.1s, which became B.1As. At Scampton a B.2 Wing consisted of No 83 Sqn (from October 1960), No 27 and No 617. The Coningsby Wing consisted of three ex-Canberra squadrons, Nos 9, 12 and 35, by 1 December 1962.

It had long been clear that high-flying bombers would not be able to penetrate Soviet airspace indefinitely. In 1954 the RAE and Avro began studies of a rocket-powered weapon that could be released at least 100 nautical miles from the target. In March 1956 Avro was chosen to co-ordinate the design and build the missile's stainless-steel airframe, Armstrong Siddeley were to produce the

BELOW *Nobody who was at the Farnborough airshow on 5 September 1952 (when this photograph was taken) will forget the amazing sight of the white delta pulling the tightest turns at roof-top height*

twin-chamber Stentor engine, de Havilland Engines would provide peroxide-driven turbines and some prototype engines, and Elliott Automation the very advanced inertial guidance. The Armament Department of the RAE was responsible for co-ordinating the megaton warhead and its arming and triggering systems. The weapon was named Blue Steel, and designed to be compatible with the Vulcan and Victor.

The first powered prototype missiles were launched from Vulcan B.1 XA903 over the Woomera range in Australia in summer 1960. In 1961 production weapons were launched from Vulcan B.2 XH539. Blue Steel was designed for release at about 50,000 ft. The boost chamber would propel it to 70,000 ft and Mach 2.5, the small sustainer taking over cruise propulsion. Maximum range was nearly 200 nm, at the reduced speed of Mach 1.5.

The first Blue Steel squadron was No 617, which achieved initial operating capability in October 1962. The other two Scampton squadrons, Nos 27 and 83, were also equipped, as were the No 3-Group Victor B.2 squadrons, Nos 100 and 139 at Wittering. These five squadrons formed the leading-edge of Bomber Command's deterrent force until the role was handed to the Royal Navy in June 1969.

Blue Steel was essentially tactical, while the US-designed XGAM-87A Skybolt ALBM (air-launched ballistic missile) was decidedly strategic. Douglas began its development in 1959, primarily for the B-52H and B-58A. The 38 ft missile had a nominal speed and range of Mach 9.0 and 1150 nm. In May 1960 arrangements were made for Britain to buy a first batch of 100, initially for a Phase-6 Vulcan

powered by 20,000-lb Olympus 301s, carrying six missiles. A great deal of work was done on strengthening the Vulcan wing, the development of a British warhead and the establishment of a 200-man British Joint Trials Force at Eglin AFB, Florida. Two Vulcan B.2s, XH537 and 538 were modified to drop dummy rounds. The whole system was cancelled without warning in December 1962, leaving the RAF with nothing.

In 1963 V-bomber training switched to intruder-type missions at very low level. The anti-flash white was replaced by grey-green camouflage, initially on the upper surfaces and later all over. Flying low in bumpy air imposed a tremendous strain on aircraft designed for high-altitude cruising flight, but it withstood this regime fairly well. The last Vulcan, XM657, was delivered in December 1964. Altogether 138 had been built: two prototypes, 45 B.1s and 89 B.2s. XM596 was never flown, but was used to provide a continuous structural audit.

Final phase-out of the B.1As began in 1964 with the OCU. The process was completed in January 1968 when the B.2s from disbanded No 12 Sqn were flown into Waddington. In the same year the two Blue Steel Victor squadrons were disbanded, leaving Scampton's Vulcans to maintain the deterrent until handover to the Royal Navy at midnight on 30 June 1969. On 31 August No 83 Sqn was disbanded. The two remaining Scampton squad-

BELOW *Many Mk 1s went on to earn their keep in other programmes. This one flight-tested the rather different Olympus engine of TSR.2 (compare the size of the jet nozzles)*

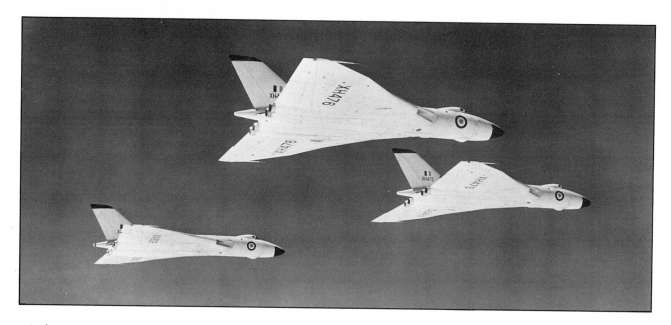

rons became part of the conventional strike force.

During the mid-1960s Nos 9, 12 and 35 Sqns were relocated at Cottesmore. No 12 was subsequently disbanded, but the other two left in January 1969 for Akrotiri, Cyprus, as a Near East Air Force (NEAF) Bomber Wing. This was the only 'permanent' overseas basing in the history of the V-force. The presence of Nos 9 and 35 Sqns was deemed politically sensitive after the Turkish invasion of northern Cyprus in summer 1974, so in February 1975 No 9 Sqn moved to Waddington and No 35 to Scampton.

After a number of crashes had occurred during low-level training, a Ferranti terrain-following radar was installed in the nose, with the antenna in a small 'pimple'. A Marconi ARI.18228 radar warning receiver was added on top of the fin. This could analyse several frequencies at once, and tell the crew not only what kind of threat they were facing, but also its azimuth direction. In 1973 four B.2s were modified to undertake maritime radar-reconnaissance with No 27 Sqn. These Vulcan SR.2As had additional tanks installed in the bomb compartment, and a variety of optical and electronic sensors.

The run-down of the Vulcan force was announced at the end of 1980. The Scampton Wing was first to go, with No 230 OCU disbanding in mid-1981, No 617 Sqn in December, No 35 in February 1982 and No 27 in March. By this time aircraft were also beginning to leave Waddington in preparation for the disbandment of Nos 9 and 101 Sqns. Then, in early April 1982, the run-down was stopped in its tracks by the Argentinian invasion of the Falkland Islands.

It was considered vital to provide the British Task Force with some kind of strategic bombing capability. Ten Vulcans were selected for modification to an agreed war standard, while selected aircrews began specialised training. A major problem was restoration of the flight-refuelling. This had not been used for over ten years, resulting in corrosion of valves and seals. Some spares were still available,

but an amazing assortment of bits and pieces had to be removed from aircraft in museums, fire-training wrecks and gate guardians. A probe and valves were retrieved from a crash-damaged Vulcan abandoned in Canada, and others from a museum aircraft in the USA. The pilots then had to relearn the techniques. Other modifications included fitting an ALQ-101D ECM jammer pod (without prepared hardpoints or matching pylons); installing Carousel inertial navigation systems (some hurriedly borrowed from British Airways' 747 stock); and changing the bomb-bay for conventional free-fall munitions. It was also decided to fit anti-radar missiles (initially Martel, later AGM-45A Shrike) to two aircraft in case it became necessary to launch strikes against surveillance radars. These aircraft carried 16,000 lb of fuel in the weapons bay.

The raids (code-named *Black Buck*) were flown from Wideawake Airfield on Ascension Island. Each involved a round-trip of 8000 nm, well beyond the normal operating range. Two fully-armed bombers, a primary and a reserve, took-off for each mission, the reserve turning back after the first outbound refuelling. Each raid was supported by as many as 11 exactly timed Victor K.2 sorties, most of which were tanker-to-tanker hook-ups. Six *Black Buck* missions were flown, but one had to be aborted because a tanker went unserviceable. Of the five missions that reached the Falklands, two carried 21 1000-lb GP bombs, two carried Shrikes and one a mix of 1000-lb HE and anti-personnel bombs for use against soft-skinned vehicles and aircraft around Port Stanley airfield. Despite the immense distances, no raid had to be cancelled due to problems with the Vulcan – although one had to divert to Rio de Janeiro after its probe failed on the return leg. With an endurance of about 16 hours, these were the longest bombing missions ever undertaken.

Meanwhile, back in the UK, No 9 Sqn disbanded on 1 May 1982 (ironically, while the first *Black Buck* mission was airborne), and Nos 44 and 101 prepared to follow. Three-quarters of the RAF's tanker fleet was committed to the South Atlantic.

ABOVE *With a span over 12 ft greater, the wing of the B.2 looked more normal*

Tanker conversions of civil VC10s had been ordered, but these would not enter service until after 1984. As an interim measure, it was decided to convert six Vulcan B.2s into single-point tankers.

A contract was awarded to British Aerospace on 5 May 1982, and the first tanker, Vulcan K.2 XH561, was flown from Waddington on 18 June. This remarkably fast turnround was achieved by keeping the modification simple. A Flight Refuelling Mk 17 hose-drum unit was installed in the former tail ECM compartment, and 24,000 lb of fuel was carried in three long-range tanks in the bomb bay. These increased the capacity to 96,000 lb, all of which could be used by the Vulcan or dispensed. The AEO's panel was fitted with an aft-facing periscope, and fuel-management controls were incorporated in the nav-radar station.

The first tanker arrived at Waddington five days after its maiden flight, and by the end of June it had been cleared for service. All six K.2s were delivered to No 50 Sqn, which gained an immediate reprieve from the run-down. But No 101 Sqn disbanded in August 1982, followed by No 44 at the end of December.

This left No 50 Sqn as the sole Vulcan unit, still at Waddington. In addition to its tankers, it was allocated four of the best B.2s, including a Falklands

veteran equipped as a receiver. These de-activated bombers were assigned as refresher-training aircraft, which allowed all aircrew grades to maintain or renew their type-qualifications without interfering with the refuelling schedule. The 'spare' B.2s also met the demand for post-Falklands air display appearances.

The six K.2s soldiered on until they were replaced by the VC10 K.2s of No 101 Sqn, which had reformed at Brize Norton on 1 April 1984. The disbandment of No 50 Sqn on 30 March should have ended the RAF's association with the Vulcan, but many display bookings had been accepted for 1984/85, and an unusually enlightened Ministry of Defence decreed that these should be honoured. While most of the remaining aircraft were flown to Marham for disposal, XL426 was retained at Waddington as the centrepiece of an 'unofficial' display unit. Two K.2s, XH558 and XH560, were inspected at Marham, and the former earmarked as a possible successor.

A small but dedicated group agreed to 'mother' XL426 at Waddington, and many displays were flown during 1984. Requests for further appearances poured in, and Whitehall agreed to continue for 'at least another year'. XH558 was returned to Waddington for restoration to bomber configuration, flying again in March 1985. It flew to Kinloss for a respray, and reappeared at Waddington on 30 November. In May 1986 it formally took over all display commitments, releasing XL426 for sale.

After the 1986 display season – during which fuel, aircrews and servicing manpower were 'borrowed' from other RAF units – the MoD decided to maintain '558 in flying condition until at least 1990, with an annual review thereafter. In December 1987 a limited budget was agreed, and the Vulcan Display Team was accepted as part of the RAF public relations effort, with enough funding to cover about 60 hours flying per year. The servicing crew was picked from Waddington volunteers, and flight crews were drawn from the Victor squadrons.

Since it became a full-time display aircraft '558 has been kept in superb mechanical condition, but

its structural limits reached a point of no return during the summer of 1992. The cost of essential wing strengthening and other remedial work has been estimated at £2.5 million, and the MoD decided not to spend this (plus at least £250,000 annual costs) in a recession. As a result, Roy Chadwick's magnificent delta has now been consigned to history.

SPECIFICATION

Avro Vulcan

Engines: four Rolls-Royce (originally Bristol, then Bristol Siddeley) Olympus two-shaft turbojets rated at 20,000 lb (301) and 17,000 lb (201)

Dimensions Span (**1**) 99 ft (30.18 m); (**2**) 111 ft (33.83 m); length (**1**) 97 ft 1 in (29.6 m); (**2**) 105 ft 6 in (32.15 m) (99 ft 11 in with probe removed); height (**1**) 26 ft 1 in (7.94 m); (**2**) 27 ft 2 in (8.26 m)

Weight Not disclosed; loaded weights probably about 170,000 lb for B.1A and 204,000 lb for B.2 and SR.2

Performance Maximum speed (**1**) about 620 mph; (**2**) about 640 mph (1030 km/h) at height (Mach 0.97); service ceiling (**1**) about 55,000 ft; (**2**) about 65,000 ft (19,810 m); range with bomb load (**1**) about 3000 miles; (**2**) about 4600 miles (7400 km)

Armament Internal weapon bay for conventional (21 1000-lb bombs) or nuclear bombs; (SR.2) none

BELOW *The Vulcan's last decade saw it with FR probe, nose-pimple radar, definitive ECM in a bulged tailcone, and camouflage that often made it conspicuous*

SNCASO 4050 Vautour

First Flight – 16 October 1952

Almost unknown to today's enthusiasts, the Vautour (Vulture) was a multi-role warplane of outstanding merit, which sustained a successful development and production programme (at a time when most other jets failed to do so) and even saw prolonged front-line service in active warfare. It was later even supposed to be a strategic bomber, but that was rather like using Vulcans against the Falklands, in that the tankers themselves needed tanker support.

At the end of World War 2 the French had a daunting task ahead. Almost all their aircraft factories had been destroyed, their design teams had been dispersed and had had little continuity of work or experience of design for six crucial years, and almost everything had to be restarted from scratch. Not least, there were no French jet engines except for uncompetitive projects by Rateau and SOCEMA which eventually ground to a halt.

The one engine that looked promising was the Atar, based on a BMW wartime design and being developed by a team of German engineers, who rejoiced in the title 'Aéroplanes G Voisin, Groupe O', the O standing for their leader, Dr H Oestrich, who had been chief engineer on the BMW 003. This was obviously going to take some time to reach fruition, and to tide things over Hispano-Suiza took a licence for the Rolls-Royce Nene and saw this used in almost every French jet from 1947 until the mid-1950s.

On the airframe side, there were still numerous private firms, but most of the factories belonged to one or other of the giant nationalised groups that had been very forcibly created in 1936. One of the biggest of these groups was the Société Nationale de Sud-Ouest (national aircraft company of the south-west), which had spent the war making the Fw 189 and major parts of the He 111. In 1946 this group flew the SO.6000, the first French jet, and followed with a spate of prototypes including the SO.4000 bomber described earlier. This non-starter shamed them into doing better, and the design team at Cannes spent 1951 working on a totally fresh design in collaboration with the general staff of the Armée de l'Air.

In June 1951 a detailed requirement was agreed, and this was noteworthy for calling for a single basic design to be produced in three versions to fly three missions: bomber, close-support and night interceptor. The design itself was a small version of the B-47, with a swept wing mounted above the mid position, underslung nacelles, a swept tail and the radical bicycle landing gear with front and rear main gears separated by the bomb bay, and small outrigger wheels outboard. From the start, the 4050 looked like being a winner if it worked.

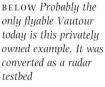

BELOW *Probably the only flyable Vautour today is this privately owned example. It was converted as a radar testbed*

Aerodynamically it was fairly conventional, with a sweep angle of 35° chosen for both the tapered wings and the tail, though the latter was bold in having a pivoted tailplane mounted half-way up the fin. The wing had a fixed leading edge, excellent Fowler flaps inboard and outboard of the nacelles, and outboard ailerons. Small fences were later added just outboard of the flap/aileron junction, and a remarkable array of two rows of vortex generators just ahead of the ailerons and another row underneath. The tail originally had a single rudder and elevators with cutouts, but the production tail had separate rudders above and below full-area elevators acting as camber-increasers on an 'all-flying tailplane'. Much later, in-service Vautours were modified yet again to have one-piece 'slab' tailplanes. All flight controls were fully powered, with artificial feel.

The 4050 was designed to be powered by the Atar, a relatively light and slim axial turbojet which promised at least as much thrust as the 5000-lb Nene, whilst fitting a rather slimmer nacelle. These nacelles were mounted at about 40 per cent semi-span, completely underslung (but not on pylons) and toed slightly inwards. Like the underside of the fuselage, everything needed for maintenance in the nacelles was at a convenient height. The front and rear main landing gears had identical twin wheels, with Maxaret anti-skid brakes, the front unit being steerable and retracting forwards, and the rear unit retracting to the rear. The outriggers had small wheels outboard of long levered-suspension links and retracted forwards into narrow vertical bays just outboard of the engines. Most of the fuel tankage was integral, construction in this context being assisted by the extensive use of metal bonding (for the first time on a French aircraft). Another unusual feature was that the fuselage had no longitudinal stringers, not even to react to the loads from the powerful door-type airbrakes on each side behind the wing.

It would be fair to claim that in the early 1950s the Vautour was the most promising twin-jet warplane in Western Europe. The only rival might have been the DH 110, but this took nearly nine years to go from first flight to operational service. In the Soviet Union the Yak-25 was an extremely close parallel, with identical layout, but this was a specialised night fighter, like the DH aircraft.

In contrast, the Vautour was versatile. Differences between the three planned versions were found mainly in the forward fuselage. Eventually three sub-types were built in quantity: the IIA single-seat tactical attack fighter, the IIB two-seat bomber and the IIN two-seat night fighter. Whereas the IIB had a glazed nose for the navigator/bombardier, the IIN had tandem cockpits with the radar operator in the back seat. Ouest-Aviation (later Sud-Aviation) made the Martin-Baker BT.4 and Y.4 seats under licence. All versions had the internal bomb bay, the IIA and IIN also having

ABOVE *When the Vautour entered service it was one of the few aircraft to be able to fire two types of guided missile: the Nord 5103 (AA.20) air-to-air weapon and the formidable AS.30 for surface attack. In the background is an MD.315 Flamant*

four 30 mm DEFA cannon fitted under the nose.

The point should be made that in the early 1950s few design teams had much experience in solving the problem of how to drop bombs out of an internal bay moving at perhaps 600 mph. The problem was extremely severe. A very few aircraft got it right, or almost right, by sheer luck. Most had to suffer years of heartbreak before everything worked properly. Some of the aircraft in this book were botched up by fitting movable flaps, rakes or rows of fingers upstream of the open bay, to break up the turbulence and give the stores inside a chance of dropping out and staying out. Possibly the best answer was the fast-acting rotary bay as first seen on the B-57. With the Vautour, success was eventually achieved by two unusual design choices. The first was that the doors translated up inside the fuselage, which, if it can be achieved, is invariably better than sticking out in the traditional manner. The other is that opening the doors automatically triggered powerful actuators which bodily moved the whole top of the bay, bombs and all, downwards close to the opening. From this point simple ejector release units could give free-fall weapons a clean separation.

The first order was for three prototypes, the first of which flew on 16 October 1952 in the hands of Jean Girard and observer Michel Retif. Development was very successful, Mach 1 being exceeded in a shallow dive on an early flight. Next came six pre-production aircraft, one being powered by British AS Sapphires and another by RR Avons, in each case much more powerful than any version of the Atar at that time. But the Atar remained the engine for all

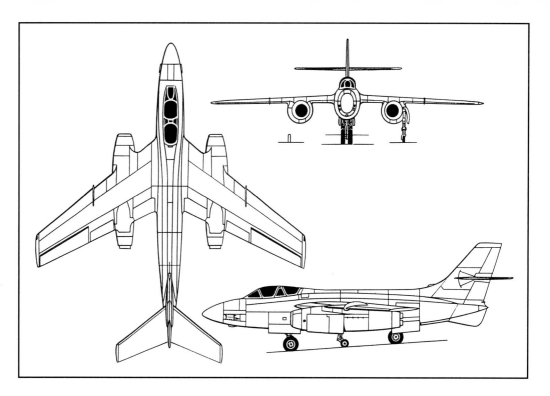

production versions, the Atar 101E-3 being not only quite a mature engine but also, with water injection, developing more than enough power for full-load takeoffs from airstrips 800 m (2625 ft) in length. A ribbon-type braking parachute was added in the tailcone to shorten the landing. Other additions included a spine linking the canopy to the fin and, on the IIA and IIB, an improved arrangement for mechanically thrusting bombs out into the airstream before release to avoid dangerous problems at high indicated airspeeds.

Originally the Armée de l'Air planned to order 300 IIAs and 140 IINs. All three versions were fully developed, the first production examples flying on 30 April 1956 (IIA), 31 July 1957 (IIB) and 10 October 1956 (IIN). In the event only 30 IIAs were built, plus 40 IIBs and 70 IINs. No IIAs entered French service, 18 being supplied at a favourable price to Israel where they enjoyed a very long and active career. The Armée de l'Air did, however, use the IIB and IIN for almost 20 years.

The IIB could carry out optically-sighted level bombing at all altitudes, as well as low-level attacks and also zoom tosses of nuclear weapons. SNCASO, which became Ouest-Aviation in September 1956 and Sud-Aviation on 1 March 1957 (and later vanished into Aérospatiale), delivered all 40 of the IIB version to the Armée de l'Air. They were assigned to the 92e Escadre (Wing), where they initially operated unpainted, with large black numbers 601/640 on the forward fuselage, and later were camouflaged dark olive green and grey.

Back in 1956 France had determined to become a political power fully equal at least to Britain, with not only nuclear weapons but also the means to deliver them. Work went ahead under a direct executive order by Prime Minister Guy Mollet that there should be a force of strategic missiles and also

a force of manned bombers, in all respects similar to the USAF Strategic Air Command. France took on board the concept of a nuclear deterrent, and named the planned organisation the *Force de Dissuasion* (deterrent force), though it was more popularly called the *Force de Frappe* (strike force). The bomber was to be supersonic, as described in the Mirage IV chapter, but something had to equip the force in the meantime, and the only aircraft available was the Vautour.

It would not be correct to say the Vautour IIB, good aircraft as it was, was ever an active element of the *Force de Dissuasion*, though if France had really had to go to war in 1958–64 the Vautours would indeed have been tasked with delivering nuclear bombs, but (assuming the targets to have been in the Soviet Union) with no hope of returning and only a slim chance of recovering to what was hoped would be friendly territory. The obvious problem was radius of action. Accordingly, while the Vautours were flown intensively in training and indoctrination missions, everything possible was done to introduce and perfect techniques of air refuelling. No attempt was made to harden them against nuclear explosions, although the problem was studied.

In 1955 the third prototype had been exhibited parked over an example of the B.10 television-guided heavy bomb, which was planned later to have a nuclear warhead. This never entered service, nor did the AS.2 Gamma stand-off weapon which had a 50-kilotonne warhead. Neither did Sud-Aviation succeed in its many planned developments of the Vautour, which included the IIBR reconnaissance-bomber (a prototype of which was flown in 1958) and a scaled-up derivative to compete against the all-new Mirage IV.

All production Vautours had underwing hardpoints which could carry bombs (see data) but were also plumbed for two tanks of 1250 litres (275 Imp gal) capacity. Flight Refuelling's French licensee, Zénith, produced 'buddy packs' incorporating a hose-drum unit, and with these, pairs of Vautours practised long-range nuclear missions in which one aircraft carried nothing but fuel to support its partner. Even in 1965, when ten Mirage IVAs had been delivered, there were still 31 Vautour IIB.1N aircraft in service, the suffix 1N indicating the slab tailplane. All had been withdrawn by late 1966.

BELOW *Vautour 329 is a IIb.1N night and all-weather fighter; the others are bombers, ready for delivery*

SPECIFICATION

SO.4050 Vautour

Two 7716-lb SNECMA Atar 101E-3 turbojets

Dimensions Span 15.1 m (49 ft 6½ in); length 15.80 m (51 ft 10 in); wing area 45 m² (484.4 sq ft)

Weight Empty 10,580 kg (23,325 lb); max take-off 20,700 kg (45,635 lb)

Performance Maximum speed (clean, S/L) 1100 km/h (684 mph), (hi altitude) 950 km/h (590 mph); combat radius (4400-lb bombload, hi-lo-hi) 1320 km (820 miles); ferry range 6000 km (3728 miles)

Armament Internal bay for one nuclear weapon or three 500-kg (1102-lb), six 340-kg (750-lb) or other bombs, plus up to 1814 kg (4000 lb) on wing pylons, subject to max total load of 2400 kg (5291 lb)

Douglas A-3 (A3D) Skywarrior

First Flight – 28 October 1952

Like most of the aircraft designed under Ed Heinemann, the Skywarrior thrust ahead into the unknown, played a major part on the world stage, had an amazingly long career, and exerted a great influence on both aircraft design and on world geopolitics. As its customer, the US Navy planned to put large nuclear-capable jet bombers anywhere on Earth, conveyed on the decks and catapults of giant carriers. At the start, the experts said Heinemann could not design the aircraft except at weights at least 50 per cent greater (the same thing was to happen again with the A-4 Skyhawk). And the number built, 282, was perhaps half as many as were really needed.

In the years immediately following World War 2 the US Navy became aware that it could fight for a broader role than it had enjoyed hitherto. At that time the whole concept of deterrence rested on the strategic bombers of the USAF, carrying nuclear weapons. The Navy realised that there were large areas of the world where these bombers could not go, but nowhere that large long-range bombers based on carriers could not go. The Navy already had the AJ-1 Savage heavy attack aircraft, with two piston engines and one jet, but believed it could field a bomber with greater speed, striking power and range. This ambitious objective was fuelled by the fact that, with the return of peace, the armed forces

ceased to be wholehearted partners, but returned to the task of each trying to out-do its rivals in the struggle for a bigger share of a drastically reduced defence budget.

To succeed the Savage the Navy considered a carrier-based version of the P2V (later P-2) Neptune, but this was big-spanned, cumbersome and slower than the Savage. Instead the Navy drafted a requirement for a completely new bomber, if possible jet-propelled, capable of operating from a carrier and of carrying an atomic bomb to a target 2000 miles distant. Of course, everything depended on what was meant by 'atomic bomb' and 'carrier'. On the second point there was no doubt. Despite the violent opposition of the Air Force, the Navy was planning a fleet of supercarriers to displace 65,000 tons and with a flight deck 1000 ft long. Funding was already sought for the first of the class, CVA-58 *United States*. As for the bomb, this was highly classified and so just described as 'a volume 5 ft by 5 ft by 16 ft, weighing 16,000 lb, to which the aircrew must have access in flight in order to perform certain operations on it prior to release.'

This clearly meant an internal bomb bay, and one far larger than anything previously considered for a carrier-based aircraft. Heinemann, Chief Engineer of Douglas Aircraft's Navy plant at El Segundo, was convinced that, as the technology developed, the

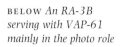

BELOW *An RA-3B serving with VAP-61 mainly in the photo role*

bombs would be made very much smaller, but he was repeatedly told the subject was classified. If he wanted to take part in the coming competition he had to abide by the huge bomb figures. What was worse was that, being a practical man, and knowing all the people involved, he had no assurance that the Navy would ever get its fleet of super-carriers. President Truman was desperately short of defence money, his senior defence adviser was Gen Eisenhower (an anti-carrier voter), and not just USAF Chief of Staff Vandenberg but also the Secretary for Defense Louis Johnson were anti-carrier. In fact, outside the Navy, nobody was for it. Heinemann could see the validity of the Navy's thinking, but decided that, to have any assurance of getting into service, he had to match the projected long-range bomber to the decks of the 52,000-ton *Midway* class, which actually existed already.

Obviously the crucial factor was take-off weight. Somehow Heinemann had to fit the required bomb bay into an aircraft capable of flying the mission at jet speed and still operate from the smaller deck. The Navy, still confident of its supercarriers, specified a weight of 100,000 lb. The Rand Corporation, the first Department of Defense 'think tank', said the mission could not be flown by an aircraft weighing less than 150,000 lb. In late 1948 eight companies responded to the Navy's RFP (request for proposals), but soon two dropped out, saying the task could not be met at 100,000 lb. Quite soon everyone had dropped out, unable to reconcile the conflicting variables, except for Curtiss-Wright and Heinemann's team. Curtiss simply had to win, because they had no other new aircraft programme, but they too did not see how it could be done at only 100,000 lb. And all the time Heinemann was driving his great team ahead producing the drawings of a bomber to do the job at 68,000 lb, and able to operate from a *Midway* deck.

When Heinemann went to Washington to show his preliminary design to BuAer (the Navy Bureau of Aeronautics) even his friend Capt Joe Murphy, head of the Aircraft Division, said 'I thought you were an honest engineer Ed; you know good and well you can't produce an airplane of that capability for that weight'. On the same day Gen Vandenberg, stung at what Heinemann was apparently trying to do, called Douglas and asked that Heinemann should be 'got out of town immediately, for making irresponsible claims'. What made Heinemann's task wholly difficult was the uncertainty regarding both the engine and the bomb, and the absolute certainty that the Navy demanded a twin-20 mm tail turret even though this, multiplied by the growth factor of 6.4, added no less than 12,500 lb to the take-off weight. Growth factor takes into account all the vicious circles of extra airframe, extra fuel and extra engine power to multiply each pound of weight added or saved.

At the end of 1948 Douglas and Curtiss were each awarded preliminary design contracts, at the

ABOVE *A new A3D-2 on test off California in 1954. It was still flying with the Navy 34 years later*

end of which Douglas had stayed at 68,000 lb and Curtiss had failed at 100,000, thus ending their aircraft manufacture. In March 1949 the keel was laid for the mighty USS *United States*, and at the end of April the super carrier was cancelled. Suddenly the Navy saw how right Heinemann had been all along, and in July 1949 Douglas received a contract for two XA3D-1 Skywarrior prototypes and a static-test airframe. Heinemann appointed Harry Nichols A3D project engineer in control of a team of highly-skilled designers and engineers. Nevertheless, one thing that worried Heinemann was that, as a visitor exclaimed, 'Heck, this is a Westinghouse airplane built by Douglas!' The giant electrical firm was responsible for the engines, electric-generating system, tail turret, radar and several secondary items.

The basic layout was eminently sensible, perhaps the only tricky item for a carrier-based aircraft being the narrow-track main landing gears folding into the beautifully streamlined fuselage. As was the case with many bombers at this time, this was because the wing was mounted high – really high, not just at shoulder level – so the main gears could not retract into the wing and there was no room for large wheels in the underslung engine pods. The wing was, as always, a compromise. Aspect ratio was a remarkable 6.75 (compared with just over 4 for the Canberra), and the sweep angle of 36° at the quarter-chord line made it look even greater. This extremely efficient wing had a thickness of 10 per cent at the root and 8.5 per cent at the tip, matched to Mach 0.85. High-lift slotted flaps occupied the inboard trailing edge, with conventional ailerons outboard, while the entire leading edge was fitted with aerodynamically opened slats. To fit carriers the wings folded hydraulically to a span of 49 ft 5 in (15.06 m), leaving room for pylons for external stores to be added outboard of the engines.

The entire nose was occupied by the navigation and bombing radar. Next came the pressurised compartment for the crew of three, beneath which

ABOVE *Three KA-3Bs, once nuclear bombers, now (in 1974) electronic-warfare and tanker platforms with VAQ-135 (Carrier Air Group 19)*

was the bay for the steerable forwards-retracting nose gear. Ejection seats looked a doubtful proposition, so at the aft end of the crew capsule a pressure door led down the main entrance/exit stairway to the entrance door. The latter was made in the form of an airbrake, which in emergency could be hydraulically driven open, at any speed which could be reached by the aircraft, to provide a dead-air region into which the crew could jump. Aft of the cockpit came the forward fuel tank, beneath which were most of the principal systems including the air-conditioning, and the electrical and hydraulic service bays. A particular feature of the A3D was that, like the B-52, it was designed to bleed very hot, high-pressure air from the engines and duct it along lagged stainless-steel pipes to turbine-driven generators and pumps in the accessory bay in the forward fuselage. Again as in the B-52 the screaming 95,000 rpm turbos were surrounded by flak curtains, but Douglas adopted them mainly on the score of supposed lighter system weight.

On top of the upper longerons came the wing, with the weapon bay occupying the entire space beneath it. A narrow gangway allowed a crew member to reach the bay from the entrance/egress chute in order to arm the nuclear weapon. The bomb doors were conventional, but flight testing showed the need for the addition of a buffet rake to stop turbulence when the doors were open at high speed, and thus allow the bombs to fall cleanly (on some flights released bombs refused to leave the bay). The rake took the form of a perforated spoiler which was forced to rotate down into the airflow just ahead of the bay, while all the stores were then thrust out by powered ejectors.

From the start Heinemann gave the A3D adequate vertical tail area, plus a yaw damper to counter any tendency towards Dutch roll, a combined uncommanded pitch/roll/yaw motion which in the early 1950s plagued many high-subsonic aircraft with swept surfaces. To fit carrier hangers

the entire vertical tail had to be designed to unlatch and power-fold over to the right, coming to rest lying flat on top of the dihedralled tailplane. All the tail control surfaces had hydraulic boost, but Heinemann insisted on the possibility of manual reversion. He even insisted on this with the ailerons, where the hydraulic boost ratio was 40:1. So that pilots should hardly ever have to use manual lateral control he added a standby lateral control system with a boost ratio of 20. From the start the A3D handled very well, and it remained a popular aircraft to fly for 40 years. On the sides of the rear fuselage were two of the biggest and most powerful airbrakes ever fitted to an aircraft, 10 ft from hinge to trailing edge. They enabled carrier approaches to be flown at high engine rpm so that ample thrust would quickly be available in the event of a wave-off. Just ahead of each airbrake was a vertical row of attachments for three (later five) ATO (assisted take-off) rocket bottles on each side, the six giving a total of 54,000 lb thrust for five seconds. Right at the back was the Westinghouse tail turret, with twin 20 mm guns, which exerted a literally massive effect on the whole design. The landing gears were robust and simple, the steerable nose unit retracting forwards and the 11-ft track main units swinging back and slightly inwards to occupy a tall, long, but narrow bay in each side of the rear fuselage closed by a large door hinged at the upper edge.

Despite consistent failure to meet any thrust or schedule targets, Westinghouse kept promising the Navy that their YJ40 turbojet was on the verge of getting well. This was important to the Navy, because it was the engine of almost all that service's new fighters and bombers. On the first XA3D-1 (BuNo 125412) it was installed with no afterburner in a nacelle of cylindrical form with the plain inlet not upright, but inclined, to improve pressure recovery at high angles of attack. After much ground running and various engine changes, the midnight-blue bomber was flown by George Jansen on 28 October 1952. So important was the XA3D that it had been secretly trucked to Edwards for its flight-test programme. Heinemann said 'The first thing we learned was that the J40 was not powerful enough'. In fact he got a small group planning for a switch to the Pratt & Whitney J57 even before first flight. The J57 was appreciably heavier, though its much better specific fuel consumption meant that the total engines-plus-fuel weight for practical missions was actually reduced. A very important secondary factor was that the heavier pod – of totally different shape – almost eliminated a potentially serious problem with wing flutter. The Navy soon threw out the J40 from all its aircraft, and the first J57-powered YA3D-1 made its maiden flight on 16 September 1953, since when the Skywarrior never looked back.

By this time Heinemann knew he had another winner, but was unsure whether he was coming or going. He had achieved the 'impossible' target of a maximum take-off weight of 68,000 lb. In any case, the A3D was designed to carry bombs far bulkier and heavier than necessary; as he had predicted, nuclear weapons swiftly became much smaller. He had matched it to *Midway* carriers, yet the Navy now had not just the promise of one supercarrier, now renamed *Forrestal*, but a whole fleet. Despite this, the Navy BuAer was convinced, first, that the Skywarrior could be loaded up to 83,000 lb and, second, that it could be qualified to fly even from the small *Essex*-class ships! BuShips fought back violently, but Heinemann was allowed to build a rig comprising A3D main gears loaded by lead weights to a total of 84,000 lb and then repeatedly slam this on to the deck of a real *Essex* carrier. Thus, while the smaller NW (nuclear weapons) would have enabled the original mission to be flown at 50,000 lb, the A3D had to be qualified at 84,000 lb, and actually took off and landed from a carrier at that weight. This is still a record for carrier operation. Three cat shots were made at this weight, the strop being hooked on two steel anchors designed to retract into the bottom of the forward fuselage on each side.

BELOW *BuNo 144841 began life as a bomber and ended it as a red-starred 'hostile' on electronic warfare training. Designation ER-3B, unit VAQ-34, NAS Point Mugu*

El Segundo built 12 pre-production YA3D-1 aircraft (130352/63), followed by 38 very similar A3D-1s (135407/44) with J57-6 engines rated at 9700 lb dry and 11,600 lb with water injection. These entered service with Heavy Attack Squadron VAH-1 at NAS Sanford, Florida, from 31 March 1956. Though fully operational, the A3D-1 still lacked many items of avionics and other equipment. All these were included in the A3D-2, the definitive version, of which 164 were built in 1957–59 (138901/76, 142236/55, 142400/07, 142630/65, 144626/29 and 147648/68). Powered by the J57-10, rated at 10,500 lb dry and 12,400 lb with water injection, the Dash-2 was also upgraded in several ways, notably in being stressed for 'over the shoulder' Labs (Low-Altitude Bombing System) tossing of an NW at low level. The last 41 were delivered as tankers, with a Flight Refuelling bomb bay tank and hose-reel pack, and with the tail turret replaced by twin ALE-2 chaff dispensers and, later, active jammers.

In the new 1962 unified Department of Defense designation system the Skywarrior became the A-3, the Dash-1 and -2 becoming the A-3A and A-3B respectively. Until 1963 both versions provided what was said later to have been 'The deterrent force that the Soviets most feared during the Cold War', in other words the NW-equipped long-range bombers on the decks of Navy carriers. They had been expected to be replaced by the A-5 Vigilante, but in fact their nuclear mission was taken over by the Polaris submarine force. Long before this, however, the Skywarrior had been developed to fly four different missions: reconnaissance, Elint/Sigint/Comint (electronic, signals and communications intelligence), air-refuelling tanker, and crew training.

For the reconnaissance mission El Segundo converted the seventh YA3D-1 (130358) into the YA3D-1P development prototype, redesignated YRA-3A in 1962. Strangely, none of the A3D-1 bombers were rebuilt for the photo mission. Instead Douglas next built the YA3D-2P (142256), which

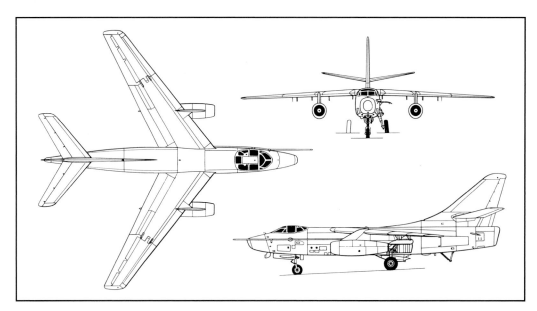

refined the exact build standard for 29 new-production A3D-2Ps (142666/9, 144825/47 and 146446/7). These had a redesigned fuselage, the pressurised area being extended aft to house a photo-navigator and recon-systems officer, and the weapon bay being replaced by additional tankage, with cameras occupying the whole bottom of the fuselage, together with photoflash bombs for illuminating targets at night. The operating units for the RA-3B were VAP-61 and -62, a few being passed on in 1974–74 to VQ-1 and -2.

The training mission was another that was fairly straightforward, though there were two distinct requirements. The principal one was to train A3D (A-3) navigators and bombardiers. While the A3D-2T was being designed for this mission, at least 12

A3D-1s were converted as A3D-1T dual-control pilot trainers. Back in the XA3D mock-up stage Capt John T 'Chick' Hayward had absolutely insisted that the engine control console be moved from the left console to the middle of the flight deck. This was so that in emergency the right-hand man could manage the power while the pilot concentrated on the flying. Now this unexpectedly paid off, in that all that had to be done was add a second set of pilot instruments and controls. After 1962 these trainers became TA-3As. The 12 A3D-2Ts, however, later called TA-3Bs, were totally different. Their cockpits were almost unchanged, but the rest of the fuselage was redesigned to be fully pressurised to accommodate an instructor and six radar/navigation/bombing pupils. Each pupil had his own radar display and bomb sight, and could actually navigate the aircraft using all available methods. Their BuNos were 144856/67.

Towards the end of the 1950s it was increasingly clear that the nuclear role would pass to missile systems, but that the Skywarrior's clearance to weights up to 84,000 lb would make possible useful roles in several other missions. One that was to become increasingly important was tanking. Following good results with the added hosereel unit in the final 41 A-3Bs the Navy converted 90 Skywarriors during the Vietnam war as KA-3B tankers or, mainly, EKA-3B aircraft able to fly the Tacos mission (tanker, countermeasures or strike). These versatile aircraft retained the 1083 Imp gal bomb bay tank and hosereel unit of the previous tankers, and added avionics which grew ever more sophisticated over a period exceeding 25 years. A typical EKA Tacos aircraft had a pressurised fuselage with the pilot and co-pilot/ARO (air refueling officer) side-by-side. To the rear were swivelling seats for four ECM (electronic countermeasure) operators all facing displays and panels occupying the entire left side of the interior. The most powerful ECM was the ALQ-86, with forward-facing antennas in two large blisters at front and rear on both sides of the fuselage. Further ECM antennas were installed in the extreme nose and tail, the antenna for the ALQ-126 deception ECM was under the nose, and at the top of the fin were radar warning receiver antennas facing to front and rear. As originally completed the EKA also had a large ventral canoe antenna for an ALQ-100 SLAR (sideways looking airborne radar), faired at the rear into the hosereel installation. These valued aircraft flew first-line missions from carriers until VAQ-134 Det 4 (USS *Ranger*) ended a deployment on 10 October 1974. Shore service followed with many units, ending on 30 September 1989 with the standing down of VAK-208 'Jockeys' at NAS Alameda.

There were many other special variants of Skywarrior, all of them conversions, of which the most important today is the ERA-3B. This flies EW (electronic warfare) missions in the Aggressor role to provide a realistic target for fleet defence systems. Like most current variants, the ERA-3B has a long flight-refuelling probe, and RWR (radar warning receiver) antennas facing to front and rear on the ends of a prominent tube on top of the fin. The main EW emitter is the ALT-40 high-power jammer, with the antennas in a Boeing canoe fairing nearly 20 ft long. Electric power for this system is generated by four ram-air turbogenerators, two in tandem along each side of the fuselage. The nose radar has a chisel radome, and the bluff tail houses the high-capacity ALE-43 chaff/flare dispenser. The ERA-3B also has wing pylons for a variety of jammers, dispensers or simulators. VQ-2 'Batmen' at NAS Rota, Spain, used nine EA-3Bs in the passive Sigint role. Several locations also operated NA-3B and NRA-3B test

RIGHT The A3D-2 first went to sea aboard Forrestal *but later EW and tanker versions served with every attack carrier in the US Navy*

aircraft into the early 1990s, VAQ-34 utilising a UA-3B used for various 'hack' tasks, and even the US Army had an RA-3B at White Sands Missile Range.

Unexpectedly, four 'Whales' of VQ-2 saw active service in the Gulf War. They were 146452/54/55, all EA-3Bs, and 144865, a TA-3B. Throughout the conflict they operated from Jeddah in support of each Carrier Battle Group strike, working on HARM targeting. Additional EA-3Bs operated from Soudha Bay, Crete, in support of USAF strikes on northern Iraq.

SPECIFICATION

A-3B

Two Pratt & Whitney J57-10 turbojets rated at 10,500 lb dry and 12,400 lb wet

Dimensions Span 72 ft 6 in (22.1 m); length 76 ft 4 in (23.27 m); wing area 812 sq ft (75.43 m²)

Weight Empty 39,409 lb (17,876 kg); combat 52,170 lb (23,664 kg); loaded (normal) 70,000 lb (31,752 kg), (maximum) 84,000 lb (38,102 kg)

Performance Maximum speed (S/L) 618 mph (537 kt, 995 km/h), (35,000 ft, 10,670 m) 591 mph (951 km/h); tactical radius on normal bombing mission 1050 miles (1690 km); maximum range 2900 miles (4667 km)

Armament Twin 20 mm guns in tail turret; internal load of bombs, mines or other stores to total of 8580 lb (3892 kg)

Saab A32A Lansen

First Flight – 3 November 1952

This book inevitably includes a mixture of aircraft which can reasonably be called bombers, and a second class generally known as 'attack aircraft'. The latter are frequently used as bombers, but they are distinguished in that they often make dive (rather than level) attacks, and to the layman they look like fighters. In general they also fly shorter missions, against hostile naval or land forces – in contrast to true bombers, which can strike at enemy heartlands thousands of miles distant. Forty years ago these tactical attack missions were most often flown by obsolescent fighters to which bomb or rocket racks had been added, but

there was a growing species that were specially designed to fly attack missions. One of the first and best of this breed was the Saab A32A Lansen.

Sweden's defence budget is what one might expect from a country with a 100-year tradition of strict neutrality and a population of less than eight million. Yet the Saab aircraft firm has managed, by never producing a failure, to fulfil almost all the operational needs of the Swedish air force, apart from heavy airlift transport. Moreover, by creating good basic designs, Saab and the government procurement machine have managed repeatedly to develop successive generations of aircraft which have been produced in different variants for attack, interception and reconnaissance. Thus, the A32A attack aircraft was the first of three production models of the Saab-32 Lansen (Lance).

Incidentally, from the start the start the Lansen was almost ignored by the rest of the world, and regarded as just another small single-jet. Few people comprehended its brilliant design, its impressive operational capability, and indeed the versatility of each of the three initial variants. To give an example of how it was misjudged, the A32A replaced the B18B and T18B, which looked like powerful twin-engined bombers. Yet, while the maximum weight of the Saab-18 family never in any version exceeded 19,390 lb, that of the smaller single-jet A32A was almost 10,000 lb heavier!

Work began in 1948, the objective being to replace the Saab-18 with an aircraft able to make precision attacks on land or sea targets in any weather, and with jet performance. The first study had two de Havilland Ghost engines, but this was replaced by the P1150 design with a single Swedish STAL Dovern axial engine. It was soon judged that the technical difficulty, cost and timescale of the Dovern could not be justified, and when the Saab-32 prototype made its first flight on 3 November 1952 the engine was an early Rolls-Royce Avon. After extremely successful development the initial production version, the A32A attack aircraft, entered production in 1954.

In general arrangement the Lansen could hardly

LEFT *One of many weapon loads for the A32A was 12 awesome Bofors 240 mm rockets*

be simpler. Its design broke new ground in that every mould line was the result of mathematical calculation, using early computers. This had many beneficial results, one of which was the achievement of a Mach number of at least 1.12 in a shallow dive on 25 October 1953, despite the fact that thrust/weight ratio was only about 0.3. The wing had a 10 per cent laminar profile and sweep of 35° at 25 per cent chord. The prototype had slats, but these were replaced in production aircraft by deep but short fences wrapped round the leading edge opposite the inboard ends of the ailerons. The latter were operated by Saab hydraulic boosters. Inboard were large hydraulically-driven Fowler flaps. During development the airflow over the wing roots at high angles of attack was improved by adding unusual triangular fences near the root just behind the leading edge. The fuselage was almost perfectly streamlined, the lateral air inlets being flush with the mould line. On the sides of the rear fuselage were added four airbrakes, while a fairing along the top provided a rectangular mounting for the powered tailplane with hydraulically boosted elevators. The nose landing gear retracted forwards and the main units inwards, the main wheels having Dunlop Maxaret anti-skid brakes.

Saab ejection seats were provided in tandem for the pilot and observer, in a pressurised cockpit under a one-piece hinged canopy. The entire aft fuselage was made detachable to give all-round access to the engine, and the Lansen soon became as popular with ground crews as it was with its flight crews. In the nose was the Ericsson mapping

TOP *From this angle the radar can be clearly seen. Note also the other antennas under the nose and above the wing roots*

MIDDLE *An AJ37 Viggen of F6 Wing formates on one of the A32A Lansens which had served the Wing so well*

RIGHT *One of the A32A development aircraft on trials with the RB 304A cruise missile*

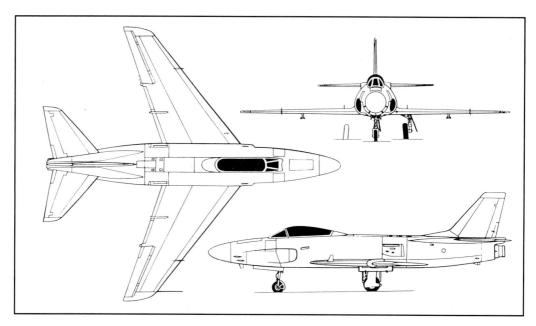

ABOVE *A32A Lansens in production at Linköping in the mid-1950s*

and navigation radar, while under the fuselage, immediately ahead of the main landing gear, was added a large blister fairing for the forward-sector antenna of the radar. This radar was associated with the Robot 304, a large cruise missile, one of which could be carried under each wing, designed specifically for the anti-ship role. The radar was used both for target lock-on and the initial programming of the missile (which had its own active terminal homing). From the start the Lansen had excellent electronic-warfare provisions. The wing was also fitted for pylons for a range of bombs and rocket launchers, including large rockets of 135, 150 and 180 mm calibre. Four 20 mm guns were fitted in the bottom of the forward fuselage.

Delivery of the A32A attack version began to wing F17 in December 1955. Deliveries were completed in December 1957, by which time the A32A equipped the 12 squadrons of wings F6, F7, F14 and F17. The A32A proved an extremely effective aircraft, maintaining excellent serviceability and a high standard of weapon-delivery accuracy. It was justly claimed that no hostile ship could approach Sweden without interception by an A32A, and that all such targets would be within one hour of a Lansen base. These aircraft began to be replaced by the AJ37 Viggen from June 1971, many then being converted as target tugs and electronic-warfare platforms.

About 450 Lansens were built, ending on 2 May 1960. Other versions were the J32B all-weather interceptor and S32C reconnaissance aircraft. Both these had much more powerful RM6A Avon engines and many other changes.

SPECIFICATION

A32A Lansen

One Svenska Flygmotor RM5 turbojet (Rolls-Royce Avon RA.7R built under licence) rated at 7920 lb dry and 9921 lb with maximum afterburner

Dimensions Span 13 m (42 ft 7.7 in); length 14.65 m (48 ft 0.8 in); wing area 37.4 m² (402.6 sq ft)

Weight Empty 7071 kg (15,589 lb); maximum 13,000 kg (28,660 lb)

Performance Maximum speed (clean, S/L) over 1127 km/h (700 mph); combat radius (max) 1600 km (994 miles)

Armament Four 20 mm cannon and up to 3000 kg (6614 lb) of underwing stores including two Rb 04, 04C or 04E cruise missiles

Handley Page Victor

First Flight – 24 December 1952

One of the most graceful aircraft ever built, the Victor was a remarkably fine achievement by a company which, in comparison with its rivals, lacked money and manpower. Its technical staff had quality rather than quantity, and in 1970 this famous name disappeared from the scene, leaving the Victors to be fostered by the company which had been their principal rival on the B.35/46 programme, the background to which was outlined in the chapter on the Avro 698 Vulcan.

In the late 1930s Handley Page (HP) moved from fabric-covered biplanes to the concept of high-speed tailless monoplanes. It built the HP.75 Manx to test the idea, but elevon power was inadequate to get the nosewheel off the ground. During the war it flew successfully, and by late 1945 the company was studying a tailless 50-seat jet to fly the Atlantic. The chosen engines were four Metrovick F.9 Sapphires, subsequently taken over by Armstrong Siddeley. Sir Frederick Handley Page then asked his top designers, G R Volkert, Reg Stafford and G V Lachmann, to study a jet bomber, and the general consensus was for a similar tailless four-jet, the wing being swept back as on most tailless designs to improve CG (centre of gravity) position with a heavy four-cannon tail turret and enhance longitudinal stability. At the same time it was realised that swept wings could raise critical Mach number, and research engineer Godfrey Lee assessed his superiors' studies in this new light.

By early 1946 the problems of simple sweepback in promoting pitch-up and tip stall had led to exploration of refined wings in which a sharply swept thick root changed towards a moderately swept thin tip. Eventually, what became famous as the 'crescent wing' was schemed, with the inboard section no less than 16 per cent thick but swept at 53°, the mid-section 9 per cent thick and swept 35° and the outer panel only 6 per cent thick and swept at 20°. This wing looked very attractive, and there were also structural and configuration benefits. The structure of the inner wing was a D-spar extending back to about 30 per cent chord. Coupled with the sharp sweep, this meant that the strong centre bridge across the fuselage could be far ahead of the CG. In turn, this meant that the bomb bay could occupy almost the entire cross-section of a slim 10-

ft-diameter fuselage downstream of an ideal mid-mounted wing. It also enabled the engines and main landing gears to be behind the main spar. Further gains were a natural form of body-waisting (local area ruling) which avoided shockwaves where the sweep effect faded out at the root, and minimal drag of wing and body at all speeds. Moreover, the structural kinks meant that under manoeuvre loads the inner wing tended to twist nose-up, virtually eliminating the tendency for a pull-out or steep turn to tighten automatically.

This work resulted in HP being one of the two companies selected in July 1947 to build two prototypes of a B.35/36 bomber, the order being placed for aircraft WB771 and WB775 in April 1948. At this time the control surfaces comprised elevons and wingtip rudders, and the crew numbered four men in a jettisonable glazed nose capsule and a gunner or ECM operator in the short tail-end. By 1949 the tailless concept, like the jettisonable nose, had been replaced by a startling T-tail (radical at that time) and a conventional crew compartment with ejection seats for two side-by-side pilots and

BELOW *There's a story behind this photo of a B.1 'dropping 35 thousand-pounders', but we won't blow the gaff*

RIGHT *Tornado prototype P.03 on tanker trials with a K.2 from Marham*

ABOVE *Portrait of a B.1 in anti-flash white. The serial is not visible*

ordinary seats for the three other crew, tail guns having been abandoned. As in the other V-bombers, the need for the three non-pilot crew to escape in emergency via a side door was never a fully satisfactory solution, though it did work on five occasions.

Like its delta rival the new bomber, the HP.80, was radical enough to need a small-scale test aircraft. This was rather a mongrel, because, though designated HP.88, it was subcontracted to General Aircraft as the GAL.63, used a fuselage purchased from Supermarine as the Type 521 and was finally constructed by Blackburn as the YB.2! It eventually flew at Carnaby on 21 June 1951, killing HP pilot Douglas Broomfield, because of resonant coupling between a bobweight (fitted as a g-restrictor at the RAE's suggestion) and the elevator power unit.

Mainly because of the crippling run-down of British defence industries after World War 2, the HP.80 took longer to emerge than had been planned. A typical bit of non-planning was that HP could not get agreement on the runway extension at Radlett until a few weeks after it had been decided that WB771 would have to be dismantled and

trucked to Boscombe Down. Here Sqn Ldr H G Hazelden at last flew it, very successfully, on Christmas Eve 1952. By this time the Radlett runway extension was almost finished, and 771 returned there in February 1953.

From the start HP had stayed with four Armstrong Siddeley Sapphire Mk 101 engines, each rated at 8000 lb, buried in the thick wing roots and fed from delicately sculpted inlets in the leading edge. The ducts passed through spectacle frames in the main spar assembled from simple 'club feet' and upper and lower 'ham bones'. They then curved gently down to the engines, whose centrelines were roughly level with the wing undersurface so that the lower portions and accessories were in blisters covered by large access doors. The jetpipes then went straight to nozzles just behind the trailing edge.

Like most of the airframe the wing structure was mainly covered in a sandwich with an outer skin spot-welded to precision-rolled corrugated stiffening panels which were then riveted to an inner skin. These panels were light, rigid, smooth and long-lived, and apart from the spars, needed little internal support. A few areas used honeycomb cores with Araldite bonding. The outboard leading edges were hinged droop flaps, depressed in low-speed flight to 22° inboard and 15° outboard. The flaps were Fowlers, in a single section on each wing, curved around under the jetpipes and running out on two tracks causing small fairings above the trailing edge. Outboard were conventional ailerons with trim tabs. Like the other flight controls these surfaces were driven by unusual Hobson power units, each a double-ended package with opposite-facing electric motor, self-contained hydraulic pump and motor and ball-screw jack. Flaps and leading edge were hydraulic.

Like other British aircraft of this time the hydraulic systems operated at 4000 lb/sq in. These also powered the main landing gears by Electro-Hydraulics Ltd, which were masterpieces of mechanical engineering. Each had a single forged leg carrying on the end of the oleo strut a pivoted bogie beam mounting four wheels each with twin tyres. The 16 main tyres, each of only 27×6.5 in size, thus enabled the weight to be carried by landing gears which retracted forwards to be housed completely within a bay less than 30 in deep, covered by a single large door hinged along the bay's outer edge. The nose gear, with twin steerable wheels castoring through 175°, was mounted far back under the leading edge, retracting to the rear, the wheelbase being only 29 ft 6 in. On each side of the fuselage tailcone was mounted a powerful door airbrake, hinged on two front arms, both being driven by a single jack on the centreline. By adjusting the depth of the drag-increasing strakes along their top and bottom edge it was possible to eliminate any pitch change at any speed or Mach number. The brakes were driven like a control surface, following the setting of the cockpit lever, and it became normal to set up a suitable power on the landing approach and adjust glidepath by the brakes. The circular ribbon-type braking parachute was housed in the tailcone.

Tail structure followed that for the wing, the swept fin carrying on its top a large bullet fairing at the junction with tiny fixed tailplanes with sharp sweep and dihedral. These in turn carried the powered elevators, which in effect were slab tail-planes. Like the ailerons, the elevators and rudder were driven by aircooled Hobson double-ended power units. All leading edges were anti-iced by hot air. The wing was fed with bleed air mixed with cold air from an inlet outboard of the engine inlet, while the tail was supplied from a jet pump mixing air from an inlet in the root of the fin (this design varied greatly during development). The engine inlets were heated electrically by Napier Spraymats.

Electrical power was generated as frequency-wild AC by an alternator on each engine, with trans-former/rectifiers converting to 28 and 112V DC. The crew compartment was pressurised to 8 lb/sq in (max cabin altitude 8000 ft), though the prototypes were at first restricted to 5 lb/sq in. The air-conditioning was mainly under the floor at the back of the flight deck, fed by flush NACA inlets on each side near the tip of the pointed nose. The floor was pressure-bearing, the giant H_2S radar filling the unpressurised lower part of the nose. A gaseous oxygen system was fitted; its associated regulator limited the normal operating height to 49,000 ft, which was well below the full-load ceiling. A total of

BELOW *Tornados ZA365 and 368 take on fuel from a K.2 tanker in 1983*

conventional bombloads might be very important. Likewise, the Type 98, an HP 80 with an airframe specially designed for low-level operations, was never built.

Flight testing in 1953 confirmed that the HP.80, named Victor, was a superb aircraft in almost all respects, and it was tragic that WB771 crashed during a fast low-level run on 14 July 1954. HP had gone to great lengths to ensure the integrity of the novel tailplane attachment and had undertaken three quite distinct types of test. Each test contained a subtle error, and the fates conspired to make all three (incorrect) results very nearly equal, confirming that all was well. The tailplane of WB771 had separated when the three bolts failed by fatigue. When WB775 began flying on 11 September 1954 its tailplane was secured by four bolts under much lower stress. Tailplane damping was a maximum at

LEFT *Unusual view of a B.1 in anti-flash white, airbrakes open*

BELOW *The strangely painted second prototype at the 1953 Farnborough airshow, with delta rival beyond*

101,360 lb of fuel was housed in Marflex self-sealing bags filling the top of the centre fuselage, a complete bay in the rear fuselage and all available space in the wing out to an end-rib at the aileron power unit on each side.

Unlike the Vulcan, the Victor bomb bay was entirely aft of the wing, and thus was able to extend half-way to the tail. Despite its great size it was closed by two simple doors, opened by a neat hydraulic drive at each end to lie out of the slipstream inside the fuselage. Nuclear weapons or 35 1000-lb GP bombs could be loaded quickly by a Houchin hydraulic lift truck. In fact the HP 80 had the capability of carrying two of the largest-size Blue Boar guided bombs, or four 10,000-lb light-case bombs or 48 standard 1000-pounders, and structural provison was made for 76 1000-lb bombs (28 in underwing containers) or 39 Type S 2000-lb mines. With typical shortsightedness, nobody in a position of authority gave a thought to the fact that, many years later, the ability to carry heavy

about 85 per cent of flutter speed, and at higher speeds fell quickly to zero. Great courage, as well as precision piloting, was shown by test pilot Jock Still and observers Frank Haye and Jack Ogilvy in measuring damping within a few knots of the disaster point. All contractor's trials were completed in March 1955 with only 140 hours total on both prototypes. By this time the first 25 B.1 Victors were taking shape on the Colney Street (Radlett) line, and two months later an order was placed for a further 33 (eight of which were completed as B.2s) at what today sounds an impossible price: £244,000 each.

The first few aircraft were initially finished silver. XA917 inadvertently exceeded Mach 1.1, making a sonic bang heard from Watford to Banbury, test observer Paul Langston becoming the first human to exceed Mach 1 travelling backwards. Soon the Mk 1s were repainted in anti-flash white, with pale markings. The Victor B.1 differed from the prototypes mainly in having a fin 15 in lower, with no dorsal fin, and a nose 40 in longer. These changes, plus addition of the massive radar, got the CG in the right place, but the reduced directional stability required addition of a yaw damper. Other changes in the production aircraft included fitting Sapphire Mk 202 engines of 11,000-lb thrust, fuel-flow proportioners in wings and fuselage, one-piece leading-edge flaps, a row of vortex generators along the top of the outer wing at 25 per cent chord, and comprehensive ECM equipment including a chaff dispenser ahead of the nose gear.

Altogether 50 Mk 1s were produced, XA917/ 941, XH587/594, XH613/621, XH645/651 and XH667. Deliveries began to No 232 OCU at Gaydon on 28 November 1957. In April 1958 No 10 Sqn became operational at Cottersmore, while three aircraft, XA923/925, were fitted with Yellow Aster reconnaissance radar, cameras, improved doppler and various passive sensors to become B(PR).1s with No 543 Sqn at Wyton. Close behind came No 15 Sqn at Cottesmore and No 57 at Honington. The Victor was extremely popular with air and ground crews. An unexpected attribute was a 'self-landing' capability. As the wingtips came close to the runway the upwash from the rest of the wing died away, causing a strong nose-up pitch. In other aircraft this is countered by ground effect lifting the tail, but the Victor's tailplane was very small and far from the ground. The result was a smooth 'hands-off' landing.

XA930 carried out trials with underwing fuel pods, and with a jettisonable and recoverable ATO (assisted-take-off) pack housing an 8000-lb thrust DH Spectre rocket engine under each wing. Neither was used on B.1 aircraft, but further development took place on the leading edge. The powerful nose flaps had required a large accumulator in the hydraulics to slam them down quickly against heavy aerodynamic loads as lift coefficient rose in a tight turn or dive pullout. Making each droop flap as a single unit was not a major change, but from before 1955 the fact that the Vulcan had incorporated a fixed droop (cambered leading edge) caused the HP team to investigate further. They discovered that, provided its inboard end terminated in an abrupt step, or 'dog-tooth', the Victor could manage with a simple extended and cambered fixed leading edge. This was retrofitted on most B.1s.

Further modifications added to the defensive avionics, and on the completion of Mod 660 the Mark number changed to 1A. The main visible change was an extension of the fuselage tailcone and increase in size of the receiver antenna at the tip. The rear-fuselage ECM boxes were originally cooled from a ventral inlet just behind the bomb bay. This tended to become blocked by chaff, so it was blanked off by Mod 2960 and replaced by a tapping from the inlet side of the tail anticing jet pump. Except for one aircraft which had been damaged, all Victors from XH587 were brought up to B.1A standard.

While the Mk 2 aircraft was being developed, as described later, many Mk 1s became redundant. For some unexplained political reason it was supposed that deploying Polaris missiles aboard submarines meant that versatile bombers could be phased out. Much thought was given to converting the Victors for reconnaissance missions. The Avro 730 Mach 2.6 recon-bomber having been cancelled in the 'no more manned aircraft' nonsense of 1957, its 52 ft Red Drover SLAR (side-looking airborne radar) was repackaged into Red Neck. This looked exactly like a 49 ft pencil, and when in 1961 two of these were hung on the 13,500-lb strongpoints already in the wing structure (for the unused fuel pods) the result amazed young spotters. The trials aircraft was XA918.

When the Valiant's grounding in 1964 left the RAF with no tankers, XA918 was turned into a tanker trials aircraft. It began work in July 1964 with a Flight Refuelling Mk 17 HDU (hose-drum unit) hung behind the bomb bay on No 11 tank stations (Nos 728/804), a Mk 20B HDU under each outer wing and a row of tanks of transfer fuel in the bomb bay. The Mk 17 was driven by a 112 V DC motor via a variable fluid drive gearbox and chains, reeling the hose in or out according to an indicated airspeed sensor. The Mk 20B pods were self-contained, driven by a windmill on the nose. Delivering at about one-third the rate of the Mk 17, they were used for fighters. A tremendous effort was needed to perfect their installation, and at an early stage they had to be moved nearer the wingtips and toed slightly inwards to keep the flailing drogues from coming too near the tail. A turbopump worked

BELOW *Boarding a Victor B.1 of No 10 Sqn 'prior to a long-range flight' (but they don't have their bags of gear, so the photo is posed)*

ABOVE *A B.2 complete with live Blue Steel cruise missile*

LEFT *B.1s carried out various test programmes, XA918 flying the Red Neck side-looking radar*

by engine bleed was added to boost fuel pressure to a precise 50 lb/sq in before feeding to the HDUs. The panic need for tankers resulted in the first B(K).1s and 14 full B(K).1As, redesignated K.1 and K.1A in 1968, the original two-pointers being designated B.1A(KP2). Wearing green/grey camouflage, these tankers served in the low-level role until replaced by the K.2 from May 1974. In hot/high places they were weight-limited on take-off, making one wonder why the RAF cancelled the Spectre rocket packs.

After shortsightedly cancelling in 1954 both the Blue Boar precision guided bomb and a number of ultra-low-level bombers being designed to specification B.126T, the Air Staff and Ministry of Supply decided what was needed was a giant cruise missile and a bomber that could release it at an altitude even higher than the ceiling of the earlier V-bombers. Presented with this problem, HP technical director Reginald Stafford schemed a series of upgraded Victors with greater span and more powerful engines. Cutting a long and involved story short, the final choice was the Phase 2A aircraft, with span increased and considerably altered systems and equipment including Rolls-Royce Conway bypass (turbofan) engines. This was called the Victor B.2. There was no prototype; it was merely decided that production would switch to the Mk 2 at the 26th aircraft of the 1954 batch of 33 Mk 1s. This aircraft, XH668, was brought forward on the Radlett line and flew on 20 February 1959.

To preserve CG position the 10 ft increase in span was added 18 in at each root and 3 ft 6 in at each tip.

ABOVE *The Victor B.2 was one of the nicest bombers of all time to fly. As it has leading-edge flap controls this is an early example. The blank square in the centre is the missing autopilot controller*

The structure had to be strengthened for greater weights and increased span, and the main structural box was made integral tankage. Further difficulty was added by the much greater mass flow of the engines. Wisely, HP designed the installation for the even greater airflow of the planned Conways, which at around 360 lb/sec, just doubled that of the Sapphire-powered B.1s. In fact, the Conway was nothing like the engine it might have been; having to fit inside the wing of the Victor restricted bypass ratio to a pitiful 0.3, instead of something like ten times greater. Of course, the leading-edge inlets and ducts, and engine-bay depth, all had to be enlarged.

The extra bay at each wing root was useful. On the left a new ram inlet inboard of the main engine intake supplied air to a Freon refrigeration system serving the enhanced avionics racking below and to the rear of the pressure cabin. On the right the new bay housed a Blackburn (Turbomeca licence) Artouste 400 hp gas turbine, fed by a retractable inlet under the wing. It provided compressed air for starting the engines. It also drove an alternator for ground electrical power, and the electrics of the B.2 were totally redesigned. Each main engine drove a 73-kVA alternator, via a Sundstrand hydraulic drive, giving 115/200 V power at exactly 400 cycles. A fifth alternator was driven by the Artouste, which was cleared for use up to 10,000 ft, and two more for emergency power were in the rear fuselage driven by air turbines spun by large ram inlets which could be opened on each side of the dorsal fin. For starting the Artouste, and sundry other duties,

two 24 V batteries were installed ahead of the nose gear in what had been the chaff bay.

In fact a convenient location was later found for the larger quantity of chaff (and later for flares) required for defence. Quite late in B.2 development, to reduce drag at around Mach 0.9 at high altitude, large streamlined bodies were added above the trailing edge of the wing just outboard of the flaps, and these could dispense anything with no part of the aircraft downstream. Other electronic defence systems were added in the rear fuselage, the most prominent (added after the B.2 was in service) being Red Steer, with six small antenna blisters round the tailcone. To increase heat-exchanger capacity a much bigger ram inlet was added at the front of a new dorsal fin (which was not fitted to the first B.2). Eventually, after much deliberation, the fixed drooped leading edge was accepted and retrofitted on B.2s already built. Another visible change was to add the big underwing tanks, cleared on the Mk 1 but never used, which could be jettisoned.

The remaining major modification was to fit the B.2 to carry the big cruise missile. Developed by Avro (Hawker Siddeley), as explained in the Vulcan chapter, the weapon was a little more difficult to load into the Victor because of the extremely small ground clearance. When recessed into the bomb

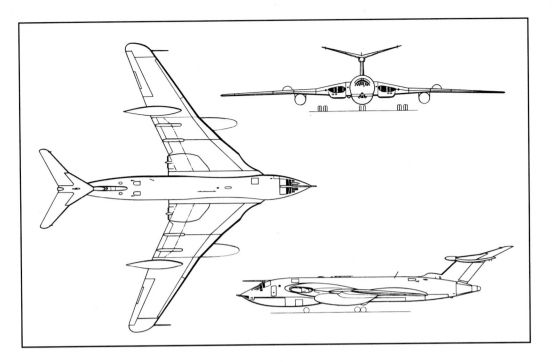

RIGHT *Victor B.2*

ABOVE *Wind-tunnel model of an unbuilt version with extended span, tip tanks and four Skybolts*

bay, with doors tailored to the missile body, drag increase was officially put at 2 per cent. Other changes included various revisions to the cockpit and other crew stations, slight increase in tank capacities and, during production, addition of a fixed flight-refuelling probe above the cockpit on the centreline, with two searchlights just below it.

Early B.2s were painted in Titanine glossy anti-flash white, often with no serial number visible except on the windbreak of the crew door (visible only on the ground). On 20 August 1959 the first aircraft, then with Mk 103 engines rated at 17,250-lb, took off from Boscombe Down for buffet tests at Mach 0.94 at 52,000 ft. It never came back. Had it been flown to a hostile country? Eventually fragments of it found in the Irish Sea demonstrated that a simple failure of the collet retaining the pitot tube

on the starboard wingtip had led to a sequence of events that the crew could not overcome. Apart from this incident the B.2 proved as good an aircraft as its predecessor.

It was the 17th, XL188, which was first to reach the RAF, at No 232 OCU on 1 November 1961. Subsequently Nos 139 and 100 Sqns, both at Wittering, became operational with Blue Steel Victors, the engines soon being uprated to Mk 201 standard at 20,600 lb, or more than double the power of the first Victor. The programme was then thrown into disarray by the American Skybolt missile, two of which were schemed as an alternative to two Blue Steels in place of the underwing tanks. While rivals said the Victor could not carry Skybolt, the Air Staff worked out that, carrying two Skybolts each, fewer aircraft would be needed, and cancelled the last six. Then a fresh order was placed for 27, on condition HP merged with another firm. The dying Sir Frederick Handley Page strove to reach a deal acceptable to his workforce and shareholders, and a merger with Hawker Siddeley was all but concluded when the last 22 Victors were cancelled. The deal fell through, and HP went bankrupt in 1970. Time was to show the cancelled aircraft would have been very valuable.

Thus, altogether 34 B.2s were built. They comprised the last eight ordered in 1954 as B.1s, XH668/675; a second batch of 18, XL158/165, XL188, XL193 and XL230/233; in 1957 increased to 24 by adding XL250/255, but these six cancelled 1960; a third batch of three, XL250/252 renumbered as XL511/513; and a fourth batch of 27, XM714/718, XM745/758, XM785/794, in 1962 the final 22 (from XM745) cancelled. The last, XM718, was delivered on 2 May 1963.

Fully modified aircraft with Mk 201 engines, fixed leading edge, trailing-edge bodies and Red Steer were often (not officially) designated B.2R, from Retrofit. The final nine were converted as extremely versatile Victor B(SR).2 bomber/reconnaissance aircraft. In order of conversion they were XL165, XM718 (which alone retained Blue Steel compatibility), XL230, XM715, XH672, XH674, XM716, XL193 and XL161. Equipment included the largest camera crate ever used by a Western air force, side-locked H_2S radar with advanced mapping and display processing, 108 of the large 3-million candlepower photoflashes and two 8000-lb bomb bay tanks. They served No 543 Sqn from 18 May 1965 until desperate need for tankers demanded their further conversion.

By early 1968 HP had schemed a complete conversion of B.2Rs to tankers, at remarkably low cost. Apart from the expected addition of two 16,000-lb bomb-bay tanks and a Mk 17B and two Mk 20B HDUs, it involved adding large tanks at the wingtips (originally designed for the stillborn Phase 6 aircraft with four Skybolts), which not only greatly increased transfer fuel but also unloaded the wing and dramatically reduced the onset of fatigue damage. The conversion also provided ejection seats for all the crew, which was increased to six: two pilots, air electronics officer, nav radar, nav plotter and supernumerary. Tragically, HP collapsed in 1970, and the job of converting tankers devolved upon the former rival, Avro (Hawker Siddeley, Woodford). Their solution was quite different, rejecting the tip tanks, removing the existing 3 ft 6 in tip extensions and rigging the ailerons 2° up, which reduced lift and increased drag. No backseat ejection seats were fitted, but 18 of the 24 main avionics systems were removed. This left three useful cargo compartments, and the tailcone became available for the fuel jettison. Fuel capacity is normally 123,000 lb (still over half the maximum weight), but theoretical total is 127,000 lb: 32,000 in the two bomb-bay cells, 36,000 in the rest of the fuselage, 32,000 in the

wing tanks and 27,000 in the underwing tanks. In addition Woodford carried out a meticulous structural audit which cleared the aircraft for 14 average years after conversion.

It had been planned to rebuild 30 aircraft as K.2s, but defence cuts in April 1975 reduced this number to 24 because nobody had the vision to see that even 30 would not be anything like enough. XL231 was the aerodynamic prototype, and other conversions (in order) were: XL232, XL189, XL233, XL191, XL163, XL190, XL513, XM715, XL511, XL160, XL188, XL512, XL158, XL192, XH671, XL162, XH673, XH669, XH675, XL164, XM717, XL161 and XH672. They performed sterling service with Marham's Nos 55 and 57 Sqns, notably in the South Atlantic (when XH675 made a 14 hr 45 min 7000-mile radar recon mission, the longest in history) and the Gulf War. The K.2 was finally retired at the end of October 1993.

SPECIFICATION

Handley Page Victor
Four jet engines: all Mk 1, Armstrong Siddeley (later Bristol Siddeley) Sapphire 202 or 207 turbojets rated at 11,050 lb; (B.2) Rolls-Royce Conway 103 turbofans rated at 17,250 lb; (B.2R, SR.2 and K.2) Rolls-Royce Conway 201 rated at 20,600 lb
Dimensions Span (1) 110 ft 0 in (33.53 m), (B.2, B.2R, SR.2) 120 ft 0 in (36.58 m), (K.2) 117 ft 0 in (35.66 m); length (all) 114 ft 11 in (35.30 m); wing area (1) 2406 sq ft (223.5 m²), (B.2, B.2R, SR.2) 2597 sq ft (241.3 m²), (K.2) 2200 sq ft (204.38 m²)
Weight Empty (1) 79,100 lb (35,880 kg), (B.2) 91,430 lb (41,473 kg), (K.2) 110,310 lb (50,037 kg); max TO (1) 180,000 lb (81,650 kg), (B.2) 233,000 lb (101,150 kg), (K.2) 238,000 lb (107,957 kg)
Performance Maximum speed (B.1, B.2) 645 mph (1038 km/h), (K.2) 610 mph (982 km/h); service ceiling (1) 55,000 ft (16,764 m), (B.2) 61,000 ft (18,590 m), (K.2) 50,000 ft (15,240 m); combat range with max bombload (1) 2700 miles (4345 km), (B.2) 4600 miles (7400 km), (K.2, not using transfer fuel) 4500 miles (7242 km)
Armament No defensive guns; max bombload (1, 2) up to four free-fall nuclear bombs or 35 GP bombs of 1000 lb, with structural provison for 28 similar bombs in underwing containers; (B.2 as built) one Blue Steel Mk 1 cruise missile

BELOW *The last V-bomber sortie was flown at the end of October 1993*

Myasishchyev M-4, M-6, 3M

First Flight – 20 January 1953

This impressive aircraft was the first Soviet strategic jet bomber, requested in 1949 to counter the future threat of the B-52 (which at that time was a turboprop). Like the B-52 the Soviet aircraft has had to soldier on ever since, but it has suffered fewer structural problems and in most respects has been an outstanding success.

The OKB (design bureau) of V M Myasishchyev had in 1949 concluded that it would be impossible to create the requested 'North America bomber' except with propellers, though a 250 t aircraft with eight M-209 turbojets appeared marginally possible. Stalin's personal 1951 demand for an aircraft to counter the B-52 implicitly stated it had to be a jet, and the OKB had little option but to design the best practical aircraft with four M-209 (RD-3) turbojets, which then were about to begin bench-testing at the Mikulin design bureau, and await the future availability of more efficient and more powerful engines.

The design was known as the M-4. Its wing was a masterpiece, aerodynamically and structurally. The basic aerofoil profile was one of the SRs series,

with a nominal thickness/chord ratio of 12 per cent at the root (though this was modified by the internal engine ducts, the 'British solution' of buried engines having been chosen), and 7 per cent at the tip. The airframe design load factor (at a weight of 140 tonnes) was of necessity quite low, namely 2g. The M-4 was not going to be particularly agile.

The wing has a three-spar centre section joined to a two-spar outer panel to give a remarkable lifting surface of nearly 175 feet span with an aspect ratio of 8.7 (compared with 8.5 for the B-52). All ribs are at 90° to the continuous rear spar, the outer-wing joint being 10.35 m along this spar from the centreline. The fixed leading edge was swept at an angle of 37°30′ to this joint, and thence at 34°48″ to the tip. The structural inter-spar box was designed with machined rectangular skin panels,

BOTTOM *An unmodified 3M Bomber, on special test programmes in 1991*

BELOW *This 3MS2 multi-role aircraft is at Monino*

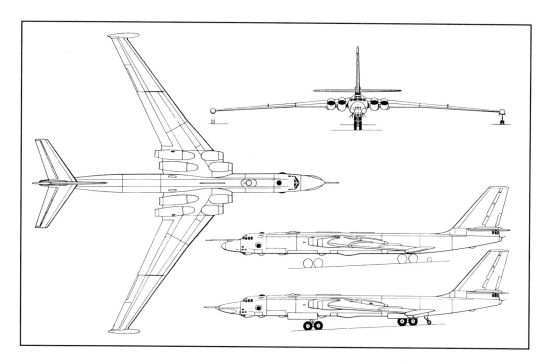

LEFT *3MS2 with upper side view of 3M*

lightweight sandwich panels being used behind the rear spar. The inboard trailing edge was set at 90° to the centreline (but occupied mainly by jetpipe fairings whose undersides are covered by a split flap). Outboard of the kink, the next section of trailing edge was swept at 25°.

The enormous double-slotted flap on each wing was made in two parts. The inboard flap runs on one track and one end-rib, while the outer flap runs directly aft on four tracks. Outboard of the flap was a fixed 2.18 m (85.8 in) gap followed by a second kink, outboard of which the trailing-edge sweep was 29°, with a powered aileron made in two sections, the inner section having a long tab on both wings. A fence on the upper surface extended from 10–85 per cent of the chord at the inner end of the aileron. From 1960, many aircraft had a larger fence further inboard bisecting the structural joint extended round the leading edge and ending at the flap.

A conventional swept tail was adopted, the horizontal variable-incidence trimming tailplane carrying powered untabbed elevators mounted part-way up the fin. The latter carried the one-piece tabbed rudder. Tail geometry, and its relation to the engines, was similar to the Valiant but on a much larger scale.

The four engines were hung aft of the rear spar on beams aligned with the aircraft centreline, their position being staggered because of sweep. Fixed flat oval inlets projected well ahead of the leading edge for each engine, the duct being carried through the spar webs while the outer fairing was arranged to taper off into the wing to reappear again around the engine. The upper cowl incorporated access doors and auxiliary inlets, the lower access doors being followed by the split flap. The four jetpipes were angled outwards, the outer pipes being much longer and angled more sharply out.

The circular-section fuselage had a ruling diameter of 3.5 m (138 in), with a discontinuity around the upper part of the joint with the pressure cabin. The latter comprised a drum housing the navigator/bomb-aimer in the glazed nose, two pilots, a radio/radar operator managing the *Rubin* main radar under his floor, and two gunners. A separate pressurised compartment was provided for a tail gunner, without a communicating tunnel (total crew being seven).

The pilot was given a sight for a fixed cannon. The forward gunners used TP-1 electro-optical sights in three bulged windows with electromechanical links to drive three turrets (front and rear ventral and forward dorsal) each with twin cannon. The Ilyushin tail turret again mounted twin cannon, and the rear gunner had the ability to take over control of other turrets in emergency.

The enormous bomb bay aft of the wing bridge was fitted with left/right double-fold doors, and equipped for four TN-9000 or FAB-9000 or lesser bombs to a maximum weight of 40 tonnes. Protected and inerted fuel cells along the top of the fuselage, full depth front and rear of the bomb bay and in the wing box, held a design total of 90 tonnes of fuel (c108,000 lit, 23,850 gal).

After studying several alternatives weight was saved by adopting a bicycle landing gear. The entire weight is supported by a main four-wheel bogie at front and rear, each with tyres 1550 mm × 480 mm, all with multi-disc anti-skid brakes and hydraulic retraction forwards into a bay with twin doors. The forward bogie is hydraulically

steerable and fitted with an extensible main strut to increase the angle of attack of the wing on take-off and landing. For stability on the ground, outrigger gears are provided, with twin wheels on long levered struts retracting forwards into tip pods with four doors. A large braking parachute occupies a box under the rear fuselage.

The hydraulic system is of the twin-duplex (four-pump) type, operating at 210 kg/cm² (3000 lb/sq in). The electric system is based on four DC 27-volt generators, with rectifiers to provide AC for the radar and deicing. Over 40 gaseous-oxygen bottles are provided. No APU (auxiliary power unit) was fitted originally, but one was added in the 1960s. Deicing is mainly by hot air from engine bleed and heat exchangers, electrothermal elements being added to the cockpit and blister glazing.

The first M-4 of a development batch believed to number 12 was rolled out on 30 December 1952. It was flown by a crew headed by F F Opadchi on 20 January 1953, 22 months after the start of design. Recognised as underpowered with AM-3 engines, the fuselage tanks were not filled, and there was no hope of meeting the full requirement until a specially developed engine became available. NATO called the new bomber 'Type 37'.

TOP *This prototype M-4 took part in the May Day flypast in 1954, with MiG-17s to give it scale*

ABOVE *Looking up at a demilitarised M6, which would shortly become an early 3MS, emphasising the aerodynamically efficient wing. All production versions had the VD-7M engine*

Generally the M-4 was an outstanding aircraft, but the OKB immediately had to start redesigning it as the M-6. The many changes included redesign of the outer wing with a straight trailing edge and pronounced washout (sharp negative incidence at the tip), adding dihedral on the tailplane and, from 1955, fitting the production engine. This had been specially developed by the bureau of V A Dobrynin to give almost double the thrust with much better fuel economy.

Other changes included fitting an RPB-4 main radar under the nose, a Loran 'towel rail' antenna and the defensive avionic system. The fixed gun was usually omitted, the turrets being modified for newer guns (AM-23 instead of NR-23), and there were numerous systems changes.

After NII testing the M-6 was qualified for DA

service in 1955, with the designation 3M. Production at Kazan is believed to have numbered 200, completed in 1959. First delivery took place in November 1955, and the 3M was operational with the DA (long-range aviation) from May 1956. The popular name was *Molot* (hammer), and the NATO name *Bison-A*.

During production the 3M was brought up to 3MS standard with further changes. These included deletion of the aft rear turret immediately behind the rear landing gear, adding ILS, a radar warning receiver system and chaff/flare ejectors, and, from 1960, a fixed flight-refuelling probe above the nose. Though popular, even the 3M was never able to fly the design mission, and by 1960 the entire force was being rebuilt to fly a dual reconnaissance/tanker role with the AV-MF (naval air force). During conversion a supposed '103-M' set a 1000-km circuit record with a 27 t payload at 1028 km/h, while another called '201-M' set 19 world records including carrying 10 t to 15,317 m (50,253 ft) and 22 t (121,480 lb) to 2 km.

Further rebuilds replaced the main radar with a large gondola with forward windows, swapped the glazed nose for a different radar, added a navigator/senso station under the cockpit with three windows on each side (linked to the ventral gondola), removed the aft turret, rebuilt the tailplane horizontal and added a flight-refuelling probe above the nose if not already present. Usual modifications also added numerous avionics antennas and rebuilt the forward part of the bomb bay to contain a large hose-drum unit requiring bulged bay doors, and the rear section to contain an extra tank. The resulting 3MS or 3MZ force served not only the ADD (successor to the DA), but also the

ABOVE Tail aspect of a 3MS2. These aircraft had no dihedral on the tailplane

AV-MF as standard heavy tanker; NATO's *Bison-B*.

The final AV-MF modification, to 3MS2 standard, rebuilt the nose to house yet another radar with an antenna in a wide lower portion of a longer but much slimmer nose carrying a fixed FR probe at the tip. Some aircraft lost both remaining forward turrets. The primary mission remained tanker until the final 40 were replaced by the Il-78 in 1991–93. NATO name was *Bison-C*.

One unmodified 3M was rebuilt as the VM-T *Atalant* to carry outsize pick-a-back loads, notably the *Buran* aerospacecraft, carried on front/rear trusses above the fuselage, with a completely new rear section and twin-fin tail. The M-28 double-deck transport version was never built.

SPECIFICATION

Myasishchyev 3MS2
Four Dobrynin VD-7B turbojets each rated at 28,660 lb (13 t)
Dimensions Span 53.14 m (174 ft) 4⅛ in); length 51.3 m (168 ft 3⅝ in), (excl FR probe) 48.76 m (159 ft 11⅝ in); wing area 351.78 m² (3,787 sq ft)
Weight Empty 82 t (180,776 lb); normal loaded 140 t (308,640 lb), max 190 t (418,871 lb); normal landing 105 t (231,480 lb)
Performance Maximum speed (SL) 620 km/h (385 mph), (11 km) 910 km/h (565 mph); service ceiling 12.25 km (40,200 ft); normal range 9440 km (5866 miles); max endurance 20 hr; TO speed/run 310 km/h, 2950 m; landing speed/run 210 km/h, 1800
Armament Maximum bomb load 40 t (88,185 lb); defensive armament originally seven NR-23 guns, today usually from two to six AM-23

Martin B-57

First Flight – 20 July 1953

Shortly after the outbreak of war in Korea, the USAF asked the British government for a private demonstration of the English Electric Canberra. This obvious interest in an overseas aircraft was virtually unique at the time, but it was necessary because the American forces in Korea desperately needed a modern tactical bomber to disrupt communist supply lines into the beleaguered southern battlefields. This task had been assigned to elderly Douglas B-26 Invaders for the first few months of the war, but their attrition rate was high and they were having only limited operational success. The Canberra demonstration was arranged at RAF Burtonwood on 17 August 1950, and during September a team of US test pilots and engineers visited English Electric's Warton factory for several days, to fly the aircraft and carry out a detailed technical assessment.

It seems likely that this first batch of trials convinced the Americans that the Canberra was ideal for the job, but in order to satisfy the US Senate a competitive evaluation of all likely contenders had to be arranged. After some weeks of internal discussion, a new 'night intruder' mission was defined by the Air Force, and five aircraft were selected to take part in the fly-off: the AJ-1 Savage

and B-45 Tornado from North American; the three-engined Martin XB-51; and two foreign contenders, the Avro Canada CF-100 Canuck and the British Canberra B.Mk2.

On 21 February 1951, Canberra WD932 was delivered from Warton to Andrews AFS, Washington, after completing the Aldergrove to Gander transatlantic crossing in the then record time of 4 hr 37 min. The actual competition was conducted at Andrews five days later. Each aircraft was given a 10 min time slot to perform a set sequence of manoeuvres, which would enable its performance and agility to be directly compared with all the others. The Canberra – immaculately flown for the occasion by Roland Beamont – was so far ahead at the end of the competition that the outcome was never really in doubt.

Despite its obvious superiority, the Canberra was still a foreign aircraft competing against home-grown rivals, and support for the project was always tempered by doubts about production availability and continued spares support. Most of these problems were resolved in mid-March, when English Electric agreed to allow the aircraft to be built under licence in the United States. This 'Americanisation' of the whole programme seemed to satisfy the big anti-Canberra lobby, and on 23 March 1951 the US Air Force issued a letter contract to the Baltimore-based Glenn L Martin Company, asking for 250 aircraft under the US designation B-57A. During the next few days a formal licence agreement was hammered out between the two principal companies, and this was signed on 3 April.

The B-57A was needed with great urgency, so the production programme was initially based on a minimum-change formula, matching the British-built Canberra as closely as possible. The US Air Force wanted to fly the aircraft predominantly in hot climates, and also planned to operate at slightly higher gross weights than the RAF, so the 6500-lb thrust Rolls-Royce Avon RA.3 engines were replaced by a pair of Wright J65s (licence-built Armstrong Siddeley Sapphires), rated at 7220 lb for

LEFT *Martin began by building B-57A bombers, with a crew compartment based on that of the Canberra, but with J65 engines*

take-off. This change resulted in re-profiled intakes, and a slightly smaller bomb bay, enabling the American aircraft to carry more fuel. Several other changes were planned, including a switch from three-crew to two-crew operation, but the basic external shape of the Canberra remained unchanged.

During August 1951 a second British-built B.Mk2 (WD940) was flown over to join WD932 as a pattern aircraft. While the production track was being laid down at Baltimore, these two machines were used extensively for performance validation, and a variety of other trials work connected with the proposed airframe changes. Everything progressed smoothly until WD932 (by then 51-17387) crashed suddenly on 21 December 1951: both crew members successfully escaped from the aircraft, but the observer was killed following a parachute malfunction. At the time of the accident the aircraft had been conducting Stage 2 manoeuvring trials at high operating weights (understood to have been 48,000 lb), and the outboard section of the port wing failed upwards during a planned 4.8g turn at 10,000 ft. This breakage was well inside the Canberra's normal structural limits, so the accident caused considerable alarm among everyone connected with the project. It was later discovered that incorrect fuel scheduling during the early stages of the flight had made the aircraft tail-heavy, and when the turn was initiated the nose pitched up very violently, exceeding the design loads by a huge margin. The aircraft structure was not at fault in any way, but the shock and uncertainty following the crash nearly jeopardised the whole programme by bringing into the open a lot of suppressed anti-Canberra feelings.

Well before signature of the original contract, the Wright Air Development Center (WADC) had asked for over 30 changes to the basic design of the Canberra, but most of these were rejected out of hand on the grounds of cost or programme delay.

Early in 1952, as part of the immediate aftermath of the accident, the US Air Force's Air Materiel Command was forced to give way under a renewed wave of pressure for these changes, and most of them were eventually accepted. At that time construction of an initial batch of 75 B-57As was already in progress, and little could be done to alter the basic configuration of these aircraft.

The first US-produced airframe (52-1418) was rolled-out at the beginning of July 1953 – ironically just a few days before the cessation of hostilities in Korea. This aircraft was equipped to the original bomber specification, but in view of the impending design changes it was one of only eight B-57As completed. The remaining 67 aircraft from the first production batch were no longer required as bombers, so they were converted on the assembly line to medium-altitude reconnaissance platforms. These aircraft retained all the basic Canberra features and were re-designated RB-57As. They were used by three tactical reconnaissance wings, beginning with the 363rd TRW at Shaw AFB, South Carolina, in late 1954. A few RB-57As were also assigned direct to the 345th Bomb Group (Tactical) at Langley AFB, Virginia, where they were used for crew familiarisation until the delayed bomber variant became available.

The structural and system changes requested by WADC were all designed to make the new B-57B a much more adaptable attack aircraft – particularly at low level. The most significant external change was a new fighter-style cockpit canopy, with tandem seating and a flat-panel windscreen which allowed an accurate gunsight to be fitted. The new transparency improved the pilot's view, and made it possible for the navigator to provide an extra pair of eyes in combat. Crew access was only possible via

the clamshell canopy, so the starboard entrance door of the B-57A was deleted, along with the glazed bomb-aiming nose. Four hardpoints for external bombs, rockets or napalm were added to both outer wing panels, and the aircraft was armed for strafing operations with four .50 calibre machine guns mounted inside each wing (after completion of the first 90 B-57Bs, this armament was upgraded to two 20 mm M39 on each side). Additional triangular speed-brake panels were mounted on the rear fuselage. These were hydraulically operated in unison with the existing 'finger' type brakes in each wing, and the combination gave the pilot much more control, improving the accuracy of low-level bomb delivery.

The B-57B was fitted with a new rotary bomb door, which the Glenn Martin company had orig-

TOP *Test pilot O E 'Pat' Tibbs surrounded by USAF ordnance all compatible with the prototype B-57B*

ABOVE *This B-57B visited the birthplace of its forbear, rainswept Warton, in Lancashire*

inally designed for its own XB-51. This device could be operated much more quickly than traditional hinged doors (complete open and shut cycle in about 10 sec), and produced far less buffeting at high speed. This again improved targeting accuracy, and allowed attack speeds to be raised slightly, which in turn reduced the time spent directly over the target. Ordnance could be pre-loaded on 'spare' doors, and the whole assembly slotted into the aircraft like a cassette, vastly reducing the potential turnround time. To guide the aircraft on its approach to the target, the B-57B was equipped with an APW-11 Bombing Air Radar Guidance System, which was used by the pilot in conjunction with the nav/bombardier's 'Shoran' system. Other changes to the baseline specification included an APS-54 radar warning receiver, and a new cartridge starting system that made the aircraft independent of all ground power units.

All these design changes delayed the overall B-57 programme and added considerable costs to the initial fixed-price contract. This was clearly not the manufacturer's fault, but the money effectively ran out after 177 of the planned 250-aircraft order had been completed. Of these, only eight were built to the original B-57A specification, and a further 67 to the alternative RB-57A standard – leaving just 102 to be manufactured as B-57B bombers. Although the Korean War had long since ended, the US Air Force quickly recognised that it had a thoroughly workmanlike aircraft on its hands, and a second large batch was ordered in 1954. These included another 100 B-57Bs (making 202 in all), 38 B-57C trainers, and 20 RB-57D high-altitude reconnaissance variants.

The new trainer was virtually a copy of the B-57B, but it had a full set of flying controls and primary instruments in the rear cockpit. It could still be used for all the normal bombing and ground attack operations, but it was not equipped for the same standards of delivery accuracy because the specialised targeting avionics were omitted in favour of duplicated flight instruments.

The RB-57D was ordered into production under the highly classified 'Black Knight' programme. In essence, the aircraft had a virtually standard B-57B fuselage, but it was powered by two Pratt & Whitney J57 turbojets, each rated at 11,000 lb thrust for take-off. The most noticeable aspect of its design was the new wing, which was extended outboard of the engines to a remarkable span of 106 ft (compared with 64 ft on the original aircraft). These machines were specifically prepared for clandestine missions over the Soviet Union and China, and the huge wing allowed them to operate at altitudes well in excess of 60,000 ft. Twenty RB-57Ds were supplied to the US Air Force and other government agencies, some of which were single-seaters, while others carried the normal crew of two. All but six were specially modified to receive fuel in flight. The first was delivered to SAC's 4080th Strategic Reconnaissance Wing in March 1956, more than a year ahead of the first military Lockheed U-2A. Operating mainly out of Emerson AFB in Alaska, Yokota in Japan, or Rhein-Main in Germany, the RB-57Ds carried out many hundreds of SIGINT/ELINT missions over potentially very hostile territory, before wing fatigue problems forced them into retirement in 1964. Some of the airframes were scrapped, but others were converted by General Dynamics into the even more bizarre

RB-57F (which is really outside the remit of this book).

The final new-build B-57s were a batch of 68 B-57E target tugs which were ordered in 1955. These were basically B-57C trainer airframes, with none of the dual controls or operational bombing equipment. Instead, the rear cockpit was occupied by the target operator, and the bomb compartment housed four large cable reels. The 9 ft × 45 ft banner targets were stored for take-off in externally-mounted canisters under the rear fuselage. To counteract the powerful drag forces generated by these big targets, all B-57Es were fitted with a hydraulically-boosted rudder and an automatic yaw damper.

By the beginning of 1957, four tactical bombing groups were equipped with B-57Bs. The two US-based units were the 345th at Langley, and the 461st at Hill AFB, Utah (later moved to Blytheville, Arkansas); the 38th TBG was operational from Laon, in France, and the nuclear-capable 3rd was assigned to Johnson AB in Japan. It was quickly evident that the aircraft seemed out of place in an American system so heavily dominated by the demands of strategic deterrence, and as a result it had a fairly short and undistinguished career. It was, after all, purchased in a hurry for one particular war, and when that conflict ended sooner than expected the whole programme seemed to lose its direction. Only four years after the B-57Bs entered service, the TBGs began to deactivate and re-assign their aircraft to reconnaissance, ECM or Air National Guard units. By the end of June 1959

BELOW *One of the first air-to-air photos of the B-57B*

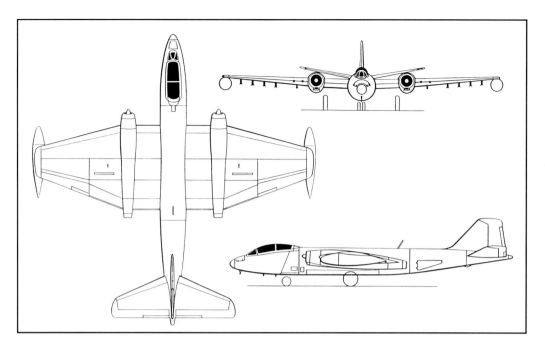

the 38th, 345th and 462st had ceased all B-57 operations, leaving only the 3rd to continue its tactical nuclear role from bases in Japan (conventional weapons only) and South Korea. Following the demise of the 345th Group, most of its aircraft were transferred to the Pakistan AF under the Military Defense Assistance Plan. Based at Mauripur, near Karachi, they formed the 7th and 8th Squadrons of the 31st Bomb Wing.

By 1964 even the nuclear strike role had run its course for the B-57B, and plans were being made for the 3rd TBG to deactivate and return to the United States. Most of the aircraft from the 90th Bombardment Squadron had already gone, and the other two squadrons (8th and 13th) were packing up prior to departure, when the government in Washington suddenly decided to escalate the US involvement in Vietnam. All the remaining B-57s were flown to Clark AB in the Philippines during April, where they waited nearly four months for clearance to deploy to a base in Vietnam itself. On 5 August 20 aircraft were flown to Bien Hoa, near Saigon, but the crews had to endure another seven months of boredom before they were given clearance to attack the enemy. During this period of waiting, the crowded airfield at Bien Hoa was attacked by Viet Cong mortars, destroying five of the valuable aircraft and badly damaging most of the others. Replacements were quickly flown in from the Philippines, but the squadrons were not allowed to hit back until 19 February 1965.

The first few months of combat operations went remarkably well, with the B-57 rapidly making its mark on enemy supply concentrations in both South and North Vietnam. Losses were few until 16 May 1965, when one of the B-57Bs exploded during start-up procedures on the crowded ramp at Bien Hoa. This started a chain reaction of fire and explosions that ripped through virtually everything parked on the airfield, killing nearly 30 men, wounding over 100 others and totally destroying

21 aircraft. After this disaster the squadrons were immediately moved to Tan Son Nhut, and replacement B-57s were flown into Clark AB from ANG units in Kentucky and Nevada.

Combat operations over the featureless Ho Chi Minh Trail presented particularly severe problems at night, and supplies were still managing to get through despite constant attempts to stop them. Following a series of trials conducted under combat conditions, 16 standard B-57B bombers were rotated back to the United States during 1969 for modification to a new B-57G 'night interdiction' standard. These aircraft were fitted with an entirely new nose section, containing an AN/APQ-139 forward-looking radar with digital moving target indicator, a sophisticated low-light television system, and an AN/AAS-26 forward-looking infrared detector. The sensors were complemented by a laser rangefinder/designator, and the wing pylons were modified to carry and release Paveway laser-guided bombs. All the guns were removed to save weight.

During the long development phase of this programme, the two standard bomber squadrons in Vietnam had reached the limit of their operational effectiveness, and both had been deactivated – the 13th returning to the United States in January 1968, and the 8th following on in September 1969.

The B-57Gs began arriving at MacDill AFB, Florida, in July 1959, where the 13th Bombardment Squadron had been hurriedly reactivated to receive them. These were among the most expensive and complex aircraft ever deployed to Vietnam, and the squadron was given just a year to train and develop appropriate tactics before they were finally committed to a nocturnal life above the steamy jungles of South-east Asia. The unit moved to Thailand as part of the 8th TFW in September 1970, and began operations against night-time supply convoys almost immediately. The new aircraft was remarkably successful in combat: the sensors worked well, and the laser designator unerringly put bombs within 10–15 ft of their intended target – in effect, this was the B-57 that the USAF had wanted for the Korean operation way back in 1950. Despite its success in the air, however, the B-57G proved to be a nightmare on the ground. As time went by it became increasingly difficult to keep the aircraft operational because the sensitive electronics simply collapsed in the sticky atmosphere of Thailand. By the spring of 1972 it was clear that the declining availability rate could not be reversed, so the squadron was withdrawn from the area and returned to the United States. The B-57Gs were quickly re-assigned to the 190th TBG of the Kansas ANG, but they fared little better in the drier climes, and two years later they were consigned to Davis-Monthan.

BELOW *In Vietnam the USAF could have done with a few hundred B-57G multi-sensor attack bombers. They had only a handful; this one (52-578) was with the 13th TBS, 8th TFW*

BOTTOM *The first B-57B loaded with dummy stores immediately upon rollout in glossy black finish*

SPECIFICATION

Martin and General Dynamics B-57 Canberra
(A, B, C, E, G) two 7220-lb (325 kg) thrust Wright J65-5 (US Sapphire) single-shaft turbojets; (D) two 11,000-lb (4990 kg) Pratt & Whitney J57-37A two-shaft turbojets; (F) two 18,000-lb (8165 kg) Pratt & Whitney TF33-11A two-shaft turbofans and two 3300-lb (1500 kg) Pratt & Whitney J60-9 single-shaft turbojets
Dimensions Span (A, B, C, E, G) 64 ft (19.5 m); (D) 106 ft (32.3 m); (F) 122 ft 5 in (37.32 m); length (A, B, C, D, E) 65 ft 6 in (19.96 m); (G) 67 ft (20.42 m); (F) 69 ft (21.03 m); height (A, B, C, E, G) 15 ft 7 in (4.75 m); (D) 14 ft 10 in (4.52 m); (F) 19 ft (5.79 m)
Weight Empty (A, B, C, E, typical) 26,800 lb (12,200 kg); (G) about 28,000 lb (12,700 kg); (D) 33,000 lb (14,970 kg); (F) about 36,000 lb (16,300 kg); maximum loaded (A) 51,000 lb; (B, C, E, G) 55,000 lb (24,950 kg); (D) not disclosed; (F) 63,000 lb (28,576 kg)
Performance Maximum speed (A, B, C, E, G) 583 mph (937 km/h); (D, F) over 500 mph (800 km/h); initial climb (A, B, C, E, G) 3500 ft (1070 m)/min; (D, F) about 4000 ft (1220 m)/min; service ceiling (A, B, C, E, G) 48,000 ft (14,630 m); (D) 65,000 ft (19,000 m); (F) 75,000 ft (22,860 m); maximum range with combat load (high altitude) (A, B, C, E, G) 2100 miles (3380 km); (D) about 3000 miles (5955 km)
Armament (A and all RB versions) none; (B, C, E, G) provision for four 20 mm or eight 0.5 in guns fixed in outer wings (very rarely, other guns fixed in forward fuselage); internal bomb load of 5000 lb (2268 kg) on rotary bomb door plus eight rockets, two 500-lb bombs or other stores on underwing pylons (while retaining tip tanks)

Douglas A-4 (A4D) Skyhawk

First Flight – 22 June 1954

Popularly called 'The Scooter', or 'Heinemann's Hot Rod', or 'The Bantam Bomber', this may be the only aircraft in history to come out weighing not more than its customer hoped (which is the norm) but less than half as much; and at the same time it exceeded the tactical radius demanded by 100 miles and the specified speed by nearly 200 knots. To be more precise, the US Navy asked in 1951 for a carrier-based attack aircraft able to carry a 2000-lb bomb, weighing not more than 30,000 lb and able to reach 400 kt. What they got was something which weighed 15,000 lb, carried a 4000-lb bombload and could achieve 600 kt.

Ed Heinemann, chief engineer of the Douglas Navy plant at El Segundo, was in the 1950s probably the most experienced designer of tactical bombers in the world. He also had experience of airliners, fighters and the first aircraft to reach Mach 2. One of his many smash hits was the AD (later A-1) Skyraider, which in Korea in 1951 was flying ten-hour missions with amazing loads of ordnance. Alongside it were fast jets, but these needed long take-offs and carried much smaller bombloads. The Navy Bureau of Aeronautics wanted something much faster than a Skyraider, with a much bigger bombload than the jets. The answer seemed to be a twin-turboprop, hence the specification.

Heinemann was busy with the A3D Skywarrior, which in 1951 was about to fly. He naturally felt that to use propellers would be retrograde, but a small jet looked like being deficient in range and bombload. So he set about the biggest rethink he could imagine, to rewrite established rules and save weight. He began with such things as hydraulic pumps and electric cable-connectors and ended with wing skins, to see what could be redesigned or, better still, omitted. In his words, 'I wanted to take the best engine I could get, stick a wing underneath and put a saddle for the jockey on top – and leave out the rest'.

He actually applied the study to a supersonic interceptor, and came out with the 'impossible' gross weight of 6000 lb. The Navy didn't want a new interceptor, but gave Heinemann 14 days to transfer the weight-saving philosophy to the required attack aircraft. So he locked himself in his office for 24 hours, and next day said to his team 'Here is a preliminary three-view. Weight comes out to 12,000 lb. I would like you all to join the team. Anyone who can't believe it, there is the door'. Nobody walked out, but the admirals in Washington thought Heinemann irresponsible. Even his closest friends thought he must be 'in need of a rest'.

Fortunately for the Navy the chief of attack aircraft procurement, Cdr John Brown, quickly

BELOW *The prototype XA4D-1 was one of the very few Skyhawks not to have the hastily contrived 'single-surface rudder' that embarrassed Heinemann ever afterwards*

TOP *No prizes for identifying the user unit of this A-4C*

ABOVE *This A-4E even draws attention to the rudder by its paint scheme*

became an enthusiastic convert. He at least managed to persuade his superiors to take the project seriously. Heinemann was told to double the bombload and increase mission radius by 100 nautical miles, and this put up gross weight to 14,300 lb. On 21 June 1952 Douglas Aircraft received a contract for two XA4D prototypes and a static-test airframe. This was closely followed by an order for nine A4D-1s, each to have an empty weight of 8136 lb and gross weight of 15,000 lb. There was still a pervasive feeling of disbelief, and the orders rested solely on Heinemann's personal reputation.

After the Mock-up Review Board in September 1952 even the doubters began to waver, and as confidence grew it was agreed to freeze the design and even tool up the factory for production of what was beginning to look like a complete world-beater. The first XA4D-1, BuNo 137812, was rolled out in

February 1954, final tweaking and instrumentation being done in the California sunshine. Bob Rahn made the first flight at Edwards on 22 June 1954. It made front pages in the media.

If the bombload of 4000 lb was borne in mind, the XA4D looked impossibly inadequate. The round-tipped delta wing was so small (27 ft 6 in) it did not need to fold. The upper and lower skins were each a single piece of metal, and the three spars were likewise one piece from tip to tip, merely bent instead of having joints. Heinemann actually designed not a wing but a fuel tank, making it look like a wing. Though the thickness ratio was only 4.5 to 5 per cent he fitted full-span slats. At the back were powered ailerons and simple split flaps. The body could hardly have been simpler, with side inlets to the 'best engine', the British AS Sapphire made by Wright as the J65, though the US version gave only 7200 lb instead of 8300. The pressurised cockpit was high to give a good view, and housed an ejection seat weighing half that of previous patterns. At the back was a simple tail, with the tailplane pivoted to the fin.

Heinemann was irritated at being told to lengthen the landing gears (because other jets had been

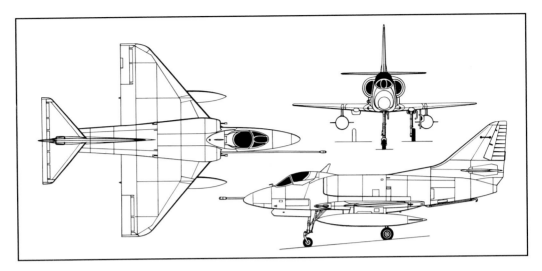

scraping their tails). This made the XA4D look stalky, perched up high, and threatened to cause trouble on rolling decks (it didn't), forcing the Menasco main legs to be shortened before retracting forwards to stow the wheel in the leading edge. The legs themselves were housed under the unbroken lower wing skin, leaving a wing so strong that later ones would pull 4g with three of the main shear-webs severed by flak. Design load factor was 7.5g, another figure that bettered the requirement. On each side of the rear fuselage was a door-type airbrake, with the sting arrester hook underneath. Catapult hooks were under the wing roots, behind the very tall forwards-retracting nose gear. In the wing roots were two 20 mm Colt cannon, and the 4000 lb bombload could be carried on three pylons, one of 2000 lb and the wing stations rated at 1000.

Flight testing was exciting and successful. Among the few fixes needed were two rows of small vortex generators along the slats and outer wing, small fences on the inner wing and slat, the addition of an extra chunk of fairing above the jet nozzle and redesign of the rudder with a single skin down the middle and half-ribs visible down each side. The last two fixes were done almost overnight. Heinemann thought them embarrassing, but nobody ever had time to redesign them 'properly'.

The second aircraft was redesignated as the first of what became 19 pre-production YA4D-1s. It flew less than two months after the first prototype, on 14 August 1954. In October 1955 one, still with a J65-2 giving only 7200 lb, set a 500-km closed-circuit record at 695.2 mph. By this time production was in hand on 146 A4D-1s, with the 7700-lb J65-4 or 4B and the three stores stations uprated to 5000 lb. Deliveries began to VA-72 on 26 October 1956. Exactly seven months previously the first A4D-2 (designated A-4B from 1962) had begun flight testing. This introduced the single-surface rudder, with powered operation, attached to a strengthened rear fuselage, but the main advantages were the addition of electronics to guide Bullpup missiles and

a rather clumsy flight-refuelling probe fixed to the right side of the fuselage. No fewer than 542 were produced, the first joining Marines squadron VMA-211 in September 1957.

This was about the time the Navy had expected to phase the Skyhawk out of production, but what actually happened was that the plant switched to the A4D-2N, with limited all-weather capability from an autopilot, terrain-clearance radar and improved gyro, LABS (low-altitude bombing system) for tossing 'nukes' and an angle-of-attack indicator. Another upgrade was the first Escapac seat. The first -2N flew on 21 August 1959. No fewer than 638 were produced, becoming A-4Cs in 1962.

From 1953 Heinemann had been searching for a replacement for the J65, and after trying to get the Rolls-Royce Avon he picked the Pratt & Whitney J52. Ten A4D-3s were ordered, but cancelled, and it was not until 12 July 1961 that Douglas flew the first A4D-5 (A-4E) with a J52-6A rated at 8500 lb. Its better fuel economy increased range by 27 per cent, but an even bigger upgrade was that there were now two pylons under each wing, for a bombload of 8200 lb. Impressive by any standard, this load was increased to 9155 lb, roughly the same as the empty weight, before entry to service in 1962! Douglas built 499 by 1966, by which time Skyhawks were demonstrating their toughness in Vietnam. About 60 A-4Es were passed to Israel, getting 30 mm guns, extended jetpipes and upgraded ECM systems.

While the Navy searched for a VAX (later the A-7) as a replacement, Douglas kept producing new A-4s. On 20 June 1967 deliveries began of the A-4F, with a 9300-lb J52-8A, steerable nosewheel, zero/zero seat, wing spoilers, braking parachute for land operations and, more visibly, a 'camel hump' filled with additional or relocated avionics. The prototype was originally to have been the 500th A-4E, and it was followed by 146 more which were the last A-4s built for Navy attack missions. But in terms of the total-build of A-4 variants Douglas were barely half-way. Two TA-4Es were built with a second dual-control cockpit instead of some fuselage fuel, and these led to 240 TA-4F operational trainers with the guns and weapon pylons. Then came eight A-4Gs for the Royal Australian Navy, 90 specially equipped A-4H and ten TA-4H for Israel, 279 TA-4J trainers used as a FAC (Forward Air Control) platform in Vietnam and as a long-serving mount in Topgun training, ten A-4Ks and four TA-4Ks for New Zealand, 30 A-4KUs and six TA-4KUs for Kuwait, and 100 A-4Ls converted from A-4Cs with A-4F avionics for the Naval Reserve.

Next came the A-4M Skyhawk II for the Marines. Powered by the 11,200-lb J52-408A, this has a completely refined structure and ECM suite, as well as a HUD, inertial platform, mission computer, braking parachute (first seen on the A-4K), better

canopy and more 20 mm ammunition. These have since been updated to A-4Y standard. Douglas built 162, plus 86 A-4Ns for Israel which had the features of the H spliced on. Fifty A-4Ps for the Argentine AF and 16 A-4Qs for the Argentine Navy were ex-USN A-4Bs updated, and they saw much action over the Falklands in 1982, 37 being claimed destroyed by the UK of which 28 were admitted.

Lockheed Aircraft Service completely rebuilt 40 old B-models for Singapore as the A-4S, plus three TA-4S with two canopies in tandem. Last of the major US rebuilds was the OA-4M for the Marines, these 23 tandem-seat FAC platforms having originally been TA-4Fs but given the avionics and many other updates of the Skyhawk II. In 1993 by far the most active programme on this evergreen aircraft is the A-4S-1 Super Skyhawk for Singapore. At first it involved 52 aircraft, but since 1991 further ex-US

ABOVE *That 'Camel Hump' on the A-4M is really big – but no bigger than it had to be*

LEFT *The RNZAF fly the A-4K and two-seat TA-4K, K conveniently meaning Kiwi*

TOP *Late M-model with five avionics upgrades*

ABOVE *Marine A-4Ms in the final year of service. Most belong to VMA-211 'Wake Island Avengers'*

aircraft have been supplied. Phase I upgrade, completed by Singapore Aerospace in 1992, involved fitting the General Electric F404-100D engine (basically an F-18 engine without after-burner, rated at 10,800 lb) which offers many advantages. Phase II, in progress in 1992–93, adds laser/inertial navigation, a GEC Ferranti HUD, a new head-down display and other improvements.

Douglas created the A-4 in the teeth of disbelief and, at prices that today seem ridiculous, delivered 2405 single-seaters and 555 two-seaters. This record speaks for itself, and the jet seems certain to serve well into the next century.

SPECIFICATION

A-4 Skyhawk

One turbojet (A, B, C) 7700 lb Wright J65-4 or -16A, (E, J) 8500 lb Pratt & Whitney J52-6, (F, G, H, K) 9300-lb J52-8A, (M, N, Y) 11,200-lb J52-408A

Dimensions Span 27 ft 6 in (8.38 m); length (most) 40 ft 1½ in (12.22 m), (M, N, Y) 40 ft 3.3 in (12.27 m); wing area 260 sq ft (24.16 m²)

Weight Empty (A) 8400 lb (3810 kg), (E) 9853 lb (4469 kg), (F) 10,030 lb (4550 kg), (Y) 10,465 lb (4747 kg); max take-off (A) 22,500 lb (10,206 kg), (E, F) 24,500 lb (11,113 kg), (export versions) 27,420 lb (12,437 kg)

Performance Maximum speed, clean (A) 664 mph (1069 km/h), (F) 675 mph (1086 km/h); with 4000-lb bombload (F) 593 mph (954 km/h), (M) 645 mph (1038 km/h); combat radius (hi-lo-hi, 4000-lb bombload, all late versions) 460 miles (740 km)

Armament On most versions, two Mk 12 guns each with 200 rounds (some export versions, two 30 mm DEFA 553 with 150 rounds); three (later five) pylons for ordnance load up to (early) 4000-lb, later increased to (most) 8200 lb (3720 kg), (M, N, Y) 9155 lb (4153 kg)

Douglas B-66 Destroyer

First Flight – 28 June 1954

The history of aviation is sprinkled with aircraft which, to save money, were intended to be merely a modified version of a previously existing type. In a very few cases it actually happened like this; examples are the carrier-based versions of the Hurricane and Spitfire and the land-based USAF versions of the F-4 Phantom II. Far more often the small modifications led to further modifications in a seemingly never-ending snowball of changes so that, eventually, the result was a totally different aircraft which would have been produced quicker, cheaper and technically better by starting with the proverbial 'clean sheet of paper'. The B-66 is a classic example.

The objective was sensible enough. Having initially laughed scornfully at Heinemann's 'impossible' weight target for the A3D, the Air Force rather suddenly realised, first, that the A3D could actually be created at 68,000 lb, and, second, that such an aircraft could fly the missions of the 100-ton B-47 over a combat radius up to nearly 1000 miles. The USAF saw that a land-based A3D could be just what it was looking for, especially for the Korean War. With the development already paid for by the Navy, the result could be 'A versatile airplane to handle the bulk of the Air Force's tactical

missions from the stratosphere down to sea level'. It was planned to adhere as closely as possible to Heinemann's existing design, and at the outset it was hoped the changes might be confined to deletion of carrier equipment and the fitting of Air Force avionics. Very soon this pious hope was forgotten, and the result was a series of totally different aircraft made in two Air Force plants which were thousands of miles apart and had never had any connection with the A3D.

As it was originally planned to stick to the A3D design, it was considered there was no need for a prototype. Accordingly, the Air Force went straight in with a June 1952 contract for 175 aircraft in two forms, to be designated B-66 in the pure bomber version and RB-66 in the reconnaissance version. Subsequently, this contract was amended as new variants were substituted. The Air Force allocated the name 'Destroyer', and Douglas the type number 1326 for the RB-66A and 1327A for the B-66B tactical bomber.

It was planned to begin with five RB-66As and then switch to the B-66B, which was expected to be the main version. The entire programme was assigned to the Douglas Long Beach plant. Today the hub of the whole Douglas empire, it was, in

BELOW *USAF 53-0454 was an RB-66, with the tail turret but no wingtip pods*

ABOVE *USAF 54-0450 was an RB-66C, with Elint receivers in the wingtip and tail pods, but retaining tail guns. It was held back as a test aircraft*

1952, a branch factory noted only for such aircraft as the C-47 and C-124, and Chief Engineer John C Buckwalter was glad that his staff had an existing Navy bomber as the basis to work on. The temptation to do better is strong, but in an Air Force versus Navy situation there is also a strong wish merely to be different. An objective assessment might conclude that 98 per cent of the changes introduced in the RB-66A were unnecessary.

Starting with the wing, this was redesigned to eliminate the fold, which was judged no longer necessary. But why stop there? The profile and detail structure were redesigned, the plan view was completely altered to give a longer root chord with a kinked trailing edge, the leading-edge slats were redesigned, and so were the slotted flaps and ailerons, there being two sections of flap on each wing and the ailerons being wider in chord but of much-reduced span, ending more than 8 ft inboard of the tip. Thermal cyclic deicing was provided for the leading edge, and then this totally new wing was set on the fuselage at 2° less incidence.

The fuselage was structurally redesigned to eliminate both the catapult hooks and arrester hook and take out the extra strength which these items had needed. Having thus begun to redesign the fuselage, the Long Beach team went the whole hog and designed a new fuselage from scratch. The pressurised crew compartment was given a totally different structure with a very deep glazed front over the centrally placed pilot, and an opaque rear section with side windows for the navigator and gunner/camera operator side-by-side behind. All three crew were given ejection seats, requiring

synchronised jettisonable roof hatches. The main radar was the APS-27, unrelated to the A3D Westinghouse set and with a radome forming just the lower half of the nose. The nose was longer and more pointed than that of the A3D, and in front of it projected a Flight Refueling Inc probe, this British system having been adopted by Tactical Air Command. The bomb bay for the B-66B was redesigned for Air Force weapons, both nuclear and conventional, while the RB housed a giant K-38 camera and a fan of three K-46 cameras, two vertical columns of photo-flash bombs and two enormous equipment racks. In the rear fuselage was a mass of further new equipment, and in the tail was a General Electric twin-20 mm ball turret and MD-1A fire-control, different even from the GE turrets of the B-36 and B-47. The tail was redesigned in detail, the vertical surfaces no longer being arranged to fold, and all leading edges having cyclic thermal deicing.

Though the Air Force had plenty of aircraft on order with the J57 engine it decided, just to be different, that the B-66 should be powered by the Allison J71. This single-spool engine was used in no other USAF manned aircraft, had marginally less power and greater fuel consumption, and offered no apparent advantage. Of course, it was given a completely new and much longer nacelle and pylon strut, and also required an across-the-board rethink of the accessory power systems. Instead of having bleed-air turbos in the fuselage, the pumps and generators were all shaft-driven and mounted on the engines. One of the very few things left alone was the integral tank in each wing, terminating at a sealed outer end rib at 90° to the leading edge and marking the former hinge axis of the wing fold; the B-66 was also fitted with plumbing and attachments for 450 US gal drop tanks outboard of the engines. Even the landing gear was redesigned, with units of different manufacture folding into

bays with totally different door geometry. A large ribbon braking parachute was added, housed under the extreme tail end. Yet a further difference from the Navy aircraft was that the USAF machines were unpainted.

In view of the immensity of the redesign task the Long Beach engineers did well to finish the first of the five RB-66A development aircraft almost on schedule at the end of May 1954, though of course this was much too late for the Korean War. George Jansen, chief test pilot on the A3D, came to Long Beach and made the first flight with 52-2828 on 28 June 1954, landing at Edwards. The five RB-66A aircraft contributed greatly to the improvements introduced in the main production versions. First, flown on 4 January 1955, came the B-66B bomber.

This was the first to have the Dash-13 engine (the RB-66A being powered by the 9,700 lb YJ71-9) and inflight-refuelling probe. Gross weight was increased, and many refinements were produced at the Tulsa, Oklahoma, plant, a USAF facility re-opened in 1951 under Douglas management to build the B-47E. Deliveries of the B-66B began on 16 March 1956. A further 69 B-66Bs were cancelled, and though these bombers took part in numerous test programmes, including the *Redwing* H-bomb drop at Bikini, they never saw front-line combat duty.

The chief production version was the RB-66B, which was the reconnaissance version of the B-66B and incorporated all the bomber's upgrades. With company Model number 1329, Long Beach built 72

ABOVE *The EB-66C and E fulfilled a vital role in Vietnam*

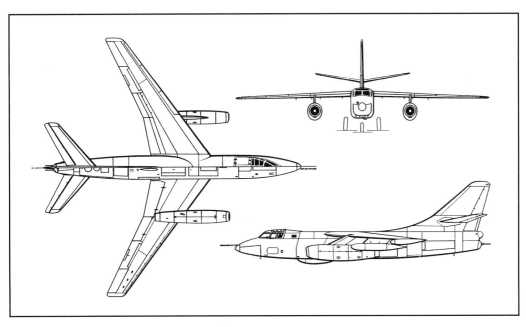

TOP *Its similar exterior belied the fact that the B-66 was a totally different aircraft from the A3D*

ABOVE *USAF 55-0311 was a regular B-66B bomber. It replaced the B-45 with the 47th BW at RAF Sculthorpe in the mid-1950s*

and Tulsa 73. This did see front-line service, principally with Nos 1, 19 and 30 Tac Rec Sqns of the 10th TR Wing in Germany. Two more versions were produced, both at Tulsa. The RB-66C was the first aircraft designed from the start for Elint (electronic intelligence). The bomb bay was replaced by a pressurised compartment for electronic-warfare systems, mainly passive receivers, analysers and direction finders, together with four extra crew. Receiver antennas were housed in the fuselage, in a large belly blister and in wingtip nacelles. The drop tanks were replaced by chaff dispenser pods, and the tail turret was later replaced by a third chaff/flare dispenser installation. A total of 36 were built, and the same number were delivered of the WB-66D weather reconnaissance platform, with a two-man data-handling compartment and various new equipment. Tail guns were retained and chaff pods fitted under the wings.

During the Vietnam period many surviving B/RB-66 aircraft were rebuilt into EB-66C or EB-66E versions configured solely for EW (electronic war-

fare). These were painted in tactical camouflage and elaborately equipped with receivers, active jammers and chaff/flare dispensers. They fulfilled a vital function, notably with the 39th Tac EW Sqn at Bitburg and Spangdahlem in Germany, finally completing the B-66's service in 1975 at the 363rd TRW at Shaw AFB, South Carolina.

SPECIFICATION

B-66B
Two 10,200-lb Allison J71-13 turbojets
Dimensions Span 72 ft 6 in (22.1 m); length (without probe) 75 ft 2 in (22.9 m); wing area 780 sq ft (72.46 m²)
Weight Empty 42,788 lb (19,409 kg); normal loaded 78,000 lb (35,381 kg); maximum 83,000 lb (37,649 kg)
Performance Maximum speed (S/L) 700 mph (1127 km/h), (36,000 ft) 594 mph (956 km/h); range 'over 1500 miles' (2,414 km)
Armament Two 20 mm guns in tail turret; normal bomb load 15,000 lb (6804 kg)

Ilyushin Il-54

First Flight – 3 April 1955

In the early 1950s the attractions of a supersonic bomber appeared in some countries to be so great as to outweigh such adverse considerations as high cost, limited bombload and, especially, very limited combat radius. Great Britain wisely organised a design competition and, after studying proposals from Handley Page, Vickers-Armstrongs and Avro, contracted with Avro for a reconnaissance bomber of extraordinarily advanced design. Unfortunately this was cancelled in 1957 because it was mistakenly thought that all manned fighters and bombers had somehow been made obsolete by missiles. The US Air Force contracted with one company, Convair Division of General Dynamics, for an exceedingly challenging bomber to combine Mach 2 speed with a useful 5000-mile range. The Soviet Union aimed rather lower, and in 1952 ordered competing prototypes for a supersonic tactical bomber from the Ilyushin and Tupolev bureaux.

The possibilities were strictly limited by the engines available. Mikulin's AM-3 was unsuitable on several grounds, and his AM-9 (later Tumanskii RD-9) was too small. The only engine really matched to the task was A M Lyulka's brand-new AL-7, and even then a twin-engined aircraft would have rather limited potential. Ilyushin elected to use the unaugmented AL-7, while Tupolev designed a considerably heavier aircraft powered by two afterburning AL-7F engines.

The original NII requirement specified a maximum level Mach number of 1.15 at 4750 m (15,580 ft), and a practical distance (translated as range, not radius) of 2400–2750 km (1491–1700 miles) with a bomb load of 3 t (6614 lb). Thus, the customer was thinking in strictly tactical terms. Extensive research was carried out on the relative merits of wings swept at 35° and 55°, the latter being selected in early 1953. The first complete general-arrangement drawing, of March 1953, showed a fuselage resembling a smaller version of the Tu-88, with an as-yet unspecified turbojet (called TRD-I) on either side at the wing root. The American Area Rule had not then been discovered, but the aircraft conformed to it, and the outer sides of the nacelles were deeply waisted (Coke-bottled) over and under the wing. At the back was a tail turret and sharply swept T-tail. One of the unconventional features was that each main landing gear was pivoted aft of the rear spar, immediately ahead

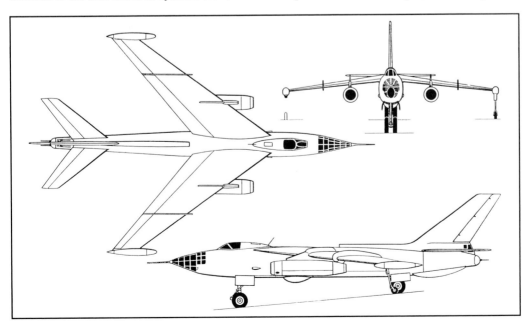

of the flap, and retracted directly forwards with the large single wheel rotating 90° to lie flat in the wing. Ilyushin did not like this, as it necessitated large wheel cutouts in the most highly loaded part of the entire aircraft, and blister fairings over the legs.

Almost immediately it was accepted that they had better start again, and after much further study a new configuration emerged in November 1953. By this time the TRD-I had materialised as Lyulka's AL-7, an outstanding engine which, with the derived AL-21, was to remain in production until 1990. One of the most vexed questions concerned the installation of these big engines, and the final answer was to hang them in external pods on underwing pylons. The other problem was the landing gear. Here the final answer was a bicycle gear, broadly similar to that adopted for the Il-30. The twin-wheel gears were mounted amazingly far apart, requiring extremely strong fuselage construction. Outrigger gears were mounted at the tips of the wings, retracting forwards into streamlined fairings. The horizontal tail was brought down to the fuselage, each tailplane having dihedral and being pivoted to serve as a primary control surface, the elevators adding camber. Despite the power of this surface it was reluctantly recognised that there was no way the pilot could rotate the aircraft to the correct angle of attack on take-off. The answer was *prisedanya* (kneeling); the forward main leg was given a double-extension capability which on take-off forcibly raised the nose. At the start of the run the angle of attack was 5°45' for low drag; as take-off speed was reached, the pilot triggered the extension circuit and within one second the angle of attack rose to the desired 10°. This novel idea was used again in the M-50.

As actually built, the Il-54 was a good-looking bomber, planned in three versions: frontal bomber, the Il-54U dual-pilot trainer (with an extra pilot cockpit in the nose) and the Il-54T torpedo carrier (with a rounded nose, a different radar and the twin guns moved right to the nose). No guns were fitted to the prototype, but it was able to carry the increased bomb load listed in the data. The leading edge was fixed, while the trailing edge had area-increasing flaps inboard and conventional ailerons outboard. At the flap/aileron junction deep fences

ran across the entire chord of the upper surface. Slightly shallower fences were experimented with, both in line with the engine pylon struts and 1 m (39.4 in) further inboard. Some drawings show a double-hinged rudder, but this was not fitted. Flight crew comprised the pilot, in a centreline fighter-type cockpit with ejection seat; the navigator/bombardier, in the glazed and pointed nose with a downward ejection seat; and the radio operator/gunner in the tail turret, again with a downward ejection seat. The forward pressure cabin had a door on the right side. An LAS-5M emergency inflatable boat was carried for ditching.

The prototype was flown by V K Kokkinaki on 3 April 1955. Most testing was very successful, but the landing gear 'complicated the fulfilment of take-off and landing'. It is not recorded whether landings could be made with the nose leg at its normal length. At the end of 1955 more powerful AL-7F engines were fitted, and in early 1956 keel area at the tail was increased by adding two inclined ventral strakes. The Il-54 passed its NII testing, but was not ordered into production.

SPECIFICATION

Il-54 as built

Two Lyulka AL-7 turbojets each rated at 5 t (11,023 lb) dry and 8.6 t (18,960 lb) with afterburner
Dimensions Span 17.65 m (57 ft 11 in); length 28.963 m (95 ft 0 in); wing area 84.6 m² (911 sq ft)
Weight Empty 23,560 kg (51,940 lb); loaded 36,820 kg (81,173 lb), maximum 38 t (83,774 lb)
Performance Max speed 1050 km/h at SL, 1170 km/h (727 mph) at 5 km (16,400 ft); range with maximum bombload 2200 km (1367 miles)
Armament Bomb load of 5 t (11,023 lb); two guns (unspecified) in nose and twin-23 mm tail turret

Il-54 (1955)

Two Lyulka AL-7F turbojets each rated at 6.5 t (14,330 lb) dry and 10 t (22,046 lb) with afterburner
Dimensions Unchanged
Weight Empty 24 t (52,910 lb); loaded 40,660 kg (89,638 lb); maximum 41.6 t (91,711 lb)
Performance Maximum speed 1155 km/h at SL, 1250 km/h (777 mph, Mach 1.18) at 5 km (16,400 ft); range with maximum bombload 2500 km (1,553 miles)
Armament Unchanged

BELOW *The Il-54's wheelbase was unbelievable*

Tupolev Tu-98

The background to this bomber is outlined in the chapter on the Ilyushin Il-54. As explained there, in the early 1950s it was extremely difficult to design a practical supersonic bomber, and in the Soviet Union the problem was compounded by a shortage of available types of engine. In late 1952, when the OKBs (experimental construction bureaux) of Ilyushin and Tupolev were both asked to build prototypes of a supersonic bomber, the only suitable engine was the Lyulka AL-7, one of the best early axial turbojets. This engine was not only of a suitable size and low frontal area but it was also the first engine to feature supersonic flow through the first two compressor stages. From the start it was intended for supersonic applications, and Tupolev naturally elected to use the AL-7F version with an afterburner and fully variable nozzle.

One of the first problems to be resolved was which of the more than 20 possible aircraft configurations should be adopted. The one selected was unusual, with a thin swept wing mounted in the mid position on a large fuselage containing the two engines in the tail, yet fed from inlets well ahead of the wing. This gave minimum frontal area and a perfectly clean and uncluttered wing, but at the same time resulted in very long engine inlet ducts and a narrow-track landing gear.

The wing profile was one of the SR-12S series, but with thickness/chord ratio reduced to a challenging 7 per cent at the root and 6 per cent at the tip. Leading-edge sweep was 60° inboard and 55° outboard, and the combination of high bending moment (resulting from concentration of mass in the fuselage) and high indicated airspeed necessitated the use of thick, integrally stiffened skins machined from stretch-levelled plate. A fence was added right across the upper surface a little way outboard of the kink. Inboard of this fence were double-slotted flaps. Outboard of it were leading-edge flaps and conventional powered ailerons.

The fuselage was finely streamlined, though its shape was severely affected by the very large engine ducts. The navigator/bombardier's glazed compartment in the nose was extended forwards to form a pointed cone with a semi-angle of only 14°. Next came the main navigation and blind-bombing radar, with a slightly bulged ventral radome over the 360° antenna. This was probably of the same type as fitted to the Il-54, and may have been the same *Argon* radar as fitted to the original Tu-88. Next, at the lower level came the steerable twin-

BELOW *The Tu-98 had a very narrow track, and suffered from major design problems*

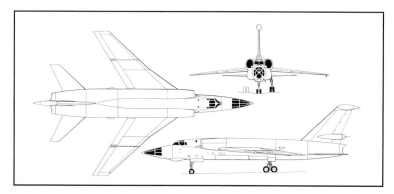

ABOVE *The Tu-98 prototype was shown to Western visitors in 1956 along with Ye-5/-6 prototypes. The visitors thought it was the 'Yak-42'*

improve pressure recovery. There was no provision for varying inlet area or duct profile. The face of each inlet was set at a slightly oblique angle to the airflow and also sloped in front view to match the angle of the adjacent fuselage surface. The ducts were widely separated until they had crossed the wing; then they curved downwards and inwards to meet the compressor inlets of the engines.

Both the vertical and horizontal tail surfaces were sharply swept. The tailplanes were mounted low and fully powered, but also fitted with geared elevators to increase camber of the deflected surface. The fin carried a fully-powered rudder, and at the top was a large circular-section pod which presumably housed the gun direction radar for the tail turret. The latter, with twin NR-23 cannon, was installed beneath the rudder and just above the jet nozzles. There was no provision for manual control of the guns. Each main landing gear comprised a very neat four-wheel bogie, with a single shock strut and a diagonal strut pivoted to the top of the leg and the front of the bogie beam. This second strut was an hydraulic jack which determined the inclination of the bogie beam prior to landing and inverted the bogie during the rearwards retraction cycle. The bomb bay, occupying the space between the landing gears, was remarkably large and very similar to that of the strategic bombers derived from the B-29. A braking parachute was housed in a compartment under the rear fuselage, and it was intended that a battery of rockets should be used to reduce the take-off run and boost speed at high altitude, but this was not fitted.

Existence of this aircraft was revealed to an American delegation which visited Kubinka in June 1956. NATO called the aircraft *Backfin*, and for many years it was for some reason thought to be the 'Yakovlev Yak-42'. Like other previously unknown aircraft unveiled on that occasion, the Tu-98 had already been rejected as a production type. Though in some respects it was superior to the Il-54, it was considered nevertheless vulnerable to defensive missiles, unlike tactical or strategic ballistic missiles. The first of two prototypes flew for two years from mid-1955. It greatly assisted the design of the Tu-28/128 interceptor, but it had a narrow track and was tricky to fly.

wheel nose gear, retracting to the rear. At the upper level were the cockpits for the pilot and radio operator/gunner, both with hinged canopies behind the vee-windscreens. All three crew had upward ejection seats. Aft of the crew was the main forward fuel tank, followed by the bomb bay under the wing with the central fuel tank above. Aft of the wing was the rear fuel tank, with the compartments for the main landing gears at the lower level.

The engines were mounted close side-by-side in the rear fuselage, with their variable nozzles closely shrouded by the aircraft structure. Overall length of the engine duct from inlet to nozzle was no less than 22 m (72 ft). Each inlet was a plain oval, though with the sharp lip necessary for supersonic flight. To avoid ingesting turbulent boundary-layer air the inlets stood well away from the fuselage, but immediately upstream a small, bulged, centrebody was added to the fuselage which, at Mach numbers beyond about 0.9, generated a fan of inclined shockwaves focused on the outer lip of the inlet to

SPECIFICATION

Tu-98

Two Lyulka AL-7F turbojets each rated at 7 t (15,432 lb) dry and 10 t (22,046 lb) with afterburner

Dimensions Span about 20 m (65/66 ft); length 31 m (102 ft); wing area about 82 m² (883 sq ft)

Weight Empty about 28 t (61,730 lb); maximum about 49 t (108,000 lb)

Performance Maximum speed 1240 km/h (770 mph, Mach 1.17) at 12 km, 1060 km/h (659 mph) in dry thrust at 6 km; combat radius with maximum bombload about 1500 km (932 miles)

Armament Two NR-23 guns, and about 6 t (13,228 lb) of bombs

Dassault Etendard/Super Etendard

First Flight – 24 July 1956

Today major air forces seem to be oblivious of the fact that their costly fixed airbases might be wiped off the map the night before the war starts, but 40 years ago they were deeply concerned about the problem. One answer appeared to be to use light tactical aircraft able to disperse away to short grass strips. NATO Basic Military Requirement 1, drafted in 1954, called for a tactical 'attack fighter' to weigh no more than 10,000 lb (4536 kg) loaded. To power the various contenders Bristol produced the Orpheus turbojet, but Britain declined to take part in NBMR-1. Eventually the finalists were the Breguet 1001 Taon, Dassault Etendard VI and Fiat G.91. The latter design won, and the French, predictably, refused to buy any.

Instead the *Aéronautique Navale* purchased a rather heavier and more powerful Etendard, the IV, whose engine was almost the same SNECMA Atar as used in the Mirage III but without an afterburner. The aircraft could hardly have been more straightforward, though the wing was swept at a sharp 45°, with powered leading-edge droop flaps, doubleslotted flaps, spoilers and powered ailerons with artificial feel. Under the fuselage were two large perforated airbrakes. The tail controls were also powered, and from the first flight of the needlenosed prototype IV on 24 July 1956, piloted by Georges Brian, the Etendard was popular for its manoeuvrability. Nor were its pilots second-class citizens, for the alleged maximum speed was Mach 1.02 at high altitude (in fact the Etendard IV had to be dived to reached beyond Mach 1).

The *Aéronvale* bought two versions, the IVM and the IVP configured for photo reconnaissance and as an air-refuelling tanker. The IVM was a light attack fighter for operation from the carriers *Foch* and *Clemenceau*. Its only odd feature was the nose. On the tip was the tiny pimple over the scanner of the Dassault Aïda radar. Above this was an even smaller infra-red sensor, while along the underside of the nose was a long blade antenna like a shallow fin. This was actually for guiding primitive missiles: the Nord 5103 for air-to-air use and the same maker's big AS.30 for attack on surface targets. The four underwing pylons could also carry various other bombs, rocket pods, Sidewinder missiles or drop tanks. Two 30 mm DEFA guns could be carried, but in practice one was usually replaced by a Tacan receiver. A retractable refuelling probe was fitted just ahead of the cockpit, and of course there were folding wings, catapult spools and an arrestor hook, and for land operation a braking parachute was fitted.

Dassault delivered 68 Etendard IVM and 21 IVP aircraft in 1961–65. The latter equipped *Escadrille* (squadron) 16F, while the IVM equipped 11F, 15F and 17F and No 59 *Escadrille de Servitude*, the training unit at Hyères on the Mediterranean coast. The IVM was too late for the Algerian war and saw little action, though it remained in carrier service to 1980, and with 59S to 1987.

The replacement was meant to be the carrier-equipped Jaguar M, but for purely political reasons Dassault succeeded in getting this rejected and replaced by a somewhat upgraded version of the Etendard called the Super Etendard. This retained almost the same airframe, though the engine is the more powerful Atar 8K-50. In the nose is the

BELOW *The prototype Etendard IVM on test over the Mediterranean in January 1959*

Thomson-CSF/Dassault Agave radar, a vast improvement over the Aïda and also giving a better appearance. The wing was refined on both leading and trailing edges, to enable take-off weight to be considerably increased. Lacking an indigenous capability, Dassault went to the American Kearfott company for the aircraft's inertial navigation system, licensed to SAGEM in France, and Thomson-CSF provided the HUD (head-up display). Not least of the upgrades was that Aérospatiale had developed a formidable anti-ship missile, the AM.39 Exocet, with a range of up to 70 km (43 miles), self-homing radar guidance and a warhead able to knock out many surface ships. Apart from a single AM.39 under the starboard (right) wing, balanced on the left side by a drop tank, other loads could include a single AN.52 nuclear bomb on the centreline or various other loads up to the limit quoted in the data. Two 30 mm DEFA guns are fitted, and over the years progressively better electronic-warfare systems have been installed.

Development was facilitated by conversion of three Etendard IVMs, Jacques Jesberger taking the first of these into the air on 28 October 1974. Dassault expected to produce 100 Supers for the Aéronavale, but escalation in price cut this total to

71, all of which were delivered by 1983. However, assiduous French salesmanship resulted in export contracts for 14 to the Argentine navy and later five (ex-Aéronavale) to Iraq. These export sales were to catapult this very ordinary aircraft into the world's headlines.

When Argentina invaded the Falkland islands on 2 April 1982 the *Comando de Aviación Naval Argentina* had received five Super Etendards and five Exocets, but the missiles had never been attached to the aircraft and, indeed, neither the armourers nor the pilots had learned how to arm or fire the formidable missile. One aircraft was cannibalised to provide spares to enable the remaining four of the *2ª Escuadrilla Aeronaval de Caza y Ataque* to fly to Rio Grande AB in the far south to try to operate against the British ships. By reading the manuals the five missiles were assembled and armed, and the pilots learned the firing drill. On 4 May a single aircraft, using flight refuelling, fired its missile against HMS *Sheffield*. By sheer chance the British destroyer was using its high-power satcom transmitter to talk to the UK and it failed to detect the approach of the Super Etendard low on the horizon, and (unbelievably) even failed to pick up the vital targeting signals from the attacker's radar. The missile struck amid-

BELOW *The 50th production IVM. The missile-guidance antenna, like an undernose fin, was a characteristic feature*

BOTTOM *First flight by the prototype Super Etendard*

ships, the crew not at action stations. Even though its warhead failed to detonate, the impact, and the pathetic damage-control systems of the ship, resulted in its total loss, along with 21 of the crew.

This was a colossal moral victory, which profoundly affected not only the subsequent dispositions of the British ships but also the weapons and defences of British surface warships (which in 1982 were all-but defenceless against close air attack). On 25 May an Exocet was launched against the large container ship *Atlantic Conveyor*. This time the warhead exploded, and the British task force lost not only a ship, but a vast quantity of stores including all but one of the vital Chinook helicopters plus six Wessex and a Lynx, and 19 men.

Iraq was supplied with *Aéronavale* aircraft Nos 65–69 in order to try to sink Iranian tankers, or even tankers of any nationality carrying Iranian crude. France trained 30 Iraqi pilots and armourers. Surprisingly, in Iraqi service the results of the aircraft/missile combination were unspectacular, though about 50 attacks were made, beginning with a Greek tanker on 27 March 1984. In the Gulf War the Iraqi Super Etendards wisely stayed on the ground, while the French carrier *Clemenceau* left her Super Etendards in France.

SPECIFICATION

Etendard IVM
One SNECMA Atar 8 turbojet rated at 4400 kg (9700 lb)
Dimensions Span 9.6 m (31 ft 6 in); length 14.4 m (47 ft 3 in); wing area 28.43 m² (306 sq ft)
Weight Empty 5.8 t (12,786 lb); catapult maximum 9 t (19,840 lb); maximum take-off (land) 10.2 t (22,486 lb)
Performance Max speed 1083 km/h (673 mph, Mach 1.02) at 11 km (36,090 ft); tactical radius (low level, no tanks) 300 km (186 miles)
Armament One 30 mm DEFA gun; up to 1360 kg (2998 lb) of bombs. Nord AS.30 missiles or other stores

Dassault Super Etendard
One SNECMA Atar 8K-50 turbojet rated at 5000 kg (11,023 lb)
Dimensions Span 9.6 m (31 ft 6 in); length 14.31 m (46 ft 11½ in); wing area 28.43 m² (306 sq ft)
Weight Empty 6.5 t (14,330 lb); maximum 12 t (26,455 lb)
Performance Max speed, clean, 1180 km/h (733 mph) at low level, 1086 km/h (675 mph) high; combat radius (one Exocet, one tank, hi-lo-hi) 720 km (447 miles)
Armament Two 30 mm DEFA guns; one AM 39 Exocet missile or one AN 52 nuclear bomb or various other loads including Sidewinder or Magic air-defence missiles to maximum of 2.1 t (4360 lb)

BELOW *Well-judged arrival by a Super aboard the carrier* Clemenceau

Convair B-58 Hustler

First Flight – 11 November 1956

In the years immediately following World War 2 the very idea of a jet bomber presupposed a limited mission radius. As for a supersonic bomber (SSB), that was a mere pipe-dream. Even a supersonic fighter appeared an almost impossible challenge. Of course, other things being equal, big aircraft tend to have longer range than small ones, but as soon as Mach 1 was exceeded, the ratio of lift to drag (L/D) was slashed by much more than 50 per cent. So the B-58, the first supersonic bomber to go into service, was a remarkable technical achievement.

To quote an imaginary example, a jet bomber designed to fly at Mach 0.85 weighing 100,000 lb might reach its maximum speed with a total installed thrust of 5000 lb, because with good design the cruise L/D might reach 20. But to accelerate to Mach 2, while the weight (and thus lift) would remain the same, the drag would reach about 25,000 lb, giving an L/D of only 4. Five times the installed thrust would mean something like five times the rate of fuel consumption; thus, even allowing for the higher speed, the mission radius would be reduced to about one-third of that of the subsonic aircraft. So nobody showed much interest in a supersonic bomber.

Quite apart from this, the propulsion system for a supersonic aircraft posed a further challenge. The simplest answer is a rocket, as was fitted to the first supersonic aircraft, the Bell XS-1, which first 'pierced the barrier' on 14 October 1947. Unfortunately, because it has to carry all the oxygen needed to burn the fuel, a rocket aircraft has even worse range and endurance than an equivalent air-breathing aircraft. This means that, to achieve the high propulsive efficiency needed by a bomber, the engine inlet and nozzle have to be variable in flight in both profile and area. This is difficult enough for the inlet, which has to be moved with high precision against enormous aerodynamic forces, but in the case of the nozzle the material has to withstand almost white-hot temperatures, because (at least until recently) supersonic engines needed an afterburner.

Despite these problems, the wish to thrust ahead with new capabilities – driven alas, by military aspirations and money – were so enormous 40 years ago that anything that looked even vaguely possible was explored in depth. One possible answer to the SSB problem was parasiting. The SSB would accept its limitations on range, and would accordingly hitch a ride either on, or under, or attached to,

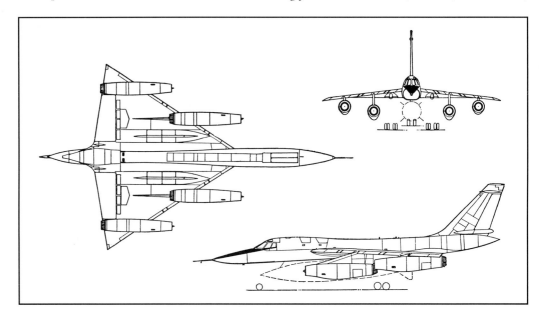

a long-range subsonic aircraft. Then it would cast off quite near the target, make its attack and return to the parent aircraft for a free ride home. Parasiting was difficult enough using fighters (to protect the B-36 parent); with an SSB as the parasite it looked like yet another non-starter.

In 1949 the USAF Air Research and Development Command held an industry competition called GEBO-II (GEneralised BOmber study #2) to obtain the best numerical data available on a manned supersonic attack system. In 1950 the answers came back, most of them proposing uninspired vehicles with from four to 16 engines, and costs to match. The best submission did not arrive until January 1951. Convair's team at Fort Worth had a factory full of lumbering B-36s, but their submission owed more to the tailless-delta work done by their colleagues at San Diego (with the XF-92 and 102). The shapely XB-46 had also been a San Diego creation.

Previously, Fort Worth had merely been a gigantic production plant, but General Manager Ray O Ryan had built up a strong design team headed by another Raymond, R C Sebold, until 1949 when he went to San Diego as VP Engineering for the whole of Convair. The programme then came under the direction of August C Esenwein. From the outset the configuration adopted was that of a tailless delta, most proposals having two very large engines under the wings. The fuselage was extremely slim, housing not much except two crew in tandem and some fuel. From the start Convair cheated by putting everything that could be burned or dropped – the bombs and as much fuel as practical – in an external pod. The idea of a giant external pod was central to the concept, because it enabled the basic aircraft to be significantly smaller,

which not only reduced drag but also made it a smaller target for hostile radars and guns.

The initial submission from Fort Worth, called FZP-110, was to weigh 107,000 lb and achieve a mission radius of 1500 nautical miles (1727 miles), with a dash speed over the target of Mach 1.7. The suggested propulsion was three General Electric J53 turbojets, the third naturally being in the tail. The biggest air-breathing engine at that time, rated at around 17,500 lb, the J53 was to be used without an afterburner. In March 1951 Convair was awarded a Phase I study contract, the system becoming USAF MX-1626. It was in competition with Boeing's MX-1712.

On 11 December 1951 Convair submitted FZP-016, recommending deletion of the tail engine but use of afterburning J53s rated at 23,700 lb, and the addition of a defence-systems operator to the crew. Intensive study had by this time confirmed that Mach 2 could be attained, that mission radius at this speed at high altitude would be about the same as at Mach 0.9 at sea level, and that the same basic design could be configured for level bombing, missile launch, reconnaissance, ground attack and long-range interception. Over the next decade Convair was aware of this versatility, to which was later added the basis for the world's first SST (supersonic transport), but never succeeded in selling any versions but the basic bomber for SAC and a dual conversion trainer.

An SSB obviously needed to have everything possible going for it, and in the early 1950s technical breakthroughs were frequent. One occurred in the field of propulsion. The J53 had been a rather pedestrian engine which obtained its power by being big. In 1951 the man who was to lead GE's aircraft gas-turbine operations, Gerhard Neumann,

ABOVE USAF 59-2433 was one of the 30-strong test fleet. Here it is carrying mission pod B-177

decided to build a prototype turbojet with variable-incidence compressor stator blades, to obtain high pressure-ratio for good fuel economy without making the engine too heavy. At the same time this would achieve higher thrust per unit frontal area, essential for supersonic flight. The Variable-Stator Experimental Engine (VSXE, inevitably called the 'very sexy') ran in 1951, and was to lead to a classic engine called the J79. The other new advance concerned the shape of supersonic aircraft. The Area Rule explained that drag would be minimised if the plot of total cross-section area, including wings, engines and pods, formed a smooth curve from nose to tail. Thus, adding a wing should be compensated by slimming down a body.

Work on the X-24A, prototype of the J79, went ahead in 1952. It was much smaller and lighter than the J53, so the Convair MX-1626 was redesigned in May 1952 with four engines in two twin underwing pods. Fierce competition with Boeing continued, the rival projects becoming MX-1964 and MX-1965. Boeing probably had as good a project as Convair, but when their B-52 was selected as SAC's future strategic bomber in preference to Convair's B-60 this inevitably had a major influence on the SSB competition. Convair were named winner in August 1952. By this time MX-1964 was in the configuration of a refined and bigger version of the F-102 interceptor, with three crew in tandem behind a deep vee-windscreen in a fuselage made even more slender by the Area Rule. Convair were to supply four types of external payload: a free-fall bomb pod (FFBP), recce pod (photo), a delta-winged rocket-propelled cruise missile called the controllable bomb pod (CBP) and an electronic recce pod (called Ferret or El Reco).

Though it had little effect on the design of the aircraft, a factor of historic importance was that the new bomber was the subject of the first Weapon System (WS) contract in history. Much earlier than in other countries, the United States had understood how rapidly-growing technical complexity was making it essential to create new systems as an integrated whole. By 1952 the notion of the WS had matured, each system comprising a basic air vehicle, plus all the onboard propulsion systems, and everything needed to support it in service (for example, spare plastic containers for fruit squash for the crew to drink), as well as everything needed to create it and train everyone to use it (manuals, films, computer tapes, simulators and even new mathematical formulae). The result was that the crucial interactions between every one of millions of parts of hardware and software could be studied and made to interface as intended.

The WS prime contractor became responsible for everything. His job was to deliver an operating system, needing nothing but the humans. In Britain the WS concept was widely misunderstood. As late as 1960 many eminent Britons professed not to understand the meaning of software, and to think a weapon system was the armament carried by an aircraft. In the case of MX-1964 the Weapon Systems were 102A and 102L, the latter being for a reconnaissance version which never went into

BELOW *Ground crews had to take care not to run the heavy access platform into the costly B-58A, or its pod for that matter*

production, though a similar aircraft was later created by conversion. WS-102A included such items as a 44 ft-diameter ribbon braking parachute, a new design of building for drying and packing it, and new ultra-clean rooms for base maintenance on inertial platforms. The system was created by 16 major subcontractors, 1223 suppliers of raw materials and standard items, over 2400 suppliers of specially designed items and facilities and more than 12,000 other companies to supply components or services. Convair was responsible for all of it. (At the same time the company was setting-up an Astronautics Division that would create an even bigger Weapon System, the WS-107A-1 Atlas intercontinental ballistic missile.)

Following receipt of final Pentagon approval, Convair was notified on 10 December 1952 that MX-1964 had become the B-58 (the name 'Hustler' was officially bestowed in 1956). Within days, letter contracts were issued for 16 B-58A weapon systems, and to GE for prototypes of the J79 engine. Subsequently, the company was to claim 'More flight time at Mach 2 than all other engines combined', though of course once Concorde was in service this claim was quickly won by the Olympus. In due course the aircraft contract was changed to two XB-58 prototypes, 11 YB-58A production prototypes for development and 31 mission pods. The two XBs, 55-0660 and 0661, had pre-production J79-1 engines, no pods and few of the required mission systems. That still left a few problems.

Convair achieved the amazingly low structure weight of 13.8 per cent of gross weight. Almost the entire wing, and large parts elsewhere, were made of aluminium-alloy sandwich, with the mirror-like skins bonded by organic adhesive. Even the leading edges had to be designed to soak during supersonic flight at 127°c (260°f), and areas subject to higher temperatures were made of stainless-steel sandwich with the skins brazed on. The wing had an almost pure 60° delta shape, though the trailing edge was inclined slightly forward to the pointed tip. The leading edge was fixed, and before first flight it was given so-called 'conical camber' (first developed for the F-102) in which the edge progressively curves downwards from the root to a maximum at the tip. Thickness/chord ratio was 4.08 per cent near the tip and a remarkable 3.46 per cent at the root.

So thin was the wing that even the specially configured main landing gears had to be stowed in a compartment which projected several inches above and below, requiring prominent fairings starting at single points 10 in behind the leading edge. Cleveland Pneumatic Tool and Menasco created the most remarkable landing gears seen up to that time, and perhaps not equalled since. The gears had to be incredibly tall, like the legs of a mosquito, because the angle of attack on take-off or landing exceeded 17°, and there also had to be plenty of room under the fuselage to load the huge pods. The vertical nose leg carried landing and taxy lamps and twin steering cylinders, and was of the gatefold type to pull the whole unit up almost vertically past the nose of the pod. The main units were double gatefolds in ultra-high-strength steel, the upper part pivoting forwards and the lower part to the rear to swing the trucks almost vertically upwards to be stowed inverted. Remarkably, total depth of the retracted gear was held to only 22 in by using eight tyres. Inflation pressure, wheel rpm and peripheral speed (the gear was qualified to 306 mph) were in a realm never before attempted.

Another record was set by the hinge moment of 120,000 lb-ft needed to move the giant trailing-edge elevons at the design indicated airspeed. With

ABOVE *Convair Fort Worth gave SAC the B-58 with four engines; Convair Astronautics gave SAC the SM-65 Atlas, with five*

a root chord of 7 ft these surfaces accounted for one-eighth of the total area of the wing, yet their power units drove them at 20° per second. The linked inboard elevons each had four power units, and the smaller outboard surfaces two. The only other control surface was the single rudder, with a power unit at the extreme top and bottom.

It was typical of the B-58 that the engine nacelles were like nothing previously attempted, though aerodynamicists had previously worked out the pressure-recovery of various kinds of inlet. The inlet adopted was circular, with a large conical centre-body faired into the centre of the engine inlet 6 ft downstream. At take-off each conical spike was retracted fully aft to capture as much air at low speed as possible. As Mach number increased, the spike moved forwards until at Mach 2 it projected far ahead to focus an inclined shock on the sharp lip of the inlet, the annular gap being reduced to the minimum. Provided the automatic inlet system worked, all was well; any malfunction and the resulting 'buzz' or inlet-unstart nearly took the offending engine off the wing. The noise could be clearly heard by the crew even at Mach 2 (the sound travelling inside the aircraft), and if it was an outer engine the load on the fin as the B-58 tried to travel sideways was enormous. The outers were almost at the tips, beyond the fuel.

Though compact to the point of being claustro-phobic – Gen LeMay emerged from the mockup proclaiming 'It doesn't fit my ass' – the three cockpits occupied nearly half the volume of the fuselage. The pilot had a stick, and a good view through very deep windows. Next came the nav/bombardier who managed the most complicated set of systems in any aircraft up to that time, the central system being ASQ-42(V) produced by Sperry. This combined seven subsystems – vertical, heading, navigation, sighting, bombing, indicator and mal-function – served principally by the nose radar, an inertial platform amidships with an astrotracker (to lock-on to selected stars) above it, a doppler radar in the tail, a radar altimeter at both ends and a bulky computer to tie it all together. The computer was of the analog type, digital technology then being far in the future.

The whole system had to interlink dozens of variables, and do it in real time. Variables in a nuclear bomb drop included anomalies in navigation, altitude above ground zero (the point vertically under detonation), burst height, winds at various heights, air densities, Coriolis effects (for example, due to Earth's rotation) and precise aircraft attitude, speed and vertical velocity at point of release. The bomb/nav could easily make the B-58 fly along any given rhumb-line or great circle, and later ASQ-42(V) was modified to fly automatic terrain-follow-ing and LABS (low-altitude bomb system) tosses in which a nuclear weapon is thrown upwards either ahead or 'over the shoulder'.

The third man was the DSO (defence-systems operator). His main concern was to manage the electronic-warfare systems, which, from the start, included radar warning receivers looking aft from the tail and wing fillet fairing, and ahead from the

wing roots. The main systems were ALQ-16, which also included active jammers, and ALR-12. The latter managed the chaff dispenser system housed in five boxes behind each main-gear bay, firing upwards. The DSO also had a display from the tail radar which enabled him to sight and fire the M61A1 gun in the tailcone, fed from a 1120-round tank further forward.

Each cockpit had an upward-hinged roof. The unique feature was that each seat was mounted inside a capsule, normally open at the front, which following failure of pressurisation or oxygen could be closed and sealed. The flight controls were inside the capsule, and windows enabled each crew-member to continue working. The real problem was emergency escape, and the USAF took the problem of wind blast at Mach 2 very seriously. For abandoning the aircraft each man would jettison his roof and fire the capsule, which was designed to protect the occupant to at least a dynamic pressure of 1240 lb/sq ft, equivalent to the B-58 IAS (indicated airspeed) limit at all altitudes. If fired at high altitude the capsule fell free to 15,000 ft, when a 32 ft parachute was deployed. The capsule was intended thereafter to serve as a survival shelter or lifeboat, containing such things as food and drink, anti-sunburn lotion and fishing tackle. Marvellous, and the idea was repeated on the F-111, but Convair and Stanley Aviation took so long to qualify the capsule that it was not cleared for use until 1963. On the final test a brown bear survived ejection at 1060 mph at 45,000 ft!

Though originally the B-58 was designed for heights greater than this, it was recognised that flying very low would avoid early detection by enemy radars, and much effort was spent investigating attack at 500 ft altitude. The production engine was the J79-3B, and at normal, MIL (maximum dry) and afterburning power it was kept at 7460 rpm. At 500 ft in MIL power thrust was 10,000 lb, and this was enough to reach the IAS limit at Mach 0.925. In fact on 18 September 1959 chief test pilot Beryl A Erickson (a man, despite the name) took a production aircraft 'faster than a .45 pistol bullet' non-stop 1400 miles from Fort Worth to Edwards at no time going above 500 ft. This is remarkable, because the structure load limits were $+2/-0$g and there was no active ride-control system to damp out turbulence.

Security on the B-58 was exemplary, and when 55-0660 was rolled out on 31 August 1956 no unauthorised person (in the West, at least) had any idea what it looked like. (There had been some funny artist's impressions, at least one with eight engines.) On that day someone took a photo from the roof of the plant and syndicated it via a news agency. The world saw something looking like a preying mantis, amazingly small and seemingly with height equal to the span. The two prototypes were not equipped for the pod, and were devoid of almost all military systems, but it still took until 11 November to clear -660 for Erickson to make the first flight. Mach 1 was exceeded on 30 December.

No fewer than 30 aircraft were needed to clear the Hustler for combat duty. Altogether Convair built 116: the two XBs; the 11 YB-58As (55-0662/0672), with Dash-5 or -5A engines and an increasing amount of mission equipment; 17 YB-58A-10s (58-1007/1023); and 86 B-58As, for inventory, made up of 36 B-58A-10 (59-2428/2463), 20 B-

58A-15 (60-1110-1129) and 30 B-58A-20 (61-2051/2080). A host of planned developments never got off the drawing board, and contracts for the B-58B, C, D and E were cancelled. The B-model (60-1109) was to have been a longer-ranged version with Pratt & Whitney J58 engines, as fitted to the Lockheed Blackbirds, and a weight of 198,000 lb. The B-58C was to have a longer body and J58s, the B-58D was an interceptor and the B-58E a multi-mission bomber and ALBM launcher. The CV-58-9 was to be a J58-engined SST with 52 passenger seats, and there were several derived SST versions which Congress considered a near miss 'as a stepping stone to the Mach 3'.

To round off the variants, Convair and the Air Materiel Areas did have a major job converting many of the 116 aircraft. Of the original YBs, nine were brought up to B-58A standard for use as attrition replacements. The second XB and seven YBs (662, 663, 668, 670, 671 and 672 and 58-1007) were converted into TB-58A conversion trainers with dual pilot cockpits, the instructor in the middle cockpit having a periscope. All 17 YB-58A-10s were either completed or converted as RB-58A reconnaissance aircraft, with the pod configured for multisensor reconnaissance.

In February 1958 Convair had received a contract for 35 FFBP pods designated MB-1, this being based on two for each YB-58A and one spare. In fact the pod situation became complex, with three main versions for the inventory selected from a host of projects. The production FFBP was the MB-1C, one of the biggest stores ever dropped from an aircraft. A finely streamlined body with four delta tailfins, it housed 3461 gal (4156 US gal, 15,732 litres) of fuel, and an integral munitions bay which usually

incorporated a B28 or, after 1963, a B53. The main alternative was the even bigger TCP (two-component pod), made up of an upper component attached to the aircraft which was recessed into the huge lower component hanging from it. The upper component was the BLU-2/B-3, containing fuel and a munitions bay usually housing a B28. Surrounding and almost completely hiding it was the huge BLU-2/B-2, filled with about 5500 gal (44,000 lb) of fuel. The usual reconnaissance pod was the LA-331A, with a choice of cameras (usually a group of KA-56) and side-looking radar. Two types of Elint (electronic intelligence) pod were qualified, containing the comprehensive Melpar ALD-4 system, but there is no record of their operational use.

On most missions all tanks were filled and the take-off and climb were performed on internal fuel. This was then replenished by a tanker, hooked up to the boom receptacle ahead of the windscreen, above the radar. Apart from its very high nose-up attitude at KC-135 speed, the B-58 posed no problems during air refuelling, and in the leading edge of the fin were an excellent row of position and IFF transmitters including one specially for tanker rendezvous. Subsequently, fuel would be taken solely from the pod(s), bearing in mind that CG position had to be maintained, and that during supersonic acceleration fuel had to be pumped from front to rear to counter the aft shift in wing lift (centre of pressure).

One of the last additions to be cleared for service was originally called MWC, from Multiple Weapons Capability. This comprised a very long, but slender bomb rack, more properly called an ejector/release unit, mounted under each wing root. On it could be carried two bombs in tandem, usually thermonuclear B43s or, from early 1968, the B61.

The B-58A joined the Air Force in December 1959, when the first production aircraft (many were flying, and it happened by chance) was assigned to the 65th Combat Crew Training Squadron at Carswell AFB, adjoining the Fort Worth plant. The first combat unit was the 43rd Bomb Wing, a three-squadron unit in SAC's 19th Air Division, 2nd Air Force. It formed at Carswell, and was declared operational on the B-58A on 1 August 1960. A month later a lone aircraft from the 43rd competed in the annual SAC Combat Competition, which was held that year at Bergstrom. To the incredulity of the B-47 and B-52 crews the B-58A was placed first in both high-level and in low-level radar bombing. Subsequently, the 43rd moved to their own base, Little Rock, ARK, and proceeded to grab headlines around the world.

Maj Henry J Deutschendorf and crew took from the Soviet Union the records for a 2000-km (1242-

LEFT *In this cubby-hole worked the WSO. Like his two colleagues, he could snap himself inside a capsule (part seen at right)*

mile) circuit with payloads of 0, 1000 and 2000 kg, flown at 1061.8 mph (1708.75 km/h). Maj Harold E Confer and crew gained the Thompson Trophy for a 1000-km (621-mile) circuit carrying a 2000-kg (4410 lb) payload at 1284.73 mph (2067.6 km/h). Maj Elmer E Murphy and crew won the trophy donated in 1930 by Louis Blériot for the first pilot to exceed 2000 km/h continuously for 30 minutes (at that time utter science fiction). Murphy's 59-2451 merely obeyed its ASQ-42(V) and described a perfect circle of the required diameter, flown in full afterburner. The result was 1073 km flown in 30 min 43 sec, equating to just over 2095 km/h for the exact 30 min.

On 26 May 1961 Maj William R Payne and crew took off from Carswell, flew to Washington and New York City at Mach 0.93 and then accelerated. Slowing to take fuel east of Greenland and near 20°W, they landed in foul weather at the Paris airshow having halved the previous transatlantic record, the time from New York being 3 h 19 min 51 sec (1089 mph). Sadly, a mechanical failure (possibly of the elevon ratio changers) caused 59-2451 (the same aircraft as flown by Maj Murphy) to disintegrate in cloud during the airshow.

On 5 March 1962 a 43rd crew flew from Carswell to a point over the Pacific west of Los Angeles, then east to New York City, back to the same point off the West coast, and back to Carswell. On both westbound legs the B-58 easily beat the Sun, and the overall figure, including enormous turns at the end of each leg, was 4 h 41 min 11 sec, for 1044.96 mph. On 18 September 1962 another crew carried a 5000-kg (11,023-lb) load in a zoom from Mach 2 to 85,360.84 ft (26,018 m), while a test crew demonstrated the launch of a satellite-inspection vehicle. In late 1961 the 305th BW became operational at Bunker Hill, IND, later renamed Grissom AFB. Their claim to fame was a tough flight from Tokyo Haneda to London Heathrow on 16 October 1963. They were credited with an average, including air refuellings, of 938 mph,

but this was based on the ideal great-circle distance of 8028 miles; the distance actually flown, mainly over the inhospitable Arctic, was well over 9100 miles, making the true average over 1000 mph.

The two B-58A wings trained at both high and low levels. One accomplishment no other SAC bomber could rival was that, from the Ground Alert 'cocked' position (inertial warmed up, for example), a B-58 could be airborne inside five minutes. The B-58 was always a very demanding aircraft. For example, the two backseaters had hardly any external view, but had such a high workload this hardly mattered, and when Convair test pilot Dick Johnson was asked 'Is it possible to land the F-111 with the wings jammed at maximum sweep?' he replied, 'Just about, it would be like a B-58'. Despite all the high demands, it was a popular aircraft, and the 43rd and 305th were distressed when on 29 October 1969 the Department of Defense announced retirement of the force with effect from 31 January 1970.

Back in 1963 when Defense Secretary McNamara had asked the Air Force for proposals for a new manned Mach 2 bomber (this at the height of controversy over the Mach 3 B-70), he was rather taken aback when the SAC Commander, Gen' Thomas S Power, asked for the B-58 to be restored to production. He called it 'One of the finest weapon systems in the world today'. He was well aware of the aircraft's heavy dependence on air refuelling, but still considered it a valuable part of the inventory. The sole reason given for withdrawal was excessive operating cost.

SPECIFICATION

B-58A

Four General Electric J79-5B turbojets each rated at 10,000 lb dry and 15,600 lb with maximum afterburner

Dimensions Span 56 ft 10 in (17.32 m); length 96 ft 9 in (29.49 m); wing area 1543 sq ft (143.35 m²)

Weight Empty (no pod) 55,560 lb (25,202 kg); max take-off 163,000 lb (73,937 kg); max after air refuelling 177,120 lb (80,342 kg)

Performance Maximum speed with pod (S/L) 701 mph (1128 km/h), (high altitude) 1322 mph (2128 km/h, Mach 2); range without air refuelling 5125 miles (8248 km)

Armament One M61A1 gun with 1120 (max 1200) rounds; up to 19,450 lb (8823 kg) of dropped stores, as detailed in text

Blackburn (HSA, BAe) Buccaneer

First Flight – 30 April 1958

As it was British, the Buccaneer was destined to be one of the most misunderstood, vilified and undervalued aircraft in history. Designed to a Royal Navy requirement of 1952 which was unique in its perceptive long-range vision, it managed to survive the 'no more manned aircraft' policy of 1957, flew in 1958 and joined the Royal Navy in 1961. Then, despite its obvious qualities of low-level structure, heavy bombload, outstanding speed and long range, it was disdainfully rejected by the RAF, which regarded 'such an obsolete subsonic aircraft' as an insult. Not even the existence of detailed projects for greatly stretched and upgraded versions made any difference, until cancellation or abandonment of all the glittering alternatives reluctantly forced this derided aircraft on the RAF in October 1969. From then on it was recognised for what it had always been; and in 1989 one 'Bucc driver' said 'The only possible replacement is another Buccaneer, with new avionics'.

To the astonishment of rivals, Blackburn Aircraft was picked in July 1955 to build its B.103 project to meet specification M.148T. In turn this had been issued to meet a Naval requirement called NA.39, of June 1952, calling for a carrier-based bomber to fly at Mach 0.85, carry a nuclear weapon internally and other weapons internally or under the wings, cruise at 200 ft altitude using avionics for open-sea navigation and attack on surface ships, and have a radius of action of 400 nautical miles even with the last 100 miles to the target flown just above the waves at about 650 mph. The requirement had been triggered by the appearance of the Soviet *Sverdlov* class heavy cruisers. Like most of its rivals the B.103 was a twin-jet, with a length of around 60 ft and weight of about 40,000 lb. Where it set completely new standards was in its use of extensive BLC (boundary-layer control) using hot air bled at high pressure from the engine compressors. This was to be blown at sonic speed through narrow slits along the trailing edge across the top of the flaps and drooping ailerons. This idea had been developed in the USA, mainly by John D Attinello, but Blackburn's team, led by Barry Laight and Roy Boot, took it much further. Soon they threw away their leading-edge slats and instead arranged narrow slits along the hot-air anti-icing pipes so that they blew from the leading edge over the top of the wing and the underside of the tailplane. The latter was

BELOW *S.2 XN980 is a few seconds away from being overhead Buckingham Palace*

ABOVE *XT287, an S.2A of No 237 OCU, parked with wings folded at Lossiemouth*

LEFT *Trials aircraft at Holme with FR probe, bomb-carrying tank door and triplets of thousand-pounders*

fitted with a hinged flap (like an elevator) which was normally locked neutral but which was automatically deflected upwards to counter the large trim change in the high-lift regime (roughly three times that of a normal unblown part-span flap). All this blowing had to be allowed for in the design of the engine, which would otherwise have far exceeded its turbine entry temperature, but the gains were enormous, for example in allowing wing area to be reduced by over 30 per cent. This transformed Blackburn's design into an aircraft which is still highly competitive today.

Blackburn had picked the Armstrong Siddeley Sapphire as the engine, fitted with jet deflection for STOL performance, but the BLC system made it possible to replace these big turbojets by much smaller DH Gyron Juniors with fixed jetpipes. A contributory factor was discovery in the USA, by Richard Whitcomb, of the Area Rule for minimum transonic drag. Incorporation of this rule, and of BLC, the use of flutter models and other new techniques, was facilitated by American assistance via the Mutual Weapons Development Program. When redesigned to conform to the Area Rule a visible consequence was prominent bulging of the rear fuselage, which increased capacity for fuel and equipment. The engines were mounted in the wing roots, causing bulges in the sides of the fuselage which, because of Area Rule, curved in from the plain inlets and out again at the jetpipes. Broad and thin, the wing swept at 40° inboard, decreasing to just over 30° at the wide tip. There was no dihedral, but the outer panels folded upwards hydraulically to reduce span to 19 ft 11 in. Between the folds primary loads were taken by three massive machined steel forgings, with spars in the wings, banjo rings round the jetpipes (the engines being ahead of these transverse structures) and strong spider frames passing over the large weapons bay. The main landing gears were very short, and with levered suspension became even shorter as they folded inwards under the jetpipes into bays closed by single wing-hung doors. The nose gear folded back under the tandem cockpits. Immensely strong

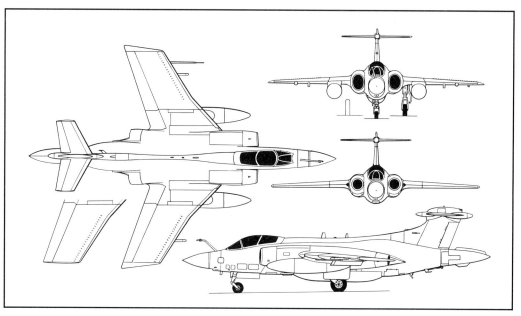

ABOVE 'Buccs' gathered at 'Lossie' in April 1988 to celebrate the type's 30th anniversary. The nearest jet belongs to No 12 Sqn, and carries a jammer-pod

and stiff, the wings had solid machined ribs and machined skins, Blackburn having to design and build their own skin mills. The double-skinned upper part of the fuselage formed integral tanks. The tail end of the fuselage was formed by prominent and powerful left and right airbrakes, driven by a single jack in the 4000 lb/sq in hydraulics, pressure in the flying-control system being reduced to 3300 to meet aeroelastic requirements. Each engine drove a 6 kW DC generator, but main avionic power was supplied by a 10 kVA alternator driven at constant speed by a bleed-air turbine.

For the first time in a British programme the sensible decision was taken to build 20 aircraft for development, and the first of these, XK486, was trucked in pieces from the factory at Brough, on the north bank of the Humber in Yorkshire, to the

Royal Aircraft Establishment at Bedford. After various problems this aircraft, painted an attractive bright blue above and white below, was very successfully flown by Derek Whitehead, with Bernard Watson as observer, on the last contractual day, April 30 1958. By this time the NA.39 or B.103, soon to be named Buccaneer, was also being seen as a possible basis with which to meet the RAF's OR.339 requirement, but the OR.339 story is told in the TSR.2 chapter.

Blackburn set up a flight-test department at Holme on Spalding Moor, 18 miles from Brough, to which the other 19 development aircraft, and all subsequent Buccaneers, were towed on their own wheels. No 3 introduced the RN specified colour scheme of dark grey above and light grey below, but the 40 S.Mk 1 (S for strike) for the Fleet Air Arm were painted in anti-flash white, with correspondingly pale markings. They were delivered in 1961–64, equipping No 700Z (the Intensive Trials Flight) and Nos 800, 801, 803 and 809 Sqns. With a thrust/weight ratio of 0.25 it took time to work up speed, Cdr 'Spiv' Leahy, CO of No 700Z, commenting 'On take-off events occur frequently enough to avoid feelings of boredom', but with cat take-offs and arrested landings in deck operation there were not many serious problems. Buffet forced addition of a prominent acorn at the fin/tailplane junction, and prolonged effort was needed to perfect the flight controls and autopilot, though the BLC system was remarkably trouble-free. It also seemed a pity that the neat retractable flight-refuelling probe had, after endless tinkering, to be replaced by a crude probe fixed permanently high above the nose on the centreline. There was also prolonged trouble with the air-turbine alternator, without which the Ferranti Blue Parrot radar went blank.

Once these snags had been cleared even the underpowered S.1 proved a valuable aircraft. Range was extended by adding flush-fitting 250-Imp gal (1136-litre) drop tanks under the inner wings. The bomb bay was covered by a rapid-action rotary door, and it was on this that stores were attached, examples being four 1000-lb GP bombs, a 440-Imp gal (2000-lit) tank or a recce pack carrying a vertical F97 night camera, six F95 day cameras (six vertical, two oblique and one forward) and/or side-looking radar or infra-red linescan. Under the wings were attachments for four pylons, each of which could carry a 1000-lb bomb, a rocket launcher or a Bullpup guided missile.

Perhaps the most fundamental problem was that, from the outset, the Gyron Junior had been only marginally powerful enough. Various later versions existed, but after studying many alternatives the decision was taken in 1960 to switch to the much newer Rolls-Royce RB.168, a specially produced military version of the RB.163 (Spey) with BLC bleeds from the HP stages 7 and 12. The air inlets were considerably deepended, but the ducts went through the original airframe structure. At the same time an equally wise decision was to throw out the air-turbine alternator and mount a 30-kVA alternator on both engines, driven by a constant-speed drive. Navigation by MRG.2 (master reference gyro) was much later transferred to an inertial platform, and extended triangular wingtips were added (sadly, later still, it was found these distinctive tips caused an unexpected stress which led to inflight front-spar failure, and they were removed).

XK526, one of the 20 Mk 1 development aircraft, flew with Spey engines on 17 May 1963, and subsequently 84 S.2s were built for the Royal Navy.

ABOVE *Standard kit on these No 237 OCU aircraft comprises bomb-door tank, Sidewinder training simulator, AVQ-23 Pave Spike laser designator (left inboard) and ALQ-101(V)-10 jammer pod (right inboard)*

A further 16, designated S.50, were supplied to the South African Air Force (SAAF), with the underwing tanks enlarged to 400 Imp gal size and with two ATO (assisted-take-off) booster rockets for hot and high airfields. These rockets were Bristol Siddeley BS.605s, each rated at 3000 lb thrust, fed with HTP (high-test peroxide) and kerosene for 30 sec. They retracted into each side of the rear fuselage beside the hook. Among the SAAF weapon fit were Nord (Aérospatiale) AS.30 guided missiles.

TOP *In the early days of a flight-test programe it is rare to photograph the first three prototypes in formation. Date, 26 March 1959*

ABOVE *The Royal Navy's S.1s were painted anti-flash white*

They could also be equipped with a flight-refuelling 'buddy pack' in the weapons bay, and in 1966 the CO of No 24 Sqn, SAAF, made a non-stop flight of over 5000 miles with two buddy hook-ups.

South Africa then ordered a further 16 S.50s, but the 1964 Labour government took great delight in forbidding this much-needed deal. At that time there was a strange situation in which the government actively hated the British aerospace industry, and did all it could to hurt it, whilst extolling the virtues of everything bought for dollars. It prevented the SAAF from ordering a second batch of 16, and even prohibited replacing a Mk 50 which

was lost during the long delivery flight in October 1965. As chief designer Roy Boot says in his book *From Spitfire to Eurofighter*, 'Those who wanted it were not allowed to have it, and those who would have been allowed to have it didn't want it ... influenced by the failure of the RAF to adopt it ...'

Normally the Air Staff have at least a rough idea of what kind of kit they want, but perhaps in 1966 they really were so fascinated by swing wings and Mach 2 that they were unable to see any merit in the British tactical bomber on their own doorstep. To recall the flavour of the time, the *Daily Telegraph* wrote on 11 December 1966, 'Mr Healey may try to force on the RAF an obsolete subsonic bomber ... acceptance of the plane would make the RAF the world's only air force operating a subsonic bomber'. Apart from the crass inaccuracy of the last statement, the writer was perhaps ignorant of the fact that with four 1000-lb bombs a Buccaneer at 200 ft was significantly faster than an F-111, Mirage IVA, Tornado or Phantom with the same load.

During the 1960s the design team at Brough had shown how several quite simple modifications could turn the Buccaneer into a bomber able to carry a heavier load than a Lancaster, and carry it further whilst using a rough 4000-ft strip and attacking at over 450 kt at treetop height. The main changes proposed were: either tandem-wheel main gears or four-wheel bogies, with a tyre pressure reduced from 230 lb/sq in to only 100; a rotary bomb door incorporating a tank of 600 gal capacity; and four pylons on altered wing stations able to carry Martel missiles or triple ejector bomb racks (or, on the inner pylons, 430-gal tanks or a Martel data-link pod). A wealth of other projects for the RAF followed, including the P.150 which with Spey 202 (Phantom) engines with afterburners and thrust reversers would have reached Mach 1.8.

What actually happened was that on 11 July 1968 the F-111K was cancelled and it was announced that a perfectly ordinary Buccaneer would be ordered instead (and to replace the defunct TSR.2 and AFVG). As the government of the day had cancelled the CV-01 carrier and announced that the Fleet Air Arm would henceforth not fly fixed-wing aircraft, almost all surviving S.2s were transferred to the RAF, starting with No 12 Sqn on 1 October 1969. By this time many FAA aircraft had been converted to carry three Martel missiles, with the necessary data-link on No 3 pylon, becoming S.2Bs, the unmodified aircraft being called S.2As. In addition 43 additional S.2Bs were ordered for the RAF, as the Blackburn B.105, delivered in 1970–76. Reason prevailed, and the four wing pylons were equipped for triple 1000-lb bombs or tandem triple 500-pounders, or a pneumatic starter pod or a Mk 20 HDU (inflight refuelling hose-drum unit). In addition the bomb doors were equipped to incorporate a tank (but of 425-gal capacity), with negligible drag penalty. Then, to save a few shillings the triple ejector racks were eventually cancelled along with the previously mentioned multi-sensor (cameras, IR and SLAR) recon pack designed to fit on the bomb door and rotated 180° when needed.

Predictably, once crews got their hands on the 'Bucc' they grew to love it. In the things that mattered – ability to fly really low (100 ft), ability to fly really fast (580 kt) and ability to fly really far (mission radius 1000 nm with typical bombloads) – this derided and supposedly obsolete aircraft was better than anything else. Indeed, in the matter of attack speed and radius it was, on most missions, better then the Tornado, which was supposed to be about two generations later.

The chief RAF units were No 237 OCU and Nos 12, 15, 16 and 208 Sqns, while seven aircraft were modified for trials at the RAE and (by Marshall of Cambridge) with Tornado avionics. Over the years updates included addition of self-defence Sidewinders (AIM-9G initially), retarded bombs, both AJ.168 and AS.37 versions of Martel, the BAe Sea Eagle anti-ship cruise missile, AVQ-23E Pave Spike laser designator, ALQ-101(V) jammer pod, 2-in, 68-mm and 3-in rocket launchers and the WE.177 tactical nuclear bomb.

To the astonishment of such people as F-15 drivers, these seemingly pedestrian aircraft proved extremely effective and elusive in *Red Flag* and other multi-national exercises. The main adverse factor was that the structure had originally been designed for the hi-lo-hi mission, and in the lo-lo-lo sortie the onset of fatigue damage was at least double that predicted; indeed, in short training missions it was treble. A further factor was an annoying triviality. One of the most severely loaded main-spar ring frames contained a 4-in hole for one of the big bleed pipes. In the change from S.1 to S.2 this frame became a fire-zone boundary, so a sealing gaiter had to be added round the duct hole. This was secured by six bolts, with 0.19-in holes. In 1971 a Buccaneer at Singapore was found to have a major crack in this crucial frame, and a prolonged investigation established that, instead of being vertical as had been supposed, the greatest stress passed right through one of the 0.19-in holes. Eventually it was decided to make two new undrilled rings for each aircraft, since when fatigue problems have been minor.

In 1985 British Aerospace was appointed prime contractor in a major S.2B update programme. Various update programmes had been studied and argued at Ministry level from 1963 onwards, but if you take no decision nobody can blame you for getting it wrong. The only trouble is, the kit in service still needs updating, and it eventually costs far more. In this case, 22 years, replacing action by talk was about par for the course. Of course, far more could have been done, and the result was severely constrained by money. Ferranti improved the Blue Parrot radar, added an inertial navigation system and linked the two together. Marconi

Defence Systems, which supplied the ARI.18228 radar warning system with passive antennas at the nose and tail of the fin/tailplane fairing covering E/J bands, added forward-facing C/D-band antennas in wing leading-edge pods together with a new cockpit display. Louis Newmark upgraded the automatic flight control system, and Tracor supplied ALE-40 dispensers for chaff on the inner side of the outer wing pylons and for flares in the underside of the rear fuselage.

Design and flight clearance was carried out by BAe Brough, but the actual retrofit programme was carried out by BAe Woodford. The 42 aircraft

BELOW *An S.2 of the Royal Navy with Bullpup missiles and rocket pods*

BOTTOM *An S.2 still with RN No 801 Sqn flying from* Victorious

involved had all been returned to the RAF by February 1990, for service in the maritime role with Nos 12 and 208 Sqns. Their primary weapon was the Sea Eagle anti-ship missile, but they retained all their original versatility. To the great regret of everyone familiar with the aircraft they are being replaced by Tornados in 1993–94.

In 1990 RAF Lossiemouth was advised that 'under no circumstances' would any Buccaneers be needed in the Gulf. On the morning of 23 January 1991 an urgent signal was received calling for Buccaneers to fly out as quickly as possible to designate targets for Tornados armed with LGBs. In three days an initial six S.2Bs were repainted Desert Sand, fitted with Mk XII IFF and Have Quick radios, and flown to Muharraq, while the ALE-40 installation was urgently qualified at Boscombe. At Muharraq the aircraft were fitted with a self-defence AIM-9L on the left outer pylon, the Pave Spike laser (AVQ-23E) on the left inner, a tank on the right inner and an ALQ-101(V)10 jammer on the right outer. Crews came from Nos 12 and 208, plus No 237 OCU, and after teaching Tornado crews how to drop LGBs the first mission was flown against the Euphrates bridge at As Samawah on 2 February. The mission was flown by two cells kept at least 45 sec apart, each comprising two Buccs and four Tornados carrying three LGBs each. The heat haze, humidity and dust made target acquisition difficult, so the technique was soon adopted of boresighting the AVQ-23E seeker dead ahead, diving on the target and aiming with the HUD. Once acquired, the

seeker was uncaged, and the Bucc zoomed back to around 20,000 ft, possibly above the Tornados.

From the first mission the combined partnership was completely successful. By 8 February 12 aircraft and 18 crews were at work, flying 679 hours in 216 missions. They directed 169 LGBs against 24 bridges, destroying every target, followed by fuel tank farms, hardened shelters, command bunkers and ammunition stores. From 21 February, the AIM-9L no longer being needed, the Buccs themselves carried two LGBs; unlike the Tornados they attacked in 40° dives from 25,000 ft, tossing their bombs into their own laser 'baskets'. They dropped 48 LGBs, hitting targets on 14 airfields at the close of the campaign. No aircraft were lost.

SPECIFICATION

Buccaneer
(Mk 1) two 7100-lb DH (Bristol Siddeley) Gyron Junior 101 turbojets, (Mk 2) 11,030-lb Rolls-Royce Spey 101 turbofans
Dimensions Span (original and post-1980) 42 ft 4 in (12.9 m), (S.2 to 1980) 44 ft 0 in (13.41 m); span (folded) 19 ft 11 in (6.07 m); length 63 ft 5 in (19.33 m); wing area (original) 508.5 sq ft (47.24 m²), (extended tips) 514.7 sq ft (47.82 m²)
Weight Empty (1) 27,140 lb (12,311 kg), (2) 29,960 lb (13,467 kg), (2B) 30,990 lb (14,057 kg); max take-off (1) 45,000 lb (20,412 kg), (2) 51,000 lb (23,134 kg), (2B) 58,000 lb (26,309 kg) [figure of 62,000 lb widely published was never applicable]
Performance Maximum speed at S/L (1) 645 mph (1038 km/h), (2B) Mach 0.92, 700 mph (1480 km/h); combat radius (4000-lb internal bombload, hi-lo-hi) 1130 miles (1820 km)
Armament Provision for bombload of 16,000 lb (4000 internal, 12,000 external) never used; normal load 4000 lb (1814 kg) internal and Paveway LGBs, Sea Eagle, Martel, rocket launchers and other stores externally

BELOW *Paul Millett taxiing out the second Mk 2, XK527, which joined the flight-test programme in September 1963. Note the conformal tanks.*

NAA A3J (Rockwell A-5) Vigilante

First Flight – 31 August 1958

Today the Vigilante is by no means a favourite among the army of military-aircraft enthusiasts; indeed, a high proportion of the younger ones may never have heard of it. This is partly because it was expensive, so not many were built, and only the first handful were designed to fly attack missions, most Vigilantes being exceedingly advanced reconnaissance platforms. Yet it was designed at a time when aeroplane technology changed dramatically on every working day, and this shapely aircraft – very much remembered with affection by everyone connected with it – was a pioneer of as much new technology as anything ever built with wings.

Among other things, it was the first to have a slim forward fuselage which disappeared into a wide rectangular box (as do many of today's supersonic twin-engined aircraft), the first to have fully variable wedge-type lateral inlets, the first to have a multimode radar and inertial navigation system, the first to have a digital computer and certainly the first to have 'slab' vertical and horizontal tails. The lateral-control system was extraordinary, and the method of dropping a nuclear weapon even

stranger. And, of course, though it was a Mach-2 aircraft weighing up to 80,000 lb, it went to sea aboard carriers.

This remarkable aircraft was the greatest of the many creations of NAA's Columbus Division. Before World War 2 the American airframe industry had been divided into Army contractors and Navy contractors, though a few of the biggest firms served both. NAA had been an Army firm (though the Navy bought many SNJ trainers), but in 1945 it began to compete for Navy orders with the NA-134 jet fighter which became the FJ-1 Fury. The Korean War provided the spur for massive expansion, and a few weeks after it began in June 1950 the company took over the huge wartime plant at Columbus, Ohio, which had been run by Curtiss. This was immediately built up to have not only manufacturing, but also design capability, and in August 1950

BELOW *The NAGPAW mock-up, which established the layout of forebody, inlets, wing, engines and tail seen in almost all the big fighters of the last two decades. The sharp-eyed will spot the twin slab vertical tails*

it was assigned complete responsibility for the AJ-2P Savage, the reconnaissance version of the AJ-1 Savage carrier-based attack aircraft. Columbus soon took on many other big programmes, but the planned AJ-1 successor, the twin-turboprop XA2J-1, was a Los Angeles programme, and a failure. In 1954 Frank G Compton, chief of preliminary design at Columbus, obtained permission to start with a clean sheet of paper and make an unsolicited proposal to the Navy for an A2J successor.

It rejoiced in the name 'Nagpaw', from North American General-Purpose Attack Weapon. From the outset it was, like the A2J, a twin-engined high-wing project, but the engines were jets and everything was swept back. Once the Navy got interested they cranked in severe demands, two of the most irreconcilable being high supersonic speed (if possible Mach 2) and the ability to take off at maximum weight with zero wind over the deck. Almost unbelievably, Compton's team succeeded. In July 1955 they received a contract for the NA-233

design and a mockup, and this was followed in September 1956 by a contract for two prototypes designated YA3J-1 and named Vigilante, plus a static-test airframe. The first YA3J, BuNo 145157, was completed impressively quickly, and flight testing began on 31 August 1958.

Today this prototype would excite little comment, but 35 years ago it was breathtaking. The fineness ratio of the fuselage (its slenderness) was startling, though it looked quite different in plan view because of the tremendous width downstream of the inlets. As already noted, these inlets were totally new, with acutely sloping sharp edges and an upper ramp

BELOW *Banking, the YA3J-1 shows one of the strange 'aileron systems' in action. The bomb/tank loading door is near the inlets*

BOTTOM *The XA3J-1 prototype over the California desert*

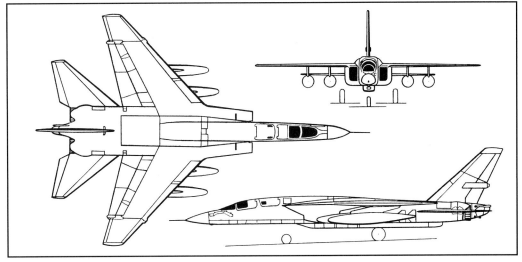

LEFT *RA-5C
reconnaissance version*

driven under computer control to angles from 0° to 23° to give maximum area on take-off and a narrow throat with focused oblique shockwaves at Mach 2. Today we see such inlets on many types of supersonic aircraft.

The engines were an obvious choice. Apart from having an air-impingement starter and a single igniter they were almost the same as the engines of the B-58A, though there were two instead of four. The same engine was picked by McDonnell for the XF4H-1 Phantom II, but with different inlets. But while the F-4 was expected to weigh about 40,000 lb, the A3J was eventually to weigh almost 80,000 lb. This in turn emphasises the challenge of catapulting at maximum weight with zero wind (a ridiculous demand). To meet it NAA had to set the wing area at 700 sq ft, compared with 530 for the Phantom II, and to use every high-lift trick going.

One could write reams on the structure. Suffice to say that almost nowhere was it ordinary. In the 1980s we heard much about the use of aluminium-lithium alloys (and that Boeing were in trouble through perhaps using it too soon), so it is worth remembering that Al-Li was used for the entire machined wing and tail skins of the very first XA3J. The most heavily stressed body frames were H-11 hot-work tool steel, previously used for the cutting edges used to machine other steels. The landing-gear legs were of a new alloy called STRUX, while the engine bays were not mere titanium, but coated with heat-reflective gold (yes, gold). Libby-Owens-Ford said the windscreen was the biggest-ever component of curved laminated glass; it cost $15,000, which was impressive in the mid-1950s.

Swept at 37.5°, the 4.9/3.5 per cent wing was probably the cleverest in the world in 1958. Only the final 65 in had to fold, and the whole wing box was an integral tank right out to the fold. The entire leading edge was carried on piano hinges along its lower edge and driven by hydraulic ball-screwjacks to −5° for cruise, −8° for loiter and −20° (−30° outboard) for take-off and landing. The inboard trailing edge comprised large plain flaps. When these were depressed to 7° or more they were increasingly powerfully blown by high-pressure bleed air, and at a maximum of 50° they more than doubled total lift. The outer trailing edge was fixed. Instead of ailerons, lateral control was by the most extraordinary system ever devised for this purpose, with a row of unique spoiler doors in both the upper and lower surfaces. The inner and central groups comprised lower doors hinged at the back and opening to 20° or 35° and upper spoilers hinged at the front and opening to 40° or 70°. Outboard, everything was reversed, the lower surfaces being hinged at the front and opened to 48° or 70°, and the upper doors being hinged at the back and opened to 26° or 42°. Thus, when rolling, the Vigilante wing had huge gaps right through it, through which passed a hurricane of air going either upwards or downwards.

What makes this system even more extra-ordinary is that the powerful tailplanes could be driven differentially, but only for lateral trimming. The primary function of the tailplanes was to control the pitch axis, while the slab vertical surface handled control and trimming in yaw. Each surface was driven by a dual hydraulic power unit with one chamber in each of the two 3000-lb/sq in systems. Signalling was of course mechanical, but fly-by-wire signals were used in parallel as a back-up. The main tailplane servos were controlled by a master actuator mounted transversely, with electrical sig-nalling for autopilot flight or trimming.

Pilot and navigator sat in tandem HS-1 seats of NAA's own design, with rocket assistance and a stabilising drogue, the limits being 0 ft/90 kt. The separate canopies hinged upwards, that for the backseater being metal with a window on each side with a sliding screen. Ladders were needed for access. A liquid-oxygen converter was fitted, lasting eight hours. Electrics were supplied by a constant-speed (8000 rpm) drive on each engine for a 30-kVA alternator, with an emergency alternator driven by the hydraulic system energised by a drop-down ram air turbine. On the left side of the nose was a very neat fold-out air-refuelling probe.

Of course, the navigation, flight control and bombing systems were the best that could be devised. Prime contractor was an NAA division called Autonetics, who were world leaders (with Sperry for ship applications) in inertial systems.

ABOVE *Carrier qualification trails were flown from* USS Saratoga *(CV-60)*

Such systems were not quite ready to be used unaided, so the Vigilante found room for Reins (Radar-equipped inertial navigation system), GD/ Electronics supplying the main multimode radar in the pointed nose. Linking this and other systems together was Autonetics' epoch-making Verdan computer, which got its name from VERsatile Digital ANalyser and not, as was said, 'very effective replacement for dumb-ass navigators'. The Navy called the system ASB-12, and its MTBF (mean time between failures) was 15 minutes in 1959, 240 hours in 1961 and 500 hours in 1964.

To say the Vigilante was a challenge is a considerable understatement. In 1954 the Navy had thought in Korean terms of low attacks with conventional weapons, but a year later the A3J was regarded mainly as a Skywarrior replacement carrying a nuclear weapon at high altitude at Mach 2. Compton's team took nothing for granted, and after studying the way hundreds of items were shoehorned into every nook and cranny in the slim fuselage, hardly leaving room for a structure strong enough for catapult shots at maximum weight and brutal landings arrested by the strong tail hook,

they began to think the last thing they needed was to cut open the underside to fit bomb doors.

Instead they devised a scheme which remains unique. Ahead of the wing they filled the fuselage with a bag-type fuel tank, and they put a flat box of fuel right across the rear fuselage above the ducts and engines. Under this, they made the whole centre and rear fuselage a three-tunnel structure. The left and right tunnels housed the afterburning engines, which were parallel and well separated. The central tunnel was fitted with a flat rectangular door, 14 ft long, which could be unscrewed from the underside. With this removed, a standard yellow Air Logistics trolley would be used to hoist a full 275 US-gal cylindrical container of fuel into the first store station in the central tunnel until rollers engaged with rails along each side of the tunnel. The tank was then rolled aft until it was stopped at the next store station. An identical second tank was loaded and connected to the first tank both mechanically and by fuel couplings. Then the linked tanks were rolled back to lock at Stations 2 and 3, the latter in the tail between the afterburners. The nuclear weapon was then loaded and locked in the first store position and firmly connected to the tank behind it to make a 'three-car train' over 30 ft long.

The Vigilante was designed to make level bombing runs at all altitudes, or to toss a nuclear weapon up from treetop height in a LABS (low-altitude bombing system) attack, in every case controlled by the Verdan computer. The ASB-12 was developed so that it could compare the radar picture with target images stored on magnetic tape to make identification certain. This was refined before first flight by an Eastman Kodak closed-loop TV system, the two wavelengths together giving clear on-board pictures of land and ship targets. At the correct moment the ASB-12, knowing from the flight-control and air-data systems every detail about the aircraft's attitude, velocity, height and atmospheric variables, would send the Fire signal. This would, in a split second, blow off the tailcone, release the latches at the three store stations and catapult the three-unit train straight out at the back by a towing system energised by a solid-fuel cartridge. The pressurised tanks, by this time empty, were intended to stabilise the bomb on its descent. Suffice to say this system seldom worked as advertised.

The central tunnel was also designed to accommodate reconnaissance systems, including cameras and a pioneer SLAR (side-looking airborne radar). Alternatively it could accommodate both cylindrical tanks and, instead of the weapon, a Buddy-pack with an air-refuelling hose-drum unit. Under each wing was provision for a pylon for a 400 US-gal (330-gal) drop tank or a nuclear or heavy conventional bomb.

In addition to the two prototypes, NAA produced 57 A3J-1 bombers for the carrier air wings. Apart from actually dropping the bomb, they were fully operational, and the engine was the Dash-4 or -8.

Like the prototypes, the first 9 were NA-247s (BuNos 146694/146702). Then came 14 NA-263s (147850/147863), followed by two blocks of NA-269s (10, 148924/148933, and 24, 149276/149299). Deliveries began in March 1960, at a unit price over $9 million; despite the low rate of production (by US standards) this was brought down later to $5.8 million. Qualification aboard USS *Saratoga* (CV-60) was completed by July 1960, and VAH-7 (Hatron [Heavy Attack Squadron] 7) worked up at NAS Sanford from June 1961, going aboard USS *Enterprise* (CVN-65) in August 1962.

By this time the A3J-1 had become the A-5A, and they were very proud to serve with the 6th Fleet in the Mediterranean as 'Peacemakers of the Fleet'. Unfortunately their reign was brief, because the Navy, already disenchanted by failure to qualify the linear bomb bay, eventually fell for the doctrine proclaimed since 1957 by Garrison Norton, Assistant Navy Secretary for Air, that strategic bombing was not a Navy mission. At a stroke this halted the A-5B, the obvious improved bomber, in its tracks.

The A-5B, until 1962 called the A3J-2, capitalised on removal of the foolish zero-WOD (wind over deck) stipulation, and on the remarkable fact that, provided it had an improved high-lift system and operated from *Forrestal* class carriers, the Vigilante could be made even heavier, the A3J-1 having been limited to much less than the theoretical 80,000 lb. The fuselage was redesigned with a hump-back which increased fuel capacity and raised the rear cockpit. Two extra pylons were added under the wings, which were redesigned with fully-blown

BELOW *An A-5A of Heavy Attack Squadron 7 in 1962. We are still designing aircraft like this today*

leading-edge flaps and bigger trailing-edge flaps, increasing the wing area to 769 sq ft. With four 440 US-gal drop tanks the range with a given payload was almost double. Maximum weight jumped to 79,588 lb (36,101 kg).

Production was halted after six A-5Bs, and the entire development and production programme became concentrated on the RA-5C reconnaissance version. This used the A-5B airframe but with the fuselage redesigned with no weapon tunnel but carrying nothing but fixed fuel tanks of greater capacity and a comprehensive suite of reconnaissance sensors. NAA built 91 RA-5Cs, and rebuilt 59 of the earlier bomber versions to the same standard. Their performance, especially in the Vietnam war, was legendary; no other aircraft could give such accurate information and send it back in real time. But then the basic aircraft was quite impressive. What other strategic bomber could go to sea aboard a carrier and also take a 2000-kg load to 91,446 ft, as did a standard A-5A on 13 December 1960?

SPECIFICATION

A-5A Vigilante

Two General Electric J79-8 turbojets rated at 10,900 lb dry and 17,000 lb with max afterburner

Dimensions Span 53 ft 0 in (16.15 m); length 73 ft 3 in (22.33 m); wing area 754 sq ft (70.05 m²)

Weight Empty 34,350 lb (15,581 kg); max take-off 61,000 lb (27,670 kg)

Performance Maximum speed (clean, high altitude) Mach 2.1 (1388 mph, 2234 km/h); combat radius (hi, two tanks) 1100 miles (1770 km)

Armament One B28 or other nuclear weapon carried internally; provision (not used) to carry two more, or two other stores up to 3000 lb (1361 kg) each, on underwing pylons

Yakovlev Yak-28

First Flight – 5 March 1958

Of all the many types of aircraft in the post-war arsenal of the Soviet Union, none have been so difficult to research as the twin-jet Yak family sired by the Yak-25. Part of the trouble has been the wealth of different versions, each in some way derived from others. Today, when almost all of them are past history, accurate specifications have yet to be published for the majority. The figures at the end of this account, referring to the basic attack bomber version of the Yak-28, first appeared in a Polish report in July 1986. Several subsequent articles (by Russians) contain errors.

The family began with the Yak-120 all-weather interceptor, first flown on 19 June 1952 with Mikulin AM-5 engines. By 1956 the production interceptor was entering service, with VVS/PVO designation Yak-25M. By this time the AM-5 had become the Tumanskii RD-9B, and the aircraft itself had matured in several respects. In addition, two development aircraft which participated in the 1955 airshow at Tushino indicated that further variants were planned.

In 1953 the Yak-125 prototype led to several versions of Yak-25, Yak-26 and Yak-27, including the -27V interceptor prototype and production -27R reconnaissance aircraft. These had Tumanskii R-11 engines, span increased from 11.0 to 11.9 m, and in the case of the Yak-27R a revised crew compartment for a navigator/camera operator in a glazed nose and a pilot aft. Another member of this family was the Yak-25RV high-altitude reconnaissance aircraft, with an unswept wing of 22 m span, just over double that of the original interceptor.

In 1957 almost all the development effort was transferred to the completely redesigned family with service designation Yak-28. The Yak-129 prototype was flown on 5 March 1958. This looked at first sight to be a mere variation on the Yak-25/27 theme, but in fact hardly any parts were common. The chief differences were that the redesigned wing was raised from the mid to the shoulder position to make room for an internal bomb bay of useful size. Other changes included more powerful afterburning engines and redesigned landing gear. The whole airframe was redesigned for greater stresses.

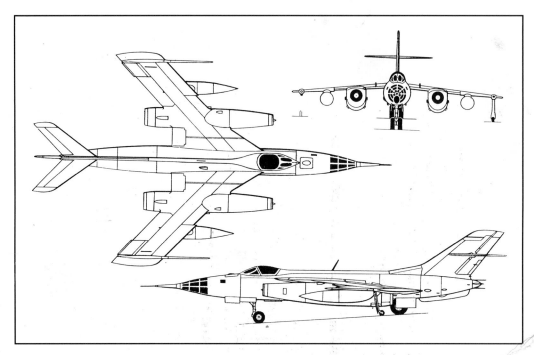

Though the wing retained the original profile of SR-9S and sweep angle of 44°, it was redesigned for much greater strength and to have the largest chord possible, to reduce the thickness ratio. Inboard of the underslung engine nacelles the leading edge was swept no less than 60° and the trailing edge redesigned perpendicular to the fuselage, giving thickness of 7 per cent at the nacelle and only 5.5 per cent at the root. Outboard of the nacelles the wing remained untapered but was given an extended and drooped leading edge outboard of a dogtooth, reducing thickness here back to 5.5 per cent. Span was increased yet again (see data). The inboard flaps were changed from the split to the slotted type, and increased in area. Most unusually, a fence was added right across the wing in line with the mid-point of these flaps, while all other fences (which had differed in the Yak-25 and 27 variants) were removed. The slotted flaps outboard of the engines were increased in both span and area, reducing the span of the ailerons, which were made fully powered with full-span tabs. On what in previous models had been the wingtips, but were now well inboard, extremely long instrument booms projected ahead of the fairings for the outrigger landing gears. Similar booms had been fitted to previous versions, but in the Yak-28 their inordinate length was apparently to assist in damping out flutter and maintain the optimum angle of attack at the tip.

The fuselage retained the original circular cross-section, but with the wing raised and the overall length again increased, this time substantially, from 15.67 m to 21.65. The greater length eased the problems of area ruling, and made possible a considerable increase in fuel capacity. Even so, still more fuel was needed in some versions, so these were equipped to carry 1000-litre pointed-nose drop tanks scabbed on below and ahead of the outer wings. The resulting increase in weight led to a remarkable bicycle landing gear with an extraordinarily long wheelbase, which in turn required major strengthening of the fuselage. In earlier versions the aft gear had borne (typically) 85 per cent of the weight, but in the Yak-28 this percentage was reduced to 60. This unit was moved as far aft as possible to allow for the greatest possible length of weapon bay disposed equally fore and aft of the centre of gravity. This short twin-wheel main gear retracted aft into a compartment with twin doors. The longer forward gear again had twin wheels with disc brakes, together with hydraulic steering. It retracted forwards into a compartment with four doors. The outriggers, with single wheels, were arranged to retract to the rear.

All versions had R-11 turbojets, almost always of the AF2-300 afterburning variety. The nacelles were completely beneath the wing and extended well ahead of and behind the wing. Most versions of Yak-28 had the inlet duct extended forwards 0.78 m so that only the tip of the centrebody was

ABOVE *Both illustrations show the Yak-27R preserved at Monino. The Yak-27R was an intermediate type between the Yak-25 interceptor and the many variants of Yak-28. Note the huge M-50 in the lower picture*

visible. This form of nacelle was also cut back at the rear so that the hinged petal flaps of the engine nozzle were visible.

The tail was not redesigned, its ancestry being traceable back through the Yak-27 and 25 to the original single-engined Yak-50 of 1949. Differences included an increase in strength, increase in length of the fixed underfin, redesign of the rudder as a single surface to give greater power in asymmetric flight, and redesign of the horizontal surface as a powered tailplane with geared elevators to increase camber, the elevators having vee cutouts to allow the rudder to move.

The Aviation Day flypast on 9 June 1961 contained several members of the Yak-27 and 28 family, and the resulting confusion among Western analysts was compounded by the NATO system of code names. To *Flashlight-A, -B, -C* and *-D* were now

ABOVE *Yet another valued Monino exhibit is this Yak-28B, with underwing tanks*

added *Mandrake, Mangrove, Firebar,* and *Brassard.* Fighters get F names and Bombers receive names beginning with B, and eventually some *Firebars* were changed to *Brassards.* Then the French pointed out that they had 310 aircraft called Broussards, so the code name was changed to *Brewer.* Even then, for anything like a proper understanding of these widely used and popular aircraft we had to wait another 20 years.

The initial bomber version was designated Yak-28B. This had the crew arranged as in the Yak-27R. The bomb bay amidships could carry various loads from 1 t to 3 t, and between it and the nose landing gear was the main radar of the RBR-3 radar bombing system. Internal fuel amounted to 3450 kg (7606 lb), which was usually augmented by two drop tanks under the outer wings. This went into modest production to replace the Il-28. In 1960 two new versions appeared: the Yak-28I, fitted with the autonomous *Initsiativa* radar navigation system for searching for targets, and the Yak-28L with the *Lotos* guidance system based on signals from ground stations, which enabled the large radar to

be dispensed with. After numerous changes both entered production, existing B-models being retro-fitted with the self-contained *Initsiativa* and redesignated BI. The bulged radome of the I and BI made it necessary to raise the aircraft on jacks to load the bombs, a procedure which usually took 90 minutes.

The second and third major production versions were the Yak-28R multi-sensor reconnaissance aircraft and Yak-28P interceptor, the latter having radar in the nose and the crew of two in a tandem fighter-type cockpit. The Yak-28U was the dual pilot trainer for all versions, with an empty metal nose and the pupil and instructor in separate stepped cockpits with almost identical canopies (but the forward canopy had to hinge to the right, there being no room for it to slide).

By 1970 all bomber and reconnaissance versions were giving way to the family of Yak-28E and 28PP electronic-warfare platforms, configured principally for stand-off jamming and electronic escort of tactical aircraft. Well over 100 Yak-28s were still flying operationally on electronic-warfare duties in 1990, but the last were due to be replaced by the Su-24MR in mid-1993.

SPECIFICATION

Yak-28L

Two Tumanskii R-11-AF2-300 turbojets each rated at 6200 kg (13,668 lb) with maximum afterburner

Dimensions Span 12.5 m (41 ft 0 in); length 21.65 m (71 ft 0 in); wing area 37.5 m² (403.7 sq ft)

Weight Empty 10,980 kg (24,206 lb); normal loaded 18,600 kg (41,005 lb)

Performance Maximum speed at 10 km (32,800 ft) 1460 km/h (907 mph, Mach 1.37); range (high altitude, with bomb load) 2570 km (1597 miles)

Armament One 30-mm NR-30 fixed gun on right side of forward fuselage; internal bay for one nuclear weapon or for conventional bombload of up to 3 t (6614 lb)

RIGHT *Though the Yak-28L looked very like its predecessors, it was actually an entirely new aircraft*

Dassault Mirage IV

First Flights – 17 June 1959; (IVA) 12 October 1961

In the story of the Vautour it was explained how this early jet bomber served in a training and support role in the formative years of France's nuclear deterrent. It is ironic that, far from being the creation of Gen de Gaulle, this nuclear force was conceived by a notably left-wing Prime Minister, Pierre Mendès-France.

In 1954 his administration committed France to the colossal expenditure needed to create a fission bomb, the development of this bomb into an air-portable form and then the design of a bomber to carry it (clearly a task for which no existing aircraft was suitable). This initial task was funded in the third post-war *Loi de Programme* of 1955–59, the final two years also paying for development of a thermonuclear device and design of long-range ballistic missiles. The fourth *Loi* of 1960–64 paid for the bombers themselves, for a silo-based IRBM and

a submarine-based SLBM. The fifth, of 1965–69 paid for operating the bombers and for building the missile force. The sixth provided funds for operating all three delivery systems, with nuclear and thermonuclear bombs and warheads.

By any standard, this was a staggering achievement. While Britain has nothing but a few SLBMs, forming one leg of the strategic triad, France has all three. At first this was called the *Force de Frappe* (strike force) but in 1961 it was restyled the *Force de Dissuasion* (deterrent force). Naturally, to reduce risk everything possible was based on the proven

BELOW *Mirage IVA bombers in final assembly at Bordeaux-Merignac. Nearest the camera is No 22. It was just after this time that visitors from Britain scorned the Spey-engined upgrade as a TSR.2 replacement*

ABOVE *Distinguished by its pointed fin, Mirage IV-01 was also smaller and less powerful than production IVA. Another obvious difference was the nose landing gear*

RIGHT *The first trial hook-up between a C-135F (then called KC-135F) and a IVA. Today, the tankers have been re-engined with the CFM56, becoming C-135FRs*

deterrent forces of the United States, including the design of two nuclear-hardened command centres deep underground, one at Taverny, on the northern outskirts of Paris, and a reserve centre at Mont Verdun, near Lyons.

In 1956 Mendès-France's equally Socialist successor, Guy Mollet, supervised the specification for the deterrent force's manned bomber. Basic requirements were the ability to carry a bomb 5.2 m (17 ft) long, weighing three tonnes (6614 lb), over a distance of 2000 km (1242 miles). The bomber was to have the capability of refuelling in flight and, to the surprise of many, supersonic speed. Indeed in an addendum, the over-target Mach number was fixed at not less than 1.7. Of course, the only likely enemy was the Soviet Union; a basic justification for the force was later explained as its ability to destroy ten Russian cities. *Armée de l'Air* Gen Pierre Gallois, who later worked for Dassault, said, 'France is not a prize worthy of ten Russian cities'. But to destroy ten Soviet cities demanded a greater range than 2000 km, and from the very start the unusual assumption was made that, quite apart from being shot down, few of the French bombers would have sufficient fuel to make the return journey.

At the outset Ouest-Aviation (previously SNCASO) thought they would probably win the bomber design contract with a stretched version of the Vautour, to be powered by Olympus or J57 engines. But in late 1955 Dassault had completed the preliminary design of the Mirage II interceptor, to be powered by two Turbomeca Gabizo engines. This was dropped in favour of the single-engined Mirage III, but it provided an almost perfect basis for scaling up to the size required to meet the bomber specification. From the outset it was self-evident that this was a fundamentally later and more attractive basis for a Mach 1.7+ aircraft than the enlarged Vautour; moreover Dassault had already begun to show the remarkable speed of development for which the company became famous. The fact that it was a private firm, and not part of the nationalised industry, was not considered to pose any particular risk, and Dassault was informed it had won the design competition in April 1957. In the same month, Britain announced that it thought military aircraft were obsolete!

The bomber, designated Mirage IV, was to be powered by two SNECMA Atar 09B engines, each with a maximum thrust of 13,228 lb. These were the most powerful French engines then available, and a single one was used in the contemporary Mirage IIIA fighter. The latter had a wing of 34.85 m² (375.1 sq ft) area, while the Mirage IV wing was scaled up to precisely double this area, rounded off to 70 m² (753.5 sq ft). The gross weight was more than doubled, to a predicted 25 tonnes (55,115 lb), which, when the aircraft was built, had grown to 26 tonnes (57,319 lb). Span and length were, respectively, 37 ft and 67 ft.

It was confidently predicted that the Mirage IV would attain Mach 2. The original Mirage III had reached Mach 1.9 with fixed inlets and a wing with a thickness/chord ratio of 5 per cent. The Mirage IIIA was expected to reach 2.2, with variable inlets and a wing 4.5 per cent thick at the root and 3.5 per cent at the tip. The Mirage IV was to have a much better fineness ratio, in other words the fuselage was relatively more slender than that of the fighter. Its radar was to be flush in the belly, so that the nose could be an acute cone. Not least, the much greater wing chord enabled t/c ratio to be set at only 3.8 per cent at the root and 3.2 per cent at the tip, the thinnest ever attempted in Europe at that time.

Dassault never had any doubt that they could create the Mirage IV very quickly, but the basic size of the bomber continued to cause much argument. Seldom have aircrew outside Japan been specifically tasked with flying one-way missions; the loose assumption that many Mirage IVs might be able to recover to friendly territory was considered unwarranted, especially as these territories might be politically forced to be unfriendly following a French nuclear attack. For this reason only a single prototype and static-test airframe were ordered.

In 1958 Gen de Gaulle was called to be President of the Fifth French Republic, and almost the first thing he did upon gaining office was to conduct a careful study of the *Force de Frappe*. Nobody in the

Armée de l'Air liked the Mirage IV, and de Gaulle quickly formed the view that the bomber had to be big enough to fly proper two-way missions. Work continued on the Mirage IV prototype, but – on top of an immense effort on the Mirage III family and several other aircraft – the design staff at St Cloud worked an 80-hour week trying to organise a much bigger bomber designated Mirage IVB.

While the Direction Technique refined the specification, discussions were held with Bristol Aero-Engines on the use of an Olympus generally similar to that being developed for TSR.2. Other feelers were put out to Pratt & Whitney. The British firm was in the throes of merging with Armstrong Siddeley, and responded feebly. In contrast, the US *motoriste* (to use the French term) immediately sent a top delegation to Paris to talk to Dassault and, especially, SNECMA, the French national engine company. The upshot was a contract to power the Mirage IVB with two JT24 (J75B) engines, each rated with afterburner at 28,250 lb, plus partnership on the new JTF10 leading to the SNECMA TF104, 106 and 306 (to be used in numerous big Mirage fighter and VTOL prototypes), as well as giving Pratt & Whitney a 10.9 per cent share of SNECMA. Later, the deal was to embrace the JT9D to power the 747 and A300B, SNECMA becoming the chief European overhaul centre for P&W engines.

This cleared the way for full development of the Mirage IVB. Wing area was to be 120 m² (1292 sq ft), and the weight began at 165,000 lb, but was brought down first to 140,000 and finally to 58 tonnes (127,866 lb). Still a two-seater, the IVB was designed for Mach 2.4.

It would have been an impressive aircraft, but the arguments continued, this time because of the cost. The deterrent bill was assuming awesome proportions, and in August 1959 the decision was taken to go back to a slightly bigger version of the original IV and to rely on air refuelling from really capable tankers. An order for 12 Boeing KC-135 tankers was transmitted to Washington, to encounter a cool reception from an Administration which condemned France's proposed deployment of nuclear weapons. For two years the *Armée de l'Air* studied ways of buying commercial 707s, if possible used ones, and converting them as tankers. At last, in October 1962 the US State Department sanctioned the sale of what Boeing called the 717-164 and France the C-135F. They were delivered in 1964.

Seldom has a design team suffered such turbulence, under extreme political pressure, as the St Cloud staff who jumped from 26,000 lb thrust to 56,000 and then back to just under 31,000! Designation of the bomber that finally went ahead was Mirage IVA. On 18 September 1959 Dassault received an order for three prototypes, designated IVA-02, 03 and 04. Meanwhile the sole Mirage IV had been completed. From 1954 the company's chief test pilot was Roland Glavany, an *Armée de l'Air* general on five years' leave. He flew the new bomber at Melun-Villaroche on 17 June 1959, without problems. On its second flight, accompanied by a Mirage III to give scale, Glavany demonstrated before a Paris Salon crowd estimated at 600,000. Indeed, the first seven flights were mere public demonstrations, because at that time the pressure was on the big IVB.

On Flight 14 Glavany reached Mach 1.9, after which he returned to the air force and René Bigand took over. The top of the vertical tail was removed, the rear cockpit fitted out with instrumentation and the Sud-Aviation (Martin-Baker) BM.4 seat, a dummy AN11 bomb recessed under the fuselage and 2500-litre (550 Imp gal) tanks added on the inner wing pylons just outboard of the main landing gears. By the end of 1959 the lone IV had sustained

Mach 1.85 at 59,000 ft, exceeded Mach 2 on the level at 37,000 ft, pulled 5 g at 818 mph at 10,000 ft and explored handling with the dummy bomb removed.

IVA-02 flew on 12 October 1961, 03 on 1 June 1962 and 04 on 23 January 1963. All were progressively closer to the production IVA, the biggest advance being 03 which as well as having the flight-refuelling probe in the nose – a uniquely simple installation – was equipped with the definitive nav/bombing system. From 1956 arguments had raged over the form this should take. Dassault's leader on this system, Jean Rouault, could do little but obey the customer, and the customer increasingly wanted an inertial navigation system. Detailed schemes were prepared for such a system, updated by radar, doppler and astro methods, but a decision was repeatedly postponed.

There were many conflicting factors. France had no inertial capability, and not even an ultra-clean assembly room. This was in the process of being created, but for test rockets and the future SSBS and MSBS missiles. It was a fundamental requirement that nothing in the *Force de Frappe* should have to rely on a foreign supplier, and in any case the State Department had made it clear that US companies would not get export licences. Further problems concerned reliability and MTBF (mean time between failures), and one of the biggest stumbling-blocks was the *Armée de l'Air*'s wish to be able to launch a nuclear strike within two or three minutes of an alarm, whereas early inertial systems needed anything up to 20 minutes to warm up and be aligned. To cut a long story short, the IVA went into production with nothing but a rather traditional

BELOW *A much later nuclear weapon is the ASMP cruise missile, which turns the IVA into the IVP. Today, the dwindling force have low-level camouflage and numerous electronic upgrades*

radar, a doppler and a twin-gyro platform. The rest was made up by the skill of the navigator.

It is appropriate here to describe the production aircraft. Like the Mirage III family it was from the outset a 60° delta, but with broader tips. At 73 per cent semi-span (measured from the centreline) a modest sawcut notch caused a vortex to improve flow over the upper surface; otherwise the wing was remarkably simple, with a fixed leading edge, and no fences, conical camber, droops, dogtooth, spoilers, high-lift devices or tabs. There were just inboard and outboard elevons, each driven by a single Dassault power unit with twin rams in separate hydraulic systems. Above and below the wing roots were door-type airbrakes carried on three arms. Structurally the wing was light alloy with a tight rectilinear pattern of spars (at 90° to the longitudinal axis) and ribs, and machined and chem-milled skin panels. The whole wing and rear fuselage was subcontracted to Sud-Aviation.

Dassault made the front fuselage, joined at the main-spar double frame. It included the semi-circular inlets, with a conical centrebody driven in and out longitudinally by a hydraulic motor and ball-screwjack. The inlet stood well away from the fuselage wall, the boundary layer escaping above and below except for a proportion rammed into the central inlet for the air-conditioning system. Managed by SEMCA, this used engine bleed air and bootstrap air-cycle machines to supply the cockpit and cool the electronics. The rear pressure bulkhead sloped back at the same angle as the back of the navigator's seat. Each cockpit had an upward-hinged canopy, that over the navigator being metal with a window on each side. The backseater could aim free-fall weapons visually using a periscope looking through a ventral blister. A liquid-oxygen system was fitted.

The vertical tail was made by Breguet. Under the single powered rudder was added a large flat vertical box (absent from the IV) for the ribbon braking parachute, produced by Aerazur. Messier were responsible for the landing gear, with a tall, steerable twin-wheel nose unit, retracting to the rear, and inward-retracting main units. Each of the latter had again to be tall, to permit the high angles needed by a tailless delta on take-off and landing. The leg swung directly inward to lie within the 12 in depth of the wing, faired by a door linked to the leg, while the four-wheel truck occupied a fuselage bay under the inlet duct. Tyres, by Kléber-Colombes and Dunlop, were inflated to 12 kg/cm² (170.7 lb/sq in), too high for unpaved strips.

The Atar engine was the 9K (or 09K), specially developed via the 09D for this aircraft. It was generally identical to the Mirage III's Atar 09C (an improved 09B) but had a greater airflow and different accessories. A special overspeed from the usual limit of 8400 rpm to a maximum of 8700 rpm was permitted to boost thrust at supersonic speeds at high altitude. Another feature was an automatic variation of the nozzle area to maintain the desired rate of descent and airspeed on the landing approach. Each engine drove the usual pumps and a 20-kVA alternator, the AC electrical system also having an emergency third alternator driven by a drop-down ram-air turbine made under licence from Marquardt. SEMCA formed a subsidiary called Microturbo to produce the self-contained gas-turbine starter, initially the 60 hp Noelle 60 and later the Noelle 002 of 80 hp. This was not used to drive accessories, merely to make the bomber independent of ground starting power.

Fuel was carried in integral tanks in the wings, between the main and rear spars and in the leading edge ahead of the landing gear. Fuselage integral tanks were between the inlet ducts, in a double-skinned fuselage section outboard of the inlet ducts, in further bays under the ducts and engines, and ahead of the main spar of the fin. Normal capacity was 14,000 litres (3080 Imp gal). As noted, the inboard wing pylons were plumbed for 2500-litre (550 Imp gal) drop tanks, and for ferrying a large tank could be attached in the weapon recess. To reduce take-off run when fully loaded provision was made for up to six SEP solid-propellant RATO (rocket-assisted take-off) bottles to be attached under each wing root, ahead of the flaps. In service, four of the six stations are used, reducing required strip length from about 11,000 to 6000 ft.

Biggest item of operational equipment, the radar originally fitted was the Thomson-CSF DRAA-8A, not very different from a small edition of the H_2S Mk 9. The parabolic scanner rotated about a vertical axis and 'looked' obliquely down through a circular radome which hardly bulged below the underside of the fuselage. Almost the only major item not made in France was the Marconi AD.2300 doppler radar, produced to Dassault's specification. Avionics items were developed by EMD (Electronique Marcel Dassault), including the analog computer, though the autopilot was by SFENA.

After entry into service Mirage IVA bombers were fitted with additional electronics, including Thomson-CSF Type BF radar warning, and a management system for countermeasures which still later included the same contractor's Remora active jammer, carried on one of the outboard wing pylons, plus a Matra Phimat chaff/flare dispenser carried on the opposite pylon. The overall equipment standard improved throughout deliveries. The main order, for 50 aircraft, was placed on 4 April 1960, three days after the first successful test at Reggane, in the Sahara, of a French 'transportable nuclear device'. A further 12 aircraft were ordered in November 1964. These had been planned to be larger, much heavier and more capable aircraft, with the SNECMA/Pratt & Whitney TF106 augmented turbofan engine. In the event they differed only in having an airframe strengthened for low-level operations, and minor changes to the avionics.

The official name for the bomber force was the CFAS, the *Commandement des Forces Aériennes Stratégiques*. Even though the active inventory of Mirage IVAs never exceeded 36 aircraft, the FAS was deliberately planned as an élite force like SAC, with first call on defence funds and organised along unique lines all geared to rapid reaction in a nuclear war. Defence Minister Pierre Messmer announced in November 1963, 'Taking no notice of foreign protests ... France will not only continue the development of fission bombs but will arm herself with thermonuclear weapons as well'. Not even the vast Sahara was adequate to test the latter, for which France was busy building a test complex in the South Pacific.

By 1963 IVA-02 had completed bombing trials at Colomb-Béchar, Algerian Sahara, 03 had completed navigation testing and refuelling trials with a USAF KC-135A, and 04 was well into acting the part of a production IVA. The first production aircraft flew on 7 December 1963, and several were delivered in 1964 to the CEAM (*Centre d'Expériences Aériennes Militaires*) at Mont de Marsan. The first unit of the FAS, EB (*Escadron de Bombardement*) 1/91, became operational and was placed on alert status on 1 October 1964.

Training of both flight and ground crews was carried out chiefly by CIFAS 328 at Bordeaux, a diverse unit which has used such aircraft as the Mirage IVA, Lockheed T-33A, Mirage IIIB, Magister, Alpha Jet and Douglas B-26B (with special electronics). The main trainer for backseaters was for many years the Nord 2501SNB Noratlas, equipped with a complete Mirage IVA radar and consoles for two students. Electric power was generated by a gas-turbine APU in an external pod

BELOW *ASMP is a supersonic fire-and-forget weapon with a nuclear warhead. Once the boost rocket has burned out it converts into a cruise ramjet*

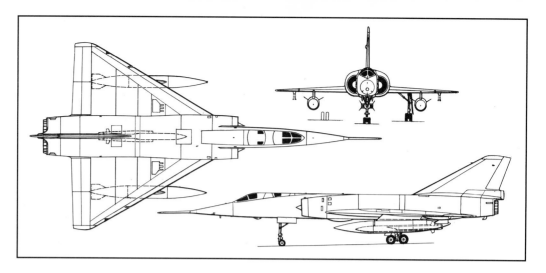

on the right side. In 1985 these were replaced by two Dassault Falcon 20s with most of the IVP avionics.

The frontline force was organised into three *Escadres* (Wings). Each Wing was dispersed between three *Bases Aériennes* (air bases). At *Base Mère* (mother base) would be one bomber *escadron* (squadron) with four bombers, and a tanker squadron (ERV, *Escadron de Ravitaillement en Vol*) with four C-135Fs. The Wing would deploy its other two squadrons at *Bases Isolées* (detached bases) each having four bombers. By 1966 the FAS Force was complete, comprising: the 91e EB, with 1/91 'Gascogne' and ERV 4/91 'Landes' at Mont de Marsan, 2/91 'Bretagne' at Cazaux and 3/91 'Beauvaisis' at Creil; the 93e EB, with 1/93 'Guyenne' and ERV 4/93 'Aunis' at Istres, 2/93 'Cevennes' at Orange and 3/93 'Sambre' at Cambrai; and the 94e EB, with 1/94 'Bourbonnais' and ERV 4/94 'Sologne' at Avord, 2/94 'Marne' at St Dizier and 3/94 'Arbois' at Luxeuil. Thus the whole area of France was dotted with groups of four bombers, all at a high alert status. As soon as the whole force was in place Gen de Gaulle announced on 10 March 1966 that France was leaving NATO's military alliance and would henceforward be an independent nuclear power.

The alert status was very demanding. Of the 62 aircraft, 26 would either be in airworthy reserve or being worked on by GERMS (*Groupe d'Entretien et de Réparation des Matériels Spécialisés*) 15/96, the FAS support unit. The other 36 would be kept either in the air (12), or at four minutes readiness (12) or at 45 minutes (12). All 36 had the nuclear weapon on board, with all associated fuzing and conditioning systems functioning. The four-minute status meant that the crew would be in the cockpit, the gas-turbine starter armed and many other systems operating. The strain on humans and hardware was severe, many air-refuelled training missions lasting 14 hours. In the first decade this small force flew well over 200,000 hours, with approximately 40,000 air refuellings, the C-135Fs having their boom modified to trail a drogue.

Among other effects, the brutal schedule was wearing out the aircraft and running up 44 per cent

of the *Armée de l'Air*'s total budget for spares! The airborne alerts were replaced by the requirement for each squadron always to have one aircraft at 15-min readiness. Moreover, in the 1960s air forces had not yet forgotten the unpalatable fact that, in any war involving nuclear weapons, airbases would be wiped off the map in a pre-emptive strike. Accordingly, the *Armée de l'Air* investigated dispersing their deterrent bombers even wider. Rocket-assisted take-offs were made from pre-surveyed rough strips which were either covered with steel mesh, a job taking six hours under combat conditions, or sprayed with a chemical agent which hardened the soil, taking only two hours. Hardened shelters were judged to be financially impracticable against the 20-kT or larger warheads that could arrive by aircraft, naval cruise missiles or many kinds of Soviet ballistic missile.

On every training mission flight refuelling loomed large. At least during the first 20 years it was normal for aircraft to take-off (normally without rocket assistance) in pairs. One would carry the bomb and empty drop tanks and the other would have maximum fuel and a 'buddy pack' hose-drum unit. At some point en route to the target they would rendezvous with a *Sous-marin* (submarine, the nickname for the windowless C-135F) which would top up their tanks to a weight of 76,000 lb (take-off limit being 69,665 lb originally, later raised to 73,799). At a further precomputed point, the 'tanker' Mirage would refuel the bomber, which would then have enough fuel to reach its target (but not necessarily enough to get back).

From as early as 1964 Mirage IVAs had practised penetration at altitudes down to 200 ft, which without a terrain-following, or even terrain-avoidance, radar was hard work, especially as the ride could be very lively in turbulence. On a very few missions for conventional warfare heavy leads of GP bombs, with or without retarder tails, could be carried (see data), but the emphasis was always on the nuclear weapon. By 1967 the AN11 was being progressively supplemented by the more refined AN22, packaged into the same streamlined case some 6 m (236 in) long and weighing about 1.4 t (3086 lb). Like the AN11 it could be dropped from high altitude, with a chronometric fuze for high burst or a radar fuze for low, or tossed or 'laid down' from low level with a parachute brake. The yield was slightly increased.

Following the elimination of the British TSR.2 in April 1965, Dassault, Rolls-Royce and British Aircraft Corporation dusted off a 1962 study for a Spey-engined Mirage IV, and on 16 July 1965 the three firms put forward a proposal for the Mirage IVS. It was a carefully considered proposal, with many good and a few bad points, but the British Air Staff, taking their cue from the government who were mesmerised by the F-111, never even took it seriously. This caused much ill-feeling with the French, to say nothing of British industry. BAC even felt justified in issuing a press release noting how the French were 'astonished at the statements made in the House of Commons and elsewhere about the Mirage IVS which are contrary to the readily ascertainable facts. They regard these misrepresentations, which seem to them to be deliberate, as an inauspicious foundation . . .'

From 1975 the previously shiny Mirages were painted with green/grey camouflage (and from 1986 the tankers, now utterly transformed by re-engining with the CFM56, have been painted blue-grey). Meanwhile, the build-up to full strength of the silo-based SSBS and submarine-based MSBS fleet enabled the CFAS to reorganise to reduce costs. The main change was to disband the 93rd Wing, which was immediately re-formed as a new unit combining the tanker squadrons ERV 1/93 'Aunis' at Istres, 2/93 'Sologne' at Avord and 3/93 'Landes' at Mont de Marsan. Rather high Mirage IVA attrition had left only 45 aircraft available, and so this force was also re-formed with unit and name changes: EB 1/91 'Gascogne' at Mont de Marsan, 2/91 'Bretagne' at Cazaux, 3/91 'Cevennes' at Orange, 1/94 'Guyenne' at Avord, 2/94 'Marne' at St Dizier and 3/94 'Arbois' at Luxeuil. Since then there have been further rundowns, 3/91, and 1/

and 3/94 having phased out their jets and been disbanded.

Remaining aircraft have been caught between the need for updating and the wish not to spend money on aircraft due for early withdrawal. By far the most significant upgrade has been to add the ASMP (*Air/Sol Moyenne Portée*, air-to-surface medium range) cruise missile. This was developed by a team led by Aérospatiale from 1978, the final configuration being that of a finely streamlined wingless weapon with lateral inlets to the integral ram/rocket. Initial acceleration is made by a solid-propellant rocket, which after burnout converts into the combustion chamber of the liquid-fuel ramjet used for cruise propulsion at supersonic speed high enough for the weapon to fly on lift from the body. Launch weight is over 840 kg (1852 lb), length 5380 mm (212 in) and range up to 250 km (155 miles) carrying a warhead of 300 kT yield.

Trials with dummy ASMPs, powered prototypes and finally guided rounds took place with various Mirage IVAs from early 1981, the first full-scale test of a guided ASMP being on 23 June 1983. This was launched over the Bay of Biscay on a low-level mission from the *Centre d'Essais des Landes*. It was planned to convert 15 Mirages to carry this weapon, but the contract with the Government *Atelier Industriel de l'Air* at Clermont-Ferrand of July 1983 actually called for 18. At first designated IVN, the modified aircraft are actually designated IVP, for *Pénétration*. The conversion amounted almost to a gutting and rework. To accommodate the missile, a deep pylon was added under the centreline. In a secondary reconnaissance role the CT52 pod was developed, housing various mixes of Omera 35 and 36 cameras, a Wild mapping camera and an SAT Super Cyclope IRLS (infra-red linescan). This pod

BELOW *The first production aircraft was flown with a dummy AN52 nuclear weapon*

was designed to fit the Mirage bomb recess, but eventually it was decided to fair this cavity over and, for reconnaissance missions, to fit the CT52 to the missile pylon.

One of the major modifications was to replace the main radar, the new set being the totally different Thomson-CSF Arcana. A high-resolution pulse-doppler set, this is itself now being upgraded with new capabilities. The EW (electronic-warfare) suite was completely replaced, new equipment including a Thomson-CSF passive radar-warning installation related to Serval, with antennas in pods on the wingtips and on each side of the tail of the fuselage. This installation searches for wavelengths from 1 to 40 GHz, giving much more detailed information than previously available, and it is linked to the active systems. The latter vary, but typically include the Thomson-CSF Barem active jammer on the left outer station and the Swedish Philips BOZ 100 chaff/flare dispenser on the right outer. There have also been major upgrades to the IVP navigation system, flight-control system, cockpits and many other items.

Today the IVP equips EB 1/91 at Mont de Marsan and 2/91 at Cazaux. EB 2/94, the only other unit, is still equipped with free-fall bombs, including AN22.

BELOW *The impressive use of ATO rockets was intended to enable the IVA force to disperse to short austere airstrips in an emergency*

Each unit now has more than the previous four aircraft, and they tend not to practise too much dispersal. France has fallen into line in believing that airbases will never be destroyed, and has even built hardened shelters for the FAS force, despite seeing in Iraq that these are useless˘ even in conventional warfare. In January 1991 it was announced that all *Armée de l'Air* nuclear-capable units were being grouped into the FAS, comprising units equipped with the IVP, Mirage 2000N, Jaguar A and SSBS missile. The IVP and IVA are scheduled to be retired in 1996, but they could see the century out.

SPECIFICATION

Mirage IVA
Two SNECMA Atar 9K turbojets each rated at 10,362 lb dry and 15,432 lb with maximum afterburner
Dimensions Span 38 ft 10½ in (11.85 m); length 77 ft 0¾ in (23.49 m); wing area 839.6 sq ft (78 m²)
Weight Empty 31,966 lb (14,500 kg); max take-off 73,799 lb (33,475 kg)
Performance Maximum speed supersonic at sea level, 1454 mph (2340 km/h, Mach 2.2) at 40,000 ft; unrefuelled tactical radius (hi-lo-hi with supersonic dash) 770 miles (1240 km); ferry range 2486 miles (4000 km)
Armament (IVA) one AN22 nuclear weapon or up to 16,000 lb (7288 kg) of conventional bombs (six under each wing, four on fuselage pylons) or four AS37 anti-radar missiles; (IVP) one ASMP cruise missile

Tupolev Tu-105, Tu-22

First Flight – September 1959

At the Aviation Day flypast over Tushino in July 1961 the biggest single shock to Western observers was the inclusion of ten examples of a previously unknown type of supersonic bomber. One of the ten had a wider nose radome and carried a large cruise missile recessed under its fuselage. It was obvious that the design was another from the Tupolev OKB, but sensible Western assessment stopped there. For over 15 years many aspects of this aircraft, most notably its combat radius, were seriously undervalued.

Its original project study dated from 1955, when work was initiated on a bomber to answer the USAF B-58. Unconventional solutions, such as those being pursued in the USA on Weapon Systems 110A and 125A, were viewed with disfavour. The objective was a conventional aircraft that could be operated from existing airbases of the DA and AV-MF, in broad terms flying missions of the Tu-16 but with supersonic speed giving enhanced ability to penetrate modern defences. It was accepted from the outset that combat radius would be somewhat less than that of the Tu-16, and that costs would be greater.

The Tu-105 design naturally had much in common with the previously completed Tu-98 bomber and Tu-102 interceptor, though it was larger than either. The wing had modified SR-5S profile, with thickness ranging from 9 per cent at the root to 7 per cent at the tip. Leading-edge sweep was 70° at the root and then 52° to the tip. Structurally this was one of the first Tupolev designs with machined skins enclosing integral tankage between spars at 10 per cent and 60 per cent chord. As noted later, the main landing gears pivoted to a trunnion on the back of the wing box, and retracted backwards into fairings. The tracked plain (not Fowler) flaps depressed to different degrees, the sections inboard of the landing gear reaching considerably greater angles on both take-off and landing. Outboard were fully powered ailerons in

two sections which moved together. There were no spoilers, and the leading edge was fixed. Single fences were located at the flap/aileron junction at about 60 per cent semi-span, and the wingtips were extended forwards to form spike antennas and pitot heads.

The enormous fuselage had a circular cross-section and, despite having 'Coke-bottle' area ruling, was beautifully streamlined (indeed the original NATO name of this aircraft was *Beauty*, later changed to *Blinder*). The side elevation tapered from the cockpit to the tail, and in plan view the taper was modified to comply with area ruling across the wing. Rather unusually, the latter was located well below the mid-position, making the weapon bay fairly shallow. The pointed nose was occupied by the navigation/bombing radar, as described later. Next came the pressurised compartment for the

TOP RIGHT *One of the first Tu-22 bombers has been set aside for display at Monino*

RIGHT *The installation of the VD-7M (later RD-7M-2) engines was unique*

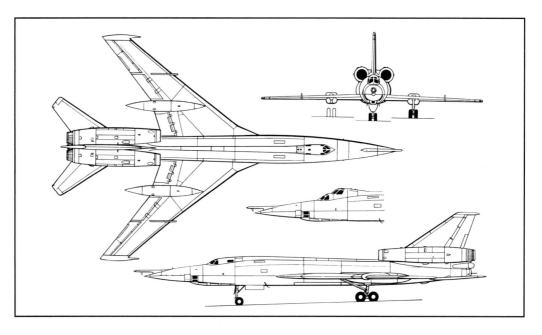

navigator/bomb aimer, with two superimposed square windows on each side giving a perfect view downwards and to the side. The pilot sat on the centreline at the upper level, with the radio systems operator/gunner behind him. All three crew entered via ventral hatches which were also used for the downward ejection seats of the navigator and radio operator. The pilot had an upward firing ejection seat. The ventral hatches were in a long blister which later housed a small tracking radar at the front, except in the Tu-22U trainer version.

At the rear this blister was faired into the compartment for the nose landing gear, which had twin wheels steered hydraulically and retracted to the rear. The main gears were very similar in design to those used later on the Tu-134 civil transport, though the bomber was very much heavier. Each had a four-wheel bogie, which in flight hung so that the bogie beam inclined downwards, the front wheels hitting the runway first. As the weight came on the bogie, the beam first rotated horizontal. Further weight then both compressed the main oleo shock strut and also swung the whole unit bodily to the rear and upwards, restrained by the long diagonal strut at the front. The latter incorporated the main retraction jack, which extended to push the whole gear to the rear, a secondary linkage simultaneously rotating the bogie beam about the leg so that the bogie unit was stored inverted inside the fairing projecting aft of the wing. The bay was closed by tandem pairs of doors. The underside of the rear fuselage was protected by a sprung steel-shod skid, which retracted fully. Immediately aft of this, anchored to the main tailplane frame, were twin braking parachutes.

The fully powered slab tailplanes were swept at 59° on the leading edge and cropped at the tip at the angle appropriate to Mach 1.5, which was the original maximum design speed. The tailplanes were built up on spars at 10 per cent and 70 per cent chord, and pivoted about a trunnion at just under 60 per cent. They were mounted at the very bottom

of the rear fuselage, whose cross-section was modified in consequence. The vertical tail likewise had sharp sweep on the leading edge, but much of this angle could be regarded as taper. The rudder was fully powered, even though it was tabbed and had inset hinges.

The unique feature of this bomber was that the engines were mounted above the rear fuselage, one on each side of the vertical tail. This installation left the entire fuselage aft of the pressure cabin (except for the wing box and weapon bay areas) available for fuel. It also eliminated the weight and pressure-loss of long inlet ducts, yet gave the engines excellent undisturbed air in cruising flight. Following model tests the decision was taken not to use the planned vee-type variable inlet but to provide each engine with a plain pitot inlet of the simplest type. The only variable feature was that, in order to provide sufficient air for take-off, the front of each inlet translated (slid bodily) forwards, the extra air being drawn in around the resulting gap. The cockpit was faired into the fin and nacelles by a dorsal spine, one of whose functions was to enclose the fuel pipes. Total capacity of the fuselage tankage was 45,000 litres, 36 tonnes. At the tail end of the fuselage was a defensive gun. This is referred in the description of the production aircraft.

In the Tupolev numbering system this was Type 105, and it was also known as Aircraft Ю (Yu). The programme was the first to be based at Kazan, Tatar SSR, which has subsequently been progressively enlarged to form the world's largest aircraft production plant. The prototypes, however, were constructed at the Tupolev OKB, where the first was flown in September 1959, by Yu I Alasheyev. All prototypes had an interim type of engine, the VD-7M, housed in an untapered cylindrical nacelle. Various changes and developments took place, notably to the avionics and weapon systems. From about the fifth aircraft the tail turret was added, plus the aft-facing radar, which was initially the PRS-3 *Argon*, but eventually settled on the same PRS-4 system as in several other bombers. Several types of main mapping radar were fitted, the usual version in the production bomber being the RBP-4 *Rubin*. The wingtip pods were enlarged, the pitot systems being relocated on the fuselage and the forward section of each tip pod housing the forward-facing passive radar warning receiver. An inflight-refuelling probe was added above the nose, the plumbing being all internal and the external probe being detachable. The internal weapon bay was fitted with twin double-hinged doors, and arranged to house two nuclear weapons or a wide range of bombs, mines or other stores.

Out of total production of some 250 aircraft, about 150 were of the missile-carrying version, designated Tu-22K by the VVS. This has the weapon-bay doors replaced by fairings cut away to permit the Kh-22 supersonic cruise missile to be recessed into the fuselage. The main radar was changed to a multi-mode type whose 2.8m rotating antenna necessitated a radome bulged out on each side. By the time this version was in production, in about 1963, the definitive engine was fitted, in a nacelle showing pronounced taper at the front and with a variable nozzle of larger diameter but with shorter petal flaps which did not project so far behind the nacelle cowl. The aft section of the wing nacelles, behind the retracted main gears, was used to house chaff/flare dispensers and strike cameras.

All of the original Tu-22 and 22K aircraft were supplied to the DA, from late 1965. Later 17 were painted in camouflage colours and supplied to Libya, initially with Soviet crews. At least one of these aircraft bombed Tanzania on behalf of Uganda. Nine were supplied to Iraq and used in action against the Kurds, who protested against Sadam Hussein's cruel rule, and then in the war against Iran. Both Libya and Iraq still have a few Tu-22s operational. In the Russian Federation about 75 remain with the Smolyensk and Irkutsk air armies, still capable of offensive operations but retained for ECM jamming and support. Their avionics have been repeatedly upgraded.

A further batch, estimated to number 60, were built of the Tu-22R multi-sensor reconnaissance version. This is operated mainly by the naval AV-MF. A fourth version is the Tu-22U (*Blinder-D*), with a stepped cockpit for a pilot instructor with a dual set of flight controls. A few remain in use with the DA, AV-MF and Libya. In mid-1993 the DA had 136 of all versions still flying. The Tu-22 was developed into the Tu-22M as described later.

In view of the fact that the Tu-22 is a traditional kind of bomber, forced by fuel and structural considerations to fly at altitude, it has enjoyed a long career. In offensive roles the long range and high penetrability of its cruise missiles has enabled it in theory to stay beyond the radius of interception. On the other hand, nobody in the mid-1950s would have dreamed that, in 1990, the Tu-22 would still be outnumbered by the Tu-16 in Soviet service!

TOP *An unusual view of an early Tu-22, lacking several later refinements*

ABOVE *Aircraft numbered from 47 to 60 forming an impressive line-up, some having servicing platforms around their RD-7M-2 engines*

SPECIFICATION

Tupolev Tu-22K
Two Dobrynin RD-7M-2 turbojets each rated at 12.5t (27,560 lb) dry and 16.5t (36,375 lb) with max afterburner
Dimensions Span 23.5 m (77 ft 0¼ in); length 42.6 m (139 ft 9⅛ in); wing area 162.0 m² (1744 sq ft)
Weight Empty 38.1 t (83,995 lb); fuel 42.5 t (93,695 lb); normal loaded 85 t (187,390 lb), max loaded 92 t (202,822 lb), max with four solid assisted-take-off rockets 94 t (207,231 lb); max landing 60 t (132,275 lb)
Performance Maximum speed (SL) 890 km/h (550 mph), (at 12 km) 1610 km/h (1000 mph, Mach 1.52); service ceiling 13.3 km (43,635 ft); combat radius (400-km full-throttle dash, hi-lo-hi profile) 2200 km (1367 miles); ferry range (internal fuel) 4900 km (3050 miles); TO run 2250 m (7380 ft); landing speed/run 310 km/h, 2170 m (with drag chute 1650 m, 5415 ft)
Armament Internal bay for up to 8 t (17,600 lb) of various bombs, or one Kh-22 cruise missile (NATO name *Kitchen*); one R-23 gun in tail turret

Myasishchyev M-50

First Flight – 27 October 1959

The OKB (experimental construction bureau) of V M Myasishchyev gained great honour from the M-4 programme, partly because it met the challenging design objectives, partly because it did so in 22 months, and partly because the basic aircraft and an upgraded Type 201M set 19 world records. Technically, this programme had presented exceptional challenges, so the same OKB was picked in 1955 to achieve the even greater task of creating a large long-range supersonic bomber and cruise-missile carrier. This programme was a direct response to the USAF Weapon System 110A, which became the XB-70.

Configuration and preliminary design were handled in partnership with the CAHI, whose team was led by Academician M V Keldysh, A I Makarevsky and G S Byushgens. V M Myasishchyev's project staff were led by L L Selyakov, L I Balabukh, I B Baslavsky, L M Rodnyansky, V A Stopachinsky and V A Fedotov. They jointly investigated more than

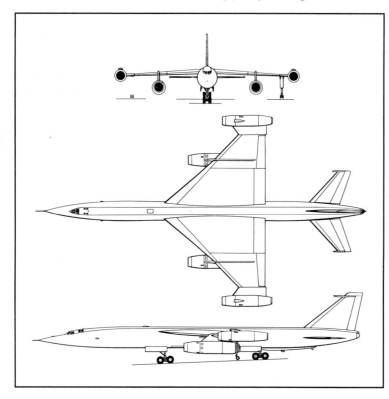

30 basic layouts, 13 of them having canard foreplanes and 16 having twin vertical or inclined tails. This total ignores the separate study made into the disposition of the engines. It was planned to use a new afterburning turbojet in the 16-tonne class being developed at the engine KB of P F Zubets, assisted by a team at the CIAM (Central Institute for Aviation Motors) led by G P Svishchyov. The design was based on the use of four of these engines.

Several times a choice of configuration seemed near, but at last, in late 1956, it was decided to use a conventional arrangement with a wing half-way along a huge fuselage, above the bomb bay and missile pylons, and with a conventional tail at the back. There were still 12 attractive ways of installing the four engines. Three schemes were examined in great detail. One was to use two engines on pylons above the wing and the other two on almost mirror-image pylons below the wing. The second was to hang two engines in pods under the wing and install the other two in the tail. The third arrangement, advocated by Fedotov assisted by Ye E Ilyenko, was to hang two engines under the wing and put the other two on the wingtips, and this was the arrangement finally adopted.

Though broadly conventional, almost everything else about this aircraft, known as the M-50, was new and challenging. At first sight it might have been thought that it was aerodynamically very much like a scaled-up MiG-21 (at the time called the Ye-6), but this similarity was illusory. Indeed, several of the features of the M-50 were much more like those of the Concorde, though the Soviet aircraft was designed ten years earlier. Among these features were the flight-control system and the supersonic longitudinal trimming system.

The wing plan adopted was that of a delta, with the tips cut off to provide mountings for the outer engines. Leading-edge sweep was 50° inboard and 41°31' outboard. The kink was located at the inboard engines, whose pylon struts were extended back across the wing to serve as fences. Thickness/chord ratio set a world record at that time for so enormous a wing, being only 3.7 per cent at the root and 3.5 per cent at the tip. This was, in several respects, the largest supersonic wing ever built apart from that of the B-70. The leading edge was fixed, and the trailing edge was occupied by four sections of track-mounted double-slotted flap, the outer sections also doubling as ailerons backed up by spoilers.

These lateral controls, and the slab tail surfaces, were naturally fully powered by hydraulic actuators. Where the M-50 certainly broke new ground was that the flight-control system was of the FBW (fly-by-wire) type, all pilot inputs being converted by potentiometers into electrical signals transmitted along mult-core cables. In the prototype M-50 this system was prudently backed up by a conventional network of mechanical linkages, but in a production aircraft it was expected that these could be removed. The weight saving was estimated at considerably more than 1 tonne (2205 lb), and further considerable savings were achieved by completely new uses of computers and mathematical algorithms to design the very thin yet heavily loaded wing. No previous data existed for such large yet thin wings of cropped delta form, and a team led by Myasishchyev himself pioneered not only finite-element analysis but also the use of computer programs which, as well as being used to design the structure, were also used to design the dynamics of the flight-control system and, at the same time, a computer-driven flight simulator. Test pilots N I Goryainov and A S Lipko were 'flying' this simulator before the end of 1958, simultaneously 'teaching the M-50 to fly' (by progressively refining the control characteristics) and also teaching themselves how to fly it.

The gigantic fuselage began with a pointed cone, which in the prototype carried an instrument probe but in a production bomber would have been a radome. Next, at the upper level, came the pressurised cockpit capsule. The crew comprised merely two pilots in tandem, the backseater normally managing the navigation, bombing and electronic-warfare systems. Each pilot sat on the centreline and entered by sitting on his seat suspended beneath the aircraft on cables, then switching the electric winch to hoist himself aboard through one of the large hinged doors in the underside of the fuselage. Next came the large forward fuselage tanks, fuel occupying all the upper part of the fuselage back to the corresponding group of full-section tanks in the rear fuselage. Another new feature was to arrange for fuel to be pumped automatically between the foremost and rearmost tanks in order to trim the aircraft longitudinally at all times, with no drag penalty, and in particular to cancel out the powerful change in trim during transition from subsonic to supersonic flight (nose-down, caused by the rearwards migration of the centre of pressure) and vice versa.

Yet another novel idea was incorporated in the landing gear. Myasishchyev had already used bicycle landing gear, so such a configuration held no terrors for him. He made the landing gear for the M-50 as similar as possible to that of the M-4, and in

TOP *This view emphasises the dramatic difference in thrust between the VD-7 and VD-7F engines in the modified aircraft*

ABOVE *Just as the M-4 had done seven years earlier, so did the first M-50 take part in a public flyby (at Tushino, 1961) accompanied by small MiGs (but this time the fighters were MiG-21Fs)*

fact the front and rear main bogie units were very similar to those of the earlier bomber, while the outriggers used the same twin wheels and tyres. The outrigger legs and geometry, however, were totally different, the legs being vertical when extended and on retraction telescoping upwards and then pivoting to the rear to lie in a narrow bay

in the pylon joining the outer engine to the wing. The novel feature was that it was apparent that the aircraft should be rotated to an angle of attack of 10° on take-off, if the run was not to be excessive, and there was no obvious way that the pilot could rotate the aircraft about the aft bogie using the power of the slab tailplanes alone. The answer was to do what S V Ilyushin had done with the Il-54 and design the front main gear not only to have a normal shock strut but also to have a second arrangement of hydraulic struts above it. This extra-extension system was triggered on take-off at a suitable speed, initially set at 300 km/h, so that without the need for pilot action the whole aircraft would be positively rotated to the correct angle. Myasishchyev called this his 'galloping bicycle'.

Despite great efforts by the Zubets bureau the engine was not ready in time for the aircraft, and in early 1959 the decision was taken to fit substitute engines. The choice fell on the ND-7, which had been developed by the KB of Dobrynin, which was then in turn taken over by Koliesov, the engine being redesignated VD-7. In the only example known of the M-50, the inner engines are after-burning VD-7F units, and the outer plain VD-7s in noticeably smaller nacelles. Each outer nacelle has a large and prominent ram air inlet on the tip, there being no corresponding inlet on the inner engines. Four VD-7s would have been inadequate, and four VD-7Fs too much. No defensive armament was planned, and in fact this prototype lacked any operational equipment.

First flown by Goryainov and Lipko on 27 October 1959, they praised almost everything, including the view, cockpit layout and simple and effective flight controls. In a brief test programme Mach 1 was passed on the interim engines, but in 1961 cancellation of the XB-70 resulted in cancellation of further development of the M-50. The prototype continued to be used in various programmes, and seven years after it first flew it was

included in the 1967 Aviation Day flypast at Tushino, causing a sensation. It was then taken to the VVS museum at Tushino, and displayed in take-off attitude. A production version would have had the Zubets engine, integral-tank wet wings, a full suite of electronics, a flight-refuelling probe and provision for launching at least two cruise missiles on pylons between the main landing gears.

In fact, the cancellation of the XB-70 was just the final straw that stopped the programme. There were many other reasons why the M-50 would probably have remained a prototype. The most basic was that it was designed to fly at high altitude. Even in its intended role as a launcher of cruise missiles it would have been very vulnerable. Another factor was that the Soviet Union was spending sums that were astronomic by any standard on ICBMs and space launchers, leaving less available for everything else. A third factor was that, when terminated, the M-50 still had a very long way indeed to go before it could have been considered an operational weapon, and it was just not worth the effort. A final consideration was that, though the Soviet Union was interested in building an SST (supersonic transport), the big Myasishchyev was absolutely useless as a starting point. But the Russians love things that are big and powerful, and this aircraft was abandoned with reluctance.

SPECIFICATION

M-50 prototype
Two Koliesov VD-7F afterburning turbojets rated at about 32,000 lb and two VD-7 rated at about 27,000 lb
Dimensions Span over engines 37 m (121 ft 4¾ in); length (approx) 57 m (187 ft); wing area 282 m² (3036 sq ft)
Weight Empty 74.5 t (164,240 lb); maximum 200 t (440,000 lb)
Performance Maximum speed (high altitude) 1950 km/h (1212 mph, Mach 1.83); radius (high altitude, no payload, subsonic) 3000 km (1864 miles)
Armament Not fitted

Grumman A-6 Intruder

First Flight – 19 April 1960

An almost exact American counterpart to the Buccaneer, the A-6 is likewise a two-seat twin-jet monoplane equipped for operation from carriers and to fly attack missions against surface targets at night or in bad weather. In virtually every other respect it is quite dissimilar. The seats are not in tandem but almost side-by-side. The engines are not turbofans but turbojets. Instead of being compact with BLC slits, the wings and tail are conventional. Instead of having an internal bomb bay everything is hung outside. And instead of having just a rather primitive radar designed to see heavy cruisers the A-6 was given what the Russians would call 'an avionics complex'.

After all, the original US Marine Corps requirement of 1956, reflecting frustration in Korea of having no air support except in fine weather, called for 'a close air support attack bomber capable of hitting the enemy at any time'. The RFP (request for proposals) was issued in May 1957. Eight companies submitted 11 designs, and on 31 December of that year Grumman's Type G-128 was announced as having won. The design team was led by Lawrence Mead Jr and Robert Nafis, the work being shared between the main plant at Bethpage and the new assembly and test airfield at Calverton some 45 miles further east on Long Island. The Mock-Up Review Board was passed in September 1959, and on 19 April 1960 Bob Smyth flew BuNo 147864, the first of eight development YA2F-1 Intruders. The designation was changed to A-6 in the 1962 unified system.

The YA2F-1 came out very much like the original unbuilt Blackburn B.103, precursor of the Buccaneer, of 1953. It had a bulging forward fuselage, twin turbojets tucked in the space under the wing roots and jetpipes arranged to tilt down to augment lift on take-off and landing. The engine selected was the 8500-lb Pratt & Whitney J52-6, hung under the leading edge and with a long jetpipe extended back behind the trailing edge, the final 10 ft being pivoted and capable of being pushed down by a hydraulic jack through 23°. On the approach, door-type airbrakes could be opened behind the nozzles, causing high drag, and with the engines at high power the approach speed could be reduced by 11 mph.

The wing was designed for good lift at modest speeds, with only slight sweepback, a long span (53 ft) and full-span leading-edge droop flaps and single-slotted trailing-edge flaps. Worked hydraulically, these reduced stalling speed to 87 kt. With nowhere to put ailerons, lateral control was effected

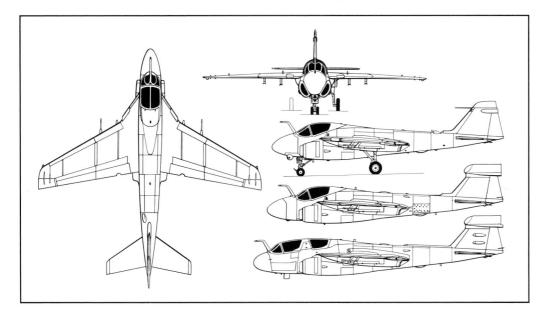

LEFT *A-6E, EA-6A, EA-6B*

TOP *Unusual view looking up at the YA2F-1 during trials with four tanks. The pivoting jetpipes are very prominent*

ABOVE *This A-6A helped train crews for the Pacific Fleet with VAH-123 at Edwards*

by flaperons, long spoilers ahead of the flaps which could also open symmetrically as spoilers and lift dumpers. The outer panels power-folded upwards about 50 per cent semi-span. The main feature of the fuselage was its fatness ahead of the wing and slimness behind. The crew sat in Martin-Baker GRU.5 seats, the radar operator (later called the bombardier/navigator) being slightly behind the pilot on the right of the centreline. A single broad canopy covered the cockpit, opened up and to the rear on steeply inclined tracks. The tail was conventional, with slab tailplanes mounted on the slender fuselage. The landing gears comprised a twin-wheel steerable nose unit, strong enough to bear the 100-ton catapult pull, and retracting to the rear, and quite tall main units each with a single wheel, with a leg stressed to hitting the deck with 20 ft/sec rate of descent pivoted at the rear of the wing box and retracting forward, the wheel being stowed in the angle between the wing root and the inlet duct. About 1950 gal (8800 litres) of fuel could be housed in the integral-tank wings and self-sealing fuselage cells.

Grumman then went ahead and built 484 A-6A Intruders for the VA and VMA heavy attack squadrons of the Navy and Marine Corps. They differed from the prototypes in having 9300-lb J52-8A or 8B engines with jetpipes fixed at a 7° downward angle, the fuselage airbrakes augmented by unusual wingtip brakes which split open to present upper and lower surfaces at almost 90° to the airflow, an enlarged rudder, five stores pylons each rated at 3600 lb (1633 kg) and the full initial spectrum of avionics. By far the largest avionic system was the nav/attack system called DIANE, from Digital Integrated Attack Navigation Equipment. Its main sensors were the Norden APQ-92 search radar and the small APQ-88 tracking radar, both feeding a Kaiser vertical display indicator giving a kind of part-real, part-synthetic picture of the scene ahead, unaffected by weather. Other parts of the DIANE included a radar altimeter and the inertial and doppler navigation systems. Litton provided the essential ASQ-61 digital computer, which processed the inputs from the sensors and presented the results either on the cockpit displays or as direct control servo signals to steer the aircraft.

The first A-6As reached VA-42 'Green Pawns' in February 1963. It is fair to describe it as the first genuinely all-weather attack bomber in history. With proper training (from NAS Oceana and later Whidbey Island), the crew could be cat-shot into a snow blizzard at night, locate, identify and destroy a target, and then land back on the carrier all without taking a glance outside the cockpit (so the brochures said). The other side of the coin was a very high burden in maintenance time and unserviceability, particularly ashore in South-east Asia, mainly at Da Nang and Chu Lai, where high-tech support was not all it might have been. Even aboard the superbly equipped carriers the Navy A-6A serviceability in 1965–66 did not exceed 35 per cent.

A colossal and prolonged effort was made by industry, backed up by the Naval Avionics Lab, to improve both reliability and performance of the avionics. After developing the tracking radar into the Norden APQ-112 it was realised it was hardly being used. Indeed, 19 Intruders were converted into day interdiction aircraft called A-6Bs, with about half the avionics removed. These flew mainly anti-radar missions with AGM-78 Standard ARM missiles. Another 12 aircraft were converted as A-6Cs, with the TRIM (trail/roads interdiction multi-sensor) in a big chin fairing housing a FLIR (forward-looking infra-red) and an LLTV (low-light TV). They were much better than the original aircraft in finding Viet Cong targets at night.

The EA-6A and EA-6B Prowler electronic-warfare aircraft, and the 78 aircraft converted as KA-6D air refuelling tankers hardly come within the scope of this book. From early in A-6A production, provision was made for greatly extending mission endurance both by fitting a fixed but removable

flight-refuelling probe ahead of the windscreen and by plumbing all five stores stations for drop tanks of 300 or 400 US gal capacity, giving a ferry range of up to 3245 miles (5222 km).

Thus, the next, and last, A-6 attack variants are all various sub-types of the A-6E. This programme began with 240 A-6A rebuilds, followed by 202 new aircraft. By far the most important type of A-6 since it entered service in 1972, the E-model is to this day the standard equipment of carrier heavy attack squadrons. The airframe differs only in detail from earlier versions, though structural audits have led to prolonged mostly minor modification to rectify or avoid fatigue damage during a lifetime roughly six times that originally planned. The flaps were made of the track-mounted Fowler type, and modified to act as flaperons, the original spoiler flaperons being retained, and the fuselage airbrakes were deleted. The P-8B version of the J52 has the same 9300-lb rating, but better life and maintainability. The seat is the Martin-Baker GRU7, which can be reclined to reduce fatigue.

By far the most important changes in the A-6E were avionic. Inside the vast nose is the Norden APQ-148 multi-mode radar, used for both navigation and attack. It simultaneously provides for ground mapping, target search/lock-on and ranging for fixed or moving targets, and terrain clearance or terrain following. It feeds an IBM ASQ-133 and Fairchild computer subsystem which is linked among other things to the Litton ALR-67 radar

warning system and the inertial and doppler navigation subsystems. Soon after the A-6E made its first flight, on 10 November 1970, Litton began delivery of ASN-92 CAINS (Carrier Aircraft Inertial Navigation System). In October 1974 the first aircraft flew with the TRAM (Target-Recognition Attack Multi-sensor) turret under the chin. The B/N (bombardier navigator) first identifies a target on the multifunction display, seen by the radar. He then slews the TRAM turret on to it, switched to FLIR and using a zoom lens. After studying the enlarged image he switches to the TRAM laser and designates the target, either for his own or for a companion's smart weapons. Of course, TRAM can also acquire targets designated by friendly lasers on the ground or in other aircraft. Virtually all Navy and Marine Corps attack units now fly the A-6E/ TRAM, which since 1981 has also progressively been modified to launch up to four AGM-84 Harpoon cruise missiles.

In the early 1980s plans went ahead for a further variant, the A-6F, with numerous airframe upgrades, the vastly superior General Electric F404 engine and new avionics. Sadly, this programme was cancelled, to some degree in the belief that the A-12 Avenger II would shortly become available. This left a major programme by BMAC (Boeing Military Airplanes Co) at Wichita to re-wing A-6Es, and the A-6E SWIP (Systems Weapon Integration Program). The last metal-wing A-6E was delivered in 1988, since when BMAC has been supplying

ABOVE *One of the early recipient units was VA-75, embarked aboard* USS Independence *(CV-62). The furthest aircraft totes AGM-12 Bullpup missiles*

graphite/epoxy wings for both new and retrofit aircraft to give a further 8800 hours without fatigue damage. Following cancellation of the A-12, BMAC expects to re-wing most of the A-6Es, but money is hard to find. The original contract for 179 wing sets still stands, and BMAC is competing for further buys.

The SWIP programme likewise applied to the final 33 new aircraft plus most of those in the inventory. It provides for eventually fitting the J52-409 engine rated at 12,000 lb, and with better fuel economy. Block 1 changes include an advanced radar, wide-angle HUD, a new night-attack navigation system, additional chaff/flare dispensers, and provision for Harpoon, Maverick, HARM, AMRAAM and advanced Sidewinder missiles, as well as various airframe improvements. Block 1A adds GPS (satellite navigation), with GPS software in the new ASN-139 inertial system, a digital (1553B) databus, a GEC Avionics air-data computer and HUD, upgraded Tacan, and new

TOP *Right-seater's view as a KA-6D tanker of VA-34 approaches that so-tiny airfield*

LEFT *One of the first A-6Es went to VA-65*

BELOW *Coming in over the stern of USS* Kitty Hawk *(CV-63) during the Vietnam War, this A-6A (probably of VA-85) shows off its wingtip airbrakes*

wing fillets housing antennas for the Sanders ALQ-126 ECM and associated receivers and dispensers. Development was proceeding on schedule in 1993 for eventual upgrade of 290 A-6Es.

The A-6E and KA-6D naturally played a major role in *Desert Storm*, operating from their carriers against sea, coastal and land targets. Ships involved were; USS *America* (CV-66), VA-85; USS *Eisenhower* (CVN-69), VA-34; USS *Independence* (CV-62), VA-196; *JFK* (CV-7), VA-75; USS *Midway* (CV-41), VA-115; USS *Ranger* (CV-61), VA-145; USS *Saratoga* (CV-60), VA-35; and USS *Theodore Roosevelt* (CVN-71), VA-36 and VA-65. Aircraft used 28 different types of weapon, including SLAM (land-attack Harpoon cruise missiles), GBU-10E/B, -12D/B and -16B/B smart bombs, Skipper II rocket-powered smart bombs, Walleye II precision glide bombs, Mk 7 dispensers with various loads, many TALDs (Tactical Air-Launched Decoys) against the intense flak, and Shrike anti-radar missiles. Three A-6Es were lost, a fourth returning damaged beyond economic repair.

TOP *Buddy refuelling, using the Douglas D-704 pack, by aircraft of VA-165*

ABOVE *These VMA(AW)-533 Intruders returning to Cherry Point all wear Gulf War bomb symbols*

SPECIFICATION

A-6E
Two Pratt & Whitney J52 turbojets: (in inventory), 9300-lb J52-408, (planned replacement) 12,000-lb Dash-409
Dimensions Span 53 ft 0 in (16.15 m); length 54 ft 9 in (16.69 m); wing area 528.9 sq ft (49.1 m²)
Weight Empty (1970) 25,630 lb (11,625 kg), (1992) 27,613 lb (12,525 kg); max TO (cat) 58,600 lb (26,580 kg), (field) 60,400 lb (27,397 kg)
Performance Maximum speed S/L 644 mph (1037 km/h); cruise (optimum altitude) 474 mph (763 km/h); range (max military load, with 300-USG centreline tank, hi-lo-hi) 1011 miles (1627 km); ferry range (tanks retained) 2740 miles (4410 km)
Armament Five hardpoints each rated at 3600 lb (1633 kg) for total load of up to 18,000 lb (8165 kg); see text for details

Tupolev Tu-22M

First Flight – 30 August 1964

Despite its shortcomings the Tu-22 had such a useful all-round capability as an in-theatre bomber, missile launcher and reconnaissance aircraft that it had an active service life more than three times as long as the B-58, which was quite a close contemporary. Nevertheless, nothing is so good that it cannot be made better, and in 1961 the CAHI and the Tupolev OKB jointly studied the prospects for fitting this aircraft (the basic Tu-105) with pivoted 'swing wings', as was also being studied at that time with the Sukhoi attack aircraft and various other projects.

At that time such wings were fashionable, and as the gains in all cases were even greater than predicted the Aviation Ministry funded a complete development prototype programme. Tunnel testing of models showed that, with minimal change to the rest of the aircraft, fitting variable-geometry outer wings (for any given weapons load) would permit combat radius to be almost doubled whilst field length would be approximately halved. Though the OKB had its own numbers for the project's different forms, it was agreed that the Service designation should be Tu-22M.

Actual design work began in the Tupolev OKB, later restyled the ANTK (Aviation and Scientific Technical Complex) named for the founder A N Tupolev, in early 1962. In fact, the planned relatively simple modification of the Tu-22 – even to the extent of starting with two existing airframes – never happened. One reason is that the task was even more difficult than expected, but a major contributory factor is that from Dr Alexei Tupolev down, everyone in the OKB was eager to produce a superior aircraft.

Back in late 1960 the engine KB of Nikolai Kuznetsov had been given the go-ahead to produce an improved power plant specifically for the 22M. The new engine, the NK-20, was an augmented turbofan based on the civil NK-8 and on the NK-22 turbojet for supersonic use. Compared with the NK-22 its mass flow was nearly 30 per cent greater, and in 1964 the new bomber engine was qualified at a rating of 20 tonnes, or 44,090 lb. This had been the design rating from the start (hence the designation, which appeared to be retrograde), and this greater power enabled the Tupolev designers, led by Andrei Kandalov, Mikhail Ulyanov and, later, Boris Levanovich, to aim for a take-off weight of 120 t (264,550 lb). This greatly upgraded the 22M's capability.

Ironically, in an interview in late 1992 Levanovich said that the designation Tu-22M was merely 'politics', implying that the weapons and mission had not changed, even though the vehicle itself was entirely new. This was at once misconstrued as meaning that the 22M was not in any way derived from the Tu-22, which is as misleading as the

BELOW Wearing code Blue 33, this Tu-22M-0 is preserved at Monino. It differs greatly from the production 22M

earlier Western belief that the first of the Tu swing-wing bombers had been a direct conversion of an existing Tu-22. The only hardware used from the Tu-22 programme comprised major fuselage and vertical tail parts, various systems components and major items of tooling, suitably modified.

The engine installation of the Tu-22 had worked well enough, but overall efficiency and high-Mach pressure recovery could be improved by using long inlet ducts leading back from fully variable intakes on the sides of the fuselage. This was agreed as desirable at the outset, and from 1962 construction went ahead at Kazan of two prototypes designated Tu-22M-0, both with the new engine installed side-by-side inside the tail end of a modified Tu-22 fuselage, with variable inlets on the sides ahead of the wing. The inboard wing retained the SR-5S profile and a leading-edge sweep of 52°, and for the first M-0 was structurally little changed.

On the tips of this inboard wing, at one-third semi-span were the pivots for the outer wings, positioned far back at almost 50 per cent of the local chord. Each pivot was a plain steel bearing of large diameter, permitting the outer wings to be set to any angle from 20° to a maximum of 65°. The maximum setting made them noticeably overswept, this having been found to combine adequate lift with minimum supersonic drag. Maximum dash Mach number at height was set at 1.89. A major structural achievement was to make the big outer panels with a thickness/chord ratio of only 3.5 per cent at the pivot and 2.9 per cent at the tip. Thus, they flex visibly even in flight through calm air.

The curved inboard leading edge of the Tu-22 was retained, with sweep at the junction with the fuselage of 70°. The outer wing was entirely new, with three sections of full-span powered leading-edged slats and full-span three-segment slotted trailing-edge flaps. Absence of ailerons meant that the spoilers ahead of the flaps had to be redesigned to operate differentially for roll control, in conjunction with differential use of the tailplanes. The spoilers could also work symmetrically as airbrakes and lift dumpers.

The tailplanes, or tailerons, were larger than those of the Tu-22, but likewise set low. Leading-edge sweep was fractionally greater at 60°, and the tips were quite different, being aligned with the airflow. The vertical tail was little altered, the sweep being 80° on the dorsal fin and 60° on the fin proper. Of course, all control surfaces were fully powered.

Tu-22M-0 No 1 was first flown by a test crew headed by V P Borisov on 30 August 1964. News of its existence was not published in Washington until September 1969, the aircraft having been identified in imagery transmitted by a USAF satellite a few weeks earlier. The NATO reporting name *Backfire* was chosen. Better definition was obtained in July 1970, when another prototype was spotted. In fact, this was M-0 No 2, which had a redesigned wing centre section.

TOP *The completely different rear end of the Tu-22M-3 includes a specially designed turret with a GSh-23-II with superimposed barrels*

ABOVE *Twin NK-20 nozzles at the back of the M-0. Instead of a tail turret this version had a giant braking-parachute box*

The new wing had a straight leading edge, with no sharp sweep at the root. Structurally it was totally different with five spars all basically at right angles to the aircraft centreline except that Nos 3 and 4 were splayed apart to leave a triangular gap for the legs of the new main landing gears. These gears were designed for considerably greater gross weight and comprised an unusual six-wheel bogie, the aft pair of wheels closer together than the front four, on three axles carried on a rocking beam pivoted at the bottom of the main leg, with the main shock strut behind and a long radius rod in front. At the top the main leg curved sharply out towards the tip to form a trunnion pivoted in a steel forging bolted beneath the wing and faired by a blister. Thus, as a breaker bracing strut pulled the gear inwards the whole assembly rose up into the wing, the bogie being housed under the wing inside the fuselage. The bay doors were hinged near the centreline, and closed on the ground, and the legs carried their own door. Tyre sizes were 1030×350. The hinge fairing was extended back to behind the trailing edge, fooling Western analysts into thinking that the Tu-22 gear had been retained.

The neat levered-suspension nose gear retracted backwards into a bay well aft of the crew compartment, with a front door on the leg and twin bay doors left open on the ground. The unit had hydraulic steering and all three gears had anti-skid brakes. In the M-0 the twin braking-parachute installation was the same in the Tu-22.

The inlets of the No 2 aircraft were refined, but retained the 150 mm (6 in) gap to divert fuselage boundary-layer air, dumped overboard through large aft-facing ducts above and below. The splitter plate was vertical, unperforated and positioned by rams to vary the duct area and profile according to Mach number. At take-off extra air was admitted through three square auxiliary doors round the outer edge. All inlet lips were sharp, the top and bottom being angled back at 60° in plan. Aft, nine further auxiliary inlets were added above the wing root admitting air round the sides and top of the duct.

The engines were members of the same Kuznetsov family as the earlier NK-8, -22 and -144. The engines were installed at an angle so that, though wide apart at the front, their nozzles were close together. The afterburner had typical primary and secondary multi-flap nozzles, the geometry being

very similar to that on the Tu-144 engine. The outer panels were visible downstream of the end of the fuselage. The complete engine could be withdrawn to the rear. The ducts ran straight in plan view, there being no area-rule waisting of the fuselage. Further details appear under the M-2.

There was much more room in the 22M crew compartment than in the 22. The crew now numbered four. The pilot (usually the aircraft commander) sat on the left, beside the co-pilot. Behind them were the large control and display consoles for the navigator/bombardier and the electronic-systems officer (*radist*), both facing forwards. All four men had their own upward-opening 'gull wing' roof door, above a KM-1M ejection seat. For high- and medium-altitude level bombing the nav/bomb officer could leave his seat and lie at a ventral blister with a small oblique forward window, but would normally study a video display giving the same view. Initially the radar and tail armament was almost the same as that of the Tu-22K. Further details are given in descriptions of later versions.

From 1966 the design team, now led by Mikhail Ulyanov, worked on the Tu-22M-1, with a modified airframe with extensions to the outer wing panels, the slats and flaps remaining at their original terminations. The AC and DC electrics, with generators driven by the main engines and an APU, and the 210 kg/cm² (3000 lb/sq in) hydraulics, were finally perfected. So was the fuel system, with a fixed but removable flight-refuelling probe above the nose. A comprehensive 'electronics complex' was planned, incorporating 23 subsystems in over 80 LRUs (line-replaceable units). Some of these subsystems were linked with the new automatic flight-control system. One was the defensive gunfire control system, with two sensors linked to the radar and infra-red warning systems and an aft-facing target-acquisition and tracking radar. The gun was the GSh-23, with twin side-by-side barrels and

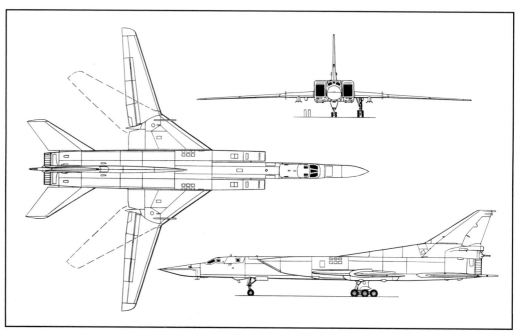

about 800 rounds. The M-1 was never built, being overtaken by the M-Z.

In 1972 series production began at Kazan of the Tu-22M-2. This did not differ greatly from the M-1 except in operational equipment. A completely new navigation and bombing radar was fitted, together with a terrain-following link and dual upgraded radar altimeters for flight at a normal minimum of 150 m (492 ft). The biggest development effort was to integrate all the elements of an almost completely new navigation and weapon-delivery system, together with computer-controlled defensive avionics. Previous ADF, doppler and inertial systems were augmented by a Glonass satellite receiver and provision for terrain-profile matching, work still not quite completed. Among the defensive aids were a powerful active-jammer, with C-VU-10-022 digital computers for energy management and transmitting antennas in the inboard leading edges and between the tail gunlaying radar and rudder, and both upward and downward ejectors for 192 chaff or flare cartridges in strips of eight triplets along each side of the rear fuselage, top and bottom. Defensive avionics usually include RWR passive receivers on each side of the nose and centre fuselage, along the inboard-wing leading edges and facing aft inboard of the tailplanes and at the top of the fin (which was raised above the rudder to house four antennas). LO-82 IR warning receivers are mounted above and beneath the forward fuselage.

Provision was made for a maximum bomb load of 24 tonnes, carried partly in the broad but shallow internal bay and partly hung on high-drag MBDZ-U9M racks along the sides of the fuselage, each with a nominal capacity of three or four triplets of bombs up to 500-kg (1102-lb) size. Alternatively, N (nuclear) or TN (tac-nuke) bombs up to 5 t weight can be carried internally. A third option is up to three cruise missiles of the Kh-22 type, each weighing some 6.3 t (13,900 lb). One can be recessed on the centreline, the bomb doors being profiled to fit snugly around the 37 ft (11.3 m) rocket. Two more can be carried on D2M (AERT-150) pylons under the wings just outboard of the landing gears, each pylon having the associated missile-conditioning system. Yet another option is 12 RKV-500B cruise missiles on an internal rotary launcher, plus two more similar weapons under each wing. The same rotary launcher can be loaded with six Kh-15P anti-radar missiles.

In 1975 the Kuznetsov KB ran the first of a largely redesigned augmented turbofan, or bypass turbojet, the NK-25. Aimed specifically at the Tu-22M, this featured a larger LP compressor handling considerably greater airflow, greater overall pressure ratio and higher turbine temperature. Rated at 25 t thrust, and with better specific fuel consumption, it enabled the weight of the bomber to be increased from 122 t (268,960 lb) to 124 t (see data), whilst at the same time reducing field length and increasing combat ceiling. Ulyanov's team

were reconciled to redesigning the inlet system for greater airflow, so they took the opportunity to switch to wedge-type inlets, which had given increasingly good pressure-recovery in the Tu-144 and were also recommended by CIAM. The upper interior wall is now the variable portion, and the lower hip is hinged. Small changes were made to the auxiliary inlets. Of course, the nozzles are also larger, requiring reprofiling of the rear fuselage.

Many other changes were also introduced and perfected in 11 development aircraft, the first of which flew in 1980. The main radar is of a new multi-mode type, again incorporating a terrain-following function but tailored primarily to maritime use, with a larger plate antenna scanning in a wider radome (with an odd turned-up-nose profile). The flight-refuelling probe is normally not fitted. At the tail a new turret is fitted with a side-mounted GSh-23 gun with barrels superimposed. The M3 is capable of routinely flying with three Kh-22 missiles, and is usually officially referred to as a rocket-launcher rather than as a bomber. Five other types of missile have been qualified on this aircraft, but are seldom carried except for the RKV-500B, Kh-15P and the Kh-31P anti-ship and anti-radar weapon.

Predictably, the NATO code-name *Backfire* was used by the US Department of Defense to justify massive expenditures on both offensive and defensive strategic systems, the Americans claiming that this bomber was intended for direct attacks on the United States. The official Washington estimate for its radius of action was 3000 nautical miles right up

BELOW *Dull blue flames are visible in the huge afterburners of the NK-25 engines as this M-3 takes off during the 1992 Farnborough Airshow. Note the nose-down attitude of the main-gear trucks*

ABOVE *Slotted flaps fully down, and slab tailplanes at an incredible angle, this M-3 grabs the last few seconds of lift before hitting the Farnborough runway*

TOP *Tu-22M-2 (No 44) has external fuselage bomb racks but no probe*

ABOVE *Everything out, down, extended and illuminated, the visiting M-3 on the approach at Farnborough in 1992*

to 1981. Not much publicity was given to the fact that a typical figure for both the M2 and M3 (depending on mission profile) is about 2200 km, or 1187 nm. Even so, alarm is now being expressed, with more justification, at the CIS's desperate wish to obtain hard currency by exporting these aircraft to anyone who can pay (Iran has been named by Western observers, a deal consistently denied by Moscow). Many used M2 and M3 bombers are available, the Kazan plant having delivered about 200 of the former and 120 M3s. In mid-1993 about 230 were in active DA units. A few are still being produced, and having little other work the Tupolev ANTK has developed an export version with modified avionics and a different radar. Clearance from the Russian government to conclude export contracts was expected before the end of 1993.

SPECIFICATION

Tu-22M3

Two Samara (Trud) NK-25 augmented bypass turbofans each rated at 25 t (55,115 lb) with full afterburner or 19 t (41,900 lb) dry
Dimensions Span (20°) 34.28 m (112 ft 5.6 in), (65°) 23.3 m (76 ft 5.3 in); length 42.46 m (139 ft 3.6 in); wing area (20°) 183.58 m² (1976 sq ft)
Weight Empty 54 t (119,050 lb); max fuel 57 t (125,660 lb); max bombload 24 t (52,910 lb); max take-off 124 t (273,370 lb); max landing 88 t (194,000 lb)
Performance Maximum speed at height 2000 km/h (1243 mph, Mach 1.9); crusing speed 900 km/h (559 mph); mission radius 2000 km (1242 miles); service ceiling (max wt) 13.3 km (43,650 ft); take-off, 370 km/h reached in 2050 m; landing, 285 km/h, with run of 1250 m
Armament One GSh-23M gun; various bomb and missile loads as detailed in the text up to a maximum of 24 t (52,910 lb)

North American B-70 Valkyrie

First Flight – 21 September 1964

Throughout the first 60 years of powered flight it was almost taken for granted that aeroplanes, including bombers, would go on getting bigger, heavier, much more powerful, faster and longer-ranged. In the case of bombers it also seemed important to fly higher and higher, to try to avoid being shot down. This process reached its pinnacle of development with the B-70, an aeroplane like no other before or since.

When the first prototype emerged from the factory on 11 May 1964 it was simultaneously the longest, heaviest, most powerful and most expensive aeroplane ever built; it was also the fastest aeroplane to take-off from the ground (instead of being dropped from a carrier aircraft) and missed, by a narrow margin, having the highest ceiling and longest range. It looked like nothing seen before, and its dazzling white finish and serial number 20001 were merely the outward appearance of the biggest package of new materials and new technologies in the history of aviation.

The challenging story began in 1954, when the first production B-52 was about to fly. The legendary commander of SAC, Gen Curtis E LeMay, could see clearly that, even though it was a jet, this great bomber would have a short life (nobody would have believed it would serve for 45 years). He was advised there were two possible replacements. Weapon System 110A was drafted, calling for a CPB (chemically powered bomber) having at least the same range as the B-52 and 'as high a speed as possible', which meant at least Mach 1+ and hopefully over Mach 2. The words 'chemically powered' were used because new fuels releasing higher energy than ordinary kerosene-type fuels appeared likely to be the key to higher flight performance. The alternative Weapon System 125A was to be an NPB (nuclear-powered bomber). This would obviously have to be huge and ponderous, and almost certainly subsonic, but it would have the advantage of being able to roam the skies for days or weeks at a time, and approach any target from any direction.

WS-125A was unique in that range was no problem. All other strategic delivery systems would have been relatively simple had it not been for the geography of Earth, which resulted in SAC establishing a baseline mission radius of 5500 nautical miles (6325 miles, 10,180 km). This multiplied the difficulties many times.

SAC naturally explored all other alternatives. The Department of Defense was funding two intercontinental cruise missiles: Northrop's subsonic SM-62 Snark got as far as equipping the 702nd Strategic Missile Squadron, but North American's fantastic SM-64A Navaho, which cruised at Mach 3, was cancelled in 1957 after the expenditure of $691 million. SAC also had the prospect of a totally different kind of nuclear delivery system, far more unstoppable than anything with wings. Until February 1954 the ballistic (wingless) missile, as pioneered by the German wartime A4 (so-called V2), was thought to be limited to ranges of a few hundred miles. Then came the report of John von Neumann's Teapot Committee, convened by the USAF, which stated that an ICBM (intercontinental ballistic missile) was not only feasible but could be created within six years. Obviously, the prospect of carrying a thermonuclear warhead over 6325 miles at 17,000 mph (27,400 km/h, or Mach 26)

BELOW *As the reptilian nose of 62-001 poked into the sunshine thousands of guests felt a sense of awe*

ABOVE *The first XB. Beautiful, maybe. Impressive, beyond doubt*

LEFT *At the back of the acres of stainless steel was a battery of afterburner nozzles whose decibel creativity was in a class of its own*

the mission to be flown at Mach 0.9, the USAF insisted that the final 1000 miles to the target should be flown at the highest supersonic speed possible. Even the most preliminary calculations sufficed to suggest that no CPB could ever take off from any practical airbase and bomb a target 6325 miles away and return, even without the supersonic requirement. Eventually, though this was not publicised, sights were set somewhat lower and for most of the CPB's life the unrefuelled range was about 7600 miles, which meant a mission radius of around 3800 miles.

Even this was still an almost impossible challenge. Ideally it demanded that the CPB should take off as one aircraft and penetrate the final 1000 miles as another. NAA decided to accept this, and their first submission comprised a huge delta-winged bomber designed for Mach 0.9, with a span of 260 ft and a gigantic fuel pod (as big as a B-47 fuselage) on each tip. The trick was that the outer wings were joined by free hinges, so that they carried just the weight of the tip pod. When all the tip fuel was consumed the outer wings were to be disconnected, leaving an aircraft tailored for a Mach 2.3 (1520 mph) dash to the target. Back at base with the weight reduced from 760,000 to only 210,000 lb, the stubby supersonic inboard wing would provide enough lift for a normal landing. But when LeMay saw the first artist's impression he removed his cigar and growled 'Hell, this isn't an airplane, it's a three-ship formation' – as indeed it was.

Boeing was likewise in trouble, and in October 1956 both bidders were told to think again. They explored variable 'swing wing' sweep and various other options, and kept falling back on the boost theoretically offered by so-called Zip fuel. Based on

seemed too good to be true. From 1954 enormous and rapidly increasing sums were voted to create WS-107A-1, a huge missile called Atlas, and WS-107A-2, a second ICBM called Titan. These inevitably reduced the money available for bombers, and eventually were to make the politicians and the public ask whether old-fashioned bombers were still needed.

In fact, the problems of creating an NPB were fairly quickly judged to outweigh the doubtful advantages. Convair and Lockheed won major WS-125A study contracts, supported by flying an operating reactor in the NB-36H, and General Electric and Pratt & Whitney spent over ten years working on two types of nuclear propulsion system, but by 1960 almost everything had been terminated. In contrast, the CPB grew into a gigantic programme. Six companies bid for it, and on 11 November 1955 Boeing and NAA (North American Aviation) were awarded WS-110A Phase I design contracts.

Even though the requirement permitted most of

ethyl borane, this costly liquid was to be produced at two huge plants which were actually built, one for the Air Force managed by Olin Mathieson and the other for the Navy managed by Callery Chemical. Zip fuel did terrible things to combustion chambers and, especially, to turbine blades, but it seemed to be the only way to get the required combination of supersonic speed and long range.

Then a miracle happened. Alfred J Eggers, an aerodynamicist at the National Advisory Committee for Aeronautics (NACA, soon to become NASA), was mowing his lawn in Virginia when he began pondering on the prospects for trapping airflow underneath a supersonic wing by boxing in the flow between an expanding body underneath it and downturned wingtips. Quickly he refined the idea, showing how at Mach numbers from 3 to 5 a vehicle with only the bottom half of a circular-section fuselage, entirely under the wing, could make the most favourable use of its shockwave pattern, provided the shapes were carefully adjusted and the outer wings were turned downwards. He co-authored a classic report with Clarence A Syvertson, which emerged with a high grade of security classification in March 1956.

Strangely, the report was not sent to NAA, but the company's CPB work qualified them for access to it, and during a literature search it immediately appeared to be of interest. Within a week NAA had found Eggers' compression-lift shapes worked miraculously. Wind-tunnel models were made with frantic haste, and when these were tested at Mach 3.5 the gain in lift/drag ratio was found to be over 100 per cent at small angles of attack and 22 per cent at peak L/D, which was reached at a smaller angle. Almost overnight the WS-110A aircraft was completely redesigned, with a 65.5° delta wing riding on top of an enormous box of jet engines, the huge wing having a completely flat upper surface and outer panels that could hinge downwards. At the back were twin powered verticals (combined fin/rudder surfaces) and projecting from just above the pointed apex of the wing was the fuselage, looking rather like the front of a serpent and carrying the trimming canard foreplane with powered trailing-edge flaps.

At a stroke, the gain in L/D ratio was so great that, not only could the bomber fly the required distance, but it could do so cruising at Mach 3 all the way. This transformed what had previously been an uncertain programme.

Boeing were told to read the crucial NACA report, but the winner of big competitions is often selected on grounds other than technical merit. It may well have been that the NAA design was better anyway, but in July 1957 NAA's biggest project, the Navaho missile, was cancelled, and 5000 technical staff were laid off. In contrast, Boeing was in such trouble trying to find a way to build KC-135s, 707s, B-47s and B-52s (to say nothing of Bomarc missiles and a second-generation ICBM) that they could

hardly have taken WS-110A on board as well. NAA was announced the winner on 23 December 1957.

On 6 February 1958 the programme was restyled the B-70, and the name Valkyrie was chosen on 3 July 1958. To the company it was the NA-278. NAA's board chairman, the great James H 'Dutch' Kindelberger, said 'I've been in this business more than 40 years, and I've never seen anything like the engineering solution to this problem'. General Electric won the propulsion contract with the J93-5, burning a special kerosene called JP-6 but with the afterburner burning Zip fuel. Six engines were needed for the bomber, while two J93s were needed for another NAA aircraft, the F-108 Rapier interceptor, which was also planned as an escort for the B-70. But difficulties with Zip fuel were enormous. On 12 August 1959, just days before the Zip plants were to go 'on stream' the entire Zip programme was cancelled. GE already had a J93-3 with an afterburner designed for JP-6. On 23 September 1959 the F-108 programme was cancelled. And on 1 December 1959 Thomas S Gates replaced Neil McElroy as Secretary for Defense and found that the decision had already been taken to abandon the idea of putting the B-70 into production.

A few days later it was announced that the programme had been 'reoriented' to a single prototype, to be flight-tested from 1962 until 1966. The Air Force Association furiously retorted that 'reorienting' really meant 'gutting'. The basic argument, as it appeared to the public, was that ICBMs had made the B-70 obsolete. Indeed, at this time yet another new weapon, the ALBM (air-launched ballistic missile), had appeared, and so-called experts in the media explained that this meant that in future SAC might as well use C-130s or even DC-3s as nuclear delivery systems.

Though not the first, the most important ALBM was Skybolt, and when this became front-page news in 1960 the B-70 was surprisingly listed as a future carrier. Moreover, in late January of that year the Air Force released a further $265 million for B-70 development, including $95 million to help develop the navigation and bombing system, which had earlier been specifically terminated. And in October 1960 it was announced that 'the B-70 has been restored to full weapon-system status'. This was a time when the Cold War was so frosty nobody wanted to cancel anything that could deliver megatons.

Then on 20 January 1961 John F Kennedy entered the White House, and in April announced that he had been unmoved by arguments to put the RS-70 into production, the designation meaning Reconnaissance/Strike. Instead, he said, the programme was being cut back to three prototypes, without military subsystems, and that even this would cost at least a further $1300 million before first flight. The order was placed on 4 October 1961, and comprised two XB-70As (62-0001 and 62-0207), with two seats and carrying nothing but test equipment, and an XB-70B (62-0208) with four seats and fully equipped as a bomber. Arguments intensified, and in January 1962 Defense Secretary Robert S McNamara was called to Congress to explain why he opposed the B-70. In part, he said, '... We have again re-studied the role of the B-70 in future strategic retaliatory forces, and again have reached the conclusion that the B-70 will not provide enough of an increase in our offensive capabilities to justify its very high cost ... The principal advantage of the B-70 is its ability, in common with other manned bombers, to operate under positive control and to deliver a large number of nuclear weapons in a single sortie. Considering the increasing capabilities of ground-to-air missiles, the speed and altitude of the B-70, in itself, would no longer be a very significant advantage. Furthermore, it has not been designed for the use of air-to-surface missiles such as Hound Dog or Skybolt, and in a low-altitude attack it must fly at subsonic speeds. In addition, the B-70 is not well suited to an era when both sides have large numbers of ICBMs. It would be more vulnerable on the ground than hardened missiles, and it does not lend itself to airborne-alert measures.

'Nevertheless, we plan to complete the limited development program outlined to the Congress last year – namely, to demonstrate the technical feasibility of the aircraft structure and configuration, as well as certain major subsystems required in a high-speed, high-altitude environment. This approach would still preserve the option of developing a manned bomber if we should later determine that such a system is required.

'The Air Force has studied the reorientation of the B-70 to a reconnaissance/strike vehicle. Such an aircraft might be useful in providing damage-assessment and reconnaissance information for the retargeting of the missile force during the attack period. It would also have a capability to attack previously unlocated, undetected or incompletely destroyed targets. Obviously this proposal will require a great deal more study to determine whether the advantages to be gained from such an aircraft are worth the great costs involved.'

Arguments persisted, a major factor in favour of the RS-70 being the work it would bring to the home states of influential congressmen. In March 1962 McNamara had to issue a further statement, in which he expressed the belief that the strategic retaliatory forces of the United States programmed through 1967 could, even after absorbing an initial pre-emptive strike, 'achieve practically complete destruction of the enemy target system'. He went on, 'The addition of a force of either 200 B-70s, which was proposed last year by the Air Force, or the 150 RS-70s now being considered, either of which would cost about $10 billion, would not appreciably change this result ...

'With regard to the wartime reconnaissance capabilities of the RS-70, we have other means of performing that function and with any adequate high-processing-rate radar system which may be developed, the B-52s and B-58s could have a considerable reconnaissance and bomb damage assessment capability incidental to their principal mission. We think that the B-52s and B-58s, arriving after our missiles have suppressed the enemy's air defense, could penetrate as well, or almost as well, as the RS-70.

'A decision by the Soviet Union to produce and deploy an anti-ICBM system could not significantly change this over-all picture, and in any event would be no less effective against the B-70 and its missiles ...' He went on to doubt the capability of developing an RS-70 high-resolution radar by 1970, to doubt the ability of communications to transmit the reconnaissance data and to doubt that humans could interpret it fast enough. Not forgetting the strike role, he opined the RS-70 would 'require the development of new air-launched strike missiles ... because of their limited size and warhead yield would have to be far more accurate than any strategic air-launched missile now in production or development'.

McNamara's 'other means' of performing the reconnaissance function was the then-secret Lockheed *Oxcart* programme, which was to lead via the A-12 to the SR-71 'Blackbird'. This aircraft, if anything flying even faster and higher than the RS-70 (the preceding number, though the letter prefix was inadvertently transposed when President Johnson revealed the Lockheed aircraft), played a significant role in reducing the need for the even more costly RS-70. In partnership with the Air Force, Lockheed produced numerous proposed derivatives of the SR-71 able to carry bombs or launch ALBMs or cruise missiles. But after the successful collaboration between Kennedy and Khrushchev to avoid World War III over the Cuban missile crisis, things changed. On the American side the Thor missiles began to be deactivated in England, Jupiter missiles were removed from Turkey and Italy, and Skybolt was cancelled. This threw the RAF into utter disarray, and also angered many US Congressmen who pointed out that they had accepted cancellation of a production B-70 only on explicit understanding that the B-52H would carry the Skybolts for which it had been designed. Worse (for the Hawks) was to come. In February 1964 Congress voted to hold the B-70 programme to $1500 million, and whereas in 1961 $1300 million bought three air vehicles, in 1964 $1500 million bought only two. The XB-70B was thus cancelled, and the sole return for more than ten years of costly work was to be two vehicles intended to gather data which might be useful for a future SST (supersonic transport).

It was the first of these two almost identical air vehicles that awed the hundreds of invited guests who sought the shade of its 6297 sq ft wing on 11 May 1964. Aerodynamically, structurally and in its

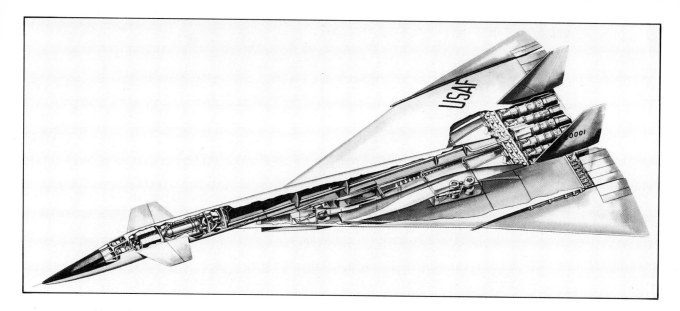

systems it was like nothing that had gone before. At this time, though computers were used en masse, everything was still done in traditional ways with answers written in books, and the elastic analysis of the B-70 – just one of dozens of aspects of the airframe's structural design – filled over 70 large volumes. About 69 per cent of the structure was made in special stainless steel called PH-15-7-Mo, and to shape this it had to be either hot-creep-formed in a furnace or deep-freeze-formed at −100°F. Never before had such an enormous structure been made by such methods, with the thickness of each part so precisely controlled (because an extra thousandth of an inch on the wing skins, for example, would add almost a ton to the weight).

There is no room here to describe even a fraction of the task of making a B-70, beyond noting that each of the mighty sheets reflected brilliantly like a mirror, had to be shaped with unprecedented accuracy, and joined by TIG-welding (tungsten/inert gas) or by brazing with a material which included a high proportion of sterling silver. Each spar had a web in the form of a wiggly sine-wave, and, whereas most aircraft wings had two or three spars, most of the B-70 wing had 54! Almost every nook and cranny formed an integral fuel tank, and when the supposedly finished structure of the first aircraft was filled with fuel and put under pressure whilst being cooked at 270°c (518°F) and flexed under simulated flight loads, fuel vapour poured in blue clouds from the joints. The trouble was microscopic porosity through numerous spot-welds, and millions of dollars were spent trying to stop fuel leaks. The narrow U-shaped No 5 tank, the rearmost of those along the centreline, was never properly sealed and was therefore left empty. Neither was the air-refuelling receptacle installed in its bay above the nose.

No 20001 spent four months on the Palmdale ramp being worked on by an army of highly qualified and often highly stressed engineers. At last on 21 September 1964 chief test pilot Al White and USAF project pilot Col Joe Cotton took the monster into the sky, rotating at 183 kt, this speed having climbed in stages over preceding months from the design figure of 150. After flying to Edwards in take-off configuration, the canard flap and landing gears were raised in preparation for going supersonic. But the gears refused to cycle, so handling was explored at low speeds using the six elevons and a 'vertical' on each wing. Each surface was driven by two power units in separate hydraulic systems operating at 4000 lb/sq in and filled with Oronite 70 which, like all the system hardware, was designed to work reliably at 332°c (630°F). Finally, the canard flaps were lowered to retrim the aircraft as the elevons were depressed to act as landing flaps, and a good landing made on the lake-bed with the three braking parachutes streamed, marred by locking of the two left rear main tyres which immediately exploded. The problem here was malfunctioning of the anti-skid system, which was governed by small sensor wheels in the middle of each four-wheel truck.

Subsequently one of the few enduring problems for the B-70 pilot was that his eyes on the nose-high landing were 100 ft in front of the main gears, and 40 ft higher. Apart from that, and the very high workload with only two men aboard, flying the B-70 was, said Cotton, 'Like driving a Greyhound bus 200 miles an hour around the track at Indianapolis'. On Flight 4 the outer wings were rotated to the 25° high-speed transition setting, and on Flight 5 to the full 65° supersonic cruise position, each row of six hydraulic drive motors being the most powerful ever used up to that time. Equally impressive was the engine box, over 7 ft deep, swelling from the sharp-edged inlets until it was 37 ft wide, and 110 ft long. At the front was a splitter like the prow of a destroyer, behind which were the perforated inner walls about the size of a large room, driven to within a thousandth of an inch against enormous aerodynamic forces to vary the duct profile and area according to Mach number. The twin steerable nosewheels retracted rearwards between these inner walls, while the ducts swept inwards around the main-gear bays, and their water cooling

systems to protect the rubber tyres. Between the ducts, on the centreline, was the bay with a sliding door in the flat undersurface which was designed to house bombs or ALBMs. At the rear the ducts led to the six J93 engines, each in a square-section compartment. Sundstrand supplied the auxiliary power units and secondary power systems.

Getting aboard was perhaps the most perilous part of the mission, because the crew door, just ahead of the canard on the left side, was almost 20 ft from the ground. Most of the structure of the fuselage was titanium, its 80 ft length being cantilevered ahead of the wing. The cosy cockpit contained side-by-side seats surrounded by what, in a split second, could become an ejected escape capsule, stabilised by two long telescopic booms. To the rear the whole fuselage was filled with avionics and with the colossal environmental control systems. These were needed to cool not just the crew and avionics but almost everything on board. These systems comprised air-conditioning plants, air-cooled radiators, and enormous tanks of water and ammonia, the latter being the secondary heat sink. The main water-cooled heat exchanger was 59 ft further back in a rare dry bay between two fuel tanks.

The second aircraft, 62-207, joined the programme on 17 July 1965. On its 39th flight it showed the kind of mission these great aircraft had been designed for, holding Mach 3.08 for 33 minutes whilst making a 2700-mile (4345-km) trip through eight Western States. By this time the missions were tasked mainly with sonic-boom research for NASA. The manufacturer's Phase I contract was to expire on 15 June 1966, after which everything would be in support of the US programme to build an SST. Just a week beforehand, on 8 June, No 2 was booked to fly a 'clean-up' mission to complete Phase I, and General Electric obtained permission to organise a formation of aircraft using their engines around the B-70 at the completion of the serious work. By 9.30am a GE-

engined Learjet had got the required pictures. The formation included a NASA F-104, flown by Joe Walker, perhaps the most experienced high-Mach pilot in the world. Unbelievably, he wandered far too close to the B-70's right wingtip, was gripped in the mighty tip vortex and hurled inverted across the top of the giant's wing. The Starfighter slammed into the twin verticals, carrying them away, before exploding in a fireball. The doomed B-70 carried on for perhaps a full minute before, with majestic lack of haste, it began a sickening oscillation which eventually went outside the design envelope. As it broke up, Al White ejected. USAF Maj Carl S Cross, on his familiarisation ride, never even initiated the ejection sequence.

The ensuing storm had repercussions which, insofar as they affected the relations between the USAF and the media, are felt to this day. The surviving B-70 continued to fly valuable research missions until, on 4 February 1969, Lt-Cols Fitzhugh Fulton and Ted Sturmthal brought it to the Museum at Wright-Patterson AFB. One of the enduring results of this intended bomber was that the Mikoyan bureau produced a fast interceptor, the Ye-155P, which led to the MiG-25 and MiG-31.

SPECIFICATION

B-70A
Six General Electric YJ93-3 turbojets each rated at 19,800 lb dry and 27,200 lb with max afterburner
Dimensions Span (spread) 105 ft 0 in (32.0 m), (65°) 78 ft 6 in (23.9 m); length 196 ft 6 in (59.89 m); wing area 6297 sq ft (585 m²)
Weight Empty about 205,000 lb (92,990 kg); max take-off 550,000 lb (249,476 kg)
Performance Max cruising speed 2035 mph (3275 km/h, Mach 3.08); service ceiling 75,000 ft (22,860 m); unrefuelled range, intended to be 7600 miles (12,230 km), actually less
Armament Never fitted, but intended to comprise up to 14 nuclear bombs, various conventional bombloads or externally carried ALBMs

BAC TSR.2

First Flight – 27 September 1964

ven in this substantial volume there is hardly room to rake over this extraordinary programme, which in almost every respect serves as a textbook example of how *not* to do it. The tale has been told many times but TSR.2 was to have been a bomber, and a bomber of uncommon ability to penetrate defended airspace, so it cannot be omitted.

By September 1957 the British Air Staff had managed to write a small document called General Operational Requirement 339, calling for a new tactical bomber and reconnaissance aircraft to replace the Canberra. At that time the Canberra's producer, English Electric Aviation, had already completed the project design of such an aircraft. Designated P.17, it had twin RB.133 afterburning turbojets side-by-side in the rear of a long but slender fuselage, a high-mounted delta wing, tandem seats for pilot and navigator and a landing gear tailored for rough-field operation. Like GOR.339 the P.17 was farsighted in combining high-altitude dash speed of Mach 2 with the ability to operate from short unpaved airstrips and fly over hostile territory at full throttle at treetop height. In stark contrast to the subsequent 35 years, the NATO air forces were at that time terrified of having their airfields wiped off the map by missiles, and the P.17 was soon developed into the P.17D which was to be lifted out of forest clearings by a VTOL platform with 60 lift jets!

To cut a long story short GOR.339 emerged soon after Defence Minister Duncan Sandys had announced that the RAF would be 'unlikely to require' any more manned aeroplanes, except for transports and trainers. Thus, the supposed Canberra-replacement was born into a world of acrimony and controversy, which was to some degree deflected into arguing about the totally different matter of the industry itself. GOR.339 had elicited 14 proposals from nine big and powerful aircraft companies, suggesting engines from five of the six biggest aero-engine firms. For reasons which are far from obvious the government thought it would be nice if the number of companies could be reduced – some said, to one airframe company and one engine firm – so it was announced that in future major contracts, such as GOR.339 and the new short-haul jet for BEA, would be awarded only to groupings of companies prepared to undertake genuine mergers, not just collaborative effort by the original firms.

So on 1 January 1959 it was announced that the Canberra replacement would be developed by Vickers-Armstrongs (Aircraft) and English Electric Aviation, who would merge into a single company, while the twin engines would be advanced Olympus turbojets developed by Bristol Aero-Engines and Armstrong Siddeley Motors, who would form another merged company. Bristol were from the start the dominant engine partner, while Vickers had the whip hand on the airframe, despite a

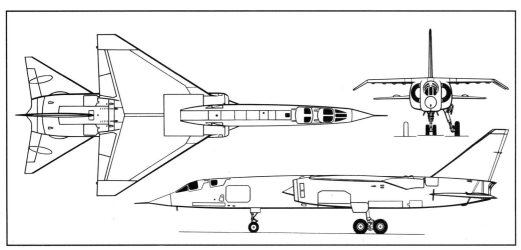

TOP *The first photograph released for publication showed the prototype TSR.2 in the Weybridge factory. The main sections from Lancashire and Southampton then had to be dismantled and reassembled at Boscombe Down*

MIDDLE *On the first take-off, seen here, 'Bee' Beamont and navigator Don Bowen were only too aware that the engines might explode at any moment!*

RIGHT *Taken from the chase Lighting T.4 during the first flight. By this time the engines were throttled back to a safe rpm range*

supposed 50/50 share of the work. The problems of who would be managing director or chief test pilot are obvious, especially as previously all the companies had been bitter rivals. The general consensus was 'Fine, so long as they do it *our* way'.

By 1959 GOR.339 had become OR.343 to describe the actual aircraft, built to specification RB.192D and designated TSR.2, from Tactical Strike and Reconnaissance. The development contract, priced at £90 million, was placed on 7 October 1960, covering nine aircraft (XR219/227). Subsequently a further development batch of 11 were ordered (XS660/670). The design was based strongly on the Vickers (Supermarine) Type 571, this company's works at Weybridge, Hurn and Itchen (Southampton) being responsible for the main delta wing and the fuselage back to station 629 (rear of the wing box) extended lower down to station 640 to include the bays for the tandem-wheel main gears. English Electric's factories at Preston were responsible for the aft fuselage and tail. The merged company was called British Aircraft Corporation (BAC). The Olympus 22R Mk 320 engines, rated at 30,610 lb with maximum afterburner, were produced by Bristol Siddeley Engines Ltd (BSEL). As for systems and avionics, these involved almost the entire accessory industry, because this was the only new warplane for many years and almost everything had to be designed from scratch.

Low-level attack aircraft need the smallest possible wing span and area, and so one of the basic challenges was how to make such a wing lift an aircraft weighing nearly 50 tons off a short rough strip. After looking carefully at pivoting swing-wings and jet lift the choice fell simply on very powerful blown flaps. The wing was basically a 60° delta, with aspect ratio of only 1.96, so that even with an area of 700 sq ft the span was only 37 ft. Thickness was 3.7 per cent, with a fixed leading edge with slight droop. At the back was the plain flap, blown over its entire span. The wing tips were tilted down at 30°. Flight control was by a fin and two tailerons, all fully powered. The tailerons, set quite low to avoid wing wake, incorporated small elevators which were unlocked and deflected upwards whenever the flaps were lowered with blowing.

No less than 5588 Imp gal of fuel was housed in the fuselage and wing, the maximum with auxiliary fuel in the weapon bay and drop tanks under the wings and fuselage being a remarkable 8188 gal. A neat retractable FR probe was installed on the left side of the nose. The seats were Martin-Baker Mk 8A, with zero/zero capability and several unique features. Electro-Hydraulics provided the landing gears, with powerful Maxaret brakes and a nose leg which for STOL take-offs could be extended by 42 in. The engines were fed by long ducts from fully variable lateral semi-circular inlets, and to confer complete autonomy a BSEL (previously Blackburn)

ABOVE *The Warton workforce turned out to welcome home what was by that time known to be a superb aircraft. This picture also gives an idea of its size*

Cumulus APU provided pneumatic, hydraulic and electrical power. Hydraulic system pressure was 4000 lb/sq in. There were four door-type airbrakes around the rear fuselage, and a braking parachute was housed in the upper pen-nib fairing between the afterburner nozzles.

The greatest of the many increasingly challenging development efforts was needed by the avionics. Ferranti supplied the multimode forward-looking radar, which provided for terrain following (in 1958 a world first), and the inertial reference system used in conjunction with Decca doppler. Navigation fixes were updated by one of two large EMI side-looking radars with the 90-in antennas in the flat sides of the avionics bay which filled the fuselage behind the cockpit, between Stations 207 and 280. The other SLAR was a reconnaissance radar, backing up the array of sensors which could be mounted on a weapon-bay pallet. Elliott-Automation supplied the central digital computer, autopilot and HUD. Smiths produced the air-data system, analog/digital converter and cockpit displays. Today there is nothing exceptional about TSR.2 avionics, but in the late 1950s none of it existed. On the other hand, the weapons fit requested was modest. Two nuclear bombs in the weapon bay and two on the inboard wing pylons were an alternative to six 1000-lb bombs internally, plus four on the pylons, or four Martel or AS.30 missiles or four rocket launchers.

Predictably, development took much longer than expected and cost many times the ludicrously small estimates. The stage was set for a melodrama in which a devoted band of engineers strove night and

day to create the weapon system the RAF had demanded, while the opposition Labour Party and, almost to a man, the popular media, stridently proclaimed that TSR.2 was a wildly extravagant scandal which ought to be cancelled at once. In 1963 the strong probability that TSR.2 would be ordered as Australia's Canberra replacement was nipped in the bud by the Labour announcement that they would cancel it if ever they came to power. Among daily vituperation by the opposition politicians were such offerings as 'TSR.2 will only drop ordinary high explosive on tanks and bridges ... new anti-aircraft weapons will be able to shoot it down by the time it is in service, so at £16 million an aircraft it is going to make Mr Amery's other blunders look like chickenfeed.... it is not the duty of the defence forces to act as a wet nurse to the overgrown and mentally retarded children in our economy ... this inherited monster has already gone on long enough'. Two media critics became famous and built successful careers on the policy of doing all they could to rubbish British aircraft (not just TSR.2), whilst extolling the virtues of anything with wings created in the United States.

When a Labour government was indeed elected in October 1964, BAC Managing Director Sir

TOP *Another view on the first flight, vortex condensation steaming from the tips*

LEFT *The penetrability of TSR.2 was never questioned. Its cancellation had nothing to do with its performance or effectiveness*

RIGHT *Once settled into the test routine the TSR.2 was a joy to fly, riding through turbulence that really shook the chase Lightning*

George Edwards expected each day to be told TSR.2 had been cancelled. When instead the axe fell on Concorde he said 'We just didn't see this one coming'. The French said they would take Britain to the International Court at The Hague, at which the new Aviation Minister, Roy Jenkins, said they hadn't really meant to cancel Concorde at all. So TSR.2 was allowed to go on generating fresh headlines each day explaining how many zillions would be 'saved' by buying the F-111 instead.

XR219, the first TSR.2, had begun its flight test programme in the hands of R P 'Bee' Beamont and Don Bowen at Boscombe Down on 27 September 1964. At that time the engine was still suffering from a potentially catastrophic high-frequency resonance at anything over 97 per cent LP rpm, but Beamont accepted the use of 100 per cent for the first two minutes of the first flight. Later, apart from unexpected problems with the main landing gears (which were soon corrected), the TSR.2 showed itself to be an absolutely superb aircraft, riding through turbulent air at Mach 0.9 to 1.12 with complete smoothness.

Beamont was due to deliver the Barnwell Memorial Lecture to the Royal Aeronautical Society on 10 March 1965, but the Ministry of Aviation instructed him not to give this lecture (in fact, they had no legal right to do this) because it would be most inconvenient and embarrassing if the test pilot were to state that TSR.2 was actually a good aeroplane. Eventually the immediate cancellation of the entire programme was announced in the Budget speech on 6 April 1965, tucked between an extra sixpence tax on cigarettes and four shillings on whisky. BAC were instructed to destroy every TSR.2 immediately, together with all jigs and tooling.

Fortunately some wicked people took it upon themselves to rescue XR219 from the gunnery range at Shoeburyness (where, it was said, the gunners deliberately failed to hit it), XR220 was put in the RAF Museum at Cosford and XR222 (still not quite completed) is in the Imperial War Museum collection at Duxford. Britain ordered 50 F-111Ks, ignoring the desperate problems afflicting the F-111 programme, and then cancelled them.

Instead it went into partnership with France on the AFVG (Anglo-French Variable Geometry) aircraft, but France then walked out, saying it had already produced such an aircraft in the various VG Mirages. It must be remembered that the British government had already announced that we would never again produce a warplane that was British. All we did produce was a succession of massive reports by highly paid experts and committees explaining that, if we must have an aircraft industry, it had better not actually produce aircraft, and we are now well on the way to accomplishing this.

According to Sir George Edwards, who has repeatedly seen world-beating British programmes torn up by the politicians, 'The battle with the enemy never stops on the civil front ... but a military cancellation does not show if you do not have a war'. So the politicians and the media were able to suggest ever more fanciful figures for the money supposedly saved by doing away with TSR.2, simply because we didn't happen to have a war at that time. And in 1986 test-pilot Beamont wrote 'The widespread smear campaign implying that TSR.2 was a scandalous technical and industrial failure, and a waste of taxpayers' money, can be seen for what it was as a monstrous manoeuvre, for political ends, from which the striking power of the Royal Air Force and the world-leader potential of British military-aviation technology have never recovered'.

SPECIFICATION

TSR.2

Two Bristol Siddeley Olympus Mk 320 afterburning turbojets each rated at 19,610 lb dry and 30,610 lb with max afterburner

Dimensions Span 37 ft 0 in (11.28 m); length 89 ft 0 in (27.13 m); wing area 700 sq ft (65 m²)

Weight Empty 44,850 lb (20,344 kg); max TO 95,900 lb (34,500 kg)

Performance Maximum speed at full load at S/L 840 mph (1352 km/h), (clean, hi, with original engines) Mach 2.05 (1360 mph, 2185 km/h); combat radius (hi-lo-hi, 2000-lb [907-kg] internal bombload or nuclear weapon) 1000 nm (1152 miles, 1853 km), (with 6000-lb internal and 6000-lb external) 460 miles (741 km); ferry range 3700 nm (4261 miles, 6857 km)

Armament Various internal and external bombloads or reconnaissance pallet as described in text

BELOW *Leaving sooty trails, XR219 arrives over its home airfield at Warton on 21 February 1965*

General Dynamics F-111

First Flight – 21 December 1964

This programme for a new tactical aircraft for the US Air Force ran roughly parallel in timing with the British TSR.2. The similarities and differences are perhaps instructive. Both were smaller than traditional heavy bombers, but much bigger and heavier than fighters. Both were powered by two powerful afterburning engines, had a crew of two, were required to fly faster than sound even at low level, to have very long mission radius and to be able to operate from short, unpaved airstrips.

In almost every other respect they were different. The British aircraft had a short-span broad wing with blown flaps, while the F-111 had pivoted swing-wings. The TSR.2 had two ejection seats in tandem, while the F-111 had seats side-by-side in an ejectable capsule. TSR.2 had turbojets, while the US aircraft had turbofans of not much more than half the thrust. Unprecedentedly, the F-111 was ill-advisedly developed as a bomber for the USAF and as a fighter for the US Navy. Not least, while TSR.2

proved to be outstandingly right from the start, to the extent that Phase I flight trials were completed in 23 flights, the F-111 proved to suffer severe and prolonged problems in aerodynamics, structure, weight escalation, systems and propulsion. Yet, such is the odd world we live in, that the British aircraft was broadcast to the world as a scandalous mistake, while the US rival was seen as a glittering prize to be coveted.

It all began in the late 1950s, when USAF Tactical Air Command was studying a next-generation tactical aircraft to replace the F-100 and F-105. These were demanding aircraft, which could operate from a 10,000-ft concrete runway but which suffered less attrition if the length available was 12,000 ft. As explained earlier, this was a time when the unpalatable truth had begun to dawn on air forces that, without any warning, and whatever the weather, their airbases might suddenly be wiped off the map by missiles – ICBMs, IRBMs, submarine-launched SLBMs or tactical missiles fired from

RIGHT *F-111A*

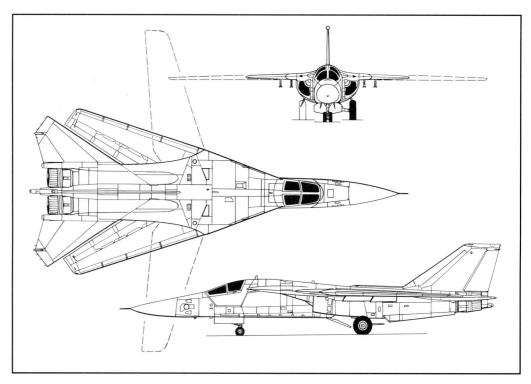

ABOVE *When F-111A 65-5701 visited RAF Wethersfield on 25 May 1967 the RAF was expecting soon to receive very similar aircraft bought to replace TSR.2*

mobile launchers. Oddly, such a possibility appears to be ignored today, but 35 years earlier it was taken very seriously indeed.

The answers seemed to be to use aircraft with V/STOL capability conferred by jet lift (which made them complex, expensive and probably inferior in flight performance), or to use ordinary uncompromised aircraft and blast them into the sky in the Zell (Zero-length launch) technique using a giant rocket (which posed even greater problems, to say nothing of how they got back to the launcher). It was agreed that maybe the best solution was to adopt the VG (variable-geometry) swing-wing, with powerful full-span slats and high-lift flaps, in order to take off in about 1000 ft, or 300 m. This still meant the aircraft would be parked on the vulnerable airfields, but the TAC generals were so used to having huge runways and blue sky that they appeared unable to picture a charred and obliterated airbase steaming gently in the rain of Europe.

There were other new factors to be considered. The British technique of inflight refuelling made it possible to deploy tactical aircraft, as well as strategic bombers, anywhere in the world in a matter of hours. By late 1959 one of TAC's growing list of requirements for its future multirole aircraft was 'the ability to fly between any two airfields in the world in less than a day'. Under USAF Director of Operational Requirements Maj-Gen Bruce K Holloway, careful study was made of such new technologies as the VG wing, jet V/STOL, augmented turbofan engines, reverse thrust, titanium primary structure, low attack using TFR (terrain-following radar), low-pressure balloon types suit-

able for unpaved airstrips and the ability to carry nuclear weapons internally and fly faster than sound at sea level. The outcome was Specific Operational Requirement 183, issued on 14 June 1960. Among its challenging numbers were a high-altitude Mach speed of 2.5, a radius of action of 800 nm (921 miles) with the final 200 nm to the target flown at treetop height at Mach 1.2, an unrefuelled ferry range of 3300 nm (3800 miles) and the ability to operate at maximum weight from a 3000-ft bulldozed strip.

It is a pity nobody had the foresight to stand back a bit from these marvellous challenges and recognise that what was really wanted was a bomb truck, that had no need for Mach 2.5 and could just as well have approached its target at 0.95. The result might then have been rather like a 'son of Buccaneer' and it would have been available on time, on budget and done a fine job. Instead, SOR-183 became popularly known as the TFX, standing for Tactical Fighter Experimental. The original requirement had called for a tactical *strike* fighter, but the crucial word was soon omitted.

This distorted the project in people's minds, and especially in the sharp mind of Robert S McNamara, who in January 1961 came from the Ford Motor Co to be President Kennedy's Secretary for Defense. He quickly gathered a team of equally bright analysts, soon called 'the Pentagon whiz-kids', determined to

ABOVE *The F-111D looked ordinary, but was actually a costly oddball because of its new-generation avionics. It served with the 27th TFW at Cannon AFB*

shake up the vast creaking DoD structure and get more defence for fewer dollars. As the biggest new project, TFX soon came under McNamara's scrutiny, and so did the Navy's requirement for a Future Air Defense Fighter to replace the F4H, F8U and F6D. He wrote 'These two planes would have many common missions and require many similar operational capabilities. After consultation with my military and civilian advisors, and independent study, I became convinced that one tactical fighter could be developed that would meet both Navy and Air Force requirements'.

His whiz-kids soon came up with a figure of one billion dollars as the potential saving from this new concept of 'commonality'. It was soon apparent that the concept was feasible, provided that each service gave up some of its critical mission requirements. After increasingly heated discussion, the Air Force and Navy Secretaries reported in August 1961 that a common design was not feasible. The USAF aircraft came out weighing 75,000 lb, 80 ft long and seating pilot and navigator in tandem. The limit on Navy length was 70 ft and on maximum weight 50,000 lb, seating the crew side-by-side behind a radar dish over 4 ft across. The Navy put the 'overall effectiveness' of the compromise TFX as 37 per cent.

This merely angered McNamara. Clearly hidebound people were being swayed by traditional rivalries, and were not even trying to give an inch here and a few per cent there in order to save a billion dollars. So he took it upon himself to tell the two services in considerable numerical detail precisely how the Common TFX should be designed. He spelt out the mould lines of the nose radome, the various lengths and gross weights, and every other area where there was divergence of opinion. Then he sent out the Request for Proposals on 1 October 1961, receiving responses from six companies on 6 December. Despite the problems, this was touted as the biggest tactical weapon programme since 1945, with thousands likely to be made for almost every Western air force and navy, with all the cost benefits not only of commonality but also of real mass-production.

Following unprecedented evaluations by up to 360 analysts the initial AF Evaluation Group recommended study contracts for Boeing-Wichita and General Dynamics (GD) at Fort Worth. Following further more detailed evaluations the Systems Source Selection Board, with representatives from every user organisation, unanimously recommended on 19 January 1962 that Boeing be awarded the development contract. There followed an unprecedented *four* further rounds of closed competition, during which Boeing was paid to switch from the GE MF295 engine to the Pratt & Whitney JTF10 and both bidders strove to correct deficiencies. As Boeing won every time, the paperwork soon referred to 'the contractor' in the singular, so most people were staggered when on 24 November 1962 McNamara blandly announced that this potentially gigantic contract had been awarded to GD. They would initially build 17 F-111As for the USAF and, in partnership with Grumman, five F-111Bs for the Navy. The programme for 1726 aircraft, including 231 F-111Bs, was costed at $5803 million.

What followed was a storm which began in Congress, soon spread to the media and provided headlines for years to come. This set the scene beautifully for the subsequent history of technical problems, programme failures and catastrophes that resulted in the media quite unfairly calling the F-111 'a lemon', which means something quite useless. A major part of the problem was that nobody had really noticed that a 3000-mile bomber can hardly be an agile fighter. And from the start things could hardly have gone worse. NASA Langley's detailed tunnel testing began in January 1963 and soon found 'high drag, low maneuverability, low directional stability and a serious transonic drag problem'. In some cases power of manoeuvre was 'about half that specified'. As for weight, the equipped empty figure for the F-111A of 36,700 lb escalated to over 42,000 lb before first flight, and eventually settled at 46,172 lb. Among many other problems was the discovery that the installation of the TF30 (JTF10) engine was a complete disaster, partly the fault of Pratt & Whitney's compressors having been designed with totally inadequate stall margin and partly because GD had designed an equally inadequate inlet and put it too close to the engine.

Not much of this had surfaced when GD rolled out the first F-111A, No 63-9766, at Fort Worth on 16 October 1964. On 21 December 1964 this aircraft was flown successfully by Dick Johnson, with Val Prahl as observer. On the second flight Johnson cautiously inched the wings to and fro, eventually exploring the whole regime from 16° to 72.5° by using the trombone-type pistol grip which provoked endless arguments over which way the pilot should move it. Compressor stalls repeatedly delayed the achievement of supersonic flight, which was at last recorded – amidst violent hiccups and bangs from the engines – on flight No 9 in March 1965. Gradually the worst problems were overcome, leaving an F-111A that was in many ways sadly deficient and no longer regarded as a fighter at all, but which introduced a wholly new and very exciting kind of combat mission in which two men could put their lives in the trust of boxes of electronics.

The F-111A and B were like no previous fighters. The former was 73 ft 6 in long, despite seating the pilot and navigator side-by-side (and not all crews liked this seating arrangement). The long outer wings, with high-lift slats and double-slotted flaps over their entire length, were held by 8.5-in diameter pivots in the bearings on the ends of the WCTB (wing carry-through box) which, like the pivot pins, was made of D6AC steel. The fixed wing glove was mounted on top of the broad fuselage. Tucked well back under the wings were the variable quarter-round inlets to the 18,500-lb TF30 engines, which were quite widely spaced. The enormous triangular tailerons, which pivoted at the top of the rear fuselage, were the primary control in pitch and roll, augmented at low speeds by the wing spoilers which also served as airbrakes and lift dumpers. The main landing gears, with huge 47 in × 18 in tyres, rested on the ground with legs horizontal (though track was still less than the width of the fuselage). The gears swung forwards, the bay being closed by a door forming a powerful airbrake. Not least of the novelties was the ejectable cockpit capsule, lowered by parachute and subsequently serving as a survival shelter or boat. The small weapon bay could house two nuclear bombs

or two 750-pounders, or an M61 gun with 2084 rounds. Provision was made for 'up to 30,000 lb of bombs or other stores on four fixed and four swivelling underwing pylons', but in practice the limit is about 13,920 lb on Pylons 3, 4, 5 and 6, the others not being fitted.

The first delivery to the Air Force was made on 17 July 1967 to the 448th TFS at Nellis, commanded by Col Ivan H Dethman. On 17 March 1968 Dethman landed at Takhli Royal Thai Air Force Base in command of a six-plane detachment from the 428th TFS called the *Combat Lancer* force. Now 12 men were to demonstrate the way they could ride the 'One-Eleven' over the mountains of Vietnam at night or in cloud, just skimming the unseen jagged peaks, and finally put down 750-lb iron bombs with better precision than other bombers could achieve by day. But still these uniquely capable aircraft got a bad Press. On 28 March, 30 March and 27 April 1968 *Combat Lancer* aircraft failed to return, and the three survivors were withdrawn. On 8 May 1968 a fourth aircraft was lost, at Nellis. What had been happening was that a vital welded joint in the left taileron power unit had

BOTTOM *Landing at Wattisham during a Tiger Meet, this F-111E belonged to the CO of the 79th FS, 20th TFW, from Upper Heyford*

BELOW *Comparative view of the F-111F of the CO of the 493rd FS (71-0889) shortly before the 48th FW re-equipped with the F-15E during the winter of 1992–93*

failed in fatigue, resulting in violent uncommanded pitch-up and roll to the left. Nor was this all. Modern aircraft try where possible to have duplicate load paths, called structural redundancy, so that if one part breaks another part will hold the aircraft temporarily together. No such redundancy was possible in the F-111 WCTB and its wing pivots, and in late 1968 it was found that the crucial pivots were cracking. GD and the Air Force toiled to incorporate structural reinforcements to cure the problem. On 22 December 1969 a Nellis F-111A pulled out from an attack, in all respects to the latest structural standard and flown correctly, and a wing came clean off. The result was an unprecedented inspection and proof test of every F-111 whilst refrigerated at $-40°c$.

Altogether GD built 159 F-111As, including the 17 development aircraft (an added 18th was completed as the prototype FB-111A). Serials were 63-9766/9782, 65-5701/5710, 66-0011/0058 and 67-0032/0114. They served at various times with the 474th, 347th and 366th TFWs, and with numerous test and training establishments. No 63-9776 was converted as the prototype RF-111A, which got no further, while 42 aircraft were gutted and completely rebuilt by Grumman as EF-111A Raven electronic-warfare platforms, able to undertake many forms of tactical jamming in support of friendly attack aircraft.

The F-111B was the proposed Navy version, tailored to fighter and interceptor missions. It differed in having wings of greater span to give enhanced low-speed lift and loiter characteristics, a

shorter nose housing the big radar of the Hughes AWG-9 weapon-control system, carrier nose-tow nose gear and hook (the VG wings did not need to fold) and naval equipment including primary armament of six AIM-54A Phoenix missiles. The Grumman-based programme flew BuNo 151970, the first of the five prototypes, at Calverton on 18 May 1965. Its escalation in weight was so severe that, despite a succession of desperate 'weight improvement programmes' and introduction of the 20,250-lb TF30-12 engine, the whole programme was terminated by Congress on 10 July 1968. Grumman had flown the five prototypes and four production aircraft by this stage.

The F-111C was ordered by Australia to replace TSR.2. A total of 24 were purchased in October 1963 for just over US$90 million for delivery in 1968, being similar to the F-111A but with the long-span wing of the F-111B, eight pylons and upgraded main landing gears as already being developed for the FB-111 and F-111K. What actually happened was that the RAAF got its aircraft in late 1973 at a cost of something over US$324 million. Something in excess of US$118 million was also spent by the two countries on a reconnaissance version, unrelated to the USAF RF-111A. For 20 years No 6 Sqn at Amberley, in

BELOW *The word 'bomber' has come to mean a platform for bombs, smart bombs, cluster bombs, retarded bombs, cruise missiles, dogfight missiles and '20-mike-mike' ammo. No 1 Sqn RAAF demonstrate*

Queensland, has operated what began as 24 Cs and later became 18 F-111Cs, four RF-111Cs and four secondhand As. In October 1992 the RAAF was authorised to purchase up to 18 F-111s pensioned off from the USAF. At first sight buying such a large force of basically obsolescent aircraft, noted for their high operating cost, might seem odd, but the extra aircraft are thought to be needed to provide spares and attrition replacements up to 2020. Details of the sub-type and price were not then announced. The recently appointed Chief of Air Staff, Air Marshal Barry Gration, said 'We could probably quickly obtain KC-135 tankers if we needed them'.

When Britain cancelled its TSR.2 it gleefully placed an order for 46 F-111K bombers and four TF-111K trainers. These were funded in 1967/68 and would have had RAF serials XV902/947 and XV884/887, respectively. They would have been like the F-111C, but with refuelling probes and other changes, but the whole programme was cancelled in January 1968. Most were scrapped, but the first two TFs were completed for research duties as YF-111As, USAF 67-149/150.

One feature of the F-111K was to have been the 'Mk II' avionics suite. This mesmerised the British politicians and was to be a feature of the next version, the F-111D, but it took so long to develop that GD switched to building the F-111E. This was basically an F-111A with the Triple Plow II engine air intake and other minor differences. GD built 94 (67-0115/0124 and 68-0001/0084), which served briefly at Cannon AFB and then for over 20 years at RAF Upper Heyford with the 20th TFW. In 1986 Grumman teamed with TRW to win a five-year $109 million contract to update the navigation and communications systems of 152 F-111As and Es. The upgraded aircraft of the 20th saw action over Libya and the Gulf.

Eventually, instead of equipping at least 315 F-111s, starting at No 100, the Mk II avionics went into only 96 F-111Ds, starting at No 216 in autumn 1970 (68-0085/0180). Prime avionics contractor was Autonetics (later called NA Rockwell Electronics), and the whole Mk II programme was a mixed blessing. It had absolutely no commonality with the other F-111s, cost astronomic sums to develop and produce, suffered poor in-service reliability and resulted in a species of F-111 which required extensive training of both flight and ground crews who then could not fly or maintain other versions. The cockpit bore no similarity at all to that of other variants, each crew-member being confronted by a huge multifunction display (basically a vertical situation display for the pilot and a horizontal one for the right-seater) and with a HUD for both men. Among many other changes came the 20,840-lb TF30-9 engine, fed by the Triple Plow II inlet, replacement of the unpopular manual scope camera by an automatic strike camera looking obliquely ahead through a window recessed under the nose, an improved environmental system and,

TOP *Party piece of the long-span F-111C of the RAAF is 'torching' – spewing fuel through the jettison pipe and lighting it with the afterburners*

ABOVE *'Ballute' (balloon-parachute) – retarded 2000-lb Mk 84 with Pave Tack equipped 'Aardvark' of 495th TFS*

unlike other versions, installation of the M61 gun. For most of their lives the D-models equipped the 27th TFW at Cannon AFB, and it is ironic that these supposedly most advanced of all versions should have been among the first to be retired to 'the boneyard'. In 1990 the USAF was striving to bring all surviving F-111s to a common avionics standard, and in the case of the D this was clearly not possible.

Chronologically the next version was the FB-111A. Having accepted that the One-Eleven was hardly a fighter, the SecDef announced on 10 December 1965 that 210 of the FB version would be purchased to replace the B-58A and B-52C/E/F versions with SAC. Of course, GD had, from 1962, been keenly aware of ways of stretching and upgrading versions with bigger engines, or three or

Painted in distinctive black, white and red, FB-111A (No 1, 67-0159) served Sacramento Logistics Center as a test vehicle

RIGHT *Polka dots for camera registration decorated this F-111A (No 18, 63-9783) and the AGM-69A SRAM missiles, on test for the FB-111A*

four engines, bogie landing gears and many other changes. In the event the FB merely featured the existing long-span wing with the bigger and stronger main landing gears, more powerful brakes, the 20,350-lb TF30-7 engine and so-called Mk IIB avionics plus an astrocompass. With all eight pylons installed the FB was designed to carry 50 bombs of 750-lb size (two in the weapon bay as an alternative to an extra 482 Imp gal of fuel) or four of the new Lockheed AGM-69A SRAMs (short-range attack missiles) on the four inboard pylons. The first of two development aircraft was the rebuilt F-111A

63-9783, which was first reflown on 30 July 1967.

By this time an initial contract had been placed for 64 FBs, but such was the escalation in price that the plan for 210 was cut back to only 76 (67-156/163·and 7192/7196, 68-239/292 and 69-6503/6514). These equipped various test and training units, and SAC's 380th BW at Plattsburgh AFB, NY, and 509th BW at Pease AFB, NH. Following the 1988 INF Treaty these two Bomb Wings were disbanded and their 61 surviving aircraft have been progressively converted by USAF Materiel Command (previously Logistics and Systems Commands) into dual nuclear/conventional tactical aircraft designated F-111G. The SRAM installation is deleted and the cockpit modified for 6.5 g manoeuvres with stick-mounted weapon-delivery controls, g-suit connectors and the Have Quick UHF radio. The G serves with the 27th TFW at Cannon, replacing the defunct D-model.

Last and best of the tactical versions, the F-111F combined the 25,100-lb TF30-100 engine and Triple Plow II inlet, giving markedly more sprightly performance, with an outstandingly good avionics suite which contrives to be much more advanced than that in the A and E, and yet simpler and more reliable than that in the D. In addition, the F was rightly picked to be equipped with the AVQ-26 Pave Tack pod, recessed into the weapon bay. When needed this is rotated through 180° to bring into action a FLIR (forward-looking infra-red) sensor, laser precision ranger and designator (or receiver of light from a designated target) and new cockpit display. Sadly, instead of 219 the USAF could afford only 106 of the F-111F model (70-2362/2419, 71-0883/0894, 72-1441/1452, 73-0707/0718 and 74-0177/0188), whose combat effectiveness is roughly four times that of an A or E. They entered service in 1972 with the 347th TFW at Mountain Home, but almost all their very active life has been spent with the 48th TFW at RAF Lakenheath.

In the Gulf War their capability with Pave Tack and various smart bombs was almost embarrassing to other Allied units. For example, when it was discovered that they were killing ten times as many tanks as the F-16s the latter were told to stop by mid-afternoon each day to allow the dust to settle before the 48th went to work at night. On the final day of the war they won a fly-off against the F-15E which gave them the honour of delivering two 4700-lb GBU-28/B Deep Throat bombs which penetrate far into the earth before exploding. The 48th's tally was: 66 aircraft flew 2500 sorties to destroy 2203 designated targets including confirmed videotape kills on 920 (and possibly 1500) tanks, 252 guns, 245 hardened aircraft shelters, 13 runways, 12 bridges and other hard targets. No other military unit has ever been able to prove such a record.

SPECIFICATION

F-111

Two Pratt & Whitney TF30 augmented turbofans, with following ratings in max augmentation: (A, EF, C, E) 18,500-lb TF30-3, (D) 20,840-lb TF30-9, (FB) 20,350-lb TF30-7, (F) 25,100-lb TF30-100

Dimensions Span max (A, EF, D, E, F) 63 ft 0 in (19.2 m), (C, FB) 70 ft 0 in (21.34 m); min (A, EF, D, E, F) 31 ft 11½ in (9.74 m), (C, FB) 33 ft 11 in (10.34 m); length (except EF) 73 ft 6 in (22.4 m), (EF) 77 ft 1.6 in (23.51 m); wing area (A, EF, D, E, F, 16°) 525 sq ft (48.77 m²)

Weight Empty (A) 46,172 lb (20,943 kg), (C) 49,345 lb (22,383 kg), (D) 49,090 lb (22,267 kg), (E) 47,400 lb (21,500 kg), (F) 47,481 lb (21,537 kg), (FB) 50,100 lb (22,725 kg); max TO (A) 91,500 lb (41,500 kg), (C, FB) 114,300 lb (51,846 kg), (D, E) 92,500 lb (41,954 kg), (F) 100,000 lb (45,360 kg)

Performance Maximum speed (hi, clean) (A, D, E) Mach 2.2, (C, FB) Mach 2, (F, when new) Mach 2.5; max speed on lo attack mission (typical) 571 mph (919 km/h); combat radius (original FB, two SRAM internal and four tanks) 1800 miles (2900 km); TO run, from 2900 ft (F) to 4000 ft (A, E), 4700 ft (FB) and 5100 ft (C)

Armament Provision for one M61A1 gun; internal bay for gun and one SRAM or B43 nuclear bomb or two B43; four hardpoints under each wing for two inboard swivelling pylons and (not normally fitted) two or four outboard fixed pylons, for loads as described in text

BELOW *An outstanding plan view of an FB, carrying just two pylons and one practise-bomb container. On tactical versions the wings are much shorter than the tailplanes. Note ALE-40 chaff/flare dispensers in tail bullet fairings, and small added radar-warning hemispheres under the nose*

LTV A-7 Corsair II

First Flight – 27 September 1965

In 1960 the US Navy thought it was time to consider a replacement for the A4D Skyhawk. Even if it had for one moment believed that the Douglas aircraft might actually remain in production until 1979, there still appeared to be a need for a VAL (V for heavier-than-air, A for attack, L for lightweight) with the ability to carry heavier bombloads and fly further. It was almost taken for granted that the VAL had to be supersonic.

Then the new SecDef, Robert S McNamara, told the Navy to think harder. In December 1962 the SBASF, the Sea-Based Air Strike Forces, study group began detailed performance and cost evaluation of 144 different hypothetical aircraft. To their astonishment the result showed clear superiority for a subsonic aircraft. Capt Henry Suerstedt of the Bureau of Weapons put it very clearly, 'If you were to take two ducks – one a fat little duck that flies only at subsonic speed and the other a larger supersonic duck – and compare the two, the supersonic duck would always have to fly higher to keep from flying into the ground. Against a duck hunter in a blind having the same angle of sight in all directions the time of exposure of the two ducks would be about the same. Both would have about an equal chance of being shot. Now the supersonic duck is a rare bird, costly to develop in both dollars and time, and you could buy three or more subsonic ducks for the same price … and the probability of them flying successfully past the hunter would be far greater than the one supersonic duck getting past'.

So the VAL requirement was drafted on 17 May 1963. Events were to show just how right was the specification for a fat little duck, because the RFP was sent out on 29 May, bids were in by September, evaluations were completed on 6 November, Congress voted funds on 8 February 1964, LTV (Ling Temco Vought) were announced winners on 11 February, a contract was signed on 19 March, the mock-up review took place on 22 June, the first A-7A off the production line at Dallas flew on 27 September 1965 and, after exhaustive testing, the first user squadron was formed a year later, on 14 October 1966.

Speed of development was important, and to ease problems LTV based their VAL submission on their F-8 Crusader supersonic fighter. In fact, no single structural part was common to the two aircraft, but their concept did save a lot of time and thought. Compared with its predecessor the A-7 had a slightly bigger wing with sweepback reduced from 42° to 35°, outboard ailerons and no provision for variable incidence, a shorter fuselage housing a

BELOW *The VAL (A-7A) was one of the first aircraft to have to meet numerical requirements for maintainability and serviceability. This photo was taken during the demonstration of 11.5 man-hours per flight-hour*

turbofan engine instead of a turbojet with after-burner, and provision for carrying more than 15,000 lb of bombs on six wing pylons. On 2 November 1965 Vought demonstrated the first two of seven development A-7As before 1000 guests. John Konrad, who in 1955 had flown the XF8U beyond Mach 1 on its first flight, rolled the first aircraft three times very rapidly in each direction whilst carrying 12 inert bombs of 500 lb and six of 250 lb. The Navy said it would carry 'more than twice the bombload of an A-4E, or carry the same load more than twice as far'.

Like the F-8A the A-7 had fully powered flight controls, but the ailerons were in the normal place outboard of the wing fold, with big slotted flaps inboard. Naturally, the wing fold came between the ailerons and flaps, with a dogtooth discontinuity at the fixed leading edge. Again, the three units of the landing gear retracted into the fuselage in the same way, but the nose gear was of the steerable type with twin wheels and stressed for the 80-ton pull of a steam catapult. The 11,350-lb Pratt & Whitney TF30-6, an unaugmented version of the F-111 engine, was started pneumatically, by an air-turbine motor. The simple fixed nose inlet to the engine duct was retained, though this had shown itself on the F-8 to be a potential hazard to deck personnel. On each side of the nose was a Mk 12 cannon, with 250 rounds, and a self-defence Sidewinder rack was added on each side of the fuselage. The belly incorporated a large door-type airbrake. About 1250 Imp gal of fuel could be housed in the integral-tank wing and fuselage cells, and a retractable inflight-refuelling probe was fitted on the right of the nose. The seat was a McDonnell Douglas Escapac.

The original contract had called for seven development aircraft plus 35 for inventory service. The second, placed in September 1965, was for 140, and a third buy of 17 brought total A-7A procurement up to 199. VA-122 and VA-174 were in full operation as the training units in late 1966, and a year later VA-147 was in action from USS *Ranger* (CV-61) over Vietnam. The stumpy Corsair II, by now popularly called the SLUF, politely translated as 'short little ugly fellah', did well, the main problems being that the aircraft was clearly under-powered and that the engine tended to suffer serious compressor stalls (for example, on ingesting gas from the guns or even steam from the catapult) and that even the seemingly good armour and systems duplication could not withstand the Viet-Cong habit of firing every gun in sight whenever hostile aircraft appeared. Accordingly, the next 196 aircraft ordered were A-7Bs, with the 12,200-lb TF30-8, which at least provided a little more power.

Designation A-7C was to have been a trainer version, but in practice applied to two quite different variants as described later. The A-7D was unexpectedly ordered by the US Air Force, which since 1966 had been studying the highly effective Navy aircraft and noting how well it stacked up against its own choice of tactical attack aircraft, which had either straight wings and propellers or afterburners and Mach 2. At first the Air Force toyed with the idea of fitting its A-7D version with an F-111 engine with afterburner. But by this time the TF30 was not only in deep trouble but Pratt & Whitney were also falling behind in their attempts to keep pace with the colossal demands for engines for the airlines as well as for huge military orders for Vietnam. From 1965 Allison had been discussing with Rolls-Royce how the RB.168 (Spey) could fit export A-7s. Suddenly it looked as if such an engine might even be picked for the A-7D. To clinch things, the engine partners produced the RB.168-62, with greater airflow and thrust increased to 14,250 lb. To cut a long story short, in February 1966 funds were voted for initial acquisition of the USAF A-7D with the Allison TF41 (another name for the RB.168-62).

This followed the F-4 Phantom II as a Navy aircraft adopted by the Air Force, but this time the USAF version was significantly better. At a stroke, the Spey-derived engine removed the propulsion problems that had plagued the A and B models. Complete autonomy was provided by adding an on-board gas-turbine starter. The seat was an updated Escapac 1C2 with rocket boost for zero/zero capability. The two ancient guns were replaced by the fast-firing M61A1, with a 1000-round drum. From the 26th aircraft the Navy flight-refuelling probe was replaced by a dorsal boom receptacle. Most important of all, the D-model introduced an updated nav/attack avionics system, with a new radar, doppler/inertial navigation, a British HUD (head-up display), projected-map display and other new features including a digital computer, a radar homing and warning system and armament controls.

BELOW *Straight from the Dallas plant and into the Vietnam War, an A-7A of VA-147 'Argonauts' is about to be launched from USS* Ranger *(CV-61)*

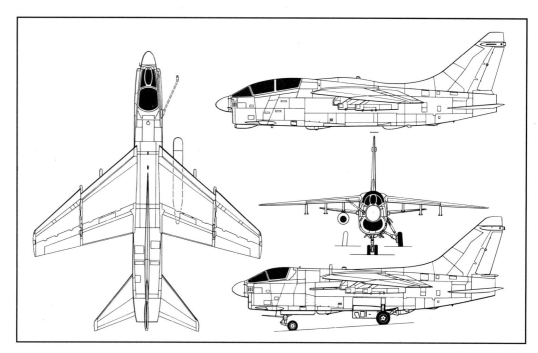

Announcement of the D caused a storm in Canada, which had wanted A-7s but been persuaded to buy the F-5 (which happened to at least five other countries, the State Department at that time regarding the A-7 as an offensive weapon). In Britain the Labour government was at pains to explain that adoption of the TF41 engine had nothing to do with any technical superiority but was merely a government-arranged offset deal following the replacement of the British P.1154, HS.681 and TSR.2 by the American F-4, C-130 and F-111. This puzzled Lt-Gen Thomas P Gerrity, USAF Deputy Chief of Staff for Systems, who said 'Offsets never entered the deal at all until the British government invented the idea; the TF41 was a distinctly superior choice, and Allison even bid a lower price'. The first two A-7Ds had the TF30, and the first with the TF41 flew on 26 September 1968. Subsequently LTV produced 459, ending in December 1976.

Whereas the original A-7 had, like the F-111,

ABOVE *In almost every respect the Air Force A-7D was a better aircraft than the Navy original. Some of the first went to the 57th FWW at Nellis*

been deliberately planned to use 'state of the art' or off-the-shelf avionics, the Vietnam war dramatically drove home the need for better nav/attack and weapon-delivery systems, especially for missions at night or in bad weather. The Navy had wished for a thoroughgoing revision of these crucial systems almost from the start, but had been thwarted by the urgent need for fast production. In 1967 pressures had eased somewhat, and it cancelled the last 257 A-7Bs and established the build-standard for a definitive and much better Navy version. This featured an upgraded TF41, the A-2 (RB.168-66), which by running slightly faster achieved a thrust of 15,000 lb with better pressure ratio. Starting was pneumatic, the Air Force gas-turbine starter being omitted. The avionics followed closely the standard

laid down by the A-7D, but modified for Navy communications, ECM and certain other items. The seat chosen was the Escapac 1G2 and 1G3. Of course, the inflight-refuelling method was by the retractable probe, and the gun was the M61A1.

The first 67 aircraft were forced by engine availability, at least temporarily, to use the TF30, and these were later designated as A-7Cs. The first true A-7E flew on 25 November 1968, and eventually LTV built 535. They played a major role in Vietnam, accounting for about half the 90,230 sorties flown by all A-7s. In December 1977 deliveries began of A-7Es equipped with a Texas Instruments FLIR (forward-looking infra-red) pod on Station 6, plus a GEC Avionics raster-type HUD. Together these made night attacks as accurate as daylight. Eventually 221 FLIR installations enabled this night capability to be achieved by about half the total US Navy inventory, in other words by one of the two squadrons embarked on each carrier.

On 17 December 1976 LTV flew the first of 60

TOP An A-7D serving with the Virginia Air National Guard. They were popular aircraft

ABOVE Also serving with the Virginia ANG, the tandem-seat A-7K. This was the last version to be built in series

TA-7C trainers, with tandem cockpits and dual pilot controls and instruments. They were rebuilds, 24 having been A-7Bs and 36 A-7Cs. The fuselage was lengthened ahead of and behind the wing, a braking parachute was added above the jetpipe and a new canopy was produced to cover both cockpits. In January 1985 the Navy began receiving 49 of these trainers after a further major rework with the TF41 engine, with an engine monitoring system, Stencel seats, automatic manoeuvre flaps and other upgrades. Six more became EA-7L electronic-warfare platforms, with the FLIR pod and extensive receiver, power-management and jamming systems, while the Marines tested FLIR-equipped TA-7Cs with the crew wearing NVGs (night-vision goggles).

One of the ironic features of the A-7 programme is that, perhaps because a subsonic bomber is less exciting to politicians than a sexy fighter (no matter what their relative values might be), only one of the 14 or 15 foreign sales that were discussed actually led to a contract for new aircraft. This was with Greece, who bought for the Hellenic AF a total of 60 A-7H and five tandem dual TA-7H Corsairs, delivered in 1976–80. They were similar to the A-7E, complete with carrier equipment, and equip two squadrons at Soudha Bay, Crete.

The KA-7F tanker and Swiss A-7G never happened, but in 1979 Congress voted funds for what proved to be the final new-build variant, the A-7K. A two-seat multi-role trainer for the Air National Guard, one was rebuilt from an A-7D and 30 were built from new. The last, USAF 81-0077, was delivered in 1983 to complete A-7 production at 1545 aircraft. The penultimate aircraft, 0076, was the first of eight Ks and 75 Ds to be fitted from 1986 with the LANA (low-altitude night attack) system including the FLIR, a GEC Avionics wide-angle HUD, terrain-following and a Singer mission computer.

Seeking to restore its lost reputation Pratt & Whitney kept improving the TF30 and in 1976 offered the TF30-408, rated at 13,400 lb and with better stall resistance. This was adopted by the Navy, some being new and others rebuilt Dash-8 engines, retrofitted to most of the surviving A-7Bs. The Dash-408 engine was also fitted to 44 A-7P and

BELOW Last of the Navy models was the A-7E, perhaps even better than the D. The Navy also bought FLIR (forward-looking infra-red) pods to equip a proportion of the force, including these two aircraft from USS Constellation *(CV-64)*

six TA-7P Corsairs purchased by the FAP, the Portuguese air force, from 1982. These were rebuilt A-7As (and several Bs), and retained the original guns but had a mix of A-7D and E avionics. They equip two squadrons at Monte Real AB.

This completes the story of a little publicised but much-liked and very useful attack bomber. From 1972 LTV strove to keep the line at Dallas open, with such offerings as the International Corsair II and III, the A-7 Strikefighter, the A-7 Plus and the YA-7F. Of these just two YA-7Fs were actually flown. Rebuilds from LANA/A-7Ds, the Fs were flown in November 1989 and April 1990. Among many changes were a stretched fuselage, a new engine bay matched to the P&W F100 or GE F110 engine, a wing-root strake, thicker skins, anhedral tailplane and Mach 1.2 speed. Instead, the USAF bought more F-16s.

SPECIFICATION

A-7 Corsair II

One unaugmented turbofan: (A) 11,350-lb Pratt & Whitney TF30-6, (B, C) 12,200-lb TF30-8 (some retrofitted, see under [P]), (D, K) 14,250-lb Allison TF41-1, (E, H) 15,000-lb TF41-2, (P, B/C retrofits) 13,400-lb TF30-408

Dimensions Span 38 ft 9 in (11.8 m); length (except K) 46 ft 1½ in (14.06 m), (K) 48 ft 11½ in (14.92 m); wing area 375 sq ft (34.83 m²)

Weight Empty (A) 15,904 lb (7214 kg), (D) 19,781 lb (8973 kg), (E) 19,127 lb (8676 kg); max loaded (A, free take-off) 32,500 lb (14,750 kg), (A, cat) 38,000 lb (17,237 kg), (D, E, H) 42,000 lb (19,050 kg)

Performance Maximum speed clean, at S/L (A) 578 mph (930 km/h), (D, E) 691 mph (1112 km/h), (D, E, with 12 Mk 82 bombs) 646 mph (1040 km/h); TO run (D, E, max weight) 5600 ft (1705 m); tactical radius (D, E, hi-lo-hi, internal fuel, 3600-lb bombs) 700 miles (1127 km); max ferry range with external fuel 2861 miles (4604 km)

Armament (A, B, C, P) two Mk 12 20 mm guns, two fuselage and six wing stations for up to 20,000 lb (9072 kg) of ordnance (see text); (D, E, H) same except Mk 12 guns replaced by single M61A1

Saab 37 Viggen

First Flight – 8 February 1967

With a population of less than eight million, Sweden has repeatedly demonstrated its ability to specify its future warplanes correctly, manage a firm development programme, and build in quantity at a unit price any other country might envy. One of the most important of these programmes was the Viggen (meaning thunderbolt or Thor's hammer).

In 1955 Saab AB had flown the prototype Type 35 Draken, aerodynamically the most advanced fighter in the world at that time and destined to support a production programme of 606 aircraft capable of flying all tactical missions at up to Mach 2. By this time, but too late for System 35, the *Flygvapnet* (Royal Swedish Air Force) could see several fundamental requirements clearly which it decided could be incorporated in the next-generation aircraft, System 37. Because the requirements were so challenging nothing was done in a hurry, and a first-flight date was not expected before the middle of the next decade.

System 37 was from the outset planned as an integrated weapons system, to operate in conjunction with STRIL-60, the nationwide electronic air-defence system to guard the airspace of one of Europe's biggest countries. Unlike the Type 35 Draken, which was planned only as an interceptor, the airborne part of System 37 was envisaged as a 'standard flying platform' which could be adapted to fly every tactical mission with uncompromised efficiency. Moreover, the first version to be developed, and built in the greatest numbers, was not a fighter but an attack aircraft, to be designated AJ37.

Indeed, so important was System 37 planned to be that it was expected to replace every other front-line type in the *Flygvapnet*, with a total production run expected to exceed 800. Another radical requirement was the ability to be operated from straight stretches of remote rural highway only 500 m (1640 m) long. With the deployment of thousands of missiles able to destroy known air-bases in seconds in a pre-war pre-emptive strike, this requirement was only common sense. It demanded high acceleration on take-off, a modest landing speed, no-flare touchdown, powerful post-landing deceleration, and the ability to steer very accurately on narrow roads even in crosswinds on ice and snow.

Full development was authorised in 1958. By 1962 all elements of System 37 either existed or were well advanced in the creation process. They comprised: the aircraft with its powerplant, airborne equipment including ejection seat, armament and ammunition, reconnaissance systems, special ground servicing and test equipment, and training equipment including simulators. Overall,

BELOW *An early delivery to F7, with tank and rocket launchers. The reversing nozzle is clearly seen*

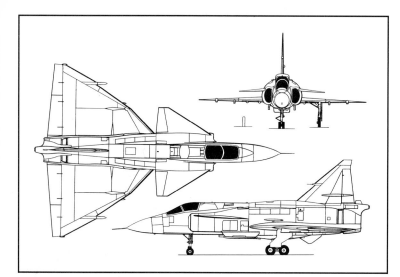

ABOVE *One of the first AJ37 Viggens to be delivered shows how the foreplane flaps help the jet perform remarkably short landings*

the project was by far the largest industrial development task ever attempted in Sweden.

By 1963 the aerodynamic design had been settled. It was as radical as that of its so-called 'double delta' predecessor, and while the Type 37 could also be called a double-delta this was for a different reason. Type 35 had been a tailless aircraft with a delta wing having very sharp sweep inboard and more normal sweep outboard. In contrast, Type 37 had an aft-mounted delta wing with modest sweep inboard and sharper sweep outboard; and the double-delta description stemmed from the fact that a complete foreplane was added, with powered trailing-edge flaps. At the time the notion of a canard (a foreplane) was revolutionary, though today it is highly fashionable for tactical fighters.

The combination of a flapped canard with a rear delta wing was judged the best way of reconciling

the conflicting demands of STOL performance, supersonic speed, low turbulence sensitivity in low-level attacks, and efficient lift for subsonic cruise and loiter. It was found that the canards could be positioned so that they generated large and very powerful vortices which would writhe back across the broad wing and enhance lift at angles of attack much greater than normal. In STOL operations its lift would add to the lift, whereas a tailplane pushes downwards to add to the weight.

Lift to high angles of attack was later further augmented by providing additional vortices from dogtooth discontinuities on the main wing. It was found that these points were good locations for EW (electronic-warfare) antennas in bullet fairings. For STOL operations it was originally planned to use blown flaps on the canard, and possibly on the main wing. Eventually all blowing was discarded, and the main wing was fitted with inboard and outboard powered elevons, and the required short landing performance was achieved by combining brutal no-flare landings at 5 m (16.4 ft)/sec rate of descent with a powerful engine reverser.

It was concluded that with suitable avionics the missions could be flown without a second crew-member. After careful thought it was also decided to use a single engine. The choice naturally fell upon Rolls-Royce, whose Avons had powered the pre-vious generations (Types 32 and 35) and whose Medway was ideal as the basis for a supersonic engine with a fully modulated afterburner. Britain at that time got everything wrong if it could. BEA foolishly forced de Havilland to make the DH.121 Trident smaller, and the Medway was replaced by the RB.163 (Spey) which was too small for the Swedish aircraft. Accordingly the Pratt & Whitney JT8D was chosen, which jointly by the US company and Svenska Flygmotor was turned into a consider-ably different engine designated RM8. This was redesigned for the Type 37, many dimensions being changed and numerous parts being made in differ-ent materials suitable for flight at Mach 2. Svenska Flygmotor designed and produced the large after-burner and fully variable nozzle, giving augmen-tation of no less than 76 per cent. Saab and Flygmotor jointly developed the reverser, as des-cribed later.

As the primary requirement was for attack and reconnaissance missions flown mainly at low level, the attainment of extreme Mach numbers – causing dramatic reduction in mission radius and endur-ance – was relatively unimportant. After studying alternatives the decision was taken to follow the formula adopted with Type 35 and use two lateral inlets of simple fixed-geometry form, but to make them appreciably larger and with the major axis vertical, standing well away from the fuselage with a gap for boundary-layer air. These inlets were placed well forward alongside the cockpit, and the canards attached along the upper edge of the duct. The ducts continued aft beside the fuselage before turning sharply in to feed the inlet face of the engine roughly in line with the front of the wing root.

Large areas of the mainly aluminium airframe were designed in bonded metal honeycomb, including the basic structure of the wing, canard flaps, elevons and rudder. Fuel was housed in a large integral tank in each wing, a tank behind the cockpit between the ducts, a saddle tank over the engine and one on each side. The cockpit was placed as far forward as possible, fitted with a one-piece curved birdproof windscreen, an upward-hinged canopy and a zero/zero rocket-assisted seat produced by Saab (who had produced seats for all their jet aircraft and for Britain's Gnat). Saab also designed the landing gears, though these were made by Motala Verkstad. The immensely strong main units had two small wheels in tandem, with Dunlop Maxaret anti-skid brakes, the legs shortening during retraction inwards so that the whole unit could be stowed outboard of the wing root. The twin-wheel nose gear retracted forward.

Electrical power was provided by a 60-kVA generator, supplemented by a 6-kVA generator driven by a ram-air turbine extended into the airstream automatically in the event of engine failure. Two independent 3000 lb/sq in hydraulic systems, each with its own pump, were backed up by an electrically driven pump to serve the flight-control surfaces, as well as the landing gear retraction, nosewheel steering and other items including an actuator to fold the vertical tail to the left for entering underground hangars secure from most forms of attack. Other items intended to be common to all original versions was a Saab CK-37 digital computer to handle navigation, flight-control and weapon-aiming calculations, a HUD produced in Sweden by SRA, and an automatic speed-control system for use in conjunction with a tactical ILS (instrument landing system).

As finally developed, the entire rear end of the fuselage, well downstream of the engine nozzle, was in the form of a heat-resistant titanium ring. A large gap was left between its upstream end and the fuselage, and normally the three gaps (one on each side and one underneath) were left open to reduce base drag. At supersonic speed the gaps were shut, and the entire tail end formed a secondary engine nozzle. After landing, the moment the nose oleo was compressed a signal was sent to the pre-armed reverser which slammed shut, to divert the thrust from the engine (in maximum dry power) diagonally forward through the three large gaps.

A little late, the first of seven prototypes made its first flight on 8 February 1967. Each prototype handled a particular range of tasks, almost all initially being in support of the initial production version, the AJ37. An all-weather aircraft, this was fitted with about 1323 lb (600 kg) of avionics in 50 LRUs (line-replaceable units), the biggest item being the Ericsson PS-37/A main radar. A monopulse set operating in I/J-band, this was flown with an

ABOVE *Aircraft 43 comes from F6 Wing, but the rest belong to F15 at Söderhamn*

inverted-Cassegrain antenna, but went into production with a mechanically steered parabolic dish, housed in a radome which could be slid bodily forwards for access.

Other equipment included a PEAB (Swedish Philips) air-data computer, Marconi HUD, Decca doppler, Honeywell radar altimeter and an advanced microwave scanning-beam blind landing system. Comprehensive radar (and later IR) warning receivers were installed, mainly by SATT, together with the AR753 set-on receiver used in conjunction with either one or two of the powerful SATT AQ31 active jammer pods and the BOX 9 chaff/flare dispenser. Nothing like this was even contemplated 30 years ago in the RAF or some other Western air forces.

The AJ37 was provided with seven hardpoints, each normally fitted with a standard 750mm (29.5-in) store ejection rack, three being under the

RIGHT *AJ37 weapons – and two types of ECM jammer – arranged around an aircraft of F15 Wing, newly painted in multicolour camouflage*

BELOW *Early deliveries went to F7, replacing Lansens*

fuselage and two under each wing. Each wing could have a third attachment, but this was left empty. Initially the biggest weapon was the rather clumsy twin-finned RB04E anti-ship cruise missile, weighing 1358 lb (616 kg) and with a 661-lb (300-kg) unitary warhead, with autopilot mid-course guidance over a range up to 20 miles (32 km) with PEAB active radar homing for the terminal phase. Three can be carried. Next came the RB05A, development of which was completed by Saab. This 672-lb (305-kg) weapon has a liquid rocket for supersonic speed over a 5.6-mile (9-km) range against ground, naval and even 'certain airborne' targets, using allegedly jam-resistant command guidance. Other early weapons included RB75 (Hughes AGM-65A Maverick), launchers for supersonic Bofors rockets up to 135-mm (5.3-in) calibre, up to 16 bombs (max load 6 t, 13,230 lb), mines, 30 mm Aden gun pods or self-defence RB24 Sidewinder or RB28 Falcon air/air missiles.

The latest weapon, RBS15F, is the air-launched version of the shipborne RBS15 which preceded it into service. Weighing about 1312 lb (595 kg), RBS15F has air-breathing (Microturbo turbojet) propulsion to achieve ranges up to 'considerably more than 70 km' (43.5 miles). Carrying a large blast/fragmentation warhead, it has inertial mid-course guidance and a terminal radar seeker by PEAB. This radar is claimed to be outstandingly difficult to interfere with, with frequency agility and various ECCM circuits. It is claimed to provide almost 100 per cent kill probability from an OTH (over the horizon) launch, and has been operational since 1990.

Inflation and other factors cut the overall System 37 programme from over 800 down to just 329 aircraft. Of these, Saab (by 1968 Saab-Scania) delivered 110 of the AJ37 attack version. The first production AJ flew on 23 February 1971, and

ABOVE *Despite the large wing needed for STOL performance, the AJ37 rides well at high speed at low level*

deliveries began four months later. The first unit was the F7 Wing at Såtenäs, which has two squadrons. Later units were F6 at Karlsborg (two squadrons) and F15 at Söderhamn (one squadron).

Subsequently Saab-Scania delivered the SF37 armed photo-reconnaissance version, the SH37 all-weather maritime reconnaissance version, the SK37 tandem dual trainer and the considerably modified JA37 interceptor, ending in June 1990. In May 1991 it was announced that SEK 300m (US$48.3m) was being voted to convert 115 AJ37, SF37 and SH37 Viggens into a uniform multi-role variant designated AJS37. These will not only have interchangeable weapon and sensor loads, including the same reconnaissance pod as carried by the JAS39 Gripen, but will also receive a new computer-based mission planning and threat-analysis system, a new databus with multiple processors, and updated ECM systems.

SPECIFICATION

AJ37 Viggen

One Volvo Flygmotor RM8A turbofan rated at 14,770 lb dry and 26,015 lb with max afterburner

Dimensions Span 34 ft 9¼ in (10.6 m); length 53 ft 5¾ in (16.3 m); wing area 562 sq ft (52.2 m²)

Weight Empty 17,900 lb (8130 kg); max take-off 45,192 lb (20,500 kg)

Performance Maximum speed (clean, high-altitude) Mach 2+ (1322 mph, 2128 km/h); max range (hi-lo-hi) 2000 km (1243 miles)

Armament Up to 15,000 lb (6804 kg) of ordnance, including 12 bombs of 250 kg, 16 of 120 kg or dispenser weapons, or three RB04E or four RB05A or two RBS15F missiles, or four launchers for six 135 mm rockets or 30 mm Aden gun pod or RB24, 28, 71 or 74 self-defence missiles

Sukhoi Su-24

First Flight – June 1967

The Su-24 was yet another example of a Soviet offensive aircraft wholly miscalculated by Western (Washington) analysts. While they got the size and weight about right, they overestimated the mission radius, and credited it with almost double the speed for which it was actually designed. As late as the 1992–93 edition, the 'bible' *Jane's* gives the official figure for maximum Mach number as 2.18, whereas it is actually 1.35. Like the Jaguar and MiG-27 the Su-24 was designed as a bomb truck with fixed inlets. For all that, the Su-24 family are outstandingly capable and mature aircraft.

Work began in 1961, when, with the inevitable aerodynamic assistance of the CAHI, Pavel Sukhoi's OKB was picked to design an aircraft to replace the Il-28 and Yak-28 in attack roles. Chief designer Ye S Felsner and his team took until 1964 to settle the configuration. The Western TSR.2 and TFX (F-111) showed that it was possible to reconcile supersonic speed, heavy bombload, long range and STOL field performance from unpaved strips. One had a fixed wing with blown flaps and tandem seats, and the other had a variable-geometry (VG) wing and side-by-side seats.

Almost from the start it had been decided to use two engines side-by-side, with long lateral inlets, and despite competition from Tumanskii the OKB remained faithful to Lyulka, who designed the AL-21 for this programme as much as for the Su-17/22. For several reasons it was decided not to use an internal weapon bay, but nevertheless to put the wing high on the fuselage and retract the main gears into the fuselage. TSR.2 exerted a strong influence, and the configuration chosen was very similar, the aircraft receiving the basic designation T-6 in the T (triangular) series. In late 1964 crew layout and STOL features were still undecided.

Considerable thought went into the first question, and several mockups were made. There was never any doubt that this had to be a two-seat aircraft. It was expected that one version would be a dual-pilot trainer, but the combat crew was to comprise a pilot (aircraft commander) and WSO (weapon-system officer). Tests showed that tandem seating, as in TSR.2, would offer lower drag, though the fuselage was in any case going to be wider than the 1.65 m (65 in) needed for side-by-side seating. It was accepted that side-by-side seating could be useful when looking ahead for an unobtrusive target, but what firmly tilted the balance in favour of the side-by-side arrangement was the wish to

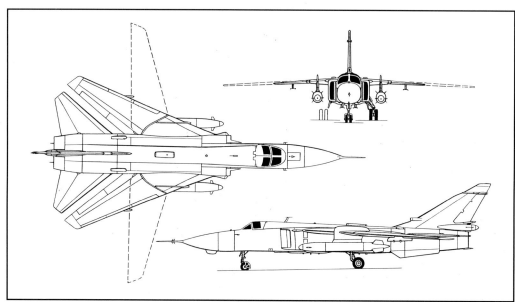

emulate the TFX (F-111) programme and enclose the cockpit in an ejectable capsule. Naturally, intense interest was taken in the design of the capsule for the winning F-111 design, full details of which were published. Unlike the US aircraft, however, the canopy was made to swing upwards, hinged at the rear in two parts, instead of in left and right 'gull wing' halves hinged at the centreline.

The big question remained concerning the wing. The favoured solution continued to be that adopted for TSR.2, with a fixed-geometry plan form with the maximum area for STOL performance but minimum span for good buffet-free penetration at high speeds in dense air. The first prototype, the T6-1 had a wing of this type; it still exists and is stored at the VVS Monino museum. This wing was in fact extremely similar to that of TSR.2, with a span of about 9.2 m (30 ft), very long root chord, delta plan shape but with squared-off tips turned down at 72° and full-span blown flaps along the trailing edge. The British bomber's choice of extremely powerful turbojet engines also influenced the selection of the Lyulka turbojet, despite the fact that CIAM (Central Institute of Aviation Motors) showed that the optimum engine for the mission would be an augmented turbofan with a bypass ratio not less than unity. Surprisingly, not only did no such engine exist in the Soviet Union in the mid-1960s but none of this size has appeared since, though two sizes of bypass turbojet (low-ratio turbofan), with a bypass ratio of 0.4, have been developed for the latest fighters.

TSR.2 influence was also seen in the shape of the aft fuselage, the sharply tapered vertical tail, and the enormous delta tailerons used for control in both pitch and roll and kept within the span of the horizontal part of the wing, the very powerful tip vortex passing just beyond the taileron tip. Like TSR.2, but unlike the F-111, the tailerons were mounted low-mid on the fuselage. Where Felsner's aerodynamicists especially followed TSR.2 rather than the F-111 was in extending the engine inlet ducts well forward of the wing, to present the engines with relatively undisturbed air. Naturally the inlets drew upon experience with the Su-15, though the latter's variable geometry was not needed and of course the inlets were larger. The inlet almost took the form of a vertical rectangle, separated from the vertical flat wall of the fuselage by a large splitter plate, behind which was left a gap of 15 cm for boundary-layer air. As in the Su-15, the duct curved upwards, in the interceptor to pass over the wing and in the bomber to pass over the retracted main landing gears.

The latter had twin wheels carried on backward-sloping levered arms pivoted to a structural leg and adjacent shock struts which were almost vertical in side elevation, but sloped outwards from the fuselage to increase track to a satisfactory 3.15 m (10 ft 4 in). Each unit retracted forwards hydraulically about a skewed axis so that the wheels came

ABOVE *Totally different from early versions, the back end of an Su-24M hides as much as it shows (for example, the anti-SAM warhead measures); among the visibles are the drag-chute tube, with* Pion *antenna feeder above and Gera-F active jammer transmitter below (a second transmitter is just above the high nav light). On each side near the top of the fin is a* Berez *passive/DF receiver, while the extended fin leading edge houses the Skip-2 (Loran-type) navaid. This aircraft was on view at the Berlin airshow in 1992*

inwards to lie beside the inlet duct. The main part of the bay was covered by enormous doors hinged along the side of the fuselage. It was a requirement to be able to operate from unpaved airfields, but even with double wheel units it did not prove possible to reduce tyre pressure to the hoped-for 7 kg/cm² (about 100 lb/sq in). The steerable twin-wheel nose gear was fitted with a wide and deep mudguard, and arranged to retract to the rear.

Provision was made for up to eight attachments for external stores, four under the fuselage and four under the wings. In addition, it was proposed to carry twin air-defence missiles on the downturned wingtips. No mission avionics were installed, though work went ahead on a PNK (attack and navigation complex) more advanced than anything previously attempted in the USSR. The prototypes did, however, have approximately the planned internal fuel capacity of 12,000 litres (2640 Imp gal). This was much less than the capacity and mass available, but matched a simple five-tank system involving the space between the inlet ducts and the widely-spaced engines. The T6-1 was fitted with a row of four RD-36-35FVR lift jets between the inlet ducts, but the appreciable reduction in field length was not considered worth the severe penalty in mission radius and general complexity.

Maj-Gen Vladimir Ilyushin made the first flight in June 1967. The 6-1 proved satisfactory, but by this time everyone was mesmerised by the F-111, and for comparative trials it was decided in 1966 to produce a swing-wing version designated T6-2IG. The outer wings were modelled on those of the US aircraft, and from the first flight in January 1970 it was judged that on balance the IG (variable-geometry) solution was better. This conclusion had almost been reached back in April 1965 when, on grounds that had nothing to do with the aircraft, Britain cancelled TSR.2 and bought the F-111. It was accepted that the VG aircraft would be heavier and more expensive.

CAHI had already done extensive tunnel testing of the proposed wing for the Mikoyan bureau, setting sweep limits of 16° and 72°. For the bigger Sukhoi aircraft the maximum sweep was reduced to 69°, partly because of the reduced (55°) leading-edge angle of the horizontal tails. The wing of both the Mikoyan and Sukhoi aircraft had much in common with that of the F-111, though instead of being merged into the top of the fuselage, the fixed glove portions were clearly defined triangles. The pivots were well aft of the extremities of this glove portion, the wings being positioned by irreversible screwjacks driven by hydraulic motors driving on the front horns, so that the jacks lie ahead of the wing carry-through box. Again the geometry resembled that of the F-111, but Sukhoi engineers commented that the T6-2IG never suffered the American aircraft's structural troubles. Some aircraft have automatically programmed and infini-

TOP The TSR.2 influence on the T6-1 prototype was soon to be even more marked when the wingtips were turned downwards

LEFT The sharp right-angled edges of the T6 prototypes are evident from this view of the aircraft preserved at Monino. This example did not have the four lift jets

tely variable drive, but those in regimental service give the pilot the choice of 16°, 35°, 45° or 69°, by push-buttons.

Each wing carries full-span leading-edge slats and full-span trailing-edge flaps, all driven by hydraulic screwjacks. Contrary to Western reports there are no ailerons, and the flaps reach close to the tip. There are three flap sections, the inner being considerably the larger, of typical Soviet track-mounted double-slotted type. Immediately ahead of the flaps on the upper surface are spoilers, used (except at the 69° wing setting) asymmetrically for roll control, backing up the tailerons, and symmetrically after landing as lift dumpers. Two airbrakes were provided under the fuselage as a result of redesigning the main landing-gear doors. The large side-hinged doors were eliminated, and instead the retracted leg was covered by a side-hinged door and the wheels by front-hinged doors which serve as the airbrakes. This was another case of copying the F-111, though that aircraft has one giant door.

Despite the fact that in many respects the fixed-wing aircraft was superior, all work on it was dropped in mid-1970, and the decision was taken to build a pre-production series of the T6-2IG. Only enough pre-production aircraft were built for a single trials unit, which was formed in early 1974. Meanwhile, Felsner's team introduced further changes, which were sufficient for the designation to be changed to Su-24, reflecting the aircraft's acceptance. Like the T6 prototypes the Su-24 was fitted with eight stores attachments. Those under the fixed wing gloves were rated at 3 t (6600 lb) each and plumbed for the second-largest size of Soviet drop tank, 3000 litres (660 Imp gal) [miscalculated by Washington as 1250 lit, 275 gal]. These giant tanks have small down-pulling foreplanes and four tail fins. There are two points on the centreline, the rear being rated at 2 t (4409 lb) and plumbed for a 2000-litre (440-gal) tank or buddy pack. The other pylons, one under each side of the fuselage and a pivoting pylon under each outer wing, were rated at 750 kg (1655 lb). Maximum external load is 10.3 t (22,700 lb), but the limit for any kind of ordnance is 8 t (17,635 lb).

TOP *This Su-24MK, reputedly having flown from Weltzow, was exhibited at Berlin in 1992. Note the Vikhr electro-optical blister behind the nose gear, and absence of a fence above the glove pylon*

MIDDLE *Walking round the same 24M we find the probe extended; beside the birdproof windscreen is one of the PVD-7 probes, behind the canopies is the dipole antenna of the ARK-15M radio compass and beside the inlet is the left-arc Berez (SPO-15S) warning receiver*

RIGHT *The baseline attack aircraft was the Su-24MK, seen here with a full load on all pylons. At this time (1983) the inlet mechanism was locked fully open*

From the outset it was agreed to fit provision for dual flight controls, and to instal a gun in the underside of the fuselage, on the right side. The gun chosen was the same as in some MiG-23/27 versions, the six-barrel GSh-6-23M, with 1000 rounds. Unlike the F-111 the gun is a permanent fit. If necessary the centreline and glove pylons can be loaded with three further 23 mm guns, the GSh-23L-2 in the SPPU-6 pod with 400 rounds and pivoted barrels. The internal gun causes a bulge in the underside which extends across the MLG door/airbrake, and the muzzle is normally faired over by small clamshell doors. A bulge on the left houses the AKS-5 ciné camera. The exceptional spectrum of external ordnance is listed in the data.

Limited production was followed from 1976 by full production of the Su-24 at Komsomolsk, building up to 65 per year. An external change in the Su-24 was that the larger afterburner and nozzle of the F-3A engine caused the rear fuselage to be sculpted closely around them instead of being a rectangular box. In turn this required addition of an auxiliary cooling inlet in the leading edge of the fin. The sides remained flat and vertical to provide a gap-free root for the huge tailerons whose range of movement exceeds 40°, with minus-24° available. Progressive upgrading in the avionics resulted in the addition of a separate air/air cooling system with the radiator in a duct above the fuselage.

All production aircraft had the PNK complex which at first integrated 10 avionics subsystems and eventually linked together 18. The initial standard aircraft had a *Relyef* terrain-avoidance radar, linked with the RV-21 radar altimeters, and inertial and doppler navaids linked via twin digital computers to the SAU-6M1 flight-control system. This was the first Soviet aircraft able to fly low-level missions under any weather or night conditions.

From the start a comprehensive group of navigation units was plugged in, as well as standard ILS, IFF and air-data systems. The latter at first used a curious three-pronged group of nose sensors, switching in the Su-24M (described later) to a long single probe. Air-data always included the UUAP-72M-13 subsystem with small vanes measuring AOA and yaw. Twin pitot probes are on each side of the windscreen.

First flown in 1972, the BKO-2 integrated defensive avionics did not reach user regiments until 1981. This retained portions of the traditional Sirena 3 system but added passive receivers at the top of the fin, facing aft, and ahead of the wing gloves, each covering a 100° forward sector. Without help from the WSO, this commands the L-167 countermeasures controller to fire the L-101G active jammer on a particular wavelength or to launch payloads from the 12 triple APP-50 chaff/flare dispensers. A visible change was a slight extension of the chord of the fin as far as the end of the metal structure, giving a kinked outline, caused by the Loran antenna. A further important upgrade was replacement of the earlier KM-1M and K-36M seats by the ligher but rocket-boosted (zero/zero) K-36D, the Su-24 being the first aircraft to be thus equipped. Either crewmember can initiate ejection, the canopy being split into left and right halves.

Despite its considerable size and power the Su-24 never had the combination of bombload and radius claimed for it by Western analysts. Especially when operating from short rough-surface airstrips, its total payload of bombs with maximum fuel, or of fuel with maximum ordnance, was less than one-quarter of the theoretical limit. Accordingly, an obvious upgrade in the Su-24M, flown in 1977, was a neat retractable flight-refuelling probe, similar to that of the MiG-31, immediately ahead of the

RIGHT *The T6-1, here seen in its final form with downturned wingtips, had a remarkable range of tailplane angles*

ABOVE *Portrait of an MK, emphasising the fence pylon. Above this is the avionics heat exchanger, behind the cockpit is the radio-compass antenna, and the guidance antenna extends beyond the fin leading edge*

windscreen and provided with night lighting. After taking off with a maximum external load, the 24M can be topped up by receiving 9 t (19,840 lb) of fuel, extending mission radius by over 85 per cent. As a tanker it can carry a UPAZ-A hose-drum unit on the aft body pylon, for transferring up to 15,000 litres.

A totally upgraded avionics suite was reflected in redesign of the avionics bays ahead of and behind the cockpit. The main radar was upgraded, and the *Kaira*-24 electro-optical (laser plus TV) sensor was added in a broad rectangular blister aft of the nosewheel bay. New defensive systems included a dome above the fuselage housing the sensor of the LO-82 infra-red missile launch warning system. The centreline pylons were modified to carry additional stores, and provision was made for giant pylons on the wing gloves forming fences extending nearly 2 m (80 in) back across the upper surface [these fence pylons were retro-fitted to various other Su-24s, and conversely absent from many Ms]. The three-pronged nose probes were replaced by a single long boom carrying pitch/yaw vanes. The Su-24MK (modified commercial) is an export version which usually lacks the FR probe and various avionics, many being earlier aircraft upgraded.

The final new-build versions were the MR and MP. The Su-24MR uses the airframe of the M, but gutted of attack subsystems and armament. Instead it houses a 'special reconnaissance complex' including a big SLAR (side-looking airborne radar) in the nose, with the antenna on the left side, a choice of cameras in place of the EO installation, and likewise causing a large blister behind the nosewheel bay, IR linescan, a new centreline pylon carrying either a 6.1-m (20 ft) multi-sensor pod or a 4 m (13 ft) flat-sided pod containing a synthetic-aperture radar, plus various Elint pods and an optional jammer/dispenser pod. About 65 MRs have so far been built, retaining the FR probe, shared between a Siberian unit and a naval regiment. The MP is a dedicated EW platform, replacing the Yak-28 in Elint, Sigint and jamming roles. It features nine antennas not seen on other versions, the most prominent being a 'hockey stick' under each side of the fuselage and a large blade under the nose.

Total production was about 940. About 220 were delivered to the AV-MF, and exports included 24 to Iraq, 15 to Libya and a planned 12 to Syria. Many more are available now for sale.

SPECIFICATION

Su-24M
Two Saturn (Lyulka) AL-21F-3A turbojets each rated at 11.25 t (24,800 lb) with max afterburner or 7.8 t (17,200 lb) dry
Dimensions Span (16°) 17.64 m (57 ft 10.5 in), (69°) 10.366 m (34 ft 1 in); length 24.53 m (80 ft 5.8 in); wing area (16°) 55.168 m² (593.82 sq ft)
Weight Empty equipped, 22.32 t (49,207 lb); max take-off 39.7 t (87,525 lb)
Performance Maximum speed (clean, low level) 1420 km/h (882 mph, M 1.159), (high) 1325 km/h (824 mph, M 1.35); TO distance at normal TO weight of 32.26 t (71,121 lb) 900 km (2,950 ft); low-level radius with 3 t (6614 lb) bombload, 650 km (403 miles); ferry range (two tanks) 2850 km (1771 miles)
Armament Armament: Internal GSh-6-23M gun with 260 rounds; missiles, four Kh-23 or 23M, four Kh-25 (all versions), three Kh-28, three Kh-29 (all versions), two Kh-58, four KAB-500, two KAB-1500L, two self-defence R-60 or 60MK; bombs, 38 AB-100, 30 AB-250 (M54) or 16 AB-250 (streamlined M62), 9 AB-500, 7 ZB-500, 8 RBK-250, or two TN-1000 or 1200 tactical nuclear; rockets, 120 S-8, 30 S-13 or 6 S-250; three SPPU-6 gun pods

SEPECAT Jaguar

First Flight – 8 September 1968

This outstandingly cost-effective tactical attack aircraft is notable on several counts. It was the outcome of two utterly disparate requirements, one by France which wanted the simplest possible subsonic trainer and light attack aircraft able to use front-line airstrips, and one by Britain which wanted an expensive *trainer* to thunder off 10,000-ft runways and fly at not less than Mach 1.8. It was the first time in history that two nations had collaborated on an aircraft right from the start of design. And the result was an aeroplane with two tiny engines and a span ten feet less than a Spitfire which could carry a heavier load of bombs from England to Berlin than a Lancaster, and deliver them more accurately, even in bad weather. It was also unusual in that the Jaguar ended up with the French partner doing all it could to stop customers buying it.

Of course, the idea of one nation wanting a cheap subsonic aircraft to fly attack missions while the other wanted a 1200-mph trainer sounds nonsensical. In fact, France had a long history of studying aircraft able to operate away from known airbases, which it realised would be the first bits of infrastructure to be wiped off the map in any war between NATO and the Warsaw Pact. As for the RAF, this had been told in April 1957 that it had better give up the idea of any future fighters or bombers, and so it hit on the idea of disguising a supersonic tactical aeroplane as a mere trainer, and issued Air Staff Target 362 in January 1963.

The most important of several British projects in this class in the early 1960s were the Hawker Siddeley (Folland), Fo 147, derived from the Gnat Mk 5, and the BAC P.45, both of which were VG (variable-geometry) swing-wing projects with the choice of either one or two engines and either one seat or two in tandem. The P.45 was an outstanding design which would admirably have met AST.362. Unfortunately, before anything could be done Britain elected a Labour government dedicated to cancelling British aircraft programmes. After it had torn up the P.1154, HS.681 and TSR.2, and replaced them with US purchases, it decided that perhaps the British industry ought in some way

BELOW *On 4 June 1974 No 54 Sqn put on view a shiny GR.1, Adour engine, spectrum of weaponry and lion mascot, at Lossiemouth*

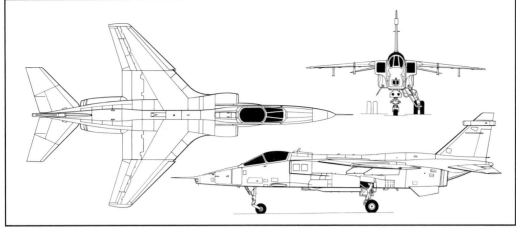

LEFT *Jaguar GR.1*
(Jaguar S)

ABOVE *The 05 prototype was the naval Jaguar M.
Successful carrier trials did not stop Dassault from
getting it cancelled in favour of the all-French Super
Etendard*

to be kept going, so it immediately began seeing
what could be done about collaboration with
France. One result was a big deal making French
Aèrospatiale helicopters in Britain at Westlands of
Yeovil. The other was to produce a joint strike/
trainer aircraft.

As said earlier, the French objective was far more
modest. In January 1964 they had drawn up a
definitive requirement for an ECAT (Ecole de
Combat et Appui Tactique), receiving proposals
from Breguet, Dassault, Nord, Potez and Sud-
Aviation. It was at this point that Britain, in the
form of Aviation Minister Roy Jenkins and Defence
Minister Denis Healey, were sent cap-in-hand to
Paris, to tell de Gaulle (who had just said his big
'Non' to Britain's application to join the Common
Market) that Britain wanted to co-operate with
France in virtually any aircraft design, and were
prepared to accept French design leadership.

So the French picked the Breguet Br 121 as the
ECAT, and BAC were then told they were the lucky
firm picked to collaborate by doing whatever the
French said. Politicians love to think they are
important, by issuing such decrees as 'The aeroplane is always to be referred to as ECAT. On no
account is any British designation to be used'. The
Br 121 was not a supersonic swing-winger but a
subsonic fixed-wing aeroplane with two tiny American engines such as the GE J85 or P&W J60. Up at

Warton – in Lancashire, where they used to call the
shots – BAC's B O 'Ollie' Heath split the P.45 into
two, one half being used as the starting point of
another collaborative project, the AFVG (which got
nowhere, as is noted in the Tornado story) and the
other being used to try to make the Br 121 a little
more like a warplane. The seeds could have been
sewn for real problems, but fortunately the French
air staff found themselves much in agreement with
AST.362 (nobody turns down a Ferrari when it's
offered, instead of a Lada) and after a lot of very
cautious discussion it was agreed that the ECAT
might be a bit more like the P.45 than the Br 121 (so
long as it was called ECAT) and actually need
engines of double the thrust. To produce the engines
Rolls-Royce (which always enjoyed a special relationship with Whitehall, unlike the airframe manufacturers) was permitted actually to make sugges-
tions in its collaboration with Turbomeca, and the
result was a very small two-shaft turbofan called
the Adour, after a French river, which bolted
together bits of the Turbomeca T.260 and bits of the
Rolls RB.172.

single-seat strike aircraft and 75 trainers, while Britain signed for 150 trainers (presumably some with carrier equipment). The commitment to 300 was a godsend for the joint company registered in May 1966 as SEPECAT, from Société Européenne de Production de l'Avion ECAT. The Adour was to be created by a British company (showing the special relationship Derby enjoyed) called Rolls-Royce Turbomeca Ltd.

An amendment to the agreement signed on 16 January 1967 enlarged the programme, though it did not reveal the extent to which British influence and design expertise had multiplied the capability of each aircraft. The new SEPECAT programme comprised: for France, 75 Jaguar A single-seat attack aircraft, 85 Jaguar E trainers and 40 Jaguar M single-seat naval attack aircraft; for Britain, 110 (instead of 150) Jaguar B trainers and 90 of a new single-attack version, the Jaguar S. Largely because the *Armée de l'Air* really needed the Jaguar, to replace the Mystère 4A, SMB.2, F-100, F-84F, Vautour and T-33, it survived the following months in which the French did all they could at the political level to put Britain down, and stop joint projects (succeeding with AFVG). But Jaguar lived.

In all essentials the Jaguar could hardly have been more conventional, though it had a relatively small wing mounted high on the fuselage and stood very high off the ground on massively strong landing gears with twin wheels able to use rough bulldozed strips. The emphasis was clearly not on training, but on easily loading heavy attack stores and then running at speed across bumpy ground. Propulsion was by the two small engines – bypass jets, or low-ratio turbofans – with afterburners for take-off and supersonic flight, but fed by simple plain lateral inlets to show that Mach numbers beyond 1 were not that important.

With a span of only 28 ft 6 in (8.69 m) but so high off the ground that many adults could not reach up to it, the wing had moderate sweep, moderate anhedral, a fixed inboard leading edge (which curved round to join the inlet duct wall at a sweep angle of 80°), a dogtooth discontinuity at the inner end of powered outboard slats, and powerful double-slotted flaps over the entire trailing edge. Roll control was thus by spoilers, augmented at low speeds by differential movement of the slab tailerons. The back end was rather like an F-4 Phantom, though the tailplane anhedral was less and the fin and rudder were taller. Between the jetpipes was a hook to catch runway arrester gear, and a braking parachute in the tailcone. The levered-suspension landing gears were by Messier-Hispano, with 70 lb/ sq in tyres and Maxaret brakes by Dunlop. Some 990 gal (4500 litres) of fuel could be housed in integral tanks in the wing and fuselage. Seats were by Martin-Baker, and like most equipment the actual pattern depended on which customer was buying. The same comment applied to the two guns, and to the stores to be hung on the five pylons.

TOP *Export Jaguar Internationals in assembly at Warton, Lancashire*

ABOVE *XZ398 of No 41 Sqn, with recon pack*

Eventually the Memo of Understanding was signed on 17 May 1965. It launched the AFVG, which the French never intended to work on anyway, and the ECAT, 'which', said the British Civil Servants, 'we shall use both in the Air Force *and Navy* as an advanced trainer to replace the Hunter and Gnat'. There followed the predictable platitudes, interspersed with cost estimates which even at the time could be seen to be nonsense (prototype R&D £9.4 million and unit price in production £450,000, for example). The one good feature of the whole deal was that, instead of traditional trickle funding in tiny drips, each nation made a firm commitment. The French signed for 75

Defensive missile rails on the wingtips were surprisingly omitted.

The work-split was just like TSR.2 in miniature. BAC made the wings, rear fuselage and tail, and the French partner the remainder. In January 1967 the French partner, Breguet, came under the control of Dassault, which smarted at having lost ECAT to Breguet in the first place and was also busy torpedoeing the AFVG programme.

In fact, the arrogantly nationalist Dassault company left SEPECAT as before, but with its own nominees on the Breguet board. Assembly lines were started at Vélizy-Villacoublay and Preston, and the first aircraft to be completed, E-01, was rolled out at Villacoublay on 17 April 1968. Then came the 'événements' of Summer 1968, which for over three months brought industry to a halt. At last E-01 was flown at Istres by Bernard Witt on 8 September 1968. E-02 followed on 11 February 1969, and Jimmy Dell flew A-03 on 29 March, exceeding Mach 1.

Despite prolonged strikes by both partners S-06 followed on 12 October 1969 and M-05 on 14 November. The first British two-seater, B-08, did not fly until 30 August 1971, showing how the RAF had at last decided its urgent need was not for a trainer version at all but for an ever-better single-seater. Reason had prevailed, and by 1971 France had gone ahead with Germany on the Alpha Jet trainer and Britain had launched the P.1182 which became the outstanding Hawk. Instead of 150 trainers the RAF finally bought 165 Jaguar S and 35 dual B-models merely to speed type-conversion.

Differences between the A, B, E, M and S were confined mainly to equipment. The A had in many ways a surprisingly low build-standard, with no attack sensors, navigation by doppler and a twin-gyro platform, two 30 mm DEFA 553 guns each with 150 rounds, a traditional cockpit and a Mk 4 seat not cleared for use below 90 kt (167 km/h). After checking out a retractable flight-refuelling probe, this was omitted from production aircraft 1 through 14! Subsequently, upgrades were fitted, notably the facility to carry the Atlis (auto tracking laser illumination system) pod in conjunction with the very accurate AS.30L smart missile.

The B had a similar nose, but with no probe, stretched to accommodate a tandem dual cockpit with two Mk 9 seats with zero/zero capability, advanced digital inertial navigation, a HUD and projected-map display, and a single 30 mm Aden

TOP *Prettiest of all Jaguars is this GR.1 of No 54 Sqn painted to celebrate the RAF's 75th anniversary*

RIGHT *Streaming vapour, a GR.1 leaves the UK for* Desert Storm. *They were painted Sand colour, had overwing Sidewinders, ALE-40 dispensers scabbed on, CRV-7 rocket pods and other updates*

ABOVE LEFT *A and E type aircraft of an unidentified* Armée de l'Air *unit queue behind a C-135F*

LEFT *Jaguar of EC11 'Roussillon' during* Desert Storm, *with tanks, Matra Belouga dispensers and self-protection Phimat jammer*

ABOVE *A-type Jag with Thomson-CSF Atlis II laser designator pod and Matra BGL smart bombs*

gun with 150 rounds. The E resembled the A but lacked the doppler, weapon-aiming system and FR probe. The M was much better equipped than the A, with Thomson-CSF Agave radar, a Ferranti laser and a Mk 9 seat, as well as a stronger hook, catapult spools, strengthened main gears with single wheels and high-pressure tyres, and various naval items. Cutting a long story short, several influential Frenchmen were determined that the *Aéronavale* would never operate the Jaguar M, and after trying to buy the Skyhawk or Corsair II the decision was taken to replace the Etendard IVM with the Super Etendard, which is hardly in the same class as the Jaguar.

Continuing with the different versions, the S was, from the start, better equipped than the A, since it had Mk 9 seats, the retractable probe, digital inertial nav/attack system with HUD and projected-map display, two 30 mm Aden guns, ARI.18223 radar warning (with a prominent receiver pod near the top of the fin, looking to front and rear) and a laser ranger and marked-target seeker looking through a 'chisel' nose. All versions could carry a 10,000-lb load of bombs or other stores, including tanks and 'buddy packs', and the S could carry a centreline reconnaissance pod housing a battery of vertical, forward and oblique cameras and an infra-red linescan.

Despite the delays, which had nothing to do with the aircraft, service deliveries began to *l'Armée de l'Air* in May 1972 and to the RAF a year later. By 1981 the former had 160 A and 40 E Jaguars equipping nine escadrons in EC3, 5 and 7, while the RAF had its 165 S (Jaguar GR.1) and 35 B (T.2) serving with No 226 OCU and Nos 14, 17, 20 and 31 Sqns in the nuclear strike role from Brüggen, 6 and 54 Sqns in the close-support role from Coltishall and No 2 (II) at Laarbruch and 41 at Coltishall with recon pods.

The Jaguar's combination of versatility, rough-field capability, long range, supersonic speed and startlingly modest costs made it of obvious interest to air forces around the world. Sadly, though Dassault made no greater proportion of each Mirage than it did of the Jaguar, the Mirage was all-French and gave Dassault far more prestige, so the effort to sell Jaguars to other customers came wholly from BAC. In August 1974 SEPECAT announced the Jaguar International, an export version which was naturally based on the British Jaguar S. It differed mainly in having the first of several uprated versions of the Adour engine, which had began life conservatively rated.

The first Adours, Mk 101, were rated at 4620 lb dry and 6930 lb with afterburner. All British and

ABOVE *Jaguar GR.1As and a T.2 of No 54 Sqn at RAF Coltishall. The perfection is routine*

French Jaguars began life with the Mk 102, rated at 5115/7305 lb. For the International the engine was the Mk 804, rated at 5320/8040 lb, and with an even bigger gain at high forward speed (eg, 27 per cent at Mach 0.9). The RAF quickly decided to buy kits to upgrade all its engines to the same standard, designated Adour Mk 104, rated at 5270/7900 lb, or with the option of 5350/8100 lb, the aircraft then becoming Mk 1A or 2A. Later, in 1979–84, the RAF Jaguars were retrofitted with the FIN 1064 inertial system, and trial installations were made of an underwing FLIR pod.

The first export sales were to Oman and Ecuador, in 1974, and eventually 139 Internationals were produced, for Ecuador (12), India (85, including 45 assembled by HAL in India), Nigeria (18) and Oman (24).

In addition, HAL in India have since 1988 been producing a further 46 Jaguars quite independently. This brings IAF deliveries up to 131, named *Shamsher* (assault sword), ten (No 6 Awn) being anti-ship versions with Agave radar, Darin nav/attack system and Sea Eagle missiles. All IAF *Shamshers* have the Adour Mk 811, which is produced by HAL, rated at 8400 lb with afterburner.

A feature available on the Jaguar International was an overwing pylon for a Sidewinder or Magic AAM for self-defence. Several Jaguar operators have used their aircraft in action, none more so than the RAF which deployed 12 Mk 1A aircraft and 22 pilots from Nos 6, 41 and 54 Sqns, plus No 226 OCU, to Bahrain during *Desert Storm*. Each aircraft was equipped with overwing AIM-9L Sidewinders, ARI.18228 upgraded to Marconi Sky Guardian, an ALQ-101 jammer pod, a Phimat chaff dispenser and two ALE-40 flare dispensers. It was soon judged preferable to attack at medium level with GP bombs instead of retarded bombs and high-velocity CRV-7 rockets instead of BL.755 clusters. They flew nearly 1000 hours in 611 sorties without loss.

SPECIFICATION

Jaguar GR.1A

Two Rolls-Royce Turbomeca Adour 104 turbofans each rated at max 5350 lb dry and 8100 lb with afterburner

Dimensions Span 28 ft 6 in (8.69 m); length 50 ft 11 in (15.52 m); wing area 260.3 sq ft (24.18 m²)

Weight Empty (1973) 16,292 lb (7390 kg), (1993) 17,012 lb (7716 kg); max take-off 34,172 lb (15,500 kg)

Performance Maximum speed (clean) up to 20,000 ft (6096 m), Mach 1.25 (720 mph, 1159 km/h), (above 20,000 ft) Mach 1.4; service ceiling 45,000 ft (13,720 m); lo-lo mission radius (internal fuel only) 334 miles (535 km), ferry range 2190 miles (3524 km)

Armament Two 30 mm Aden; two Sidewinder AAMs; up to 10,000 lb of stores

Panavia Tornado

First Flight – 14 August 1974

Subject of the biggest multi-national pro-gramme (of any kind) in history, the Tornado began rather uncertainly in 1967 to see if anything could be rescued out of the shambles of British aircraft procurement. The government had cancelled all the British programmes, bought the F-111, cancelled that, set course with France on the AFVG (Anglo-French variable-geometry) and then watched that collapse as France walked out. Nobody then could have dared hope that a frail infant called MRCA (Multi-Role Combat Aircraft) would lead to a programme which would produce nearly 1000 aircraft in 20 years, with a fair chance of a good many more. Though this book is concerned mainly with aircraft rather than politics, this tale, if we had room for the politics, would be ten times longer and be packed with the usual lessons on how difficult it is for people to take either a multi-national view or a long-term view. The marvel is that something really did come out at the other end.

The original Memo of Understanding was signed on 25 July 1968 by Belgium, Canada, West Germany, Italy, the Netherlands and the UK. A month later the first numerical proposals were submitted by Canadair, Messerschmitt-Bölkow and BAC. Everybody said they wanted the maximum of everything, to the extent that it was stipulated the MRCA had to land in hot-day conditions (to give the fastest touchdown and lowest reverse thrust) on an icy runway (to give poorest wheel braking). NAMMO (NATO MRCA Management Organisa-tion) was formed on 15 December 1968, and the industrial airframe group called Panavia was formed on 26 March 1969, with offices at Munich. Soon Belgium, Canada and the Netherlands walked out, and Italy so wavered that the development phase was signed for by Britain and Germany alone, on 22 July 1970 (Italy signed three months later). The shareholdings and hence work-shares were: West Germany 42.5 per cent, Italy 15 per cent, UK 42.5 per cent. This reflected planned buys of 320–420 for Germany (they originally said 700), 100 for Italy and 385 for the UK.

From the start the partners thought in terms of a twin-engined aircraft with variable-geometry swing wings, but they carefully studied every possible alternative. For example, MBB spent much time looking at single-engined versions, while (mainly because of the Italians) until 24 March 1970 there were to be two main versions, the single-seat Panavia 100 and tandem-seat Panavia 200. Dropping the single-seater reduced time and cost, and the number of prototypes needed; the original total of 13 was cut to seven, and then increased to nine. Of these, four were to be assembled at Warton, three at Munich and two at Turin.

As engine supplier for the defunct AFVG Bristol Siddeley had never stopped working on a suitable engine, even after the takeover by Rolls-Royce in 1966. Keeping an ear to the ground the team at Bristol, led by Gordon M Lewis, made their proposed engine smaller but with even lower fuel consump-tion, taking the bold step of going from two shafts to three. Designated RB.199, it finally won over the Pratt & Whitney JTF16 on 4 September 1969, and a month later Turbo-Union was formed to manage the engine programme. Shares were held by Fiat (now FiatAvio) 20 per cent, MTU 40 per cent and Rolls-Royce 40 per cent, though the agreed work-split was Fiat 15, MTU 42.5 and Rolls-Royce 42.5. The first complete RB.199 ran in September 1971, an engine flew in a pod (which incorporated the right side of an MRCA fuselage, complete with gun)

RIGHT *A GR.1 inside its HAS (hardened aircraft shelter) at RAF Honington in 1981*

surface, but during development Krüger flaps were added. The wings each had three sections of powered slat covering the entire leading edge, and four sections of double-slotted (fixed-vane) flaps covering the trailing edge. Lateral control was effected by differential movement of the huge tailerons, augmented at low speeds at intermediate and low sweep angles by spoilers which after touchdown serve as lift dumpers. All three landing gears were designed to retract forwards into the fuselage, the nose unit having twin steerable wheels and the main legs each carrying a single wheel with a low-pressure tyre and Goodyear anti-skid multi-disc brake. At the rear was an arrestor hook.

The contract for the main radar was won by Texas Instruments, whose muti-mode set operates through two completely independent antennas, a big flat plate with straight top and bottom for the GMR (ground-mapping radar) and, below, a smaller circular antenna for the TFR (terrain-following radar). Cooling was liquid, and the antenna drives hydraulic. The installation devised was excellent, because the radome was arranged to hinge wide open for access to the antennas, which in turn were mounted on a second portion of aircraft nose which itself hinged wide open for unrestricted access to front and rear. This complete installation was fortunately common to all users, and is one of the 351 hinged or removable panels which cover almost the entire external surface and make Tornado one of the easiest aircraft to service.

In general, systems were conventional, though the two quite independent hydraulic systems operated at 4000 lb/sq in. What was unusual was the excellence of the SPS (second power system) for which the supplier was KHD (Klöckner Humboldt Deutz). For a start, each engine drove an accessory gearbox, which in turn drove the hydraulic pumps, oil-cooled brushless generators and other units. Second, cross shafts enabled each engine to drive the entire SPS in the event of single engine failure. Third, on the right side was added a KHD gas-turbine APU (auxiliary power unit) which could start the main engines and provide secondary power on the ground; strangely, the APU has not been required to drive all the accessories following double engine failure.

It was obviously essential to adopt the best possible avionic architecture that could be afforded (the RAF wanted more, for example a main X-band radar, a fine-grain Ku-band and a laser, but were out-voted). In the event the agreed initial standard comprised the GMR/TFR already described, and a laser ranger (added to many aircraft after 1985), inertial and doppler navigation with Kalman filtering for the best combined accuracy, Tacan, ILS and other approach aids, communications, air-data computer, standby attitude/heading reference (and on some aircraft, Spils to prevent stall/spin departures in extreme manoeuvres), triple-redundant CSAS (command stability augmentation system),

under a Vulcan in April 1973, and a pair of early RB.199-01 engines powered the first MRCA prototype on 14 August 1974.

In all major respects MRCA was conventional. The only slightly advanced features of the otherwise aluminium-alloy structure were that the wings were pivoted through Teflon-coated bearings to a carry-through box of EBW (electron-beam welded) titanium, and the rudder and aft section of each taileron were metal honeycomb. The centre wing box formed an integral tank, as did the structural boxes of the wings (right out to the tip), front and rear fuselage and (in RAF aircraft) the fin, the two fuselage tanks being Uniroyal self-sealing multiple cells. Total capacity was 1285 Imp gal (RAF aircraft, 1406 gal, 6392 litres). During development it was decided to make provision for a retractable inflight-refuelling probe housed in a quickly-attached package along the right side of the fuselage just below the canopy.

The amazingly short engines were installed close together in the rear fuselage, each with a twin-bucket reverser forming part of the airframe. The inlet ducts were long and almost straight, leading back under the wing from wedge inlets standing well away from the fuselage, each with a fully variable upper wall and two large suck-in auxiliary doors in the side which open on take-off. Each wing glove was originally simple, with no movable

autopilot/flight director, and various radar homing and warning systems. These were arranged to feed to the Litef central computer, which in early aircraft had a memory of 64K, later upgraded to 224K and eventually to be standardised at 256K. This computer in turn was required to feed the cockpit displays, which in the standard aircraft serve a pilot in front and navigator behind on Mk 10A zero/zero seats. The initial standard for the pilot included a HUD (head-up display), HSI (horizontal situation indicator), TF display, moving map and radar-warning display. For the navigator the initial standard included a central combined display, with a small stick radar controller, flanked by left and right tabular displays for mission planning, nav/com control, stores management, systems monitoring and inflight navigation, as well as a BDH (bearing/distance/heading) display and various radar warning and defensive systems displays.

From the outset the MRCA was designed to fulfil

TOP *Touch-down by one of the German aircraft used by the TTTE at Cottesmore, England. Instructors, pupils and aircraft are tasked without regard to nationality*

RIGHT *Portsmouth Aviation supplied the special bomb-loading trollies for use inside HASs*

BELOW *Luftwaffe JaBoG aircraft parked outside their HASs, showing the Cold War to be over*

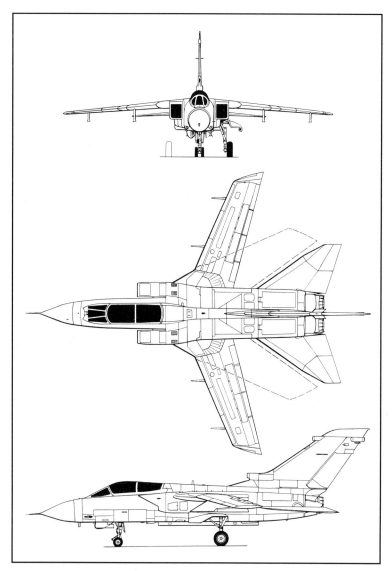

seven basic missions: deep interdiction, counter-air (against airfields), BAI (battlefield air interdiction), CAS (close air support), reconnaissance, maritime strike/attack and point interception. No customer wanted all seven, but the aircraft had to meet all the requirements; moreover, it had to carry any of more than 70 different kinds of store (possibly an all-time record) which were, in many cases, specially designed. Another specially designed item was the gun, all customers having agreed on the fit of two cannon. The contract went to Mauser-werke, whose MK27 is a very powerful weapon of 27 mm calibre, each gun having 180 of the large rounds. No internal weapon bay was specified, there being no fewer than seven pylon hardpoints for a total of 11 stores: a single ERU (ejector-release unit) on the centreline, three ERUs on each so-called fuselage shoulder pylon and single ERUs on the inboard and outboard pylons under the wings, all four of which slew automatically according to wing sweep. Maximum external stores load is academic, the brochure answer simply being 'more than 9 t, 19,840 lb'. Defensive systems are discussed later.

The first aircraft, assembled by MBB at Manching and flown by BAC's Paul Millett, with MBB's Nils Meister in the back seat, opened the flight test programme on 14 August 1974 with a flawless 30-min mission. Like most of the nine prototypes, aircraft 01 was painted white with red trim, but it bore registration D-9591, later changed to 98 + 04. Subsequent prototypes introduced the complex mission subsystems, equipment, armament and the production Mk 101 engine. The first of the pre-production aircraft (PP11-PP16) flew on 5 Febru-

BELOW *The* Aeronautica Militare Italiana *sent* Desert Storm *aircraft from Nos 154, 155 and 156 Gruppi. Two are taking fuel here from one of the hard-worked KC-135Rs*

ary 1977, by which time emergence of the ADV (Air-Defence Version) had resulted in the original aircraft becoming the Tornado IDS (InterDiction Strike). The first production IDS aircraft flew on 10 July 1979 (UK), 27 July 1979 (Germany) and 25 September 1981 (Italy). The first service delivery was made on 1 July 1980 to the TTTE (Tornado Tri-National Training Establishment) at RAF Cottesmore, where all Tornado aircrew were trained.

Subsequently deliveries were made to the four original customers, in each case starting in 1982. The RAF received 229 IDS aircraft, comprising 164 GR.1, 14 GR.1A and 51 Mk 1 dual-pilot trainers (including one PP aircraft). The *Luftwaffe* received 157 IDS attack aircraft (including two PP), 35 ECR and 55 dual. The *Marineflieger* received 112 IDS including 12 dual. The AMI (Italian AF) received 88 strike (including one PP) plus 12 dual. Production was brought up to 732 of this version by a Saudi Arabian order for 28 IDS for the RSAF, plus six R/IDS (equivalent to the GR.1A) and 14 dual.

All IDS versions have structural provision for the FR probe and two guns, but the avionics and weapons vary according to the customer. Defensive avionics not only vary but are subject to upgrade. The radar warning receiver was usually the Elettronica ARI.23284, with fore/aft fin antennas, but the GR.1 and 1A now have the Marconi Hermes system. Chaff/flare dispensing is by the Swedish BOZ 100 series pods (Germany Type 101, Italy 102, RAF 107). Each BOZ spews chaff from an annular slit and IR flare cartridges directly to the rear through 14 launch tubes; usually a single BOZ is carried on an outer wing pylon, but occasionally two are needed. With two BOZ, any jammer pod has to go on a weapon station. The usual jammers are the Telefunken Cerberus II, III or IV or, on RAF aircraft, Marconi Sky Shadow. Aircraft from No 556 (Batches 6 and 7) have an STD-1553B digital data bus and upgraded ECM.

Luftwaffe aircraft equip eight Staffeln, two each with Geschwadern (wings) JBG 31 at Nörvenich, 33 at Büchel and 34 at Memmingen and one each with JBG 32 at Lechfeld and 38 at Jever. Standard camouflage is dark grey, dark green and medium green, and principal weapons include B61 nuclear bombs, the MW-1 anti-armour dispenser, AGM-65 Maverick (various), AGM-88 HARM and self-defence AIM-9L. All frontline aircraft have lately been retrofitted with the Dornier Olmos (On-board Life-MOnitoring System), and following several years of testing, the very advanced LATAN (Low-Altitude Terrain-Aided Navigation) is nearing the operational stage, presenting the pilot with a digital picture of the terrain good enough for blind navigation through mountains or even blind landings. *Marineflieger* units were originally two Staffeln with MFG 1 at Jagel and two with MFG 2 at Eggbeck, one of the latter being equipped with an MBB/Alenia multi-sensor pod and tasked with reconnaissance as well as attack. The MFG is

ABOVE *Sand-coloured ZA411 of No 20 Sqn, Laarbruch, zooming with 'Hindenburger' tanks and a pair of Alarms (nine can be carried)*

transferring 40 aircraft to the *Luftwaffe*, reducing its strength to two Staffeln. Standard camouflage is Basalt grey and light grey, and main weapons Kormoran 1 (Kormoran 2 from 1995), BL 755, HARM and AIM-9L.

The *Aeronautica Militare Italiana* was late in getting the Tornado in service, partly through a lack of navigators. Of the 100 aircraft, 54 are assigned to the three Gruppi, 154 (6° Stormo at Ghedi), 155 (50° Stormo at Piacenza) and 156 (36° Stormo at Gioia del Colle). Of the rest, 36 are in active reserve and others at the TTTE or trials units. Camouflage is dark green and dark sea grey, and main weapons B61, MW-1, AGM-65D, HARM, Kormoran 1 (Gruppo 156) and AIM-9L. RAF GR.1s equip the Brüggen wing (Nos IX, 14, 17 and 31 Sqns), Nos 27 and 617 Sqns at Marham, plus TTTE Cottesmore, TWCU Honington, Strike/Attack Opeval Boscombe Down, A&AEE Boscombe Down and DRA Bedford. Camouflage is dark green and dark

ABOVE *At the TTTE at Cottesmore mixed crews train on aircraft of all partner air forces*

sea grey, standard equipment includes a laser ranger and marked-target seeker in a chin fairing and weapons include the WE.177B nuclear bomb, JP 233, BL 755, 1000-lb GP, Paveway II, Alarm and AIM-9L. From 1993 Nos 27 (renumbered 12) and 617 Sqns will replace Buccaneers in the maritime role with Sea Eagle stand-off missiles. No IX Sqn carries the TIALD Thermal-Imaging Airborne Laser Designator.

The GR.1A has the guns replaced by an advanced no-camera reconnaissance installation (small blister behind the laser) with a side-looking infrared and IR linescan, plus real-time recording and ground data-link. The GR.4 is the GR.1 after an MLU (mid-life update). This began in 1990 with addition of RAM (radar-absorbent materials), Have Quick 2 secure radios, NVG (night-vision goggles) filters, Mk 12 Mod 4 IFF, Navstar GPS navigation and provision for 500-gal (595 US gal) tanks. The update adds a new Marconi defensive electronic system, GEC Avionics Spartan terrain-referenced navigation (with terrain following), a new HUD and new HDD (Head-Down Display), advanced video recording and a new weapon-control system. Lack of money may prevent over 100 GR.4s also receiving TIALD, despite its proven value. The Royal Saudi AF received 34 standard plus 14 dual IDS, equipping Nos 7 and 66 Sqns, each unit having six aircraft equipped to GR.1A standard for reconnaissance. They are finished in an overall disruptive pattern of sand, green and brown, and main weapons are JP 233, GP 1000-lb, Sea Eagle, Alarm and AIM-9L.

Tornado ECR is an Electronic Combat Reconnaissance version first flown in 1988 and used by the *Luftwaffe* (35) and AMI (16, all conversions). Tornado ADV is an Air-Defence Variant developed at British expense for the RAF (197), produced as

F.2 (18 including 6 dual) and F.3 (179 including 46 dual), plus Saudi Arabia (30 including 6 dual). Tornado 2000 is a proposed successor to the IDS with a longer fuselage with single-seat cockpit, greater internal tankage, faceted nose and different intakes to reduce radar signature.

Tornado IDS aircraft played a crucial role in the 1991 Gulf War. Overall, the RAF modified and repainted in Desert Sand overall 87 GR.1 and 1A aircraft and deployed 62 to the theatre. They were drawn from Nos 2, 9, 13, 14, 15, 16, 17, 20, 27, 31 and 617 Sqns, and were based at Dhahran, Tabuk and Muharraq. They were tasked with deep penetrations of Iraq to crater airfield runways using JP 233, and to destroy the aircraft themselves in their HASs using LGBs. The JP 233 attacks were made from very low level, but subsequent bombing was almost entirely from about 20,000 ft, which the weapon-delivery system had not been designed for.

Altogether over 1550 bombing sorties were made, dropping over 4200 bombs of 1000 lb (usually carried eight at a time under the fuselage) and 2000 lb, about 975 LGBs, over 100 JP 233 loads and firing 123 Alarms in defence-suppression. Six GR.1As crewed by Nos II and 13 Sqns located Scud launchers with the real-time IR sensors. Other units flew the F.3 interceptor.

Italy's AMI prepared 12 aircraft and sent eight, from the three Tornado Gruppi (154°, 155° and 156°) based at Al Dhafra (Maqatra). The Royal Saudi AF deployed No 7 Sqn and newly formed No 66, both at Dhahran. With the Italians, they too hit Iraqi airfields. Such was the nature of these demanding missions that the IDS force suffered proportionately much higher losses than any other element of Coalition airpower. The RAF suffered three pre-war losses, six in combat and one non-combat loss; Italy suffered one combat loss and Saudi Arabia one non-combat loss. Their achievments spoke for themselves.

SPECIFICATION

Tornado IDS

Two Turbo-Union RB.199 Mk 103 augmented turbofans each rated at 9100 lb dry and 16,075 lb with max augmentation (ECR has Mk 105, 9656/16,960 lb)

Dimensions Span (max) 45 ft 7½ in (13.91 m), (min) 28 ft 2½ in (8.60 m); length 54 ft 10.3 m (16.72 m); wing area (to centreline at 25° sweep) 286.3 sq ft (26.6 m²)

Weight Empty equipped, 30,620 lb (13,890 kg); max TO (clean) 45,000 lb (20,411 kg); max 61,620 lb (27,950 kg)

Performance Maximum speed (clean, high) Mach 2.2 (1454 mph, 2340 km/h), (low level, clean) over 800 kt (902 mph, 1480 km/h), (low, max bombload) 691 mph (1112 km/h); runway requirement, less than 2950 ft (900 m); combat radius ('heavy weapons load', hi-lo-hi) 863 miles (1390 km); ferry range 2420 miles (3890 km)

Armament Two Mauser MK 27 guns each with 180 rounds (not on GR.1A); up to 'more than 19,840 lb, 9 t' of 54 types of external store, see text

Rockwell B-1B Lancer

First Flight – 23 December 1974

One of this bomber's many predecessor projects, AMSA, was said to mean America's Most Studied Airplane. No aircraft in history has ever sparked more controversy – mainly for the wrong reasons – nor taken so long to go from the drawing board to combat duty, a matter of over 24 years. Indeed the history of the B-1 reflects the traumatic changes that have fundamentally and irreversibly affected the concept of a bomber.

The story really began in 1962, when it became evident that the B-70 was not going to enter the USAF inventory. This bomber had been designed for the greatest possible supersonic speed, greatest altitude and longest range. Its astronomic cost focused media attention on the supposed fact that bombers were no longer needed in an age of long-range missiles, ICBMs and SLBMs. In fact, it was self-evident that (in 1962, and even in 1993) missiles are incapable of doing anything except destroy a fixed target whose location is known. Bombers were still needed to destroy mobile targets, search for targets whose exact location was unknown and, not least, undertake recce missions both before and after a strike.

Later the Department of Defense hit on the concept of its strategic striking power being deployed by a triad, the image being that of a table with three legs. These legs were the ICBM, the SLBM and the manned bomber. Take away any leg, said the Pentagon, and the concept of strategic deterrence falls over.

Far more valid than the supposed obsolescence of the manned bomber was the unpalatable fact that the development of SAMs had swept away for ever the notion that a bomber could avoid being shot down by flying faster or higher. Though most early SAMs were not noted either for their quick reaction time or their reliability, they had, by the late 1950s, demonstrated their ability to intercept simulated or actual bomber targets out to distances up to 75 miles and at heights well above the ceiling of any practical bomb-loaded aircraft. The only alternative appeared to fly as low as possible. to put off for as long as possible being detected by hostile air-defence radars.

There followed a prolonged study of what kind of bomber was most cost/effective. One family studied, SLAB (supersonic low-altitude bomber), concen-

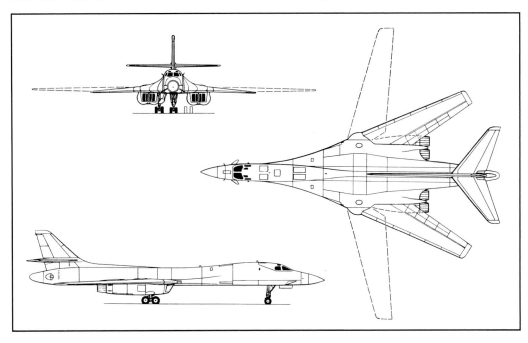

trated entirely on the highest speed at the lowest height, which in turn meant a bomber resembling either a paper dart or a projectile with hardly any wing. No aeroplane of traditional form could fly faster than sound at low level without 'shaking the crew's eyeballs out', and also burning so much fuel that its radius of action would be uselessly short. Eventually, after evaluating over 300 aircraft configurations including several with nuclear propulsion, it was reluctantly decided that the 'far out' ideas were for various reasons impractical, and that the only cost-effective strategic bomber would have conventional augmented turbofan engines and an airframe notable only for having a VG (variable-geometry) swing wing, spread out with full-span slats and flaps for take-off and landing, and folded back to an acute angle for the low-level supersonic dash to the target.

One remaining major decision was whether the future bomber should fly at something like Mach 2 at high altitude as well as at high subsonic speed at low level. This was one of the principal factors addressed in the AMSA study of 1965, which actually stood for Advanced Manned Strategic Aircraft. The decision was taken in 1968 that the AMSA should possess both capabilities, and this profoundly affected the design parameters of the engine and its inlet system. It also resulted in the decision to require a crew-capsule escape system similar in concept to that of the B-58 and F-111.

The point could be made that the existence of Project *Oxcart* at the Lockheed 'Skunk Works' affected the perceived need for AMSA. The highly secret Lockheed effort was directed towards a reconnaissance aircraft with speed and height capabilities far beyond anything previously known, and this had already done much to kill the B-70. The AMSA studies increasingly concentrated on penetration of hostile airspace at treetop height,

which only the much smaller and shorter-ranged F-111 could do. AMSA was from the start seen as the B-52 replacement, and at all times the most difficult requirement was to achieve anything like the older bomber's combat radius.

Eventually the USAF sent out its RFP (Request for Proposals) on 3 November 1969. It quickly narrowed the field to three airframe and two engine finalists, and (to the surprise of some) on 5 June 1970 picked North American Rockwell for the airframe and General Electric for the engine. NA Rockwell's Los Angeles Division received a contract for five prototypes of a bomber called the B-1 under the 1962 DoD multi-service numbering system, plus two structural test airframes, while GE's Military Engine Division at Evendale, Ohio, received a contract for 40 F101 turbofan engines. But controversy continued, and with the unpopularity of defence funding in the late Vietnam era the contracts were reduced in January 1971 to three flight and one ground test aircraft and 27 engines.

Even the prototype programme involved more than 3000 suppliers in 47 states, which muted criticism of the aircraft in Congress. An idea of the effort involved is given by the fact that during the review of the engineering mockup in October 1971 there were 297 RFAs (Requests for Alteration). Rockwell had by this time restructured to form North American Aircraft Operations, with a special B-1 Division at the main plant (formerly called Inglewood) in Los Angeles, though all B-1 assembly took place at the USAF Plant 42 at Palmdale. Here the first B-1, 74-4058, was rolled out on 26 October 1974 and flown by Charles Bock and crew on 23 December, landing at Edwards. Soon afterwards authority was given for a fourth flight article (76-0174), while SAC prepared to build a force of 240 B-1s.

The first three prototypes were initially finished in

anti-flash gloss white, with a black radome, candy-stripe nose probe and dark unpainted engine nozzle petals, but aircraft No 4 was completed in an unusual camouflage of green, brown and sand (tan). This reflected the growing importance of low-level operations, and these were also responsible for major design alterations, though these were not particularly obvious externally. The engine nacelles were subjected to major revision, and the inlets were completely redesigned with different geometry eliminating the previous variable ramps and instead concentrating on reducing radar cross-section. The complex crew capsule was replaced by four Weber Aces II ejection seats, and the forward fuselage, wing root and aft avionics bay were redesigned to accommodate the LRUs (line-replaceable units) and antennas of the enormous defensive avionics system, for which AIL Division of Cutler-Hammer had been contracted in January 1974.

It was increasingly evident that, despite the years of study, the B-1 was not quite right. The fourth prototype was a giant step in the right direction, but very much more could be done. Meanwhile, the debate in Congress and throughout the country ceased to say that missiles had made bombers obsolete; instead the arguments were polarised around the supposition that SAC's missions could be flown by long-range cruise missiles launched from the existing force of B-52s, which would accordingly not even need to cross an enemy frontier. There were many flaws in this argument, notably that not even the cleverest cruise missile could hit a moving target, or a target of uncertain

location, or fly a reconnaissance mission, but to the chagrin of many the argument was accepted by President Carter, who on 30 June 1977 terminated all plans to procure the B-1. Oddly, as air-launched cruise missiles had been used since 1916, he described the ALCM as 'a new kind of weapon'. Fortunately, he also directed that B-1 testing and development should continue.

Rockwell worked hard to update and improve the B-1, and also carried on flying the three prototypes, No 2 reaching Mach 2.25 on 5 October 1978. By this time the B-1 was beginning to be reassessed as an important third leg of the Triad, and instead of being called a mere bomber – which was considered passé – it became the LRCA, for Long-Range Combat Aircraft. Each of the first three aircraft was continued on development of particular systems, joined on 14 February 1979 by No 4 which was alone able to assist refinement of the defensive electronics, which far transcended anything attempted previously. Boeing Military Airplanes was assigned the prime contract for the OAS (offensive avionics system), many elements of which were similar to, or derived from, the OAS developed for the B-52G/H.

At the same time (1979) Congress funded a deep

and prolonged BPE (Bomber Penetration Evaluation). The practical airborne part of BPE was ended with the last flight of the No 4 aircraft on 29 April 1981, after which the four prototypes were stored at Edwards. They were kept airworthy, and following delivery of a massive BPE report on 30 June of that year a special LRCA steering committee met on 17 September. On 2 October 1981 President Reagan announced that 100 improved bombers, designated B-1B, would be procured for service with SAC. Rockwell received a $2.2bn contract in January 1982, the Air Force vote for 1982 through 1986 funding 1, 7, 10, 34 and 48 aircraft per year to make up the total. Prototypes Nos 2 and 4, now restyled B-1As, were brought as nearly as possible to B-1B standard, 02 (retaining the original crew capsule and inlets) being used on weapon tests and 04 for avionics. The first B-1B (82-0001) flew at Palmdale on 18 October 1984, and the first delivery (of 82-0002) took place to the 96th Bomb Wing at Dyess AFB on 7 July 1985.

Apart from the engine inlets, the B-1B appeared be very similar to the B-1A. Another difference was seen in the fuselage tailcone, which became blunter and more capacious to accommodate aft-facing elements of the defensive avionics. Incorporating this vast system was one of the three principal changes between the B-1B and the No 4 prototype. The other two were a considerable increase in internal fuel capacity (reflected in much higher gross weight and the need for stronger main landing gears) and redesign of the weapon bays and addition of external fuselage hardpoints, as described later. As before, almost the entire airframe

TOP *This Lancer hails from the 96th BW. Failure to participate in* Desert Storm *was said to be because B-1B crews were 'not proficient in conventional-ordnance delivery'*

ABOVE *Another 96th Lancer takes off from George AFB during a period punctuated by severe problems, including grounding due to dangerous engine difficulties*

was made of 2024 or 7075 aluminium alloys, though with considerable amounts of GRP (glass-fibre reinforced plastics) and titanium alloys, the whole aircraft being electronically and structurally hardened against nuclear radiation and overpressure.

Another change was expected to be a reduction in available wing sweep, but eventually the outer wings were unchanged except for being strengthened, with a leading-edge sweep range from 15° to 67.5°. Each wing was fitted with full-span slats in seven sections, six sections of single-slotted flaps extending to 40°, terminating well inboard of the tips (where there had once been planned to be ailerons) and four sections of spoiler ahead of the four outer flap segments, used for lateral control and as airbrakes and lift dumpers. The centre section could almost be regarded as a wider part of the fuselage, because (as in NA Rockwell's losing finalist in the F-15 programme) the wing and fuselage were designed to be blended by giant fairings mainly of GRP. These provide reduced drag, reduced radar cross-section and volume for extra fuel and for much of the defensive avionics. The wings were pivoted by pins of 6Al-4V titanium in large spherical steel bearings carried at the tips of the very wide and deep carry-through box also made of 6Al-4V alloy. Like the wing boxes the carry-through bridge was sealed to form an integral tank.

Most of the 195,000 lb of fuel was housed in the fuselage, which was designed in five sections of which the aft two were made by LTV. Titanium was used to skin these rear sections, and also for engine bays and firewalls, and various other parts subject to high temperature and/or stress. At the front the capsule was replaced by a conventional pressurised section for the pilot and co-pilot, both with fighter-type sticks, and, behind them, the operators for the defensive and offensive avionics. Above each seat was a jettisonable roof panel, normal egress being by a retractable ladder immediately aft of the nose gear. A requirement not envisaged in the original design was the need to scramble in minimum time, from an airfield under SLBM attack with only a few minutes' warning. The first crew-member to reach the aircraft thus would hit a button on the nose gear which would immediately initiate the main-engine start sequence, using a Garrett APU in each engine nacelle to provide starting power to both adjacent engines at once.

The F101-102 engines were developed from the B-1A's Dash-100 version, the emphasis being on simplicity for long life at reduced cost. In particular, this philosophy affected the variable nozzle, though augmentation (afterburning) in both hot and cold flows was retained. The engines were mounted in widely-spaced pairs under the back of the fixed inboard wing. It was desirable to get them as near the CG (centre of gravity) as possible, for stability in turbulent sea-level air, but with space between them to allow the main landing gears to retract inwards. CG considerations also demanded an advanced fuel-management system, by Simmonds, a need highlighted by the loss of the No 2 prototype on 29 August 1984 entirely due to loss of control caused by mismanagement of the fore/aft disposition of the fuel. The inflight-refuelling socket, compatible only with a high-speed boom, was placed above the nose.

Each engine was arranged to drive a hydraulic pump to provide four completely separate systems with the baseline pressure at 4000 lb/sq in, the B-1 being one of the first American aircraft to use this pressure. Main services driven included the wing sweep, by four motors turning two screwjacks linked by cross-shafts (though on at least one occasion one wing pivoted too far forward and ruptured the port flank tank inboard of the pivot); other hydraulic items include the bomb doors, landing gear and all flight controls. The latter were designed with traditional mechanical signalling, except for the outer spoilers which were fly-by-wire. Strangely, fly-by-wire was added only as an emergency back-up to the tail controls. The latter comprised left and right tailplanes, driven together for pitch and differentially to augment the spoilers in roll, and three sections of rudder, one being below the tailplane.

In addition, from the start of design of the original prototypes, it was judged prudent to add a completely automatic system to even out bumps in low-level tubulence, which would otherwise rapidly degrade the capability of the crew to do their job. At first this was called LARC (Low-Altitude Ride Control), but the title eventually became SMCS (Structural-Mode Control System). It was soon evident that this subsystem could not operate via the main flight controls. The area to be stabilised was the crew compartment, so swept canard foreplanes were added here, each with 30° anhedral, driven by hydraulic power units signalled by vertical and lateral accelerometers in the forward fuselage. The anhedral enables the vanes to damp out motion in yaw as well as pitch.

The landing gears were conventional. The steerable twin-wheel nose unit was by Menasco, and retracted forwards, a Tu-160 designer commenting that putting the gear under the crew compartment unnecessarily increased the cross-section of the fuselage. The main gears, by Cleveland Pneumatic with a four-wheel bogie, Goodyear wheels and carbon brakes, was arranged to fold inwards and to the rear, the stowed wheels being vertical. Goodrich tyre pressure of 275 lb/sq in precludes operation except from strong pavements.

BELOW Nose-gear doors, slats and flaps still deflected, a B-1B Lancer cleans up on departure from RAF Mildenhall in 1990

From the start defensive guns were judged not worthwhile, all reliance being placed on the avionics. The biggest element in the offensive system, the main radar, was surprisingly derived from that of the small F-16 (so was the Singer Kearfott inertial navigation system). The Westinghouse APQ-164 operates in all its ten modes via a low-observable phased-array antenna in the extreme nose. The APQ-164 is really two radars, one being on instantly available standby, the only unduplicated parts being the antenna, video signal processor and radar target indicator. IBM provided successively better ACUs (avionics control units) including two for terrain following based on the B-52 LRUs. But the crucial installation was always seen as the ALQ-161 defensive electronics. Originally this comprised an RF (radio frequency) surveillance system and corresponding ECM subsystem, a tail-warning function, an ASQ-184 defensive management system and an expendable countermeasures system totalling 108 elements, the main cartridge ejection packs being in the top of the fuselage. From the start ALQ-161 included a large number of Northrop jamming transmitters linked to Raytheon phased-array antennas, most in the inboard leading edges and tailcone. An EMUX (electronic multiplex) data bus system using millions of signals passed along pairs of twisted wires, enables all elements to be controlled by a network of digital computers, which allegedly could be programmed easily. The system was progressively upgraded to counter additional frequency bands and include a repertoire of new jamming techniques.

As completely redesigned, the B-1B internal weapon carriage comprises a double bay forward of the wings with a length of 31 ft 3 in (9.53 m) and a single 15 ft (4.57 m) bay aft, all with conventional doors driven hydraulically. The forward bay incorporates a non-structural bulkhead which can be moved axially to tailor the length of each compartment according to the load. The longest item is the AGM-86B ALCM, eight of which can be carried on fixed beams or on a CSRL (common strategic rotary launcher) driven hydraulically. Other internal loads can include 24 AGM-69A SRAMs (short-range attack missiles), 12 B28 or 24 B61 or B83 nuclear bombs, or 84 Mk 82 500-lb bombs or Mk 36 500-lb mines. A normal load in the conventional role is 64,000 lb (29,030 kg). Under the fuselage can be attached six racks for a further 12 ALCMs.

Delivery of the 100 aircraft was completed in April 1988, at a published unit price of $282m (then £167m). These have ever since equipped four Bomb Wings, the 96th BW at Dyess, Texas (29 aircraft supplied), 28th BW at Ellsworth, SD (35), the 319th at Grand Forks, ND (17) and the 384th at McConnell, Kansas (17). Predictably, in view of its interest to the media, the B-1B, named Lancer, followed the F-111 in being the object of unthinking derision and ridicule, even the normally responsible *Armed Forces Journal* calling it 'The world's first self-jamming bomber'. Obviously, with a system such as ALQ-161, there were going to be problems, probably taking years to resolve.

Painted two shades of dark grey and a dark green, the remaining aircraft in the inventory (about 78 available at any one time, of a total in 1992 of 94) are thoroughly shaken down and their crews very experienced in simulating missions with nuclear and conventional bombs and SRAM missiles. ALCM is not carried, and the AGM-129 ACM (Advanced Cruise Missile) is not scheduled for B-1B wings. Moreover, B-1Bs have done well in the annual SAC bomb/nav competition, so it was rather surprising that no B-1B unit was deployed to the Gulf War in 1991.

SPECIFICATION

B-1B Lancer

Four General Electric F101-102 augmented turbofans each rated at 17,000 lb dry and 30,000 lb (13,608 kg) with maximum augmentation
Dimensions Span (max) 136 ft 8½ in (41.66 m), (min) 78 ft 2½ in (23.84 m); length 147 ft (47.8 m); wing area 1960 sq ft (181.1 m²)
Weight Empty 192,000 lb (87,090 kg); max take-off 477,000 lb (216,368 kg); max landing 360,000 lb (163,300 kg)
Performance Maximum speed clean at 500 ft (152 m), Mach 0.99 (652 kt, 750 mph, 1207 km/h); normal penetration speed 600 mph (966 km/h); max unrefuelled range 6300 nm (7255 miles, 11,675 km); mission radius (typical) 3000 miles (4820 km)
Armament See text

Sukhoi Su-25

First Flight – 22 February 1975

Perhaps alone among the aircraft in this book, the Su-25 was not created in response to a demand by a customer air force. On the contrary, it resulted from the insistent lobbying by Pavel O Sukhoi himself, in the teeth of opposition from both the VVS and Soviet research organisations and industry. In World War 2 Sukhoi had seen his Su-2 attack bomber largely replaced by S V Ilyushin's Il-2 'Stormovik', which was built in numbers greater than any other type of aircraft (36,163). Subsequently Sukhoi's own Su-6 family had consistently failed to replace the Il-2 in production, despite being on some counts superior.

This traumatic period drove home to Sukhoi the value of a tactical aircraft able to fly over the battlefield with a fair degree of impunity, whilst killing tanks and knocking out other difficult surface targets. Stalin had said 'The Red Army needs the Il-2 like it needs air and bread'. Yet, from the early 1950s, Frontal Aviation had no aircraft in this category. Prompted by his designer Zhurii V Ivanshezkin, Sukhoi was convinced that this was a mistake, but he found few people prepared to listen until, 20 years later, the USAF organised an 'AX' competition, which resulted in the production of

713 Fairchild A-10A Thunderbolt IIs. This was almost exactly the style of aircraft Sukhoi was campaigning for, and quite suddenly his arguments ceased to be regarded as those of a silly old man trying to sell a silly product, and instead were taken seriously. In 1972, the year in which the rival AX prototypes first flew, the Sukhoi project was allowed to go ahead. Internally it was the T-8, one of the 'triangular' rather than one of the S (swept) series, though at first glance this 'plank wing' aircraft would not be thought of as a delta, though all taper is on the leading edge. Even stranger was the later VVS designation of Su-25, odd numbers being reserved for fighters.

The T-8-1 prototype was flown by bureau chief test pilot Vladimir Ilyushin (son of S V Ilyushin) on 22 February 1975. Just over six months later P O Sukhoi died, and the Su-25 programme passed to Vladimir P Babak. He explains that from the start there were five main design objectives: the greatest possible invulnerability to fire from high-velocity weapons of up to 30 mm calibre; the greatest weapon lethality from a simple and cheap aircraft; outstanding manoeuvrability and pilot view; the ability to use short unpaved front-line airstrips; and

LEFT *Su-25T*

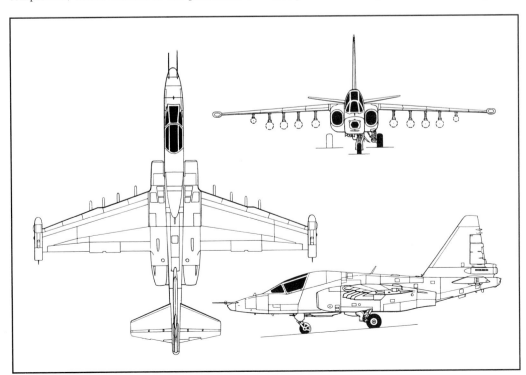

independence of ground support. All requirements were fully met, the only regret being that the engines had to be turbojets instead of fuel-efficient turbofans.

The wide-span wing is tapered on the leading edge, which is fitted with full-span slats set by the pilot to one of three positions: take-off/landing, normal flight or active manoeuvres. A dogtooth kink at mid-span results in increased chord outboard. The trailing edge is occupied by double-slotted flaps and powered ailerons. On each wingtip is a flat pod, the aft part of which splits open into upper and lower airbrakes. The fuselage incorporates a titanium 'bath' with a thickness of 24 mm (0.95 in) completely surrounding the cockpit, except from above. Similar titanium armour protects many other crucial parts. The engine bays on each side under the wing are clad in stainless steel, and like the fuel tanks in the fuselage and inner wings are protected by Freon gas bottles and reticulated plastic foam. Special forms of airframe structure were adopted to minimise the effect of damage. The rudder and elevators are manual, and like the powered ailerons all pilot demands are conveyed by duplicated titanium push/pull rods, separated as widely as possible. The levered-suspension main gears are matched to almost any frontline strips, and retract forwards to lie flat under the simple air inlet ducts. Tyre size is 840×360 mm, suitable for soft, rough strips. The nose gear is offset to the left, with a hydraulically-steered wheel with 660×200 mm tyre with mudguard, retracting forwards.

There was never any doubt the correct number of engines was two, but their location was a careful balance between asymmetry, propulsive efficiency, weight, drag and accessibility. Ladders or trestles are almost never needed except to enter the cockpit, and every part of the engines can be reached from the ground. The flying prototypes were initially fitted with obsolescent Tumanskii RD-9A turbojets of 5732 lb thrust, recognised as inadequate. They were also fitted with a 30 mm gun in an external gondola with twin barrels which could be angled down by the pilot, but this proved unsuccessful. The second aircraft, the T-8-2, had the R-95Sh engine derived from the Tumanskiii R-13. With a take-off thrust of 8818 lb, the R-95Sh engine was still only marginally adequate, especially in hot and high-altitude operations in Afghanistan, which is where the first test unit (200th Guards) was sent in 1978. This unit of 12 aircraft was blooded in the harsh school of real warfare, operating in concert with Mi-24/25 helicopters and using any available frontline fuel including MT petrols and diesel oil.

By 1984 the ancient and almost derelict factory at Tbilisi was getting into its stride, and the Su-25 was fully operational in Afghanistan in large numbers, including the Su-25K export version. By this time a laser ranger and target designator, had been fitted, integrated with a HUD sight, and many other additions. The main armament comprises a very powerful twin-barrel 30 mm gun, with 250 rounds and firing at 3000 rds/min, and eight underwing stores pylons for a total load of 4400 kg (9700 lb). Every kind of Soviet tactical free-fall weapon or rocket can be carried, as well as various air/ground missiles including LGBs (laser-guided bombs). Using LGBs the error on a point target at a stand-off range of 20 km (12.5 miles) is typically 5 m (16 ft). Rocket launchers can accept all calibres from 57 to 370 mm (14.6 in) calibre, while another type of store is a GSh-23 gun pod, with a 260-round magazine of 23 mm sequenced ammunition and twin barrels depressed downwards for attacking ground targets.

From the outset manoeuvrability was judged excellent. Rate of roll is surprisingly high for such a wide-span aircraft, and sustained turns can be pulled at 5.2 g with the maximum weapon load,

and at 6.5 g with a load of 1.5 tonnes (3307 lb). With a little experience pilots found they could orbit the battlefield whilst keeping their eyes continuously on ground targets. In 1984–85 two aircraft were lost to Redeye missiles, but this primitive missile was easily countered by increasing the available supply of IR decoy flares to a total of 256, in four 64-tube strip dispensers above the engine nacelles and aft fuselage. The Stinger missile proved much more difficult to counter, and here the modifications assumed that the missile would hit the aircraft and explode. Almost all Stinger strikes were in the jetpipe area, so sheets of 5 mm (0.2-in) steel armour were added inboard of the jetpipes to protect the aft fuselage tanks, This completely stopped any further losses, and in fact the immaculate Su-25K exhibited at the 1989 Paris airshow had been severely damaged by a Stinger and two Sidewinders in Afghanistan. By the late 1980s the Sukhoi OKB had no doubt that, because of its nine years of actual battle experience, the Su-25 is more difficult to shoot down than any other tactical aircraft. The final score of 23 Su-25s lost from all causes during the campaign equates to one per 2800 hours of actual combat missions.

The Su-25 and -25K have twin cruciform braking parachutes, which are almost never used but can reduce the landing run from 600 to 400 m (1300 ft). The pilot has a K-36D seat, almost universal in Soviet combat aircraft, and an exceptionally bulletproof windscreen and side-hinged canopy. The Su-25UB dual-pilot trainer has tandem K-36D seats, the pupil being approximately in the original position and the instructor behind at a much higher level. Each cockpit has its own canopy, hinged to the right. To balance the increased side area, the vertical tail is raised on top of an added root portion. The dogtooth on each wing leading edge is replaced by a gentle kink which does not generate a vortex. The Su-25UT unarmed

ABOVE *This Su-25 served in the 'frontline' against NATO at Demmin, then in East Germany. Tip pod noses were scarlet, and fin top green. Code 'Red 9'*

trainer version is slightly shorter (15.36 m, 50 ft 4.8 in), powered by the R-95Sh, and much lighter and cheaper; the export designation is Su-28. Hundreds were expected to be produced as the future advanced trainer for DOSAAF, but like other versions production ceased in 1991 for lack of money. A single example was produced prior to 1991 of the Su-25UTG, an unarmed UT version fitted with catapult and arrestor hooks for trials at Saki naval airfield and the carrier *Kuznetsov*. Another variant, the Su-25BM, is used for towing targets and for firing from its underwing pylons target rockets on which fighter missiles can home.

Two-seaters have been flying since 1985, but it was not until 1989 that production at last switched to the definitive engine. This, the R-195, is not only more powerful than the R-95 but it was designed almost from the start to be much more resistant to ground fire. To reduce IR signature cool upstream bleed air is expelled from the tip of the turbine tailcone. In fact the Tumanskii engine bureau consider that many of the design techniques and materials of the R-195 can now with advantage be applied to other engines. Sukhoi and Tumanskii engineers said in 1989 that the R-195 had at that time 'demonstrated its ability to keep running after suffering battle damage in eight places'. Following tests under severe hot/high conditions, including some in Afghanistan, it was found that with R-195 engines the underwing stores load could be increased to 6.4 tonnes (14,109 lb). Most Su-25Ks are being re-engined, and by 1990 this had become the routine maximum for Su-25 operations. By this time the self-contained maintenance and ground-support system was also in use with every Su-25

ABOVE *Su-25 9013 of the Czech AF stopped at RAF Honington en route to Boscombe Down. The front half sported a colourful camouflage of sand, yellow, turquoise and two shades of green*

regiment. This comprises four pods, carried like any other store, which render the aircraft totally self-sufficient in any climate for up to 12 days. The equipment includes all covers and blanking plates, electric generating plant, fuel transfer pumps and onboard systems checking and test devices.

Whereas manufacture of all earlier Su-25 versions were terminated in 1991, a further variant is expected to continue in production. This incorporates all the lessons of the Afghan war, and its similarity to the Su-25 and 25K is only superficial. Known as the T-8K to the Sukhoi OKB, it is the Su-25T to the customer, and an export version would be the Su-34. The airframe is basically that of the UB, with the taller vertical tail, but retaining a dogtooth on each wing. The fuselage has a redesigned centre portion with a single cockpit similar to that of the instructor in the UB. Behind is a humped section housing an enlarged tank which increases internal capacity to 3840 kg (8470 lb) despite enhanced protection systems. The GSh-30/II gun is permanently mounted in a gondola under the right side of the fuselage. This frees the widened nose for TV, laser ranger/designator and optical sight with up to × 23 magnification, plus a pod-mounted low-light TV and FLIR (forward-looking infra-red), giving comprehensive weapon capability at night or in bad weather. Other equipment includes a KN-

23 doppler/inertial navigation system. Target tracking and weapon release are automatic. Other avionics include an outstanding system of mission communications, monitoring and recording, plus what is predictably one of the most comprehensive warning and self-protection suites in any tactical aircraft, including various countermeasures in the wingtip pods, rear fuselage and a large cylindrical compartment above the jetpipe to defeat all known IR missiles. Apart from the gun, weapons can include up to 16 Vikhr tube-launched anti-tank missiles, Kh-25ML laser-guided missiles, Kh-29L attack missiles, Kh-58 anti-radar missiles and many other stores including two SPPU-22-01 pods each housing a GSh-23 gun and 260 rounds. Moreover, service life of this aircraft has been published as 1500 hours or 7 years, which is a new departure for a Russian aircraft.

SPECIFICATION

Su-25K, Su-25T

Two 4500 kg (9921 lb) R-195 turbojets

Dimensions Span 14.36 m (47 ft 1½ in); length 15.53 m (50 ft 11½ in); wing area 33.7 m² (362.8 sq ft)

Weight Empty (25K) 9.5 t (20,950 lb), (25T) 9.8 t (21,605 lb); maximum take-off (25K) 17.6 t (38,800 lb), (25T) 19.5 t (42,990 lb)

Performance Maximum speed (clean, S/L) 950 km/h (590 mph); combat radius with 2 t (4400 lb) external weapons (low) 400 km (249 miles), (high) 700 km (435 miles); take-off/landing run on rough strip 600/700 m (1970/2300 ft)

Armament One AO-17A gun with 250 rounds and up to 4.4 t (9700 lb) of ordnance on eight pylons, (Su-25T) same but gun GSh-30/II

Lockheed F-117A 'Nighthawk'

First Flight – 18 June 1981

As the first LO (low observables) or 'stealth' aircraft (except for a small research aircraft which preceded it) the F-117A has generated enormous interest around the world. When nothing was known about it except its existence it became the subject of official disinformation and unofficial guesswork, which embraced not only its shape but even its designation. When at last the real aircraft was revealed, the truth was much stranger than the fiction. It looked rather like a flying pyramid, or something made from folded black paper.

As noted in the chapter on the B-2, attempts to make aircraft invisible date from 1913. In 1935 the 'father of radar', Sir Robert Watson Watt, pondered on how aircraft designers could counter his new invention. In 1936 he wrote a classified note on what we would today call 'reducing radar cross-section'. RCS ought to have governed the design of every subsequent warplane. Instead, it was virtually ignored for the next 40 years, despite the fact that throughout that time radar was the sole means of detecting the presence and location of hostile aircraft at great distances or at night.

By 1970 Lockheed Advanced Development Projects, the so-called Skunk Works, had completed considerable preliminary investigation of methods of minimising RCS, and had also assigned individual engineers to study the problems of reducing noise, visual signature (ie, to try to make aircraft invisible) and, by no means least, IR signature. By 1972 it had been concluded that the likely success with each method varied very greatly. RCS showed the promise of reductions of at least 100-fold if not 1000-fold. IR signature showed almost as encouraging a picture, though it looked as if an enemy equipped with sensitive IR receivers would continue to have little difficulty in detecting aircraft from certain aspects. In this case all that could be done was to use the coolest possible engines, screen all hot parts of the structure and so shape the aircraft that, when approaching a target, all hot regions were completely hidden from the target area (but

BELOW *The F-117A conjures up thoughts of flying saucers, especially in such a landscape. They were seldom parked out in the open at Tonopah*

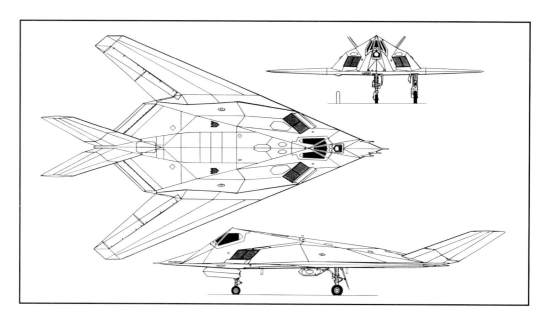

they might be in full view of a hostile interceptor or AWACS overhead to the rear). Reducing noise and visual signature to useful levels looked exceedingly difficult, which among other results led to the conclusion that even LO aircraft should not be used by day unless they could avoid a close approach to the target. Put another way, there did not appear to be any LO answer to the problem of anti-aircraft systems using guns or missiles against an aircraft clearly visible at close range.

By 1972 the Skunk Works, headed by C L 'Kelly' Johnson, had completed a further amount of fundamental research, aided by practical results from RCS-reduction methods used on its SR-71A 'Blackbird' aircraft and, especially, on the Mach-4 D-21 reconnaissance RPV which the SR-71A could launch. Throughout, the Skunk Works kept in close touch with the Defense Advanced Research Projects Agency, and DARPA increasingly provided funding. By 1973 a specially designed lightplane, the Windecker VE-5A, was being used in full-scale flight research into glassfibre construction with RAM (radar-absorbent material) coatings. By 1974 LO research was really taking off. Most of the giants of the US aerospace industry became involved, but the Skunk Works had by far the most experience. And in 1975, the year in which 'Kelly' Johnson retired and handed over to Ben Rich, that remarkable team devised an RCS-reduction technique called faceting. Using powerful computers it was possible to design any aircraft so that its entire exterior surface was made up of flat surfaces. Even the top of the wing, normally a smooth cambered curve, could be formed from flat surfaces, provided there was no very large change in angle from one panel to the next.

Flat surfaces reflect electromagnetic waves such as radar strongly, but almost entirely in a particular direction, like a mirror. The Lockheed engineers reasoned that if about 99 per cent of the energy was reflected away where it could do no harm, then hardly any could be reflected back to the radar that sent it out. It was simply a matter of choosing the

correct angles, avoiding any inside corners or curved surfaces, and making the exterior surface of the aircraft in flight as smooth as possible and without any discontinuities or gaps such as are often found at the edges of doors and hatches. Such rules precluded the normal rounded wing leading edge. It was clear that a faceted aircraft would not only look strange but would also be aerodynamically inferior to other aircraft. But this was not really a problem, provided one had a long runway. Once flying, a faceted aircraft could pull g and be quite agile, though of course the need for cool jets and nozzles eliminated the use of afterburners. This would tend to make the aircraft subsonic, but what was the point in supersonic speed if the aircraft could not be detected?

By 1976 Skunk Works testing was suggesting signature reductions to about one-thousandth the RCS of conventional aircraft. DARPA thereupon committed greater funds, launched a major research project called Have Blue to test-fly the first LO aircraft, and in March 1977 contracted with Lockheed for a number (variously reported as two, five and seven) of Have Blue XST (experimental stealth technology) aircraft. These were simplified scale models of a planned future LO attack aircraft (the F-117A). Powered by two 2850-lb General Electric CJ610 turbojets, they were in the 12,000-lb gross weight class, and strongly resembled the full-scale machine except in having rudders mounted outboard of the jet nozzles and canted inwards. Landing gears were of F-5E type. Bill Park, who had played a major role in the SR-71 programme, made the first flight in January or February 1978 from Groom Lake, Nevada. Two XSTs were lost, for reasons unrelated to their special design, but testing against captured Soviet radars and other defence systems proved most encouraging.

By mid-1978 it was clear that even the first and crudest form of LO design, faceting, worked as predicted. This was a discovery of the very greatest importance (one only marvels that it was not made 40 years earlier). Accordingly a high-priority programme was launched to develop the full-scale aircraft for the USAF inventory. It was launched only three months after the start of XST testing, as a Black programme (ie, hidden even from Congress, and with its funding 'lost' in other votes) of the USAF, not DARPA. Its name, *Senior Trend*, has been continued throughout the life of the programme, though the designation of the aircraft is the inexplicable one of F-117A. Later the name 'Nighthawk' was bestowed officially on the aircraft itself, not the programme. As the F-117A has no gun and cannot carry air-to-air missiles, to call it a fighter is obviously nonsensical. Moreover, US fighter designations began at 1 in 1962 and by the late 1970s had reached 18, not 116! Clearly, the correct designation would have been A-11.

There was never any doubt that Lockheed would win the contract, which was placed in November 1978. It included five FSD (full-scale development) aircraft and two for static test. Bill Park had been injured ejecting from an XST, so the first flight was made by his successor, Hal Farley. It took place at Groom Lake on 18 June 1981, the amazingly rapid development (even by the standards of the Skunk Works) giving an indication of the priority assigned to the *Senior Trend* programme. Despite the rapid pace, and the unprecedented design of the entire aircraft, hardly any really large changes were necessary. Indeed, almost the only major change to the future production programme was to cut the number bought from 100 to 59, purely on budgetary grounds. There is not the slightest doubt that the Bush administration regreted this, and after 1993 the USAF could certainly use more than 100, even though they are not multi-mission aircraft.

It is a fundamental feature of LO aircraft that, by their very nature, their 'invisibility' means that their flight performance can be compromised. There is no need for STOL capability, supersonic speed or 9 g agility. The entire design of the F-117A was tailored to minimal radar and IR signatures. Having said that, it is truly remarkable that it handles like any other tactical aircraft, can mount sustained operations from existing airbases, and is described by its pilots as pleasant and smooth to fly. Obviously, as the wing does not have an ideal aerofoil profile, take-off and landing speeds are high, and care must be taken never to let speed bleed away, especially at high weights. This is particularly to be watched when pulling successive turns, because the thrust/weight ratio is only 0.41 and speed must be allowed to build up again between one sustained manoeuvre and the next. Perhaps the only other basic factor for the pilot is that the F-117A flies combat missions at night, always against high-value point targets, so the work-load upon the single crew-member is high.

In a bizarre way the aerodynamics and structure of the F-117A are conventional. The cockpit is at the front, the wide fuselage rides on a low-mounted swept wing and the tail is at the back. Among the

other conventional features is the underlying structure, mainly of aluminium alloy, designed and machined by computer in order to obtain the dimensional accuracy needed for an LO exterior. Highly-stressed or hot parts of the structure are steel or titanium, and there is a fair amount of graphite composite, but less than in some other modern aircraft. This skeletal substructure serves as the strong and rigid foundation on which are individually attached the absolutely flat and separate skin facets. All edges and joints are, of course, geometrically sharp and precise, traditional curved joints or

BELOW *A newly delivered F-117A on acres of concrete at Tonopah. The last thing it wanted was a 'hot and high' airbase*

fairings being scrupulously avoided. Finally, almost the whole exterior, except for the cockpit transparencies and the engine nozzle, are covered with RAM. It has been widely surmised that this takes the form of a polymer binder heavily laden with a fine powder of carbonyl iron or other ferritic material. The very few gaps or joints are then sealed with RAM applied like putty or stripped on as adhesive tape. In 1990 Holloman AFB commissioned a computer-controlled RAM-respraying building in which the entire coating can be perfectly renewed without human intervention. But it must be emphasized that the F-117A is 'the Wright Flyer of the stealth age', and later LO aircraft are not so compromised by flat facets and RAM coatings, though Ben Rich denied the suggestion that the coatings are heavy.

Even though the F-117A is subsonic, the need for all edges to be sharply angled away from 'the bad guys' results in a leading-edge sweep of no less than 67.5°. The leading edge is sharp, and the underside is flat as far back as the first chordwise change in angle. This flat underside takes in the fuselage as well as the wing, as if the aircraft had made a wheels-up landing on sandpaper. The tip again follows exact angles parallel to other parts of the aircraft. On the trailing edge are inboard and outboard elevons used for pitch and roll. The tail comprises two rudders (not ruddervators), each canted out at nearly 45° and swept at exactly the same sharp angle as the wings. There are no tail elevators.

Far more than any previous aircraft the F-117A was designed to meet a specific operational requirement – near invisibility – which resulted in it being an almost non-flyable vehicle. The flight-control computers were then programmed to make it not only flyable but highly manoeuvrable. There were, nevertheless, problems and penalties. Farley said 'As this was the first airplane designed by electronic engineers it's not surprising a number of aerodynamic sins were committed. In fact the unaugmented aircraft exhibits just about every mode of unstable behaviour possible: longitudinal and directional instability, pitch-up, pitch-down, dihedral reversal and various other cross-axis couplings. The only thing it doesn't do is tip back on its tail when parked.'

For a start, the wing aerofoil profile looks (to an aerodynamicist) a sick joke. The pressure profile round it is quite unlike that of a 'proper' wing, there being no strong negative-pressure area to provide lift, but instead, small spikes of reduced pressure along each of the facet lines. The faceting made the whole airframe much more vulnerable than normal to acoustic vibrations, requiring special attention to skin design. Surprisingly large stressing problems were posed by the unique engine nozzles, described later, and by fuel transfer removing the inertial relief provided by the wing fuel. There was no way the huge elevons could be drooped for take-off or

landing, and the simple answer was to use long runways. The fly-by-wire control system, derived from that of the F-16, was modified with totally new software, and also altered from a force-sensing sidestick to a position-sensing conventional stick.

In addition to what was probably the most exhaustive flutter test programme of all time, the F-117A needed prolonged flight-testing to overcome its natural instability. To provide constant mastery over the severe yaw instability, the twin canted rudders were added, and made powerfully all-moving. During development their size had to be increased by 50 per cent. Final proof that the system worked came when a USAF pilot testing store compatibility in severe sideslips suffered explosive failure of the right rudder (and the left very nearly departed also). He brought the aircraft back successfully. One of the fundamental problems was how to reconcile the sharp sweep needed for LO with the efficient high aspect ratio needed to achieve a L/D (lift/drag ratio) high enough to achieve the necessary mission radius. The answer was to keep prolonging the wing to the rear, and this combined with the large elevons needed for pitch authority resulted in far greater roll power than the structure could safely accept, so roll authority is deliberately restricted.

Obviously, the F-117A flight controls depend crucially on the air-data input. No stealthy air-data sensors existed in the 1970s, and the ideal solution – flush 'invisible' sensors such as pressure ports around the forward fuselage – proved virtually impossible to achieve. Each such port has to sense pure AOA (angle of attack) or pure sideslip, whereas in every F-117A location the sensed pressure was a mix in which each variable was a function of all the others. This would have demanded very complex correction coefficients in the flight-control system. The answer adopted was to fit four finger-like probes projecting ahead into undisturbed air, giving pure readings with adequate redundancy. They look simple. Each terminates in a tiny forward-pointing pyramid with a microscopic sensor hole in each of its four faces. The simplicity is deceptive. For one thing, these probes had to be made of special materials in an unconventional shape. Ability to prevent icing was vital, and the only possible method was heating (the trivial IR radiation being no problem). But when the heat was switched on, the initial probes cracked. The next design did not crack, but the changed temperature shifted the calibration, and it was soon realised that quality control on these probes had to be exceptional. A seemingly unimportant (microscopic) difference in the hole alignment was found to feed back a sensed sideslip, which when 'corrected' by the flight-control computer resulted in the aircraft flying left-wing down. There were many similar unexpected problems with the air-data system.

Equally prolonged flight-test was needed on the propulsion system. General Electric's F404 found

yet another application in this aircraft, but a little money was found to modify it for this unusual tasking. What was needed was maximum thrust from the coolest jet, and the F404-F1D2 was rebuilt as a turbojet. Thus it gives maximum thrust for the minimum mass flow, which eased the problems of designing the inlet and nozzle. There was no simple way of hiding the highly reflective engine from hostile radars ahead without fitting a conductive metal mesh grill across the inlet. This made it possible to mount the engines in a simple way beside (or inside) the fuselage, above the wing, with the inlet straight in front. Each inlet is a sharp-edged paralellogram, swept back in plan and side eleva- tion. The grid design had not been finalised when production began, and different kinds could still be seen on the flight-line in late 1990. All are some form of criss-cross mesh of sharp-edged V-sections, with RAM coating. As the mesh gauge (0.625 in, 15 mm) is less than hostile radar wavelengths, the grid acts like an electromagnetic barrier. Any signals that do go past it are absorbed by the duct's RAM lining. Avoiding inlet icing was one of the few real problems encountered during the F-117A flight-test phase. The pilot can illuminate each inlet, and can switch on non-emissive alcohol sprays.

Downstream of the inlet is a large hexagonal door in the top of the duct through which extra air can be drawn on take-off. This door hinges inwards, but in normal flight is sealed as flush with the surrounding skin as possible. Above each engine is a flush exit, with a radar-absorbent mesh, for engine-bay cool- ing air. Downstream of the engine the jetpipe is connected to a large mixer, similar to those down- stream of modern turbofan cores, which rapidly

mixes the hot jet with a much greater flow of cool air which has passed around the engine. The mixed flow is then spread out and flattened in the unique nozzle, which terminates as a two-dimensional horizontal slit, 5 in (0.13 m) high and 65 in (1.65 m) long. The lower edge of the nozzle extends further aft than the upper lip, and is curved upwards, masking the entire nozzle from an observer below. No serious pitch-moment problem is caused by varying engine power. Inside the nozzle is a row of 12 vertical guide vanes which help to squeeze out the jet but whose main purpose is to tie the top and bottom of the heavily stressed and high- temperature nozzle together and stop it bulging. Part of the nozzle is coated with Shuttle-type ceramic refractory tiles, to avoid high temperatures which could cause distortion.

The pilot sits very near the pointed nose. It was judged that his need for good undistorted view ahead through the attack HUD outweighed the drawback of having a flat windscreen, but as this is sharply inclined it reflects radar upwards. It forms the front of the canopy, which is hinged upwards at the rear. Like all other transverse joints, the front of the canopy has a zig-zag edge. At its pointed top is an aft-facing light to illuminate the inflight-refuell- ing receptacle in the top of the fuselage, which rotates through 180° to close with a smooth external surface. Just ahead of it are two ILS antennas, which likewise retract flush when not needed. The seat is an ACES, and exceptionally powerful rams are needed to blow off the heavy canopy before firing the seat. The neat landing gears, designed for 225 mph (362 km/h) take-off speeds, all retract forwards into bays covered with serrated-edge doors. Above the tail is a box for a braking parachute, usually with a black canopy, while underneath is an emergency arrestor hook.

The purpose of the F-117A is to find, identify and destroy high-value point targets at night. To do this it can, says the USAF, 'carry the full range of tactical munitions', which obviously includes nuclear. The principal weapon is the 2000-lb (907-kg) GBU-10E/B or BLU-109 LGB (laser-guided bomb), two of which can be carried side-by-side in the weapon bays. These fill the lower part of the centre of the fuselage, and are 69 in (1.75 m) wide and 15 ft 5 in (4.7 m) long. Left and right bays are each sealed by a saw-edged door hinged on the centreline. Another important weapon, especially in its AGM-65D (IR) and -65E (laser) versions, is Maverick. Of course, free-fall weapons can also be delivered with considerable accuracy.

The primary navaids are inertial and GPS Navstar, either of which will give accuracy on a typical F-117A mission measured in feet. For target identification an advanced FLIR (forward-looking infrared) is used. The seeker optics for this are housed in a large ball below the windscreen, shielded by a flat grid of much finer mesh than the engine inlets because it has to be transparent to IR wavelengths only. Being entirely passive (receiving, but not emitting), it does not compromise the aircraft's stealth qualities as would a radar. The ball is steerable, and the pilot can select two magnifications, which will be in the region of × 3 and × 15. He will use the lower magnification, giving a wide FOV (field of view), to search for the target. Having found it, he will switch to the narrow high-magnification mode, select the aim-point and lock the optics on. The weapon release system will launch the selected weapon so that it falls into a small 'basket' above the target, within which it will either home automatically or be capable of homing on a laser-designated target. In the latter case an aft-firing laser under the nose is used to illuminate the target (not with visible light, of course) so that the LGB will home on the aim-point automatically. The laser is boresighted parallel to a downward-looking IR receiver, which in turn is linked to the FLIR which is already locked-on to the target, so in theory the system is foolproof.

The 59 F-117As for the inventory were delivered between June 1982 and 12 July 1990. Total programme cost was $6265m, most of this being for R&D (research and development). Ben Rich

BELOW *No 843 'HO' from the 49th FW landing at RAF Lakenheath en route from Saudi Arabia to the USA for maintenance*

BOTTOM *Aircraft 830 of the 37th FW parked at Mildenhall during Air Fete 92*

seems not to have been boasting when he said that (again) the Skunk Works had developed something 'in significantly less time and for less cost than comparable programs'. Indeed, in accepting the 59th aircraft the USAF Chief of Staff, Gen Mike Dugan, said 'The F-117 program is a model of success.... On time, on schedule (actually two months early) and on performance. In fact, it has exceeded performance, and come in under cost.' Average fly-away unit cost, including GFE (Government-furnished equipment) was $42.6 million.

Tail numbers of the five prototypes are believed to have been 79-780/784, and of the production aircraft 79-785/843. All are finished in a dull greyish black, with low-visibility markings and insignia, and with the canopy transparencies treated to reduce visual and radar reflectivity. The initial deliveries were made to the 4450th TG (Tactical Group) at Tonopah Test Range, Nevada, a unit which also used A-7Ds, partly as a security cover and partly for use as trainers, chase aircraft and for special purposes. The unit's immense workload was not helped by missions being restricted to hours of darkness, which was an almost impossible burden in midsummer. On 10 November 1988 the Department of Defense admitted the aircraft existed, revealed its designation and also released a blurred retouched photograph. This allowed the 4450th to fly around the clock, and the A-7Ds were replaced by T/AT-38s.

In October 1989 the unit was redesignated as the 37th Tactical Fighter Wing, a fully operational unit comprised of the 415th and 416th Tactical Fighter Squadrons and the 417th Tactical Fighter Trainer Squadron (all three of which in World War 2 flew Beaufighter night fighter and attack aircraft noted for their quietness). Part of TAC's 16th Air Force, the 37th was tasked 'for real' on 19 December 1989 when six aircraft flew, with tanker support, non-stop to Panama to take part in Operation *Just Cause*. In the event, only one target required to be attacked. Two aircraft each had a single BLU-109. In both cases the weapon-aiming system worked as advertised, but because of a misunderstanding the second bomb was about 1000 ft off-target. This rammed home the lesson, taught perhaps 1000 times in the past, that a method that works in the clear skies of California or Nevada may not work in conditions of fog, rain or smoke.

Iraq's invasion of Kuwait led to the 'Black Jet' flying actual combat missions against some of the most heavily-defended targets in the world. The first group, from the 415th TFS, rested overnight at Langley AFB and then flew with tanker support non-stop to Khamis Mushayt, Saudi Arabia, on 19 August 1990. Having just delivered the last aircraft Lockheed had none left to fly to the Farnborough airshow in September, but it was allowed to screen an informative video. It showed the 37th TFW's computerised mission planning, the long 198-mph take-offs (admittedly Tonopah is a 'hot and high'

place) and quite impressive inflight manoeuvres. The latter caused clouds of vapour to form above the wings and stream from the tips, which at most radar wavelengths would multiply the radar cross-section several times. Less obvious was the fact that, tricky as it may be in some respects, the -117A is reputedly the easiest aircraft to air-refuel in the USAF. Ben Rich, who had just handed over Presidency of the Skunk Works to Sherman Mullin (who had previously been in charge of the YF-22), said Lockheed had done remarkably well to achieve an average fly-away price of $42.6 million, which was surely an understatement!

In December 1990 aircraft from the 416th went to the Gulf, followed by the 417th in January. Thus, by the start of Operation *Desert Storm* on 16 January 1991 a force of 45 Black Jets was in place at Khamis Mushayt, with about 60 pilots. They were tasked to destroy all the most localised and hardened targets such as Saddam Hussein's command bunkers, communications towers, Ministry of Defence building, and (though the 37th had not trained for such targets) bridges. Most were in the Baghdad area, defended by a known 60 SAM sites and about 3000 AAA pieces. In 1271 combat missions a total of 2000 stores were dropped, almost all 2000-lb GBU-27 (Paveway III) or GBU-10E/B (Paveway II). These were launched from various heights, and in virtually every case scored a direct hit. In nearly 7000 combat hours no aircraft suffered a single hostile strike, and none even reported being 'painted' by hostile radar.

In 1991 the House Armed Services Committee added $140 million to continue development of the F412 (see A-12 Avenger) and retrofit it to the F-117A. This would increase mission radius by 28 per cent and reduce take-off distance by 13 per cent. At the same time the troublesome inlet and exhaust system would be replaced by a new system entirely. In 1992 the 37th TFW moved to their permanent base, Holloman AFB, New Mexico. This has been upgraded with special facilities including simulator buildings, mission planning centres and the computer-controlled RAM respraying installation.

SPECIFICATION

F-117A
Two General Electric F404-F1D2 turbojets (not turbofans) rated at 11,800 lb
Dimensions Span 43 ft 4 in (13.2 m); length 65 ft 11 in (20.08 m); wing area reported to be 1140 sq ft (105.9 m²), which seems an over-estimate
Weight Empty, said to be c.30,000 lb (13,608 kg); max take-off 52,500 lb (23,814 kg)
Performance Maximum speed (all heights) normally c.Mach 0.9 (at S/L, 684 mph, 1100 km/h); unrefuelled combat radius (hi-lo-hi with 5000 lb 2268 kg, weapons) 600 nm (691 miles, 1112 km)
Armament Up to more than 5000 lb (2268 kg) of 'the full range of USAF tactical munitions' carried in internal bays as described previously

Tupolev Tu-160

First Flight – 19 December 1981

The Soviet Union was often forced by American weapon developments into producing direct counterparts. Physically the largest contemporary example of this is the Tu-160, the world's biggest and most powerful bomber (the B-36 of 45 years ago had greater span, but was nothing like so heavy or powerful). Rather unusually, the former Soviet Union, in the person of VVS Col Evgeni Vlasov, frankly admitted that the 'Aircraft 70' programme was launched solely because of the existence of the American B-1. The Tupolev bureau carried out the initial planning in 1973, being given authority to start with an absolutely clean sheet of paper in order to create the best possible aircraft. A key factor at this time was the recognition that there were several advantages in making the aircraft somewhat larger than the B-1.

As the initial work was on a low budget, the planning and detail design of Type 70 continued even after the B-1A had been terminated in June 1977. Indeed, it was during this very period, when it looked as if no B-1 would enter service, that the VVS ordered the prototypes of the Tu-160 to be built and tested. Leader of the team was Vladimir I Bliznuk, and the work was increasingly not at the original site of the then very large ANTK named for A N Tupolev (led at that time by his son, Alexei), but at the colossal bomber development and production facility at Kazan, capital of the Tartar SSR. According to Col Vlasov this programme was 'an expensive countermeasure ... the price of rivalry'.

Further, he points out 'Looked at from the outside, the Tu-160 and B-1B are similar. This similarity can be explained by the main features of the two design objectives: long radius of action despite major equipment and stores load, capability of deceiving enemy air-defence systems at low altitude at transonic speed or at high altitude at supersonic speed, and meeting the requirements for minimal radar/IR/acoustic signatures and optical visibility. However, they only bear resemblance from the outside. Though both aircraft were designed at about the same time (the Soviet aircraft somewhat later), the differences between them are fundamental'.

The most basic difference is perhaps the engine. Though the Soviet bomber follows exactly the same layout as the B-1, the greater mass flow and power of its engine enabled it to start life at considerably greater weights, and to have increased potential for development. Its huge engine is the last to bear the initials of famed General Constructor Nikolai Kuznetsov. Derived from the NK-32, the NK-321 is the biggest and most powerful military engine of all time. A three-shaft engine, with three-stage fan, five-stage LP (low-pressure) and seven-stage HP (high-pressure) compressors, it was developed for the greatest thrust with the lowest fuel consumption. Not too much effort was expended in minimising noise or infra-red radiation when in full afterburner. Inlet diameter of this great engine is 1450 mm (57 in), and mass flow at take-off 365 kg (805 lb)/sec. Thus, take-off thrust is 79 per cent greater than that of the engine of the B-1B!

A second fundamental difference is that, whereas the USAF put all the B-1B effort into improving low-observable qualities at low level, at the cost of subsonic speed, the Soviet choice was maximum performance yet, according to Vlasov, and to Col-Gen Boris F Korolkov, the distant radar signature of the giant Soviet bomber is actually significantly less than that of the B-1B, even discounting the large increase in radar signature caused by the B-1B's external carriage of missiles. The Tupolev bureau are particularly proud of their engine inlet, which is claimed to have minimal radar signature despite being fully variable and able to achieve ideal compression both externally (with inclined shocks) and internally. As a result, the Tu-160 is much faster than the B-1B at low level (being able to reach just over Mach 1) and getting on for twice as fast at high altitude.

The four engines are installed under the rear of the enormous fixed inner wing, which has a continuously curved and well-rounded leading edge which at the front reaches a sweep angle of 90° and thus merges imperceptibly into the forward fuselage beside the cockpit. Outboard are the swinging outer wings, with several sweep angles selected by buttons from 20° to 65°. Thanks to an enormous amount of tunnel testing of every part of this aircraft, the Tupolev bureau consider they have achieved the most aerodynamically efficient supersonic aircraft ever built. Each outer wing has straight taper from root to tip, full-span hydrauli-

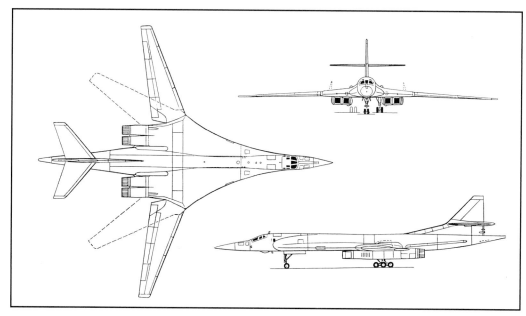

ABOVE *One of the first good photographs of the almighty Tupolev to be released, in 1990*

cally-driven slats (really Krüger flaps, which at the root become cambered as on the 747 when fully extended), and almost full-span double-slotted flaps. At maximum sweep the inner portion of each flap hinges up to form a giant fence. The small section of trailing edge outboard of the flap is 'a simple aileron', used at all speeds for roll control and backed up by the differential tailerons mounted half-way up the fin. The rudder is a one-piece surface forming the entire vertical tail above the horizontal surfaces. The ailerons droop 20° with flaps down.

Despite being 10 m (33 ft) longer, the Tu-160 fuselage is claimed to offer lower drag than that of the US bomber. This is partly because its nose radome is more pointed, with a smaller cone half-angle, partly because the overall cross-section area is much less, and partly because, throughout the entire design, the Tupolev bureau eliminated every

excrescence and used special computer routines both to achieve the optimum shape and also to program the machine tools to ensure that this shape was reached in production. Even before applying special surface treatments, including overall precisely controlled thicknesses of RAM (radar-absorbent material), the -160 is considered to be the smoothest and most accurately made bomber of all time (before the B-2, at least). Unlike the B-1B there is not a single fence (apart from the 'flap fins') or vortex generator anywhere. Moreover, though the Soviet bomber has 'the largest and most comprehensive electronic-warfare system ever designed' almost every antenna associated with it is flush with the aircraft's surface.

The engines are installed in pairs in rectangular-section nacelles. The complete convergent/divergent variable nozzle projects behind the nacelle, which itself projects far behind the wing, and each engine can be removed straight out to the rear. The inlets are broadly similar to those of the B-1A (though of course larger), and unlike those of the Tu-144 and Concorde. Each twin inlet has a curved V shape in plan view, the vertical central splitter leading back to an inner wall in each duct which is variable in both profile and throat area. It is claimed that this inlet offers lower drag and higher pressure recovery over the full range of Mach numbers from 0 to 1.9 than any other inlet currently flying. The outer side of each duct is also vertical, and incorporates five large suck-in auxiliary doors to admit additional air on take-off and during penetration at full throttle at low level. Particular care was taken to minimise the radar signature when these inlets are open.

The nose landing gear carries landing and taxy lamps and has twin wheels with high-pressure tyres steered hydraulically through ± 55° and retracted to the rear. Beside each wheel is a spray/debris deflector. The main gears have much in common with those of the Tu-154, though they are larger and stronger. Each has a massive steel oleo leg pivoted just inboard of the engine box, which restricts track to only 5.4 m (17 ft 8 in). The leg carries a six-wheel bogie; unlike the Tu-22M family the wheels are all in line. The unit is swung up hydraulically, the bogie rotating 90° to lie parallel to the leg to be housed in a narrow but deep box between the engines and the fuselage, projecting above the wing in a prominent 'canoe' fairing. A braking parachute is stowed in a drum in the rear of the fairing between the horizontal and vertical tails. The entire aft end of the fuselage is packed with avionics, the cable looms for which are carried past the huge integral tanks in the rear fuselage inside prominent duct fairings on each side which must significantly increase radar cross-section.

One of the greatest contrasts between the Tu-160 and B-1B is the maximum fuel capacity. Whereas the limit for the American bomber is 195,000 lb, or about 88 tonnes, the Soviet bomber can load 130 tonnes (287,600 lb), and still carry its maximum weapon load. The inflight-refuelling capability is thus hardly ever required. According to Vlasov the combat radius at Mach 1 in the terrain-following mode is almost identical to that at Mach 1.9 at high altitude. In either mode he claims the giant Soviet bomber to have markedly better handling and flight characteristics than the B-1B, which he states has many problems including 'a nose-down tendency in TFR flight, severe limitations on AOA (angle of attack) and even more severe limitations on weight caused by a tendency to fall off uncontrollably on one wing whenever AOA approaches the stalling angle'. Certainly the Tu-160 is claimed to have no flight limitations, so that the pilot can perform 'carefree' manoeuvres.

One of the reasons for the smaller cross-section of the fuselage is that the pressurised crew compartment is not placed above the bay for the nose landing gear but ahead of it. The flight crew enter via the nose-gear bay and then walk forward. The crew of four comprise two pilots (one the aircraft commander), a navigator/bombardier and an electronic systems officer. Each has his own K-36 series

LEFT *Three of the crew pose for the camera at the disputed Tu-160 unit at present in the Ukraine. Ground locks secure four air data attitude/temp sensors. The tailplane attitude is more obvious than the defensive electronics which fill the leading edges*

ejection seat. The forward windscreens give an outstanding view ahead, which can be augmented by a video camera, one of the sensors of which can be aimed at the terrain ahead through an optically flat window at the front of a blister on the underside. The Tu-160 was designed to meet the same speed/mass birdstrike requirements as the Su-24 and other supersonic low-level aircraft. As in the Vulcan and B-1, the pilots have fighter-type sticks.

Having commented on the failure of the B-1B electronic-warfare system to meet requirements, Vlasov continues 'The EW systems installed in the Tu-160 fully meet the purpose of the aircraft. They are easily removable and maintainable, and the modules are quickly replaceable. The navigator's panel is provided with eight computers, complex bomb-release systems, radar displays and long-range navigation systems, linked with Glonass satellites. A computer generates the actual flight route on a topographic chart. There are more than 100 computers operating aboard the aircraft, serving various purposes. The automatic air-combat and defence system is capable of interrogating several targets at the same time'.

Apart from the M-50, the Tu-160 is the first Soviet bomber to have no defensive firepower. Studies were made of the effect on drag and weight of a tail barbette (a manned turret was not considered), but, as in the case of the B-1B, the decision was taken to rely on the various electronic and IR defensive systems. The passive receiver systems are new, and the overall power-management system is said to be 'a generation later' in conception than that of the B-1B. Batteries of active emitters occupy the curved leading edge of the inboard wing and the tail end of the fuselage, whilst magazines for more than 1000 chaff/flare cartridges are arranged in groups above the nacelles and strips along the side of the rear fuselage. The systems officer has a large display on which is grouped all information on hostile threats. He can elect to take over manual control of the active defence systems in situations where automatic responses might betray the aircraft's presence.

Another contrast with the B-1B is that the Tu-160 was designed to carry all its weapons internally. The two enormous weapon bays extend from the nose landing gear to the engine nozzles. Each is 33 ft long, one being ahead of the structural wing bridge and the other aft of it. Normal outward-hinged doors are used. The limitation of 16,330 kg (see data) is merely the optimum capacity. A considerably greater load could be carried if it were considered necessary. Each bay can be equipped with a rotary launcher for either six RK-55 long-range (3000 km, 1864 miles) cruise missiles or Kh-15P SRAM (short-range attack missile) type weapons 'for annihilating enemy air defences', or 12 smaller RKV-500B missiles.

According to Vlasov there would be no major problem in modifying the Tupolev bomber to carry

TOP *Slow fly-past by an unpainted Tu-160. Seeing the actual aircraft underscores its size, compared with the B-1B*

ABOVE *The electronically scanned radar is hidden, but ahead of the nose gear is the enormous window of the forward electro-optical sight system*

additional weapons externally. In his view such extra load is unnecessary, cuts radius of action by at least 1000 km (620 miles), and so increases radar cross-section that the aircraft can be detected 'as much as 2.5 times earlier'. And, of course, it reduces flight speed and thus gives defences rather more

ABOVE *Aircraft 20 tucks away its landing gear on departure from Dolon AB. From this angle the multiple cable conduits past the rear-fuselage integral tanks are clearly seen*

time to react. One pilot said 'we prefer to remain undetected'.

The first of the two prototypes was completed in 1981, and was photographed by American reconnaissance satellites on 25 November of that year. It was then parked next to Tu-144s (being re-engined) on the special test airfield at Zhukovskii. Flight testing began on 19 December 1981, and was generally most successful, though the geometry of the tail needed modification and several nitpicking criticisms (for example of the Tupolev OKB's speed of response to problems) have appeared in Russian newspapers. Production of 100 was authorised at Kazan in 1985. The 12th off the line was inspected by US visitors at Kubinka on 2 August 1988, when the smooth white exterior caused favourable comment. Another Tu-160 flew over the crowd at the 1989 Aviation Day. Later that year regular service aircraft were used to set records carrying 25 t loads round 1000 and 2000 km circuits at Mach 1.58 and 1.63, and various height/ load records. At that time 20 were in service with the 184th Regiment at Priluki, Ukraine, crew training being carried out at Dolon AB, Siberia. In the event production was terminated in late 1992 at about No 50. They equip DA regiments at Engels (Saratov oblast), Mozhdok (Caucasus) and Ukrainka (Far East).

Ten aircraft formed the development fleet, most of which were based at the NII Zhukovsky test centre. Seven of these were still there during the public Mosaeroshow in August 1992, when it was noted that five have been abandoned as not being worth bringing up to the standard of production aircraft. These five are now being cannibalised for spares. Training of Tu-160 crews was carried out partly with development and early production aircraft, and partly with a fleet of 16 converted Tu-134 transports, made up of Tu-134UBL pilot trainers and Tu-134BSh bomb/nav trainers. Both have the Tu-160 radar, which the pilot needs for terrain following. The UBL serves at Priluki, home of the 184th Regiment; the BSh, which has underwing pylons for practice bombs, equips the Tambov school which also trained Tu-22M crews.

SPECIFICATION

Tu-160

Four Samara/Trud NK-321 augmented turbofans rated at 35,300 lb dry and 55,115 lb maximum

Dimensions Span (20°) 55.7 m (182 ft 9 in), (35°) 50.7 m (166 ft 4 in), (65°) 35.6 m (116 ft 9.8 in); length 54.1 m (177 ft 6 in); height 13.1 m (43 ft 0 in); wing area 340 m² (3660 sq ft)

Weight Empty about 118 t (260,000 lb); maximum take-off 275 t (606,260 lb)

Performance Maximum speed, at high altitude Mach 1.88 (2,000 km/ h, 1,243 mph), at S/L Mach 1.02 (1,250 km/h, 777 mph); cruising speed 850 km/h (528 mph); service ceiling 18.3 km (60,000 ft); max unrefuelled combat radius 7,300 km (4,535 miles)

Armament Typically six RK-55 ALCMs ('AS-15' or 'AS-19') on forward rotary launcher plus 24 RKV-500B ('AS-16') SRAMs on two aft rotary launchers, or 16,330 kg (36,000 lb) of bombs

AMX

First Flight – 15 May 1984

This aircraft is unusual in several respects. First, in contrast to obsolescent fighters kept in service for ground-attack duties, or fighters able to carry air/ground weapons, or armed versions of trainers, it is an example of a 'fighter type' aircraft explicitly designed for tactical attack and reconnaissance. Second, and partly in view of this objective, no attempt was made to fly at supersonic speeds, in order to make the aircraft more cost-effective in its designated role (in which supersonic speed is virtually impossible anyway). Third, it was the joint creation of Italy and Brazil, countries which had not collaborated previously, nor had designed aircraft in this class, unless one includes the light Fiat G.91.

The original requirement, dating from early 1977, was stated by the AMI (Italian air force). It called for 187 of a new design of tactical aircraft to replace the G.91R in the close-support attack/reconnaissance roles, the G.91Y and F-104G in the interdiction role and the F-104S in multiple tactical roles. The counter-air duties were to be shared with the longer-range Tornado; other missions were to be assigned to the AMX entirely. Work went ahead at once by Aeritalia, with Aermacchi as associate contractor.

These partners completed the detailed definition phase in March 1980. Later that year the Brazilian Government announced that it would participate in the programme, and in September 1980 Embraer of Brazil became an industrial partner. The work split

finally agreed is: Aeritalia (team leader with 46.5 per cent by value) is responsible for the centre fuselage, nose, fin/rudder, tailplane/elevators, ailerons and spoilers; Aermacchi (23.8 per cent) is responsible for the forward fuselage (including gun and avionics integration), canopy and tailcone; and Embraer (29.7 per cent) is responsible for air intakes, wings, slats, flaps, pylons, drop tanks and reconnaissance pallets. Every part is made at one source only, but there are production lines in both countries.

The basic AMX single-seater is a conventional aircraft made mostly of aluminium alloy by traditional methods. Features include a deep fuselage with plain air inlets just aft of the cockpit to feed the unaugmented turbofan engine, a shoulder-high wing with traditional (12 per cent) thickness and slight (27.5°) sweep, and damage-tolerant structure throughout (for example, three main wing spars and multiple load paths throughout the fuselage). The relatively large tail includes honeycomb-filled carbon-fibre construction for the fin, rudder and portions of the horizontal surface.

The flight controls and movable high-lift surfaces were thought out carefully for maximum survivability. The wing has full-span slats and almost full-span double-slotted flaps, the latter being track-mounted but differing from the Fowler type in having no fixed wing above. All these surfaces are driven by hydraulic screwjacks with electrical signalling. Outboard of the flaps are very small

BELOW Aircraft of the Brazilian FAB are dark sea grey and pale grey. They have a gun on each side of the nose

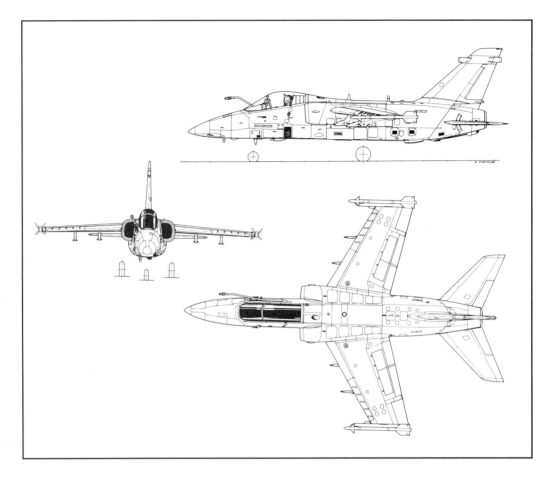

ailerons, used for roll control together with two spoilers on each wing ahead of the flaps. Again all these surfaces are hydraulically powered, with electrical signalling. The spoilers are also used symmetrically as airbrakes and, after landing, as lift dumpers. The fin/rudder are conventional, but the horizontal tail appears to comprise an all-moving 'slab' on each side, with a large tab. In fact the tailplane is hydraulically driven for trimming only, and what appear to be tabs are in fact the small elevators. Aeritalia shares in manufacture of the GEC Avionics flight-control computer.

The Spey 807 engine was selected because of its toughness, proven reliability and good fuel economy. It is made under licence by groups of companies in Italy and Brazil. Because of the limited range of flight Mach number it was possible to use simple round-lipped inlets, with the ducts curved sharply inwards to the engine. Access to the engine, or its removal, is achieved by disconnecting the rear fuselage, complete with the horizontal tail. A total of 3440 litres (757 Imp gal) of fuel is housed in bag tanks in the fuselage and integral tanks in the wings. Under each wing are hardpoints for two pylons, all four being plumbed for drop tanks. The usual size is 1100 litres (242 Imp gal) inboard and 580 litres (128 Imp gal) outboard. On Italian aircraft a fixed inflight-refuelling probe, with inbuilt

floodlight, is attached to the right of the large one-piece birdproof windshield.

The pressurised cockpit contains a Martin-Baker Mk 10L zero/zero seat, and is covered by a canopy which hinges open to the right. Electronics are digital, and the pilot has HDDs (head-down displays) and a HUD (head-up display). All three levered-suspension units of the landing gear retract into the fuselage. The steerable nose unit goes forwards and the main units swing forwards and inwards whilst turning to lie with the wheels almost flat under the inlet ducts. No braking parachute was thought necessary, but an airfield arrester hook is standard. The mainwheel tyre pressure of 140 lb/sq in was chosen to permit sustained operation from unpaved surfaces.

Predictably, the aircraft for the AMI and FAB (Brazilian AF) differ in their avionics and weapons. Both nations agreed that the bulk, weight and cost of a multi-mode radar was not justified, though (as explained later) a radar-equipped two-seater is planned. Instead of fitting a laser, both air forces chose to instal in the nose a simple ranging radar. The Italian package is an Israeli Elta radar made in Italy by FIAR, while the Brazilian radar is by Technasa/SMA. Navigation is inertial, with a standby attitude/heading reference system, plus Tacan and VOR/ILS. Quite comprehensive ECM

ABOVE *One of the first AMI recipient units was the 51° Stormo. Colour is pale blue-grey overall*

(electronic countermeasures) are fitted, triggered by fore/aft passive receiver antennas at the top of the fin. Following Italian practice, the active counter-measure is usually a windmill-driven jammer pod mounted on one of the outer pylons.

Most of the avionics racking is along the under-side of the fuselage, on both sides. Everything possible has been done to make it easy to change boxes or to replace them by different equipment. The Brazilian aircraft has a gun on each side, whereas the Italian has a different gun on the left only. On the other hand, the M61 gun chosen by Italy needs a large drum magazine mounted trans-versely which, together with the liquid-oxygen converter, takes up an entire bay in the nose. There is no internal weapons bay, but a bay on the right side under the cockpit floor is available for recon-naissance sensors. Brazilian aircraft have a choice of three Aeroeletronica pallets housing various vertical, forward and oblique cameras or other sensors, these boxes being variously bulged or flush with the fuselage mould line. In addition an IR (infra-red) and EO (electro-optical) reconnaissance pod can be carried externally on the centreline pylon.

Seven prototypes were built, three by Aeritalia, two by Aermacchi and two by Embraer (as well as a static-test specimen). A01, assembled at Turin-Caselle by Aeritalia, made the first flight on 15 May 1984. It was lost on its fifth flight, on 1 June, but this had no significant impact on the programme. YA-1, the first Brazilian-assembled prototype, flew on 16 October 1985. The first production aircraft flew at Turin on 11 May 1988. The production phase is expected to comprise 252 single-seaters, 187 for Italy and 65 for the *Força Aérea Brasileira*, plus 65 two-seaters (51 for the AMI and 14 for the FAB).

The AMX has been cleared to Mach 0.9, and to perform all normal manoeuvres at AOA (angle of attack) up to 45° with no fewer than 25 different kinds of external store. Self-defence AAMs (air-to-air missiles) are carried on rails on the wingtips. Missions have been flown by day and night and in poor visibility, and it was a design requirement that sustained operations should be possible from damaged bases offering no ground support other than fuel and weapons.

On 14 March 1990 the prototype two-seat AMX made its first flight. This has a raised rear cockpit which replaces the forward fuel tank and requires relocation of the ECS (environmental control system). Some two-seaters will be dual-control

ABOVE *Development aircraft formate for the camera, with contrasting loads*

AMX-T trainers, but work is going ahead on the AMX-AS maritime attack version. In this the backseater will be a navigator, managing a multi-function attack radar (the FIAR Grifo in Italian versions) and also provided with a Ferranti video monitor to record the HUD for subsequent playback. Primary armament of the AS version would be the AM39 Exocet missile. Other changes might include the 13,125 lb Spey 821 engine and slightly extended wingtips

SPECIFICATION

AMX (single-seat)
One 11,030-lb Rolls-Royce Spey Mk 807 turbofan
Dimensions Span (excluding AAM rails) 8.874 m (29 ft 1.37 in); length 13.575 m (44 ft 6.4 in); wing area 21.0 m² (226.05 sq ft)
Weight Empty (operational) 6640 kg (14,638 lb); loaded (clean) 9600 kg (21,164 lb); maximum take-off 13 tonnes (28,660 lb)
Performance Maximum speed (S/L, clean) 565 kt (1047 km/h, 651 mph, Mach 0.854); attack radius (6000 lb/2721 kg bombload, full reserves, lo-lo-lo) 528 km (328 miles)
Armament Up to 3800 kg (8377 lb) of external weapons, including self-defence AAMs (Italy two AIM-9P, Brazil two MAA-1 Piranha) plus (Italy) one M61A1 20 mm gun or (Brazil) two DEFA 554 30 mm guns

McDonnell Douglas F-15E Strike Eagle

First Flight – 11 December 1986

For many years generally regarded as the best fighter outside the Soviet Union and successor states – and thus the rightful heir to the status enjoyed by its ancestor, the F-4 – the F-15 is an example of how a good design can be made into a multi-role aircraft. It is also an example of how an air force can make a 180° U-turn in policy.

The story began in 1965 when, worried at the emergence of new Soviet fighters, the USAF requested funding for a new fighter programme, the FX. RFPs (Requests for Proposals) were sent to Fairchild Hiller (the vanished Republic Aviation), McDonnell Aircraft and North American Rockwell. After a close-fought contest McDonnell was announced winner on 23 December 1969, and the first F-15A flew on 27 July 1972. The first TF-15A dual trainer (subsequently redesignated F-15B) flew on 7 July 1973.

Predictably, the F-15 was a blend of new and old. Most of the structure was aluminium alloy or titanium, though movable surfaces and wingtips incorporated metal honeycomb. In configuration the F-15 followed what had become a new shape set by such aircraft as the MiG-25 and F-14, with a high wing, twin engines fed by fully variable wedge inlets on each side of the forward fuselage and a twin-fin tail carried on long beams outboard of the engines. The wing was remarkable for its size (over 600 sq ft), for its completely simple leading edge devoid of a single droop, slat, dogtooth, fence or vortex generator, and for its plain flaps inboard, traditional ailerons outboard and lack of spoilers. The two large vertical tails incorporated small inset rudders, while the horizontals were slabs with giant dogteeth, used for pitch only.

Pratt & Whitney won the propulsion contract, using their JTF22 core as the basis for the F100-100, rated at 23,830 lb with maximum augmentation. Predictably this engine began indifferently (though far better than its predecessor, the TF30) and over the years matured into perhaps the longest-lived and most reliable fighter engine in history. In 1985 the F100-220, with digital control, was qualified after an accelerated mission test of 4000 cycles, and has ever since powered the F-15C, two-seat F-15D and multirole F-15E with the most crucial elements, the HP and LP turbines, overhauled on a basis of 4300 cycles, typically equivalent to nine years of normal operations.

BELOW *Long an exponent of the F-111F, the 48th FW now flies the superior F-15E. They usually carry only one Lantirn pod*

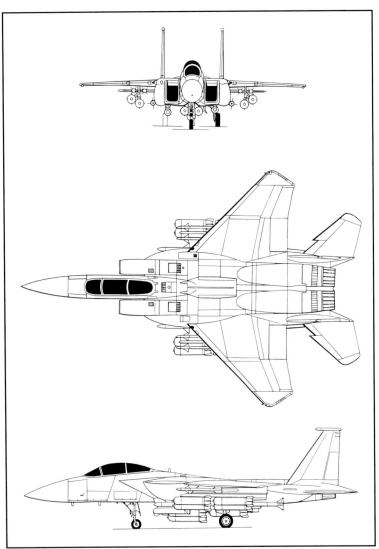

The three units of the landing gear all retracted into the fuselage, and each had a single wheel with a high-pressure tyre. This reflected the USAF policy of assuming that, even in wartime, they would never be short of long paved runways at locations that would not be destroyed by the enemy. Armament comprised an M61 gun in the starboard wing root, fed by a belt passing over the right inlet duct from a 940-round drum in the fuselage, and four Sparrow medium-range radar-guided missiles carried on the square flanks of the fuselage. In addition four close-range Sidewinders could be carried on twin underwing pylons which could also carry 500-gal (600 US gal, 2309 litre) drop tranks, a third such tank being on the centreline. A receptacle for an air-refuelling boom was provided above the fuselage, ahead of the single giant door-type airbrake.

Likewise the main radar, the Hughes APG-63, was welcomed by pilots as setting a new high standard. This equipped the F-15A when it entered service in November 1974. Again, over the years this radar, the signal processor, computer memory, software and other crucial elements were utterly transformed to multiply capability. The improved radars equipped the F-15C and two-seat F-15D from 1979, but another major upgrade in these versions was the ability to add a conformal fuel tank on each side of the fuselage, not only adding a total of 1248 gal (5678 litres) of extra fuel, with very little drag

BELOW *The commander's aircraft proudly proclaims its unit as the 405th TTW. This passed out all F-15E crews at Luke AFB before merger into the 58th FW*

penalty, but also enabling 12 bombs of 1000 lb or four of 2000 lb to be hung under the tanks, and various reconnaissance or weapon-aiming sensors to be installed inside the tanks. From 1988 AIM-7 missiles have been progressively replaced by AIM-120 AMRAAM. One could write a large book on how the avionics of the F-15 have been developed, but most of this was directed towards the air-to-air role. Indeed, the ruling philosophy behind the F-15 was that its design was not to be compromised in the slightest degree by any pretensions at air-to-ground capability. A popular slogan was 'NOT A POUND FOR AIR-TO-GROUND!'

It was the horrifying and totally unacceptable thought that the USAF might buy the European Tornado as its Enhanced Tactical Fighter, to replace the F-111, that prompted McDonnell to launch the idea that the F-15 might, after all, be turned into an attack aircraft. Under the name Strike Eagle, McDonnell modified the second F-15B (71-0291) as a supposedly all-weather dual-role aircraft, with the rear cockpit containing four multi-function displays for navigation (including terrain following), weapon selection and monitoring of hostile threats. Test and evaluation of the proposed improvements in 1982–83, followed by evaluation against the F-16XL, led to selection of the F-15E on 24 February 1984. The first F-15E flew on 11 December 1986, and deliveries began to the 4th FW at Seymour Johnson on 29 December 1988. The planned buy of 392 was cut to 200, plus three *Desert Storm* loss replacements, and 48 for Saudi Arabia.

The F-15E reflects the USAF's philosophy of unhindered operations from giant airfields, command of the sky, and the ability to dictate how a war is waged. The main tyre pressure of 305 lb/sq in is hardly suitable for a bulldozed strip, and when it comes to quoting field length everyone has been careful never to reveal what this might be at maximum weight. Of the 200 USAF aircraft, the first 134 have the same 23,450-lb engine as the F-15C/D, though the engine bay was designed also to accept the much more powerful GE F110-129. From No 135 the vastly improved Pratt & Whitney F100-229 is fitted, one of its numerous advantages being a take-off thrust of 29,100 lb, and this does a little to improve behaviour and field length with a full load of bombs and fuel.

The radar is the Hughes APG-70, about two generations later than the Dash-63, with synthetic-aperture design for high resolution. Automatic terrain following is governed by a Lear Astronics triple-redundant flight control system. The main night and all-weather navigation and weapon-aiming system is LANTIRN, with a navigation pod hung under the right inlet duct and a targeting pod under the left. The nav pod houses the terrain-following radar and a fixed-imagery sensor (a forward-looking infra-red) whose picture can be presented on the wide-angle holographic HUD. The targeting pod houses a second FLIR, with wide and narrow fields of view, slaved to a laser ranger/designator, both slewed under crew control. There is considerable additional equipment to accommodate, which meant the internal fuel capacity was

BELOW *The second two-seater, 71-0291 – in which the author once had an exciting ride – was later rebuilt as the first F-15E, then called Strike Eagle*

ABOVE *More Luke aircraft, from the 405th TTW's 550th TFTS. They are off to practise with real bombs*

slightly reduced, and the gun ammunition drum reduced in height.

The F-15E thus retains the gun, and the ability to carry the same air-to-air missiles as the C/D. Obviously, its huge fixed-geometry wing is totally unsuited to full-throttle flight at treetop height, though with a heavy bombload the combination of higher wing loading and much-reduced top speed (490 kt) makes response to turbulence less violent. Certainly the F-15E stands very high in any listing of dual-role aircraft, with its combination of excellent avionics, a very heavy load of almost any kind of tactical store and exceptional air-combat capability in the clean condition.

SPECIFICATION

F-15E Eagle

Two Pratt & Whitney augmented turbofans, (1-134) F100-220 rated at 14,670 lb dry and 23,450 lb maximum; (135-200) F100-229 rated at 17,800 lb dry and 29,100 lb maximum

Dimensions Span 42 ft 9.8 in (13.05 m); length 63 ft 9 in (19.43 m); wing area 608 sq ft (56.5 m²)

Weight Empty equipped 31,700 lb (14,379 kg); max fuel (internal and external) 34,768 lb (15,771 kg); max take-off 81,000 lb (36,741 kg)

Performance Maximum speed (clean, high altitude) Mach 2.5; low attack with max bombload 490 kt (564 mph, 908 km/h); max combat radius 790 miles (1270 km); max ferry range 2765 miles (4445 km); field length; about 8000 ft (2440 m)

Armament One M61A1 gun with 512 rounds; provision for up to 24,500 lb (11,113 kg) of ordnance on tangential attachments along lower edge of conformal tanks, centreline and one pylon under each wing, each with provision for triple ejector rack

JAS 39 Gripen

First Flight – 9 December 1988

During the 1970s several of the 'non-super-power' countries around the world began to plan totally new designs for future fighters. Among them were China, India, Israel, Sweden, Taiwan and Yugoslavia. Fashion dictated that all should be single-engined single-seaters (though with the possibility of a dual version), with a rear delta wing and forward canard. Alone among them, the Israeli Lavi was planned as an attack aircraft with a secondary fighter role. The rest were seen as fighters with secondary attack and reconnaissance roles. The Lavi production programme was cancelled, and the other projects had made only slow progress by 1993. In contrast, the Swedish aircraft has been developed with all the skill and assurance expected from that country.

From the outset it was agreed that, mainly for budgetary reasons, Sweden's future aircraft would be smaller than rivals in the superpowers and Western Europe, and thus it was planned around the use of a single engine of similar power to those used in rival twin-engined aircraft. It was further taken for granted that the aircraft would have to operate from the Swedish Class V90 highways, because unlike more unimaginative air forces the *Flygvapnet* can see that in any future war its aircraft could not survive unless they were dispersed to hundreds of remote locations. The V90 public roads are of course paved, but the required field length is 880 m (2625 ft), which can be a challenge in a Swedish winter. Every part of the aircraft had to be maintainable by a short-service conscript wearing large fur gloves. A further basic requirement was that it should fly fighter (Jakt), attack (Attack) and reconnaissance (Spaning) missions, hence its designation JAS 39. The prime requirement was to replace any remaining J35 Draken aircraft, and the AJ/SH/SF/JA/AJS versions of the Type 37 Viggen, in that order.

In late 1980 the industry group IG JAS was formed by the prime contractors: the Saab-Scania Military Aircraft Division, Volvo Flygmotor, Ericsson Radar Electronics and FFV Aerotech. In 1981 the detailed proposals were submitted to the programme co-ordinator and customer, the FMV (Swedish defence material administration). Designated Saab 2105, and then Type 2110, it followed the same layout as the Viggen, with a canard and rear delta wing (and, after much thought, a single vertical tail), but was significantly smaller and slimmer and powered by a single General Electric F404J engine, to be developed in collaboration with Flygmotor and produced in Sweden as the RM12.

The programme agreed on 30 April 1982 specified procurement of 140 aircraft including about 25 dual two-seaters by the year 2000. The first of five prototypes, 39-1, was rolled out on schedule on 26 April 1987 and flew on 9 December 1988. The long

BELOW *Second production aircraft, called 39-102*

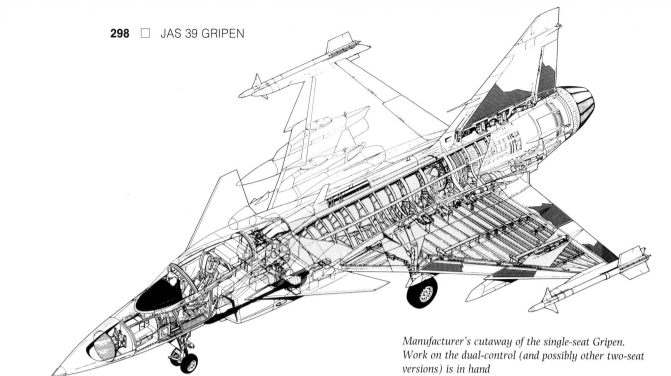

Manufacturer's cutaway of the single-seat Gripen.
Work on the dual-control (and possibly other two-seat
versions) is in hand

period spent checking the systems before first flight reflects on the complexity of even the smallest modern combat aircraft, but sadly, despite such care, there was a fault in the software and 39-1 was damaged beyond repair when landing on 2 February 1989. Subsequently 39-2 has tested the near-definitive fly-by-wire control system, 39-3 the Ericsson/GEC Ferranti PS-05/A multi-mode radar, 39-4 all the remaining avionics and 39-5 the final production-standard avionics and flight controls.

An agile and attractive aircraft, the Gripen (Griffin) has a modern structure with over 30 per cent made of CFRP composites. British Aerospace produced the first $3\frac{1}{2}$ carbon wing sets, subsequent wings being made by Saab. The leading edge, swept at 45°, has a prominent dogtooth and comprises three sections of droop slats driven by Lucas 'geared hinge' actuators. The trailing edge comprises three powered sections, the short inboard section acting as a flap and elevator, the middle section as a flap and elevon and the outer as an elevon (elevator and aileron) only. The broad square tip carries a missile rail. The foreplanes have a leading-edge angle of 43° and are the primary pitch control. Like the wing boxes and vertical tail they are carbon composite.

As in the Viggen, the foreplanes are mounted at the top of the lateral inlet ducts, higher than the mid-mounted wings. Fuel is housed in integral tanks formed by the entire wing boxes and by integral main and collector tanks in the fuselage; Intertechnique supplied a fuel-management system giving active CG control. The three landing gears are by AP Precision Hydraulics, the single-wheel main units retracting forwards and the steerable twin-wheel nose gear retracting to the rear and having its own anti-skid braking system. There is no hook, braking parachute or reverser, but airbrakes can be opened on each side of the rear fuselage, and after landing the foreplanes go into 'snowplough'

mode at a nose-down angle almost broadside-on to the slipstream.

Compared with the F404 the RM12 has a greater fan airflow and 105°c higher turbine gas temperature. It was also designed to meet more stringent birdstrike requirements, calling for increased redundancy to ensure sufficient 'get home' power. GE supply about 60 per cent by value of the parts, but in turn Volvo supplies parts to GE for other F404 applications, and carries out all RM12 assembly and test. The inlets are almost rectangular and of simple fixed-geometry form, showing that extreme-Mach performance was not a requirement. Engine control is digital, via one of three MIL-1553B buses.

The seat is a Martin-Baker S10LS. Ericsson developed the three head-down displays, Hughes the wide-angle HUD and GEC Ferranti the associated video camera. Honeywell provide the laser-inertial navigation system, Lear Astronics the FBW flight controls (two-channel digital with single-channel analog standby), BAe the standby attitude/heading 3-axis strapdown gyros, and Ericsson the central computing system which has 40 processors and works faster than that of the F-15E, with the same storage capacity. The main radar serves all fighter and attack functions, including terrain following. It is augmented on most missions by a FLIR (forward-looking infra-red) pod hung under the right inlet duct, which can be replaced by a laser ranger. Comprehensive EW (electronic warfare) equipment is carried, with active jammers and dispensers carried both internally and externally.

A single Mauser gun is carried in a slightly bulged section of fuselage with its muzzle just inboard of the bottom of the left inlet splitter plate. Seven attachments for ordnance are provided, those on the wingtips normally being for self-defence RB74 (AIM-9L Sidewinder) missiles. Other air-to-air weapons can include Sky Flash, Active Sky Flash and

LEFT *What, no bombs? Weapons get more sophisticated, but the Gripen can still drop the dumb 'iron' variety*

ABOVE *First production aircraft, retained by Saab to replace the lost first prototype*

AMRAAM. In the attack mode initial weapons include bombs (free fall, retarded and smart), rockets, MBB submunitions dispensers, RB75 (Maverick) and the big RB15F anti-ship cruise missile. FMV has proposed developing a new TSA (heavy guided attack-weapon) with a warhead weighing about 500 kg (1102 lb) for use against particularly large or hard targets.

The *Flygvapnet* have a requirement for 340-350 Gripens, to equip 21-23 squadrons. The first 30 were ordered along with the prototypes on 30 June 1982. Authority for the next 110 was given on 3 June 1992, and this total included 14 of the dual-control JAS 39B, the go-ahead on which was authorised in July 1989. This retains almost unchanged avionics and fuel capacity, and has a 0.5-m (20-in) fuselage plug. In late 1992 the remaining four prototypes had made over 600

flights, 39-3 flying to Farnborough for static display (demonstrating the programme is on schedule) and 39-4 performing impressively in the flying. At that time all aspects of performance had been cleared to equal or better the specification, the sustained turn of 9g being exceeded. Except for the RBS15F all weapon trials had been completed satisfactorily. Remaining problems with avionics cooling, the fuel system, the Microturbo gas-turbine APU (auxiliary power unit) in the left wing root, control stick and flight-control memory were all perfectly normal, and capable of early solution.

Because of its firmly managed development and modest size, JAS 39 is certainly the cheapest

ABOVE *First take-off (on 4 March 1993) by Gripen No 102, which was to have been the first to be delivered to the Royal Swedish AF. Up to a further 349 may follow for the same customer*

LEFT *Formating on the photo aircraft, the first Gripen delivered to F7 Wing demonstrates its powerful leading-edge droop slats, driven by internal Lucas 'geared hinge' actuators*

Flygvapnet livery. At least a hiccup in the programme has resulted from the loss of 39-102 during a flypast in Stockholm on 8 August 1993, which was caused by the excessively harsh control inputs. The first unit will be F 7 at Såtenäs, which will carry out pilot conversion and weapon training. The JAS 39C is a planned upgraded version with a longer fuselage, higher-thrust engine and enhanced data-handling avionics. There is no reason to doubt that this multi-role aircraft will not only be a success in the *Flygvapnet* but also the first big military export success for Sweden's aircraft industry.

warplane of its type, and the proposed 39X export version is said to be priced at well below US $30m in operational trim. When Germany temporarily abandoned EFA it was allegedly quoted a JAS 39 price of DM89m. Saab suggest that in frontline service the total operating cost should not be higher than SEK (Swedish Kronor) 17,000 per flight hour, which is typical for a bizjet and a fraction of the cost levels recorded by rival aircraft.

Deliveries are to begin in late 1993, though flight development will continue at least until 1995. The first production aircraft, 39-101, joined the flight-test programme on 10 September 1992, painted in

SPECIFICATION

IG JAS 39 Gripen

One Volvo Flygmotor RM12 augmented turbofan rated at 12,140 lb dry and 18,100 lb with maximum augmentation

Dimensions Span 26 ft 3 in (8.00 m); length 46 ft 3 in (14.1 m); wing area not released

Weight Empty 14,600 lb (6622 kg); clean gross c.17,635 lb (8t); max 27,500 lb (12,473 kg)

Performance Max speed 'supersonic at all altitudes'; no other data

Armament One MK 27 gun; maximum weapon load 4 t (8818 lb)

Northrop B-2

With this bomber, military aviation takes a giant step into a new era. This step is manifest in many ways. One is that, considered as a simple trucking system, the B-2 is probably the most efficient bomber in history, moving more 'payload' further on any given amount of fuel than any previous bomber. But that is a side issue. The central reason for its existence is that it was designed from the start to be almost impossible to detect until it was very close to its targets – relative to other bombers – thus posing almost insoluble problems to defenders. This LO (low observable) or 'stealth' quality is bound to be an essential requisite for all future aircraft designed to penetrate hostile airspace. It is more difficult to accomplish than anything else in the history of warfare. The costs are so high that, as the B-2 nears combat duty with the USAF's Air Combat Command, most Americans are asking 'Is any airplane worth $2000 million each?'

Stealth technology goes back (at optical wavelengths) to 1913, and at radar wavelengths to 1936. After being surprisingly ignored, it was gradually brought back into the procurement process from 1958 (with the Lockheed A-12/YF-12/SR-71) and made the central design factor from 1974 (with the same manufacturer's XST and F-117A). When President Carter cancelled the B-1A in June 1977 he was aware that the USAF was already convinced that, because of LO technology, neither the B-1A nor any upgraded version of it (such as the B-1B) could with any certainty be regarded as a definitive strategic bomber. In 1977 work was already in hand to study to what extent a totally new ATB (Advanced Technology Bomber) might be able to incorporate the maximum amount of LO technology and thus be far more difficult to detect than any previous bomber. The work was no 'ivory tower' long-term research programme; even before the election of President Reagan the Air Force was urgently studying how the new knowledge could most rapidly be used to underpin a new ATB to succeed the B-1. The entire programme was Black, ie not mentioned in Air Force funds and hidden from Congress, except for a handful of special committee members.

The ATB programme was launched in 1978. Its existence was 'leaked' by the magazine *Aviation Week & Space Technology* on 11 August 1980, and confirmed by Defense Secretary Harold S Brown 11 days later. Nothing more was said, however, and the ATB was officially described in 1988 as the most closely guarded secret since the Manhattan Project to develop the atomic bomb. No announcement was made when the newly elected Reagan Administration gave the full go-ahead in June 1981, selecting a Northrop/Boeing proposal over a rival one from Lockheed/Rockwell, nor when in November 1981 the contract for FSD (full-scale development) was signed. This contract included one prototype, and named Northrop as prime contractor, assisted by Boeing, LTV and General Electric. The Reagan Administration did, however, state that to build 110 ATBs would cost about $30 billion in FY81 (Fiscal Year 1981) dollars, and that the aircraft was of 'flying wing' type.

In June 1986 Defense Secretary Caspar Weinberger announced that the USAF had stated a requirement for a force of 132 ATBs, and that these would cost an estimated 36.6 billion, again in FY81 dollars. On 19 November 1987 the first production contract was awarded, priced at approximately $2bn. The ATB was (as expected) redesignated the B-2, and in May 1988 Northrop's Advanced Systems Division, at Pico Rivera, Los Angeles, renamed as the B-2 Division. A month earlier, in April 1988, the DoD had released an artist's impression of a B-2 in flight, and – in contrast to the disinformation practised with some other programmes – this proved to be accurate, with just a few areas such as the sensitive engine nozzles 'fudged'. Much later it was disclosed that Northrop at that time had contracts for 13 airframes, six for flight test, two for structural testing and five for the SAC inventory.

The USAF took the view that, in contrast to what happened with the SR-71, A-12 and F-117A, it was not practical to confine B-2 flight testing to a remote area at night, and so – long before it was ready for flight, incidentally – the first prototype was publicly rolled out from Northrop's engine test hangar at Air Force Plant 42 at Palmdale on 22 November 1988. It was a serious rather than 'ballyhoo' occasion, and the limited number of guests were permitted only a nearly head-on view of the new bomber. Predictably, the magazine which had first leaked

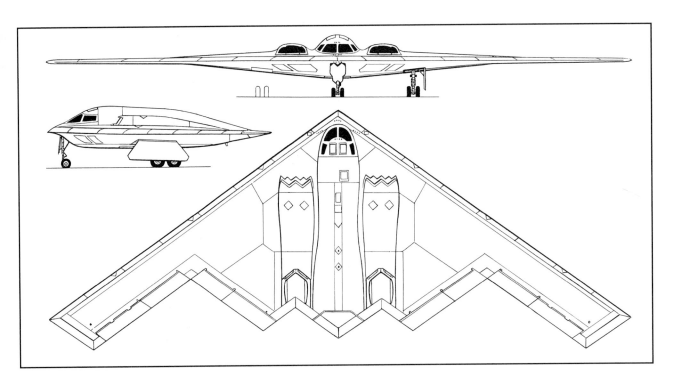

the project in 1980 hired a Cessna and took perfect photographs from all angles including directly overhead.

USAF serial 82-1066 was like nothing seen before, though many observers noticed that by chance it had exactly the same span as Northrop's YB-49 all-wing bomber of 40 years previously. Whereas the YB-49 had looked merely futuristic, the B-2 looked menacing and unearthly, like something from another planet. It also belied its size, appearing much smaller. It was also obvious that it had been designed along principles which were completely different from those which governed the design of the first 'stealth' warplane, the Lockheed F-117A 'Nighthawk'. That aircraft had been designed with an external surface made up almost entirely of flat surfaces all meeting at carefully chosen angles. Instead the B-2 showed an exterior of amazing smoothness, made up entirely of curved surfaces. Moreover, whereas the F-117A relied heavily on RAM (radar-absorbent material) coatings, to the extent that one radar expert rather inaccurately commented 'It's like a lead sled, with a half-inch coating of the stuff all over', the B-2 was designed to have such an amazingly small RCS (radar cross-section) to start with that RAM is limited in general to the thin finish coat of dull blue-grey 'paint'.

Of course, LO technology aims at making an aircraft difficult to see, hear or detect from its IR (heat) emission from its engines. All these factors are important, but RCS (radar cross-section) dominates the design because, whereas an oncoming aircraft might be seen or heard up to five miles away (usually much less), it could be detected by radar

200 miles away. Simple arithmetic shows that, in the opinion of many impartial experts in the US government an aeroplane that can get close to its target before being detected is worth every cent of $530 million, which was the predicted price including R&D (research and development) in FY89 dollars. Of course, as is the case with every weapon in a free society, there are plenty of opponents to the programme, and later it will be emphasised that not even the Air Force actually expects that 132 B-2s will be funded.

This is a bomber in which LO technology has driven every facet of the design. Of course, it has to be able to use ordinary USAF airfields, and fly reasonably far and fast, but such considerations as wing sweep, aerofoil profile and propulsion parameters have had almost nothing to do with striving for the last decimal point of Mach number or the last thousand feet of altitude. Having said that, the B-2's flight performance compares favourably with that of other jet bombers (see data). Indeed, there are many who consider the B-2 the final vindication of Jack Northrop's conviction that the all-wing aeroplane cannot be beaten for efficiency, even though in this case the configuration was adopted for totally different reasons.

The wing is unlike anything seen before, in both plan and aerofoil profile. The leading edges, swept at 35°, are absolutely straight and (uniquely) sharp. The profile of the upper surface is conventional, forming a cambered lifting surface, but (amazingly) the undersurface begins with a concave form before curving back in a more normal convex underside. Again, the wing is unusual in consisting of distinct inner and outer sections. The outer section is

conventional, with constant chord and almost constant thickness out to a point where the trailing edge is swept forward at 35° to give a symmetric pointed tip. Inboard, the trailing edge is again swept forward at 35°, and as thickness/chord ratio increases slightly from this point in to the centreline it follows that the depth of the wing increases enormously. Seen from the front, the upper surface slopes slightly up from tip to root, while the lower surface slopes very sharply down, so that when the aircraft is parked the pregnant belly is barely a tall man's height from the ground. Along the upper centreline is a large rounded bulge which takes the place of a fuselage. The YB-49 had no such bulge, and its presence in the B-2 is not because the crew or rotary launchers required it but because it helps to give the best overall shape. The bulge lies closely between the two almost equally wide but flatter bulges caused by the engines and their inlets.

Obviously, propulsion is one of the greatest challenges facing the designer of an LO aircraft. Nobody is particularly bothered about noise or even visible smoke, and early flight testing of the B-2 showed that the aircraft puts out its fair quota of both commodities. Smoke emission is being reduced close to zero, and in high-altitude flight it does become important to eliminate obtrusive contrails which would render the whole LO concept pointless. The USAF has commented that use of particular fuel additives, such as chlorofluorosulphonic acid, can almost eliminate contrail formation at visible wavelengths. The jet trails would still be visible to infra-red or on ultra-violet wavelengths, and in any case not a great deal can be done if the enormous output of water from the engines turns to crystals of ice, as almost always happens at high altitude.

Where propulsion is concerned the effort has been directed against signature at radar and IR wavelengths. The four engines are turbofans derived from the F101 which powers the B-1B and the F110 used in fighters. Of course, instead of an afterburner, the efflux is discharged direct to atmosphere in a way which, without losing significant thrust, reduces the temperature of both the jet and the nozzle and surrounding structure as much and as rapidly as possibe. For a start, the required thrust must be generated at minimal TET (turbine entry temperature), and this means making the mass flow (weight of air passing through the engine per second) and pressure ratio as high as possible. A slim fighter engine such as the F110 is poor in this respect. An airline-type turbofan, with a bypass ratio of eight or more, is very good, but the resulting fan – perhaps 8 ft in diameter – would not fit inside the B-2 and would present an enormous target to hostile radars. The best compromise was to hold the overall diameter close to that of the F110, in order to make the engine fit inside the B-2 wing, and use modern fan technology, with wide-chord blades, in order to achieve the highest possible airflow and fan pressure ratio.

The F101 has a mass flow of 350 lb/sec and fan pressure ratio of about 2, with a diameter of 55 in. The F110 fighter engine has an extra fan stage, but

ABOVE *The strange monster emerges to blink at a dark world from brightly lit Building 42 at Palmdale*

a much smaller diameter of 46.5 in, so while pressure ratio went up to over three, the airflow fell to 270 lb/sec. In dry thrust the F110 gives a maximum of 17,000 lb. In contrast the B-2 engine, the F118, gets something like the airflow of the F101 through the diameter of the F110, and with appreciably greater pressure ratio than either of the earlier engines. This means that it is in the 19,000 lb thrust class, without any augmentation, and with a substantial reduction in maximum gas temperature. Thus, the jet issuing downstream of the turbine is already relatively cool, and it is very rapidly cooled further by emerging as a flat sheet which is expanded across the prominent black structure downstream. It has been surmised that these are RCC (reinforced carbon/carbon) structures, but the modest temperatures involved do not call for RCC and the black colour may have another explanation. For example, in contrast to the dull blue-grey elsewhere, the entire leading edge and all fixed portions of trailing edge are of shiny black material, with a width (measured perpendicular to the edge of the wing) of about 3 ft. Similar RAM coating is seen covering the entire structure below and around the sides of the engine nozzles.

Clearly a large cooling airflow surrounds the jets and keeps these black structures quite cool. This air is taken in through the main inlets, and through the boundary-layer inlets immediately below. The entire inlet is above the wing, square-on to the airflow. The sharp lips, however, are of zig-zag form, the side of the inlet curving up from the wing while leaning slightly back and then sharply sweeping back at 40° to form a V-shape. Thus, there is a forward-pointing V at the mid-point of the twin-engine inlet, but the splitter to separate the flows is downstream, almost unseen externally. The lower lip, 3 in or 4 in above the wing surface to swallow

the boundary layer (which in cruising flight would be laminar anyway), has an extra V on each side, giving a total of three triangular apices pointing forward, again at 40°. The main and lower ducts all curve down to meet the engines, which are mounted horizontally inside the wing. A straight line drawn horizontally through the bottom of the inlet just misses the top of the engine, which is a basic objective of LO design. At high power at low speeds (certainly up to 200 kt) additional air is taken in through a large square auxiliary inlet in the top of the duct just in front of each engine. These auxiliary inlets are covered by powered doors which open on diagonal axes. Just outboard of the left engine group is a triangular door in the upper surface of the wing which opens to serve the Garrett APU (auxiliary power unit).

Outboard of the engines almost the entire structure forms a series of integral fuel tanks. Their outlines can be seen clearly in the upper skin. Additional fuel is carried ahead of the inlet ducts and in two tanks aft of the weapon bay between the jet nozzles. Total capacity is about 170,000 lb (77 tonnes, 96,250 litres, 21,200 Imp gal). This is much less than that of the B-1B, but because of the all-wing bomber's greater aerodynamic efficiency it flies further (see data). A flight-refuelling receptacle can be opened in the normally smooth top of the 'fuselage'. The high unit cost of the B-2 was a major factor in prompting the USAF to at least attempt to convert from the widely used JP4 fuel, which has always presented a fire hazard, to JP8 fuel. JP8 is a new specification for a kerosene-based distillate very similar to JP1 and 2 of over 40 years ago.

Flight control of the B-2 is a modernised version of that used over 40 years ago on the YB-49. While the sharp leading edge is fixed, and incorporates no fixed slots either, the entire zig-zag trailing edge is hinged and power-driven under multi-redundant control. The two inboard surfaces on each side, hinged to the forward-swept trailing edge of the inner wing, are elevons used in slow-speed flight, combining the functions of elevators, ailerons and flaps. Immediately outboard, hinged to the inboard half of each outer wing, are elevons used in normal flight, serving as elevators and ailerons. The outer-most surfaces are split into upper and lower halves, and are called 'drag rudders' (on the YB-49 they were called decelerons). Surprisingly, they are slightly open at most times, even during take-off. In normal flight the lower half of each drag rudder can be depressed to 90°, while the upper half is opened to the extent needed to execute each manoeuvre. On the landing approach the drag rudders are set at +45°/−45°.

The almost triangular surface forming the centre of the trailing edge (ie, the tail end of the fuselage) is driven automatically as a gust-alleviation surface. It has been reported that it is driven in partnership with at least some of the elevons. If this is true it undoubtedly involves the outer elevons, which have maximum effectiveness in cancelling out wing bending. A surface on the centreline has little effect on wing bending, but a big effect on fuselage ride quality. This 'beaver tail' is the B-2's equivalent to the SMCS foreplanes of the B-1B, but it is a generation later in concept. An industry official is quoted as saying 'The device is of a unique design, and you would not intuitively understand how it works just by looking at it'.

All movable surfaces are controlled by integrated flight-control and stability-augmentation systems, which use many computers all linked to the central 1553B digital data buses. Surface commands are transmitted along quadruple FBW (fly by wire) and optical-fibre links giving unprecedented redundancy. In general terms the B-2 is the most computer-controlled aircraft in history (and, as

described later, its design and manufacture are also computerised to a previously unknown degree). All data buses and FBW links are hardened against EMP (electromagnetic pulse) from nuclear explosions. In the manual mode the pilots can fly the aircraft using fighter-type sticks. The air-data system, which among other things feeds the flight instruments, does not use pressure or static heads, as on the F-117A, nor external vanes for angle of attack or yaw. Instead it uses computers to process the pressures sensed at various points in the aircraft, including 28 flush 'invisible' sensors arranged in seven groups of four around the nose. Their ice protection may be by intermittent hot air.

The landing gear is conventional, and in at least the first two prototypes is based on existing products for Boeing commercial transports (nose gear by Menasco for the 757, main gears by CPT for the 767). The nose gear is modified to retract to the rear, the upper part of the leg carrying a RAM-coated door with zig-zag edges. A larger door hinged to the fuselage covers the rest of the unit. The main gears are also modified, in this case to retract forwards. Thus, they occupy a long but narrow bay which is covered in flight by a single enormous door hinged inwards from just outboard of the leg, and thus open on the ground. The original 767 gears retracted inwards, but in the B-2 the engines immediately alongside make this impossible. Approach speed is a modest 140 kt, and no hook, braking parachute or reversers are installed.

Structurally the B-2 has been described as multiple-spar, but in fact almost all the strength resides in the two principal spars, with the weapons bay between them. The all-wing configuration distributes the loads and stresses from tip to tip, resulting in spar-bending moments much less than

BELOW *Another view of 82-1066 near Edwards*

ABOVE *Perhaps the strangest sight in the sky, the No 1 B-2A tucked in behind a test KC-10. Here the trailing yaw line is clearly visible*

those of conventional aircraft such as the B-1B. The fast-acting active control system, and gust-alleviation system, combine to reduce stresses still further. Nevertheless, at the start of ATB design it was shortsightedly thought that, with so small a radar cross-section, this bomber could fly all its missions at high altitude. When in 1983 it was at last recognised that this belief was nonsensical, the B-2 did require structural modification in order to withstand possibly violent manoeuvres in dense air during flight at full power in the terrain-following or terrain-avoidance modes. A much more difficult task was to redesign the most crucial of all parts from the radar cross-section viewpoint, the leading edge, to withstand severe low-altitude birdstrikes. This resulted in unavoidable but modest slippage to the programme.

Birdstrikes, solar glint and both radar and IR reflectivity posed problems in the design of the cockpit windows. Remarkably, the two forward windows are among the largest and heaviest ever produced for an aircraft, giving an all-round view better than in almost any commercial transport. Drag, reflectivity and birdstrike problems are to some degree eased by the very sharp slope of the giant forward panels, which begin only just behind the sharp horizontal prow of the aircraft. Of course, the capacious cockpit is pressurised and air-conditioned, and in summer the ECS (environmental control system), located ahead of the right main landing gear, will be kept running on the ground to keep the avionics cool. This is important, partly because the avionics are so widespread and expensive (and vital) and partly because there are no

windows that can be opened. Even the entrance door, immediately aft of the nose-gear bay, is normally closed. When opened it reveals a telescopic ladder which is pulled down for boarding. The crew of two climb vertically up between the main avionics racks and walk forward to their ACES II seats. Most unusually, the aircraft commander (or instructor) sits on the right, and the pilot on the left. In a combat mission the left-seater does the flying and the right-seater manages the mission – for example, the electronics, the weapons and the navigation – and gives the orders. It has long been surmised that the work-load of a 10-hour mission against strong defences would preferably be handled by a crew of three. There is no customer requirement for a third man, but Northrop has left room for a third seat and provided a third jettisonable hatch in the roof, aft of the commander.

As noted, both pilots have sticks, and each has a left-hand set of engine controls and trimmers. All flight information is displayed on eight 8 in × 8 in colour tubes. Normally three of those in front of the commander would illustrate navigation and target information, hostile threats and weapon status, but quick menu buttons can enable either crew member to fly the mission unaided. To ease workload a unique three-position switch acts as a master, controlling several hundred items simultaneously. When set to TAKE-OFF it puts every system and equipment item into the correct mode, transfers the mission data tape, carries out the checklist and prepares propulsion and flight control for normal flight. Switched to GO TO WAR it mutes every onboard emitter, puts the flight controls in the stealthy mode, readies all weapons, and performs many other tasks. The third position is LAND, which reactivates emitters and other systems, restores flight controls to normal, and performs the appropriate checklists.

Navigation is of course inertial, backed up by Navstar GPS satellite receivers. Other equipment includes Tacan and ILS. Little has been disclosed regarding mission equipment beyond the fact that Hughes is prime contractor for the APQ-118 main radar. This radar is naturally of a very special type, because there is no point in fitting an almost undetectable aircraft with radar that broadcasts like a lighthouse. The APQ-118 is one of the first covert, or LPI (low probability of intercept), radars. One could question why even this radar is thought necessary, because today a bomber with no radar at all, nor any other kind of active emitting system, can navigate at low level with precision and aim free-fall bombs with equal precision. It probably would need a special LPI radar altimeter, used with various passive sensors, in order to follow the undulations of the terrain. These undulations would themselves be an important aid to precise navigation, backing up such passive systems as laser-gyro inertial and satellite-based Navstar.

Be that as it may, the B-2 has two very large

dielectric areas on the underside of what might be called the nose. These areas measure about 12 ft wide × 6 ft high on each side, and as well as following the 35° sweep angle they are inclined down at an average of about 45°. Each probably covers some thousands of modules forming an active array, but specially controlled to hop from one frequency to another, to emit exceedingly brief pulses, and aimed to avoid sensitive target areas. Quite distinct from this large radar, photographs of the first B-2 show flush antennas distributed along the leading edge. On each side of the centreline the shiny black leading edge is divided by structural lines into eight sections. Along these are spaced the antennas, which are of square shape but set at 45° (this could be called a diamond shape). On each side the first is just beyond the first structural join, and is completely in the upper surface. The remainder are evenly spaced, and fall within the third, fourth and sixth leading-edge sections. These outer three antennas are wrapped around the leading edge, to 'look' straight ahead. When the first B-2 prototype was rolled out in 1988 these eight antennas could hardly be detected, because they were the same shiny black as the rest of the leading edge. When the same aircraft made its first flight they appeared a contrasting greyish blue, while photographs taken from the left side on the same occasion make them appear bright orange-red! These spectral changes may indicate a surface structure made up of exceedingly fine wires or grooves, giving a diffraction effect. To confuse things even further, a photograph of three production B-2s in the Palmdale assembly building show seemingly complete

airframes finished in white all over, with no trace of leading-edge antennas.

Different parts of the structure are made of aluminium alloy, titanium alloy, steel and other metals, including honeycomb-stabilised sandwiches. By far the greater part, however, is of composite material, mainly graphite (carbon) fibre bonded with epoxy resin adhesives. Extreme care has been taken to seal gaps, to make every access door or other skin aperture seal perfectly, and as far as possible to give an exterior perfect for dimensional accuracy and smoothness. The B-2 Division at Pico Rivera is believed to be the world's greatest concentration of computer power and graphics displays, with over 400 terminals in 30 display rooms. This, for the first time, has made it possible to put the entire design on a fantastic three-dimensional database. This database contains many billions of items which define every part and shape, and will remain in use not only in design and manufacture but also for engineering support throughout the B-2's service career. It almost eliminated the need for mock-ups, avoided countless problems by providing a perfect interface with subcontractors and suppliers, and not least was instrumental in achieving the unprecedented dimensional tolerances. It enabled the prototype to be made on schedule in production tooling, with maximum tolerance over the whole 172 ft span of

BELOW *November 1990 photo showing the pilots' cockpit of the No 1 aircraft. Aircraft for the USAF inventory have four video displays per pilot, not three*

6.3 mm (less than $\frac{1}{4}$ in). In most sensitive areas skin dimension is within 1 mm. The computer base determined the optimum locations and arrangement of every part, and incidentally showed that instead of 3000 lb/sq in the hydraulic system should operate at 4000.

Despite the development of the Convair AGM-129 ACM (Advanced Cruise Missile) and Boeing AGM-131A SRAM II (advanced Short-Range Attack Missile), both of which are LO stealth weapons, no attempt has been made to fit the B-2 with external stores pylons. So perfect is the entire concept that everything is carried internally, and in practice it is thought almost impossible that this should ever prove a handicap. The spacing between the two principal wing spars of the B-2 was matched exactly to the length of weapon bay needed by the Boeing AARL (Advanced Applications Rotary Launcher). There are two such bays, one on each side of the centreline in the pregnant-looking belly. Each launcher can be loaded with eight ACMs or SRAM IIs. Other weapons include B61 or B83 free-fall NWs, up to 80 Mk 82 GP bombs of 500 lb size, or such other free-fall weapons as M117 750-lb fire bombs or Mk 36 1000 lb sea mines.

Of course, no provision is made for defensive armament. As for internal EW (electronic warfare) systems, such as offensive and defensive avionics, the whole point of the B-2 is that, if the enemy does not know you are there, such things are not needed. At the rollout of the prototype B-2 an unnamed 'senior Air Force official' was quoted by *Aviation Week* as saying 'The ALQ-161 electronic counter-measures system used on the B-1B is a non-existent issue as far as the B-2 is concerned. By focusing on reducing the aircraft observability problems you accomplish the same objective even better than you could with electronics'. This does not mean, however, that no EW or defensive equipment is carried.

The most convincing (unofficial) cutaway of the B-2 to be published, in *World Airpower Journal*, shows rear radar and ECM equipment bays on each side immediately ahead of the beaver tail. In February 1990 the outgoing USAF Chief of Staff, Gen Larry D Welch, commented that, while a sophisticated enemy would be aware of an impending strategic attack by B-2s, he 'could not track the bombers with enough accuracy to stop them'. And incoming Air Force Secretary Donald B Rice said that the new bomber's stealth qualities did not rely on any single characteristic or system, and that an enemy 'would require more than the occasional blip they would get on their radars' to find a B-2.

The first B-2 prototype, 82-1066, took rather longer than expected over its ground testing but finally made a 2 hr 20 min first flight on 17 July 1989. It was flown from Palmdale to Edwards by Northrop Chief Test Pilot Bruce J Hinds and the director of the USAF Combined Test Force Col Richard S Cough. Based at Edwards, the Flight

Validation programme was completed as planned in eight flights, totalling 31 hr 25 min, by 22 November 1989, including a refuelling from a KC-10A. Block 1 testing, covering aerodynamic performance and airworthiness, was completed on 13 June 1990 in 16 flights totalling 67 hours, 8 hours less than planned. After a layup for preparation, Block 2, the crucial testing of LO (low observables) began with Flight 17 on 23 October 1990. Aircraft #2 (82-1067) flew on 19 October 1990. Tasked with loads test and envelope expansion, this has a non-standard LO configuration and is planned to be the only B-2 not to join the USAF, being assigned to permanent testing. Aircraft #3 (1068) has full mission avionics, including APQ-181 radar; #4 (1069) is handling avionics, LO and weapons testing, #5 (1070) is conducting weapons trials and #6 (1071) is assigned to operational testing. All six trials aircraft were delivered by 1993 to the 6520th Test Squadron at Edwards.

The trials aircraft are B-2A Block 10. Except for No 2, all will be modified to the production standard, B-2A Block 30. The original USAF goal was 133 aircraft, the 132 for the inventory being sufficient for a force of four Wings. By 1991 the more realistic target of 75 had been accepted for two wings, the first being the 509th BW. Previously a Minuteman II missile wing, this was activated in 1989 at Whiteman AFB, 45 miles from Kansas City. By 1992 the above-ground area of Whiteman had been transformed, notably by the building of 34 hangars, one for each B-2A. These are not hardened, but are carefully air-conditioned to protect the aircraft external surface and avionics. In parallel, Oklahoma Air Logistics Center was prepared as the primary depot facility, backed up by Hill, San Antonio and Warner-Robins.

There has been speculation that this aircraft was 'the straw that broke the camel's back' in forcing the Soviet Union to abandon competition in strategic weapons, thus bringing about the policies of *Glasnost* and *Perestroika*. There is no doubt that the collapse of confrontation between the superpowers has led to a new perspective on defence in the United States. In January 1990 Defense Secretary Richard B Cheney ordered 'a reassessment' of the B-2. In October 1991 Congress froze the whole programme. At that time funding had been voted for the six for development (five for inventory) in 1982, plus three in 1988, three in 1989, two in 1990 and two in 1991. In 1992 the Air Force lowered its sights to a minimum force of 20 aircraft, and it will achieve this with one funded in FY (Fiscal Year) 1992 and four in FY93. The last four probably would not have been voted had the defence budget not been before Congress immediately before the election of Congress as well as the President.

Following the $2 billion voted on 19 November 1987 to start production, the 75-aircraft programme was estimated (in then-year dollars) to cost $64.7 billion. In 1992 the cost of a 20-aircraft

ABOVE *Rare view of two B-2As following the test tanker in 1992*

programme was put at $44.4 billion (not much more than the $41.8 billion for 15), or a total programme cost of $2,220 million per aircraft. Bare flyaway price per aircraft is less than half this at $1020 million.

Predictably, numerous opposition groups have switched their attacks from the B-1B and Trident to the B-2. All kinds of media pundits have gone to remarkable lengths to proclaim that LO will not work, or that it has been proved that it does not work. So far there is no known evidence for these claims, and the fact that no F-117A was once 'painted' by Iraqi radar in 1271 deep-penetration sorties (7000 hours) suggests that even this more primitive LO *does* work. Other criticisms have been that the B-2A will have to reveal its presence while looking for moving targets, or else rely completely upon target data provided by satellites such as KH-12 and Indigo Lacrosse. Of course, target information is essential. While missiles can take out all fixed targets, such as airfields, they are useless against relocatable or mobile targets, and the B-2A is seen as the only weapon able to attack such targets in heavily defended airspace. It is for this reason that the advertised LPI (low probability of intercept) quality of APQ-181 is crucial.

For the moment, the test programme has, on the whole, gone well. Far from being a sluggish or tricky aircraft, Col Cough describes the B-2A as 'a very nimble aircraft . . . a lot of fun to fly'. According to Gulf Coalition Commander Lt-Gen Charles Horner, 'Two B-2s, without escorts or tankers, could have performed the same mission as a package of 32 strike aircraft, 16 fighters, 12 air-defence suppression aircraft and 15 tankers'. Conversely, the cost of these aircraft is widely held to be unaffordable. Senator Warren Rudman – by no means as anti-bomber campaigner – says 'It's time to start looking at a 2½-leg Triad: one leg ICBMs, one leg SLBMs and half a leg the B-1B with cruise missiles'.

SPECIFICATION

B-2A
Four General Electric F118-100 turbofans 'in the 19,000 lb class'
Dimensions Span 172 ft 0 in (52.43 m); length 69 ft 0 in (21.03 m); wing area (lower surface) just over 5000 sq ft (464.5 m²)
Weight Operating 175,000 lb (79,380 kg); maximum fuel 170,000 lb (77,000 kg); normal loaded, originally to be 358,000 lb (162,386 kg), increased 1992 to 371,330 lb (168,433 kg); max take-off 400,000 lb (181,437 kg)
Performance Maximum speed (S/L) 495 kt (570 mph, 917 km/h); service ceiling, c.50,000 ft (15,240 m); unrefuelled range (37,300 lb weapons, eight SRAM II and eight B83, hi-hi-hi) 6300 nm (7255 miles, 11,675 km); hi-lo 1000 nm, 1152 miles, 1853 km-hi, 4400 nm (5067 miles, 8154 km); (24,000 lb, eight SRAM II and eight B61 at weight reduced to 358,000 lb, hi-hi-hi) 6600 nm (7600 miles, 12,231 km), (hi-lo [as before]-hi) 4500 nm (5182 miles, 8339 km); range with one refuelling over 10,000 nm (11,515 miles, 18,532 km)
Armament Up to 50,000 lb (22,680 kg) of weapons as detailed earlier; normal loads 24,000 or 37,300 lb. To be equipped for precision-guided weapons, 16 at 2000 lb or 76 at 500 lb

General Dynamics/McDonnell Douglas A-12A Avenger

Never Flown

In contrast to the Lockheed F-117A and Northrop B-2, this 'stealth' aircraft was developed with virtually no publicity at all. Indeed, in early 1991 almost the only information released comprised a list of subcontractors and a flood of news concerning the troubled management of the programme. Sadly, a dissatisfied Defense Secretary cancelled it in consequence. It is included here because of its great technical interest.

It will be noted that the A-12A repeated the name of one of the most famous US Navy attack aircraft, a product of Grumman. In 1987 that company could look forward to many more years of work as a principal – perhaps *the* principal – supplier of carrier-based aircraft to the US Navy. For fighters the F-14D seemed likely to remain in production to the year 2000, while for attack aircraft the A-6F Intruder II was the obvious choice. A mere two years later, in 1989, both programmes had been cancelled. For a fighter the Navy expected to buy a derivative of the YF-22 or YF-23, in neither of which Grumman has a share. As for attack, the Navy organised a competition for a totally new ATA (Advanced Tactical Aircraft). This was a programme Grumman simply had to win. Instead, on 23 December 1987 the Navy announced it had selected the ATA submission made jointly by General Dynamics and McDonnell Douglas, again with no Grumman participation. Salt was rubbed in the wound when it was announced that the A-12A would be named Avenger II (later the II was dropped). Moreover, President Bush flew the *Grumman* Avenger.

As the last of the three known LO (low observable) 'stealth' aircraft to be designed, the A-12A was in some respects the most advanced. It clearly drew very heavily upon the technology of the B-2 bomber, and had almost exactly the same form of wing aerofoil profile. In plan, however, the Navy aircraft was different, in that it was a perfect delta (triangle). It had to comply with previously existing requirements for carrier-based aircraft, namely that it was stressed for nose-tow accelerated launch by steam catapult and for wire-arrested landing, and had folded dimensions compatible with elevators and carrier hangars.

Before assembling the fullest description of the Avenger possible in 1991, it is desirable briefly to review the programme. The ATA began not later than 1985 as a 'Black' programme, launched by Navy Secretary John Lehmann. He concurred with many admirals and civilian staff who were convinced of two things: that the A-6 or any upgraded version of it was obsolescent, and that its replacement should be a 'clean sheet of paper' design based totally on stealth principles. At that time, and today, the total Navy force of A-6 Intruder aircraft in carrier air wings numbered about 350. From the start the Navy thought in terms of a total buy of 450 ATAs, which it hoped would cost not more than $45 billion including R&D. The Marine Corps surprisingly chose not to be involved.

Without any announcement an industry competition was mounted, which finally resulted in two finalist proposals, one by a team of Northrop, Grumman and LTV, and the other by GD and McDonnell Douglas. So far as is known, there was no engine competition. The finalists set up the PPO (Principal Program Office) at GD's Fort Worth Division, the McDonnell Douglas project design work being centred at St Louis. The Department of Defense awarded a preliminary development contract valued at $241m, pending a further review in January 1988. Following this review a fixed-price incentive contract valued at $4.379 billion ($4379m) was allocated to complete the R&D. This sum, modest by comparison with some other contemporary programmes, included the prototypes and static-test airframes. The designation was announced as A-12, the same as that of the first Lockheed 'Blackbirds' of 1962. There was no A-11.

When this programme was revealed to Congress, at the time of the initial contract award, Congress began to apply pressure to the USAF to buy a land-based A-12 as its next major attack aircraft, replacing the FB-111A. Many observers commented that the Air Force would rather design its own aircraft, but in November 1988 the A-12A prime contractors were awarded a $7.9m contract for an 11-month study of a USAF version. Three months later, at the start of 1990, the Assistant Chief of Naval Operations, Vice-Adm Richard M Dunleavy, said that the Navy planned 'better than one-for-one replacement' of the A-6 by the A-12A. He said the Navy had 'never bought the number of A-6s it needed'. At that time unofficial estimates for the A-12A ranged up to $96.2m per copy. A few days later it appeared that the highest guess was accurate, the Navy announcing that its initial procurement plans through FY94 (Fiscal Year 1994) involved 106 A-12A aircraft at a cost of $10.2 billion. The total procurement was set at the remarkably high figure of 858, expected to take up to the year 2005.

In early 1990 a list of principal subcontractors was released. It was exceedingly informative, and revealed a tremendous amount about the Avenger. The list consisted of AiResearch, Ball Aerospace and Loral Randtron Systems (door mechanical drive group), Bendix (main landing gear, wheels and carbon brakes), Garrett (air-data computer), Garrett Auxiliary Power Division (airframe-mounted accessory-drive gearbox system), General Electric Aircraft Electronics Division (missile warning system), Harris (multi-function antenna system), Honeywell (digital flight-control system), Honeywell/Litton (integrated inertial sensor assembly), Litton (inertial navigation and ESM [electronic surveillance measures] systems), Martin Marietta (navigational FLIR [forward-looking infrared]), Parker Bertea Aerospace (inflight-refuelling probe), Swedlow subsidiary of Pilkington (cockpit transparencies), SCI Technology (amplifier control intercommunications), Sundstrand Turbomach (APU [auxiliary power unit]), Teledyne Ryan Electronics (radar altimeter), and Westinghouse (multi-function radar and combined function FLIR).

In mid-1990 a blurred near-head-on illustration of the Avenger was released, followed by two much more informative views (seemingly pictures of a model) at the end of that year. These enabled at least a preliminary description of the aircraft to be attempted.

The A-12A Avenger was a subsonic twin-jet carrier-based aircraft designed for attack at night or in bad weather. It was to replace the A-6E Intruder, and was roughly in the same category as regards weight, flight performance and mission load. It had rather more engine power, very much better fuel economy and about one-hundredth of the radar cross-section. Because of its shape the dimensions were not quite the same (see estimated data), the wing area being much greater and the length less. Overall, the two aircraft were in a similar size class.

Aerodynamically, the perfection of the delta layout was uncanny. It showed an amazing ability to reconcile the needs of LO stealth technology with the practical needs of good handling in the most arduous bad-weather carrier operations, not even excepting the need to perform sharp agile manoeuvres while in hostile territory. In all LO aircraft the sweep angle of the wing leading edge is crucial. By May 1991 the only released illustrations had been carefully selected to make it difficult to determine this value (the same was done with the F-117A). Wildly differing guesses have been published, and the figures that follow are simply those

calculated by the author. They work out to a leading-edge angle of 50°, and this is not unreasonable. It is virtually certain that the leading edges of all doors were designed with a zigzag plan shape with the edges parallel to the same angles.

Like the B-2, the upper surface was cambered like a conventional wing, and the line from tip to tip could be drawn with a ruler. In contrast, the undersurface had marked dihedral, so that depth increased unnaturally rapidly all the way from the tip to the swollen belly. Thus, at the expense of a less than optimum aerofoil profile over the inboard sections, the wing could accommodate everything in the aircraft, with the exception of the head and shoulders of the pilot and navigator. These men were to sit in tandem Martin-Baker Mk 14 NACES seats, firing upwards. The natural curve of the wing put the backseater at a higher level. Swedlow were credited with 'transparencies' [plural], but the available pictures made it look as if there was one giant canopy incorporating the windscreen. The entire unit had to be proof against birdstrikes at maximum speed at low level. Such aircraft as the F-16 use flexible polycarbonate, but the Avenger had the problem of eliminating solar glint and radar reflectivity, whilst at the same time appearing to be the same temperature as the sky or sea background. Normal crew entry and egress was through the canopy, which appeared to be surrounded by a wide opaque border and could in some way hinge upwards. A photograph of a mockup cockpit naturally showed electronic displays: three plus a large HUD in the front and four in the back. More surprisingly, this mockup appeared to have dual flight controls.

Virtually the entire structure of the Avenger was of composite material, the ruling choice being graphite (carbon)/epoxy. The available illustrations suggested that the exterior was entirely pale grey on top, and a darker colour underneath, which is what one would expect. As in the B-2, everthing possible was done to seal joints or gaps, and finally to add a (probably thin) layer of RAM (radar-absorbent material). Several chordwise lines crossed the wing, one pair suggesting that the outer wings folded to give a width of about 28 ft. A simple upward fold would result in an overall height of about 17 ft, which was acceptable; or the outer wings could fold through almost 180° to lie on the inner wings, though this might cause RAM skin damage problems. The digital flight controls obviously had quadruple electrical or optical signalling, and appeared to do everything with surfaces on or above the trailing edge. The illustrations showed a rectangular surface at the centre of the wing, which could only be used for control and trim in the longitudinal plane (and possibly for gust alleviation and ride control). Further out was a gap, where the engines were (and propulsion is something that by early 1991 had been kept under wraps). Then came four large rectangular surfaces on each side, two in the

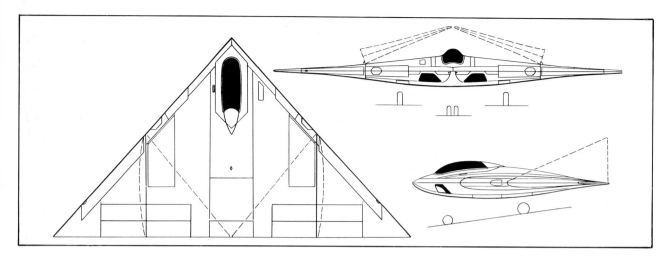

ABOVE *Unofficial three-view, drawn from released model photos and artwork*

inboard wing and two in the folding outer panel. Each pair were perfect rectangles, and arranged in tandem. Thus, each pair could comprise a flap or aileron with a same-size spoiler upstream. In the leading edge of the outer wing was what looked like a giant slat or leading-edge flap, but this outline may have had another explanation.

When this was written, little A-12A quantitative data (apart from costs) had been disclosed. Nevertheless, it was obvious from the shape of the aircraft that its wing area was much greater than that of the A-6E, or FB-111A. The A-6 wing has an area of 529 sq ft, and the wing loading at maximum weight is just over 114 lb/sq ft. The SAC version of the F-111 had an area of 550 sq ft, and at maximum weight the wing was loaded to no less than 207 lb/sq ft. In contrast, the Avenger would have had about twice as much wing, and the loading was only 61 lb/sq ft (see data). This would have been splendid from the viewpoints of inflight agility and slow carrier landings, but it is just what you do not need when making attacks at full throttle at sea level. The higher the wing loading, the smoother the ride. Even at 600 mph, which is much slower than a Buccaneer or clean Tornado, a wing loading of less than 60 lb/sq ft could (as the saying goes) 'shake the crew's eyeballs out'. Obviously, advanced sensors of air data, vertical acceleration and some form of active control system were incorporated in order to give an acceptable ride.

Propulsion was to be provided by two F412 engines. These had been developed by General Electric specifically for this aircraft, using most of the core of the widely used F404. It will be recalled that a version of the F404 was used to power the very first stealth warplane, the F-117A. In that case not very much was done to the F404, except convert the engine to a turbojet, remove the afterburner augmentation and provide for jet dilution with large flows of cooling air. The F412 is a more optimised engine. It would have introduced a new hi-temp, high-pressure core, and also have a new fan giving 37 per cent greater mass flow and

higher pressure ratio. Thus it should be able to give a take-off thrust of about 13,000 lb (compared with 11,800 lb for the F-117A engine) at a remarkably low jetpipe temperature. As in the B-2, the leading edge of the inner wing was unusual in that its underside sloped sharply downwards aft of a sharp beak-like lip. The engine inlets were in this bluff sloping section. Each had a roughly rectangular shape, with a sharp lower edge parallel to the leading edge of the wing but much further aft. As this was a smaller aircraft than the B-2 there was less chordwise length in which to do clever things with the inlet duct, and no hint has been given of how the inlet would have fed the engine efficiently whilst screening it from any hostile radar. Likewise, nothing was revealed regarding the engine nozzles, beyond a faint suggestion of flattened ovals in the trailing edge. Clearly the jets must have been heavily diluted with cool air, and in view of the geometry of the installation it would have lent itself well to thrust vectoring and probably thrust reversal.

There is little point in surmising the unknowns, such as the landing gear and systems. One of the subcontracts was of especial interest. Harris have made a special study of the most advanced kinds of multi-function array antennas, in which the antenna is made up from anything from 500 to 5000 small active modules each with a size somewhere between a cucumber and a frankfurter. In the Avenger these were clearly arranged conformally, so that they are flush with the skin (almost certainly, in the leading edge, as described later, and in the 'nose', between the engine inlets). Another point to note is the profusion of passive receivers, such as FLIRs and a missile warning system. These do not imperil a stealth aircraft, because they do not emit. As for the radar altimeter, which is hard to avoid in a low-flying and terrain-following aircraft, it would have fired very brief pulses aimed straight downwards, and so would be very difficult for an enemy to detect.

The Avenger was to carry all its weapons

internally. It has been said that 'both air-to-air and air-to-surface radar modes and weapons are included', the only surprising thing here being that a stealthy attack aircraft tries to avoid air-to-air modes entirely. The task of the structural designers was made more onerous by the demand for AAMs to be carried in separate bays. Indeed, it was the design of the weapon carriage system that was primarily responsible for the collapse of the programme.

A side issue was the requirement for snap-action doors. Most of the Avenger's targets would have been extremely heavily defended, with both anti-air sensors and weapons. Moreover, this aircraft would usually have had to approach much closer to its targets than would usually be the case with a B-2. For example, it could often have found itself in the midst of a hostile surface fleet, and at wave-top height. Even at night or in bad weather this would be perilous, and to 'unmask' by opening a cavernous weapon-bay door would be suicidal. This would still be the case even with a flush bay on the underside. In addition, opening a bay door, on either side of the centreline, would cause an asymmetric yawing moment and seriously degrade inflight stability. This explains why three large companies should all have been named as supplying a 'door mechanical drive'. Such industrial strength was needed because the bay doors were quite new in both geometry and drive system. Even the largest door had to open and close within a fraction (possibly 0.5) of a second. To get large stores to separate cleanly within such a period at 600 mph is no mean challenge. Hence the need for three contractors on the drive, two of them electronics companies. A further problem is that the doors were very highly stressed, yet had to preserve their precise shape so that they could close without the slightest gap around their zigzag edges. Such considerations underscore the fact that no possible development of the A-6, with external weapon carriage, could hope to survive in a future conflict.

Despite its size, and its wish to avoid air combat, the Avenger was designed to a positive load factor of 9g. Because of its advanced quad-redundant flight controls and its low wing loading it should have been one of the most agile aircraft ever built. The released artwork showed what appeared to be extremely large circular dielectric areas wrapped round the leading edge at mid-span, and these could have been the locations of the Harris multi-function arrays. Far more than any previous aircraft the Avenger used integrated avionics, several subsystems being linked by computer and multiplex distribution to particular LO skin antennas. Two more of these regions were wrapped round the leading edge nearer the tips, having the form of black squares at the outer ends of what appeared to be slats or leading-edge flaps. They could have been the receivers for the GE passive missile warning system. The artwork gave no hint of how the

retractable inflight-refuelling probe was installed.

The programme prime contractors chose to site the final-assembly facility at the former Douglas plant at Tulsa. In spring 1990 the Secretary of Defense, Dick Cheney, announced a major Pentagon review, following which large teams of Navy and DoD evaluators descended on Tulsa and saw the prototypes in final assembly in May 1990. The first was expected to be rolled out in September 1990, and to fly before the end of the calendar year, with all eight prototypes due to be completed by 30 June 1991. The major review cut back production from the planned 858 to 620, to be priced at $51.96 billion, the US Navy carrier force being reduced from 15 wings to 12. But trouble of a serious nature was surfacing, and on 11 June 1990 Cheney summoned the chairmen of the two prime contractors to explain why these problems had escaped the review. He was said to have been 'furious', and to have emphasised the urgent need of both services for the Avenger. The explanation of the problems, which put back the first flight to 'later in 1991' was blandly given as 'complexity, and delay in the tooling required'. This was a childish comment, as was the later explanation that the contractors were finding 'difficulty in making the structure withstand the stresses of cat launches and arrested landings' (because that is a basic design requirement for carrier-based fixed-wing aircraft, other

ABOVE *The first artist's impression, suggesting an A-12 over the Fleet*

than the Sea Harrier). Navy sources also hinted at a problem in meeting weight limits, and this was in fact the real killer. Later the DoD issued a Cure Notice, with solutions to be demonstrated in early January 1991.

Remarkably, on 7 January Cheney announced complete termination of the programme. Part of the trouble was fiscal, and the Secretary and contractors were clearly far apart on what extra costs might be involved and who would pay. The crucial problem was that what appeared to be unnecessary design requirements had made the structural weight reach unacceptable proportions. It was said in May 1991 that the Avenger was required to carry no fewer than 24 Mk 82 bombs internally, plus AMRAAM missiles in separate bays. Obviously, this was yet another case where figures were plucked out of the sky and subsequently treated as if they were carved in stone. There was no reason why 24 bombs had to be carried; an Avenger with 18 would be more effective than a cancelled programme. Likewise there was no earthly reason why self-defence AAMs had to be carried; LO aircraft do not stop and fight! The result was that the entire underside of the aircraft, by far the most highly stressed part of the entire structure, was composed of nothing but huge cutouts, for bomb bays, missile bays, landing-gear bays and engine bays. There was nothing to carry the enormous loads except the two widely separated spars, and inevitably these spars had to be extraordinarily strong and therefore heavy. It will be remembered that a crucial feature of LO design is that the zigzag edges of all doors have to close with no gaps. By October 1990 structural weight growth was forcing studies of alternative engines, and also threatening to violate the carrier elevator limit of 27,600 lb for the empty aircraft. This was just the most severe of several serious difficulties.

Described as 'the biggest cancellation in history' (which it was in monetary terms), removal of the Avenger left both the US Navy and Air Force without the slightest chance of putting a modern attack aircraft into service before the first decade of the 21st Century. At first there was even loose talk about trying to redesign the F/A-18, or the F-14 or even the A-6 to try to fill the gap. The Navy recognises that – if not now, then certainly by 2000 – such exercises are pointless. Instead it is trying to formulate an AX medium attack requirement, but in spring 1991 had no clear idea how far AX should be a LO aircraft, whether it should be supersonic, what engine might fit, and even whether the

aircraft could be based on the Air Force Lockheed F-22A fighter (which seems an odd way to develop a carrier-based attack aircraft). All published indications were that, by suggesting a unit price ceiling of $63 million (on a run of 575) and permitting stores to be carried externally, the Navy had already given up trying to get an aircraft designed for the missions. By 1992 the Navy decided it would need to replace the A-6 force with an estimated 400 to 500 aircraft from 2002, or even earlier depending on fatigue life of the new A-6 wings. Industry was invited to submit bids for the A-X by September 1992, the responders being: GD/McDonnell Douglas, a modified A-12; Grumman/Boeing/Lockheed, a new design; Lockheed/Boeing/GD, a modified F-22A; and Rockwell/Lockheed, a new design. Requirements include a 12,000-lb ordnance load including every USN and USAF tactical store except AIM-54 Phoenix, and a tactical radius of 700 nm (806 miles, 1297 km). The Navy planned to select a single design and contractor team in May 1993, followed by dem/val (demonstration and validation) in 1994 and FSD (full-scale development) in 1996. However, despite the imminent election of both the President and Congress, the Defense Budget in October 1992 suffered efforts to reduce costs of future aircraft. The modest request for $165 million for A-X was approved, but prototype strategy was revised to include further study and prolonged evaluation of competing proposals.

As a trivial closing comment, not only did the Avenger have a lower RCS than any other aircraft in history but it also posed unique problems to the writer of serial numbers and insignia. The released artwork showed a very faint NAVY just ahead of the starboard outer control surface, and an equally unobtrusive Modex number 303 behind the inboard leading edge (read 'the other way up', ie as seen from head-on).

SPECIFICATION

A-12A Avenger
Two General Electric F412-400 turbofans, each in the 13,000-lb class
Dimensions Span 70 ft 3.3 in (21.42 m); span (folded) 36 ft 3.25 in (11.05 m); length 37 ft 3 in (11.35 m); wing area 1308 sq ft (121.55 m²)
Weight Empty equipped c39,000 lb (17,690 kg); max take-off 80,000 lb (36,287 kg)
Performance Maximum speed at S/L about 580 mph (933 km/h); combat radius (hi-lo-hi with 12 Mk 82 bombs) 932 miles (1500 km)
Armament Internal bays for up to 15,000 lb (6804 kg) of weapons, including 24 Mk 82 500-lb bombs and four AIM-120A AMRAAM missiles in separate bays

Index